D1432064

# TITO AND GOLIATH

*By Hamilton Fish Armstrong*

THE CALCULATED RISK

"WE OR THEY"

WHEN THERE IS NO PEACE

CHRONOLOGY OF FAILURE

EUROPE BETWEEN WARS

HITLER'S REICH

TITO AND GOLIATH

By HAMILTON FISH ARMSTRONG

# Tito
## AND
# Goliath

"None can pierce the vast black veil uncertain
Because there is no light behind the curtain."
James Thomson,
"The City of Dreadful Night," 1874

The Macmillan Company: New York · 1951

WITHDRAWN

*7589*

*Copyright, 1951, by Hamilton Fish Armstrong*

All rights reserved—no part of this book may be
reproduced in any form without permission in
writing from the publisher, except by a reviewer
who wishes to quote brief passages in connection
with a review written for inclusion in magazine
or newspaper.

PRINTED IN THE UNITED STATES OF AMERICA

*First Printing*

327.49
Ar735x

# ACKNOWLEDGMENTS

A NUMBER of friends have helped me with this book, and I wish to record my gratitude to them. Mention of their names, however, should not involve them in any responsibility for the views I express in it or for whatever faults or errors it may contain. Mrs. Ruth Amende Rosa of Barnard College, Professor Philip E. Mosely of Columbia, Professor Cyril E. Black of Princeton and Professor Alex N. Dragnich of Vanderbilt have all read sections of the manuscript and given me valuable suggestions. Both Meyer S. Handler, the highly competent correspondent of *The New York Times* in Belgrade, and Gaston Coblentz, Balkan correspondent of the *New York Herald Tribune,* have done me many favors, not only personally but by their first-rate reporting over considerable periods of time. Mme. Slavko Grouitch, who is devoted to the Jugoslav people under whatever régime they may be living, has had no part in shaping this book but the memory of her keen observations on the life and character of her adopted nation has stayed with me and proved useful. I should have liked to name the many members of the American Foreign Service who have shown me hospitality, but forbear for fear of perhaps doing them a disservice in their present or future posts. The same caution must prevail regarding the officials of other countries. In my own office, I am particularly indebted to Mary H. Stevens and Elizabeth Bryant for their protracted work on both manuscript and proofs, and to the Library staff of the Council on Foreign Relations, notably Donald Wasson. Jean Gunther has prepared the index. My colleague Byron Dexter has given me wise and patient advice throughout.

*H. F. A.*

7589

# CONTENTS

| | | |
|---|---|---|
| PREFACE | OUT OF THE SHADOWS | ix |
| I | THE IMPOSSIBLE SPLIT | 1 |
| II | JUGOSLAVIA CHOOSES FREEDOM | 5 |
| III | TITO RIDES THE WIND | 18 |
| IV | WHO, WHOM? | 35 |
| V | STALIN AND TITO | 47 |
| VI | TITO AND STALIN | 61 |
| VII | HERESY | 72 |
| VIII | ECHOES OF OLD WARS | 82 |
| IX | ISOLATION | 88 |
| X | IMPASSE | 100 |
| XI | TITO ON THE TIGHTROPE | 111 |
| XII | STRONGHOLDS OF POLISH INDEPENDENCE | 130 |
| XIII | A POLISH TITO | 144 |
| XIV | POLES, RUSSIANS AND GERMANS | 157 |
| XV | RELICS OF NATIONALISM IN THE LAND OF MASARYK | 171 |
| XVI | MACEDONIA: OLD STRUGGLES IN NEW DISGUISES | 185 |
| XVII | BULGARIA CONTAMINATED | 199 |
| XVIII | PRESCRIPTION: FORCE | 211 |
| XIX | FROM SUB-SATELLITE TO SATELLITE | 223 |
| XX | WARNING IN BUDAPEST | 237 |
| XXI | HIS OWN MEPHISTOPHELES | 245 |
| XXII | "LET THE SPARROWS TWITTER" | 256 |
| XXIII | STALIN ON THE DEFENSIVE | 273 |
| XXIV | IF STALIN TAKES THE OFFENSIVE | 284 |
| | INDEX | 301 |

## OUT OF THE SHADOWS

IN his dying statement Lenin called Nikolai Bukharin "the greatest and most valuable theoretician." Stalin agreed, so long as Bukharin's theories agreed with his. But by April 1936, when I met Bukharin in Paris, the two were definitely at odds and Bukharin was no longer a member of the Politburo. He still was editor of *Izvestia*, however, and still a revered Communist oracle. Sitting on the edge of the bed in his room at the Hotel Lutetia he set forth a Communist dogma which would, if it were true, be revolutionary in the relations of states. Its correctness or error could not be demonstrated then; but now the situation has changed, and the truth appears.

Looking at me with the amiability of a tired professor, but with complete assurance, Bukharin explained at length that national rivalry between Communist states was an impossibility—"by definition an impossibility." "What creates wars," he said, "is the competition of monopoly capitalisms for raw materials and markets. Capitalist society is made up of selfish and competing national units and therefore is by definition a world at war. Communist society will be made up of unselfish and harmonious units and therefore will be by definition a world at peace. Just as capitalism cannot live without war, so war cannot live with Communism."

Badly outclassed in dialectics, I managed nevertheless to express doubts. Could one explain national rivalries so neatly and dispose of them so rationally? Would groups of men with different inheritances, aptitudes and standards, possessing different natural resources and different productive machines, agree on what constitutes the common good and on how it should be divided?

Bukharin shook his head, but slightly, as if to imply that such queries were too feeble to deserve notice.

What tribunal of mere men (I persisted) was to decide the common good? And when they had figured it out down to the last decimal point of the master plan and up to the final plateau of the master graph, mightn't rebellious human nature upset all their calculations? People are quixotic. Even enlightened self-interest assumes unexpected forms at different times and places. History shows that often a nation chooses to lay down its life to save it.

Bukharin's answer was bland but final. The ultimate tribunal would be "the consensus of Marxist truth." What is truth? It does not need to be interpreted, only expounded. The unity and harmony of Communist society were not a theory but "*eine spontane Realität*" —"a spontaneous fact."

About ten years were to pass before it became possible to test the accuracy of these dogmatic statements. At that time there was no Communist state except the Soviet Union, thus no Communist international society and no way of ascertaining whether Communist nations *because they are Communist* abandon competitive struggles, are content with the station in life to which they are assigned, cheerfully fulfill the tasks appropriate to that station and live together in harmony and peace.

After the Second World War, however, a Communist international society came into existence. Now there were other Communist states in addition to the U.S.S.R., and Moscow was called on to establish relations with them—states that were not bourgeois, capitalistic and therefore naturally antagonistic, but Marxist, brotherly and therefore deserving equality of treatment.

Hardly had these new conditions come into existence when the whole structure that Bukharin had reared in his mind collapsed. Within three years, one of the principal states belonging to the new Communist family was being branded as reactionary, bourgeois and nationalistic and its fellow members were being instructed to shun it politically, economically and culturally. When the Communist chief of that Communist state attempted to explain his course, the simple fact that he dared enter a defense at all was taken as an added crime as well as an affront to the individual whose orders were canon law for the Cominform, the supreme tribunal of the Communist international society.

According to the formal resolution of the Cominform, published at the end of June 1948, Marshal Tito of Jugoslavia had been guilty of breaking "the unified Communist front against imperialism" and his Party had "taken the road to nationalism." Tito's reply was that not he but the Bolsheviks themselves had succumbed to nationalist temptations. He said that they had attempted to dominate the Jugoslav Communist Party and had aimed to exploit Jugoslavia as a Russian colony in the old capitalistic and imperialistic tradition.

Bukharin was no longer there to explain this rude contradiction of his maxim that rivalry and competition between Communist states is an impossibility—"by definition an impossibility." Early in 1938, two years after I had been sitting with him in the Hotel Lutetia, Lenin's favorite theoretician had been tried by Stalin for his particular deviation from the consensus of Marxist truth, and shot.

# I

## THE IMPOSSIBLE SPLIT

*All truths wait in all things.*
Walt Whitman

How did one of the young Communist states come to deny the "spontaneous fact" of Communist international solidarity and create the "impossible" split? Why were traits of individualism and independence which had been crushed long ago in mighty Russia able to live along in a mere dependency, as Stalin of course considered it? And today, when the impossible has become the real, how is Tito able to survive the attacks of the Stalinist press and the smothering Stalinist boycott? How far has his revolt tempted other restless Communists to emulate his daring? When we have found the answer to these questions we shall be in a position to decide what it means to us.

The answer can be in ideological terms, that a dogmatic faith breeds heresies and that heresies are contagious. Or it can be in humanistic terms that Stalin's dictatorship, like Hitler's, underrates the everlasting determination of people to be themselves, live their own lives, work for themselves and not somebody else, make their own mistakes and follow their own star. Or it can be in historical terms, that people with different experiences have different values which cannot easily be reduced to a common denominator—that Serbs, for instance, were individual landowners and free citizens while Russians were serfs, and that Croats and Slovenes were impregnated with Western culture, belonged to a Western church and shared in Western technological progress, while Tolstoi was explaining in "Anna Karenina" how Russian peasants would not use the iron plough that Levin brought back to them "from Europe." Or, finally, the answer can be in terms of personal power, that the veteran dictator in Moscow and his apprentice in Belgrade were bound to fall into dispute for the possession of Jugoslavia, and that for various reasons the man on the spot won out.

Each of these answers contains a part of the truth. The parts differ in size, of course; and the importance attributed to each by one side or the other tends to alter as time goes by and propaganda purposes change. Some of the answers seem definitely incongruous. But all of them had their share in deciding Tito to reject Stalin's efforts to boss him and use Jugoslavia for Russian purposes, and all helped make it possible for him to do it successfully. The fact that his heresy appeals to so many kinds of people gives his independent Communist régime added significance. Fanatical Communist purists; patriotic idealists; foreign radicals who had discovered that Stalin's kiss was political death and were delighted to regain respectability by accepting the Belgrade version of the Marxist gospel; reformers, mercenaries and adventurers—all find something there to attract them.

Of course Tito may be assassinated, with unpredictable results for his régime and his heresy. An attempt is rather more likely now than it was earlier, when the Soviets were less anxious to kill him than to disgrace and ruin him, or at any rate to disgrace and ruin him before killing him; death alone was too good for him, and not good enough for Soviet purposes. But as the hope that he could be disgraced and ruined by propaganda and economic pressure has faded, the temptation to get rid of him and the tremendous nuisance which he represents by one sharp act must have increased. He is guarded, naturally, but assassination even of a dictator surrounded by guards is not impossible if the men chosen for the job are ready for certain death. Regardless of what may happen to Tito now, however, he is sure of a permanent place in Communist history—if Communists continue to maintain the fiction that they recognize history. For whatever might happen to his régime after he had disappeared, and even if it were denied that he had ever existed, the fact that he and his heresy could have existed will continue to exert its influence on all subsequent Communist development. World Communism will never again be quite the same.

This does not mean that Tito's significance is solely doctrinal or will appear chiefly in the history books. His movement is important politically now and Jugoslavia's place in the balance of world forces is important strategically now. In both cases the importance grows, and clearly will not, as things stand, diminish.

The Stalinist press furiously denies that the signals which the Jugoslav rebels flash from their citadel to fellow-Communists abroad bring answering signals; but the frequent arrests of native Communist leaders throughout Eastern Europe, charged with Tito's crimes, refute the denials. To increase this satisfactory confusion, Communist intellectuals, fellow-travellers and radicals of various sorts in Western countries are exchanging charges and counter-charges of bad faith and of deviations from orthodox Marxist principle. The debate reaches the point where the question is whether Tito or Stalin is the heretic. Even behind the blank walls of the Kremlin there must be ideological dispute, and if there is that, we can judge from past events that there also is acute political effervescence, and—again from precedent—we may legitimately hope that this will not end without some shooting.

Tito's present influence in the Communist world has been compared with that of Martin Luther in the European world of the sixteenth century. It is even more like that of Henry VIII, I think, for although no wives are involved the purposes on either side are more temporal than spiritual, more hierarchical than theological. But whether he is more like Luther or Henry VIII, in attacking the inner morale of the church militant Tito has impaired its physical strength also. This is a matter to which we shall return later, for it constitutes one of the most important factors, I believe, in the international politics of our time and in our military strategy.

At the time of which I shall write first, however, during the war and in the early days afterwards, Tito had no idea that he was cast for a world-shaking rôle. He simply believed that his status as a national leader was different from that of any of the other Communists in Eastern Europe, and he felt that he, his Party and his country deserved to have the fact recognized. To substantiate his belief, Tito could point to the manner in which he had organized the Partisan movement, to its independent contribution to the victory over the Nazis, to Jugoslavia's key geographical position and to his own de-

4 ]                                    TITO AND GOLIATH

cisive leadership. But starting from these truths he went on to error.
He supposed that if his services and qualifications for national leadership distinguished him from the other satellite leaders his standing
in Stalin's eyes must be different from theirs. This was the beginning
of the situation which Bukharin said could never arise between
Communist states. Tito expected to be treated as an equal. Stalin
never dreamed of granting him or anyone else equality and indeed
was incredulous when Tito seriously claimed it.

Most of us did not notice that the elements of conflict were present
in this situation and that the physical conditions were such that it
could come to a head. Tito's relations with Stalin were masked by
the usual totalitarian control of the press and all other media of information and discussion and by Communist discipline, which is
ironclad until it shatters. Also, a catalytic agent was needed to stimulate the reaction, and it did not seem credible that either side would
supply it.

Stalin eventually did supply it, with the complacency of the man
who has forgotten that he can be crossed. He of course recognized
that Tito was different in caliber from the slavies he had sent to do
his housekeeping and run his errands in the other satellite states—a
Gottwald in Czechoslovakia, a Pauker in Rumania or a Bierut in
Poland. But the objective differences on which Tito in the end came
to rely, the physical strength of Jugoslavia's position and of his position in Jugoslavia, were items which simply had no meaning for
Stalin, the political and military genius who permits no rivals,
accepts no partners, never accords favors and never fails. From sheer
incomprehension, Stalin committed one of the most magnificent
blunders of his career and experienced one of his nastiest surprises.

# II

## JUGOSLAVIA CHOOSES FREEDOM

> Patriotism to the Soviet state is a revolu-
> tionary duty whereas patriotism to a bour-
> geois state is treachery.
>
> Trotsky, "The 3rd International After Lenin"

TITO's feeling of superiority to his Com-
munist colleagues in the other capitals of Eastern Europe was well
grounded. To begin with, his country's rôle in the war had been different from that of the other satellites—different in origin and different in accomplishment. Jugoslavia had not been one of Hitler's
allies like Hungary, Bulgaria and Rumania, "liberated" late in the
war by the Red Armies. Her course had not been the essentially passive one that Czechoslovakia adopted for understandable enough
reasons after Beneš was deserted by his great allies in 1938 and the
country became a *Protektorat*. Little Albania was not even a satellite in her own right; native opposition to the Italians, and to the
Nazis after the Italian capitulation, was organized there in part with
Jugoslav help, and after the war Communist Albania became a
moon to the Jugoslav sun. Poland had shown the way in resisting
the Nazis, but in the end her achievement did not match Jugoslavia's. The Beck régime accepted the risks of war voluntarily, but
its conceit and stubbornness wasted the heroism of the Polish people
and brought them to swift defeat; after that, Polish patriots fought
in exile abroad and joined in desperate uprisings against the occupying forces at home, but for reasons which will be mentioned later
the Polish underground sacrificed itself in vain without being able
to take a decisive lead in the moment of liberation. The Jugoslavs
defied Hitler open-eyed; and though the German invaders quickly
defeated the Jugoslav Army as they had the Polish Army, and

occupied the Jugoslav cities and key strategic areas, they never possessed the country as a whole or governed it with security. The Jugoslav terrain was ideal for guerrilla warfare. Well-organized Jugoslav bands, at times totalling forces numbered in six figures, constantly cut German and Italian communications and joined in pitched battles with the occupying troops. Divided though they were by internal conflicts, Jugoslav resistance forces always held considerable parts of the national territory; and that section which Tito commanded and manœuvred to supremacy participated in the final liberation as an equal ally of the Red Army. Thus it came about—a crucial point—that Jugoslavia escaped occupation by Soviet troops, the only East European state to enjoy this good fortune.[1]

To these historical factors geography contributed another which was decisive. Jugoslavia was further from Russia than any of the five other nations marked to revolve in the Soviet orbit. Also, in consequence of the manner in which the zones of occupation in Germany and Austria were allotted after the war, she was the only one of them which remained in direct contact with several non-Communist nations and possessed besides an open sea frontier. She thus was physically situated to evade, if her leaders wished, the bear hug that enveloped the rest.

Before we attempt to understand why her leaders did so wish we must see how it was that the group of men exercising power in Jugoslavia at the end of the war happened to be Communists. How did Tito and his Communist followers, allies of the Soviet dictatorship, succeed in getting control of a people so notoriously nationalistic and individualistic as the Jugoslavs? The contradiction seems the stranger because it was only after Jugoslavia had become involved in the war that the Communist Party there put forward any claim to being patriotic. No Communists anywhere were supposed at that time to be patriots. Not until after Hitler had attacked him did Stalin resurrect the heroes and saints of past Russian struggles—Nevsky, Suvorov, Kutuzov—to help him wage the Great Patriotic War; not until then did he allow Communists to begin coöperating with patriotic movements in Eastern Europe or permit them to

---

[1] Soviet troops were in Czechoslovakia for a year, until November 1945, and although this was not called occupation it had the same effect.

summon up the shades of their heroic past to encourage resistance to the new national enemies. Among the Jugoslav Communists patriotic spirits were certainly to be found—men who had become disillusioned with the slow progress of social and economic reform under the semi-parliamentary or semi-dictatorial régimes of the interwar period and who hoped to translate the Marxist slogans of social revolution into terms of national progress. In general, however, the Jugoslav Party before the Nazi attack was simply a small unit in a great supra-national revolutionary organization which appealed to the ambitions of oppressed classes rather than to stirrings of national fervor.

Although handicapped by having to build on these foundations, Tito managed to transform the Communist Party of Jugoslavia into a fighting body which received the support of many non-Communist nationalists and patriots. Step by step, by fair methods or foul, he was able, as we shall see, to lead his Partisan bands to a position of ascendancy over their non-Communist rivals, despite the fact that these had been first in the field as defenders of the national soil and in many cases had long records of proven patriotism. In the end, he displaced the Jugoslav Government-in-Exile which had begun the war as the fighting ally of both the Western Allies and Soviet Russia, and which was never officially disowned throughout the struggle; and as a climax he unseated the Karageorgevich dynasty which early in the nineteenth century had led the Serbs to freedom and after the First World War had brought the South Slav peoples together in a united state for the first time in history.

These were feats of daring and deceit, political acumen and political legerdemain, and could have been performed only by a man possessing remarkable resourcefulness and determination. Such a man would not be likely in after days to relinquish control of the government which he had organized gun-in-hand to outsiders claiming to know more than he about his domestic political situation, about the correct ideological basis for his social program and about the duty which he owed to them in comparison to what he owed to himself.

From these inflammable materials there suddenly in 1948 blazed up a conflagration which lighted all the Eastern sky and illuminated

for the benefit of fascinated outsiders recesses of the Stalinist world
heretofore deeply obscure.

For the prologue we must go back to March 1941. In this second
year of the Second World War the Jugoslavs were still free, but isolated in the widening Axis flood. The United States, of course, was
still neutral; but in January encouraging messages had been brought
to Belgrade by Colonel William J. Donovan on behalf of President
Roosevelt, supporting (if that is not too strong a word) the somewhat vague offers of help being made by the British in the event that
the position of Prince Regent Paul and his Government became desperate and they decided to fight. On February 9 the United States
Government had again attempted to encourage the Jugoslav Government to oppose the Axis. In a message to the American Ambassador in Belgrade, Secretary Hull gave details of the enormous increase in American war production, indicated that much of it would
be at the service of Britain and other opponents of the Axis, and
ended by quoting a sentence of President Roosevelt's with the evident hope that when it was repeated to members of the Jugoslav
Government it might stiffen their resistance: "We know now that a
nation can have peace with the Nazis only at the price of total surrender." [2] But even if the United States had been in the war at that
time it could not have done much more than exhort and encourage
an ally in Jugoslavia's geographical position ; and the British promises
necessarily looked to a distant and—given current German military
successes—almost incredible future.

Hitler's and Mussolini's threats and promises, on the other hand,
were concrete and immediate. In every direction that Prince Paul
looked he saw their massed bayonets, planes and tanks. Prime Minister Cvetkovich has described [3] how he tried to stave off the menace
by asking the Soviet Government to supply Jugoslavia with arms
and to make representations on her behalf in Berlin. Much was
promised, he records, but nothing done; and eventually even the
Soviet Ambassador in Belgrade who made the promises disappeared
to Moscow and never came back. Cvetkovich also tells of a meeting

[2] "The Memoirs of Cordell Hull." New York: Macmillan, 1948, Vol. II,
p. 929.
[3] *Le Figaro*, Paris, April 4, 1950.

between representatives of the British, Greek and Jugoslav chiefs-of-staff in Athens on March 8 and 9 to try to agree on common measures in case the Nazis should attack Greece (as they did shortly) and of how it had no concrete results. On March 25 the Jugoslav Government succumbed to Axis threats and signed the Tripartite Pact, concluded by Germany, Italy and Japan the previous autumn and already avidly accepted by Jugoslavia's neighbors, Hungary and Rumania.[4] To its credit, it did not accept the Axis offer of the Greek port of Saloniki, and it insisted on inserting a clause to the effect that the Axis Powers should not demand "either right of passage for German troops to traverse Jugoslav territory or the use of roads or railroads for military purposes."

Forty-eight hours later this decision was reversed. On the night of March 27 a band of patriots led by General Dushan Simovich, head of the air corps, and including a staff officer named Colonel Drazha Mihailovich, overthrew the regency, brought young King Peter to the throne and put an end to any idea that Jugoslavia would play an Axis rôle.

The Jugoslav Communist Party, which had been outlawed in 1921 for attempting to assassinate Prince Regent Alexander and Premier Pasich and for murdering Minister of the Interior Drashkovich, took no part in this patriotic undertaking. Its underground headquarters were in Zagreb and the official in charge was the Secretary-General of the Central Committee, Josip Broz, formerly called Walter, at this time passing under the alias of Babich or Tomanek, later to be known as Tito. In this period Stalin was still Hitler's ally; and as a disciplined Communist Tito was to this extent Hitler's ally also.

Hitler by nature could not put up with any defiance which he thought he could beat down, but his first move was to gain time. He

[4] The date of the Tripartite Pact was September 27, 1940. The Hungarian Government adhered to it November 20, and the Rumanian Government three days later. German troops had already moved into both countries. The Bulgarian Government concluded a special agreement with the German Government March 1, 1941, regularizing the entry of German troops which had already occurred. Italy, who had annexed Albania in the spring of 1939, attacked Greece on October 28, 1940. Thus when Jugoslavia finally adhered to the Tripartite Pact she was already surrounded on every frontier (except that with beleaguered Greece) by Axis-controlled states occupied by German and Italian troops.

offered the new Simovich Government the port of Salonika in return
for its help in the war on Greece. General Simovich did not accept,
but he tried to mollify Hitler by stating that for the time being there
would be no change in Jugoslavia's international engagements, including the Tripartite Pact signed by his predecessor. Meanwhile
Hitler was arranging for the transfer of the necessary additional
troops to execute a punitive expedition, and on the morning of April
6 without warning his planes appeared in a cloud over Belgrade
and reduced great parts of it to ruins. Invasion followed, and by
April 15 the Jugoslav High Command was forced to surrender.
Though these operations in themselves were quite satisfactory to
Hitler they had consequences which he does not seem to have considered important but which in the event affected the whole course
of the war. The German campaign against Russia had been scheduled to begin the middle of May. However, the necessity of dealing
with Jugoslavia postponed it until June 22. This delay was decisive,
for it meant that the German forces failed to reach Moscow before
winter came to the Red Army's aid. They failed to capture the city
then, and the reprieve gave the Russians time to strengthen its defenses to resist all subsequent assaults. Thus the coup d'état in Belgrade, carried out by men who were as thoroughly anti-Communist
as they were anti-Nazi, had the ironical result of saving the Communist capital.[5]

The attitude of the Jugoslav Communists just following the Nazi
attack of April 6 is the subject of much speculation and dispute, as
is indeed natural since the Soviet position at the time was, to say the
least, ambiguous. In Moscow on the evening of April 5 Stalin signed
a treaty with the Jugoslav Ambassador promising to respect Jugoslavia's independence and to maintain friendly relations in case she
were attacked. This may have been either a last-minute attempt to

---

[5] German authorities have stated that the Nazi war machine never wholly
recovered from this setback. Vice Admiral Kurt Assmann, German military his-
torian, calls the Nazi failure to take Moscow "the turning point of the war."
Hitler's unforeseen campaign against Jugoslavia drew off nine divisions which
had been earmarked for *Barbarossa* (code name for the invasion of Russia). The
German High Command had estimated that the chastisement of Jugoslavia
would delay *Barbarossa* by four weeks. Actually the delay turned out to be 10
days longer than that. (See "The Battle for Moscow," by Kurt Assmann, *Foreign
Affairs,* January 1950.)

deter Hitler or, as Churchill calls it, "an amiable grimace." If meant as a deterrent it failed, for the bombardment of Belgrade began within a few hours. Perhaps it is on the basis of this treaty that Brigadier Fitzroy Maclean, head of the British military mission at Tito's headquarters in 1943 and 1944, speculates whether Stalin had not become wary of Hitler even before the attack on Russia and might not have been sending Tito instructions "not altogether in accordance with the spirit of the German-Soviet Pact." [6] He does not give grounds for this supposition. The generally accepted view is that the men in the Kremlin, though warned specifically by the British intelligence and in more general terms by the Department of State,[7] did not credit the possibility of a direct attack on Russia. Stalin had said in December 1939 that not Germany but Britain and France were responsible for the outbreak of war. Although Soviet relations with Germany had deteriorated after November 1940, the Soviets continued to provide the Germans with economic assistance and the Communist line everywhere was still to denounce Britain's last-ditch stand against the Nazis as the "Second Imperialist War." That is how Jugoslav Communist publications described the war throughout 1940. The captured German documents give no hint that Berlin suspected Jugoslav Communist elements of acting against German interests before Hitler actually attacked his Russian partner.

Since his break with Stalin in 1948 Tito has specifically claimed credit for patriotic Communist activities against the Nazis in the period between the Nazi conquest of Jugoslavia in mid-April and the Nazi attack on Russia on June 22. Addressing the Fifth Congress of

[6] "Eastern Approaches," by Fitzroy Maclean. London: Jonathan Cape, 1949, p. 312. The American edition, published by Little, Brown, Boston, 1950, has the title, "Escape to Adventure."

[7] In January 1941 Secretary Hull began receiving secret information from Berlin about Nazi preparations for an attack on Russia, and after deciding that it was authentic passed it on to the Soviet Ambassador in Washington, Mr. Oumansky. The last specific warning was given Oumansky by Under Secretary Welles on March 20. (Hull, *op. cit.*, Vol. II, p. 968.) The Soviet Government may have shared the view of its Ambassador in Berlin, Dekanozov. He held that Hitler was making fake plans for an attack on Russia, intending that they should become known to the Soviet intelligence, as a means of influencing the Soviet Government to make further economic concessions. (Cyrille Kalinov, "Les Maréchaux Soviétiques vous parlent." Paris: Stock, 1950, p. 31.)

the Jugoslav Communist Party on July 21, 1948, he said that the
two-month period in 1941 "was used by all Party organizations in
the country for final preparations for the uprising, for diversions, for
gathering arms, etc.," as well as for rallying "all those who thought
honestly and who were ready to fight against the invader." He stated
further that when news came of the "sneak attack" on the Soviet
Union by "Hitler's Fascist hordes" (until that moment Stalin's
allies), the Central Committee of the Party met and decided to
issue a proclamation calling for "a general people's uprising," asking all patriots to contribute to the struggle for liberty "under the
leadership of the Communist Party of Jugoslavia" and telling them
that "the struggle of the Soviet Union is your struggle as well."
According to Tito, this proclamation incidentally informed Party
members as follows: "We knew that the Fascist criminals were preparing against the Soviet Union and working mankind. . . . We
are accepting this struggle for we expected it and we are ready for
it." Moscow must have been as deaf to warnings from Tito as to
those from London and Washington.

A friend in Belgrade has supplied me with two proclamations
which he states were issued by the Central Committee of the Communist Party on April 15 (the day of the surrender) and May 1.
If authentic, these would support the thesis that the Party leadership
did not feel it necessary to condone the German attack because
Hitler was then Stalin's ally. The first told the peoples of Jugoslavia
who were "fighting and dying in the struggle for independence" to
remember that eventually the battle would be crowned with success
"even if you now succumb to the superior enemy," and asserted that
the "Communists and the whole of the working class of Jugoslavia
will hold out in the front rank of the people's struggle against the
conqueror." The second said that the "terrible disaster" was due
to the "criminal policy of the Belgrade rulers who while in power
had cared about nothing but their own capitalist interests," had
neglected the country's defenses, had "tied themselves to the Axis
bandits" and had neglected "to conclude in time a pact of mutual
aid with the great and strong Soviet Union in the interest of peace
and the independence of the peoples of Jugoslavia." This lends
support to the claim that the Jugoslav Communist Party rallied

to the idea of resistance, but fails to show that it distinguished between Prince Paul's "capitalist rulers" and the patriots who overthrew them on March 27, or that its policy aimed to strengthen the latter. It ignores the treaty signed by Stalin and the Jugoslav Ambassador in Moscow a few hours before the Nazi planes bombed Belgrade, and passes over Stalin's failure to make any move under that treaty to help Jugoslavia in her hour of agony.

An anecdote related to me by Tito is interesting in this connection. Between Jugoslavia's defeat in April and Germany's attack on Russia in June, he came from Zagreb to Belgrade—in disguise, of course—and by chance encountered the Soviet Military Attaché in the street. He had been avoiding any Soviet contacts, even secret, in order to maintain his own disguise and in order not to risk embarrassing the Soviet representatives. But the chance opportunity was too good to miss and he informed the Red Army officer that he was preparing a scheme of guerrilla resistance against the Nazis and asked if he could count on receiving Soviet assistance. According to this anecdote, the officer readily promised Soviet help, although none ever was actually forthcoming.

The nearest to anything like outside confirmation of the claim of the Communists to have acted as patriots and nationalists before the Nazis attacked Russia is contained in the documents presented by Foreign Minister von Ribbentrop in support of his note to the Soviet Government on June 21, 1941. In excusing Germany's attack on her ally he mentioned among other grounds for complaint the fact that the Soviets had carried on anti-German propaganda in various European countries. The Nazi-sponsored newspaper appearing in occupied Belgrade gave details of the charge in so far as Communist activities in Jugoslavia were concerned.[8] For example, a

[8] *Novo Vremye*, Belgrade, June 23, 1941. Most but not all of the charges printed in Belgrade are to be found in the voluminous documentation presented in the *Völkischer Beobachter* of Berlin in connection with the German note as read by Ribbentrop over the Berlin radio. The *Völkischer Beobachter* also printed additional accusations based on Jugoslav documents said to have been found by German troops in Belgrade. One was a report from a Jugoslav representative in Moscow named Georgevich that the Soviet Government regarded Germany as the "powerful enemy of tomorrow." Another was to the effect that the Soviet Chief-of-Staff had told the Jugoslav Military Attaché in reply to a request for arms in November 1940: "We shall supply all that is requested, and at once."

Communist pamphlet issued in Slovenia on August 23, 1940, the anniversary of the German-Soviet agreement, was said to have attacked the Jugoslav Government for drawing closer to Berlin and Rome and "attempting to hitch itself to the imperialist chariot of Germany and Italy;" one issued in Zagreb accused Machek, leader of the Croat Peasant Party, of selling out to Germany and Italy; and another circulated in Slovenia in November, on the anniversary of the Russian Revolution, protested Jugoslavia's "flirtation with the imperialists in Berlin and Rome." To reënforce the authenticity of these pamphlets, Ribbentrop gave the text of a circular supposedly issued by the Ljubljana provincial government, August 5, 1940, warning local officials that Communist manifestations in the near future, unlike those in the past, would probably be directed against Germany and Italy. He further cited a report from the German Legation in Belgrade, September 13, 1940, conveying information that Moscow propagandists were assuring Communists in Zagreb that various territories then under German occupation, Jugoslavia included, would eventually become Russian protectorates, "following the expected military weakening of Germany." He also published a propaganda document allegedly found in the Soviet Embassy in Belgrade assuring the Serbian people that the "U.S.S.R. will react at the right moment" to the German expansion into Rumania and Hungary.

Now it is true of course that the Soviets were attempting to keep or extend their influence in Eastern Europe in the fullest degree that Berlin would tolerate within the limitations of continued Soviet-German coöperation.[9] Yet the Ribbentrop charges constitute a pretty flimsy sort of proof on which to build a case for Germany's attack on her ally. And even supposing that what Ribbentrop said about scattered Communist leaflets and dispatches from Moscow were accurate, it is unconvincing as evidence that the Jugoslav Communist Party as such—in distinction from individual Party

[9] *Cf.* the Soviet protest against the Ribbentrop-Ciano decision of September 7, 1940—the so-called Vienna Award—giving about a third of Rumanian Transylvania to Hungary; the competition between Berlin and Moscow for control of the Danube; and the Soviet demand for a "security zone" in Bulgaria in November 1940.

members, radicals labelled as Communists or agents-provocateurs —was following a different line toward Germany from that followed by Communist Parties elsewhere.

The suggestion that nationalist sentiments were stirring among Jugoslav Communists as far back as 1940 is not, as we shall see, inherently improbable. On the other hand, the natural thought of the Party leadership at first would have been to turn the unexpected developments of March 27, 1941, to its own purposes by dividing and confusing non-Communist groups. There has been printed in various places what purports to be a proclamation of the Central Committee of the Party published on March 30, 1941 (three days after the coup, and two weeks before the date of the first of the two proclamations cited above), calling on the Jugoslav people to resist the Simovich "clique" who had seized power with the help of "British agents" and were making Jugoslavia a tool of foreign "imperialists." Further, one of Brigadier Maclean's British officers who indicates that he had access to Communist archives (might it perhaps have been through the police dossiers on Communist leaders?) has published a secret directive allegedly drawn up by Tito in that same interval between the patriotic coup and the Nazi invasion.[10] In this Tito instructed his followers to aid "all elements" which were "trying to overthrow the existing monarchical régime," regardless of their "ideological outlook and character," and especially to "disorganize the resistance of the Jugoslav Army." The authenticity of this text has been denied to me by Tito's official spokesman.

One of Tito's chief assistants, Milovan Djilas, has gone so far as to say that the overthrow of the Cvetkovich Government and the Jugoslav refusal to join the Tripartite Pact were effected by the Jugoslav people "under the leadership of the Communist Party of Jugoslavia." [11] This is of course pure fantasy. Tito himself is more cautious. As we have seen, he claimed in his speech of July 21, 1948, that following the Simovich coup the Communist Party at once be-

[10] "Whirlwind," by Stephen Clissold. London: Cresset Press, 1949, p. 27. Published also by the Philosophical Library, New York, 1950.
[11] *Borba*, Belgrade, May 7, 1948.

gan preparing for resistance to the Nazi attack which seemed to him inevitable. He even went so far as to state that "the people's uprising" after the surrender of the Jugoslav Army was "organized and led by our Communist Party alone." But as to the coup itself, the first step in the chain of great events, he limits himself to stating in general terms that the Cvetkovich Government fell "under pressure from the masses," that this "did not find our Party unprepared," and that "on that day our Party was complete master of the situation during the great demonstrations in Belgrade." On that day Tito himself was in Zagreb.

It is not possible at the present time, and perhaps never will be, to judge among all the *ex post facto* accusations and claims put forward by the Jugoslav protagonists and their friends and enemies, at home and abroad. Nor is it necessary to do so here, for this account aims to show merely how the resistance leaders in Jugoslavia came to be irretrievably divided and how by the end of the war the Communists were in control, even though the Jugoslav people had always been strongly individualistic and nationalistic and therefore would have been most unlikely subjects for successful Communist propaganda in normal times and by democratic political methods.

What is beyond dispute is that the coup which actually overthrew Prince Paul's government was carried through without participation of the Communist organization of Jugoslavia, and that even if the Communists had offered support to the Simovich Government, which nobody seems to claim they did, it would certainly have been refused. When Hitler suddenly turned on his Soviet ally, however, Tito's attitude automatically became one of resistance also. He has stated in his speech to the Fifth Party Congress, already mentioned, that he determined on June 27 to set up headquarters in Belgrade for organizing "National Liberation Partisan Detachments," and that he continued to work in Belgrade "up to the middle of September 1941." This would not indicate that he conducted activities on any great scale in this period, since Belgrade was occupied by German troops and swarmed with Gestapo agents. But in September the Partisan headquarters and the Central Committee of the Communist Party "went into the field," establishing themselves first at Krupanj, in Western Serbia, where an area had been cleared of hostile elements, and then at Uzhice. From that time on the operations of the Partisans against the Germans and their Italian allies were almost continuous—sometimes forays to secure munitions and food, sometimes rear-guard actions as they moved from one area to another, sometimes hand-to-hand battles.

# III

## TITO RIDES THE WIND

> I seem to see lies crowding and crushing
> at a narrow gate and working their way
> in along with truths into the domain of
> history.　　Samuel Butler, "Note Books"

DRAZHA MIHAILOVICH, the General Staff
officer who had supported the anti-Axis coup of March 27 and
refused to obey the headquarters command to surrender on April
15, was already in the field. In fact, as he had denounced the surrender, taken to the mountains and issued an appeal for continued
resistance as early as May 10 his admirers claim that he never quit
the field. Around him he gathered ex-soldiers and peasant volunteers
in guerrilla bands which called themselves Chetniks, the name used
by their Serb forefathers in old struggles against the Turks. From his
mountain headquarters in Serbia and eastern Bosnia he directed the
Chetnik operations—harassing German garrisons and disrupting
German railway connections, especially the important line by which
the enemy was transporting troops and supplies southward for use
against the Allies in Greece and the eastern Mediterranean.

By comparison with Mihailovich, then, Tito evidently started his
resistance career at a disadvantage. His embarrassment was the same
as that of Communist leaders in other Allied countries after Hitler's
attack on Russia changed the struggle from the "Great Imperialist
War" to the "Great Patriotic War." Communists who came into the
French Resistance had a hard time shaking off the albatross of the
Nazi-Soviet Pact; and only their repeated deeds of valor made their
countrymen forget how basely Moscow's French agents—Thorez,
Marty and the rest—had acted at the time of Munich and afterwards when France was going down to defeat before the armored

divisions of Stalin's partner. In Poland the blood of the most idealistic Polish Communists never could quite wash out the memory of how Molotov congratulated Hitler when the Nazis captured Warsaw, after the slaughter of hundreds of thousands of Polish soldiers, and of how he received Ribbentrop in Moscow with the Nazi salute. Everywhere in the Allied camp Communists become patriots had to pay for Stalin's miscalculation that he could strike a bargain with Hitler, and for his crime in demanding a cut in the blood-money of murdered nations.

Many events in Jugoslavia during the war remain deeply obscure. Jugoslavs will never settle among themselves just how the various national elements and leaders behaved under the pressure of competing national, sectional and class interests; and foreigners will certainly never settle it for them. At least three wars were in progress simultaneously, and they frequently overlapped. There was the patriotic war against the Nazi invaders, their Italian partners and their Hungarian and Bulgarian camp-followers. There was the long-standing feud between Croats and Serbs, turned into what at times amounted to a civil war by the anti-Serb excesses of the Croat pro-Axis militia (Ustashi), and further complicated by special Slovene, Montenegrin, Bosnian, Macedonian and other regional interests. Thirdly, there was the social war between Communists and anti-Communists. Tribal rivalry and social revolution thus superimposed separate and shifting patterns on the national struggle for freedom. Under these kaleidoscopic conditions Tito succeeded in shedding the anti-national reputation which had belonged to him and other Communists in the first phase of the war and in converting his movement, smelling at first of the Ribbentrop-Molotov Pact, into a militant organization which patriots felt they could join to defend the homeland.

In time the complexities and obscurities of the Jugoslav situation worked to favor Tito abroad also. The conditions under which policy was made in some of the Western capitals lent themselves to this. Most of the top Allied statesmen, already harassed by the responsibility of making final decisions in a great number of areas, were quite innocent of any knowledge of Balkan history and of course had had no direct experience with Balkan problems. Sometimes they were advised by officials who though sincere and painstaking were themselves equally inexperienced and, in turn, perplexed by conflicting reports and importunings from their agents in the field, many of them newcomers themselves to the Balkans. When an eminent strategist in desperation sent off some crony or trusted relative to report the truth to him direct the confusion became worse confounded. Some Americans felt that in London undue weight was given to immediate military projects in the Balkans in contrast to considerations of long-range policy. In Washington, difficulties arose because the information and policy-making functions of the Office of Strategic Services were never satisfactorily determined in relation to those of the State Department, and because O.S.S. officers in Jugoslavia were sometimes at odds with each other as well as with the home office, which sometimes might also be at odds with the State Department. It is easy to see that functions of information and policy-making which in a large measure had to be improvised in a great emergency, and which never were satisfactorily correlated, could become confused in dealing with the situation in Jugoslavia, where confusion was the keynote. Tito's reputation improved in the foreign as well as the domestic confusion, especially among those who, knowing or caring little about the past, fixed their eyes on current estimates of the military situation and felt that the political future must take care of itself.

The following were the chief characters in the Jugoslav drama, which even a librettist for Verdi would have considered complex:

General Nedich, the Serb Pétain, established his headquarters in occupied Belgrade in August, four months after the Jugoslav Army's surrender. He attracted outright traitors, opportunists and defeatists who felt that the country could not survive another prolonged resistance and slaughter like that of 1914–1918.

In Zagreb, Hitler and Mussolini set up Ante Pavelich as puppet leader of Croatia. This was in April, some months before they could find a satisfactory collaborator in Serbia. Pavelich, who was a long-time international spy and professional assassin, gushed with egotistical Croat nationalism; but as the Führer and the Duce, who had chosen him to run the "Kingdom of Croatia" for their absentee Italian princeling, required that he pay them constant court, his patriotic pose did not remain convincing for very long. He preached racial purity and racial hate and killed Jews and sent out his ferocious Ustashi bands to massacre such of the Serb population of Croatia as refused to be "converted" from the Orthodox Church to Catholicism in order to save their lives. But he could not disguise that he was the hireling of Croatia's two hated enemies and as such he was hated by patriots.

The political organization formerly all-powerful in Croatia, the Croat Peasant Party, gave no inspiring lead against either Pavelich or the Nazis. Its chief, Dr. Machek, had been lukewarm to the coup of March 27, partly, no doubt, because it was led by Serbs and partly because in practical terms it seemed (and was) foolhardy. After some hesitation, Machek did join the Government formed by General Simovich, but when the Jugoslav Army was defeated he refused to accompany King Peter and most of the Ministers into exile and remained in the Pavelich state, under house arrest, but unharmed. Like the bulk of his followers he belonged to the Roman Catholic Church, and it was inevitable that his Catholic hate and fear of Communism should extend to the Communist-led Partisan movement. He did not fall into the error of supporting Pavelich on the grounds that he too was an enemy of the Communists, but some of the clerics connected with the Peasant Party did; they said field masses for the Ustashi troops and were photographed at Pavelich political rallies. For one reason or another, then, the Croat Peasant Party remained an essentially negative factor throughout the patriotic struggle.

Tito exploited this situation in Croatia, of course, to make himself the protagonist of both Orthodox Serbs and anti-Pavelich Croat patriots against the Ustashi and their German and Italian allies. At first, however, almost all his followers were Serbs—one Serb enthusiast, now a high government official, told me that in the early days the proportion was 95 percent. Gradually the number of Croat Partisans increased, and came to include Catholics and even priests. Though Tito was frankly a Communist, and though his men wore the red star on their caps, he deprecated too open talk about establishing an eventual Communist dictatorship. Even had he not seen the wisdom of this himself, he would have followed instructions to that effect from Stalin, who desired to avoid offending British and American democratic susceptibilities. In any event, Pavelich's fawning dependence on Hitler and Mussolini made it not too hard for patriots to persuade themselves that, by comparison, Tito's links with Moscow were unimportant. Moreover, there still lingered in Croatia, and even more in Montenegro and Serbia, strains of nineteenth-century Pan-Slavism, the effect of which was to surround Russia—any Russia—with a rosy aura and to make association with her, regardless of any social theories involved, more attractive than with any other nation.

The other leading figure in the Jugoslav drama was, of course, Mihailovich. His Chetniks were mainly Serbs and loyal to the Karageorgevich dynasty, which had ruled in Siberia longer than in other parts of the country. As we shall have cause to note, Stalin, no lover of kings, did not lose sight of the importance of the dynasty's hold on Serbian hearts; and Churchill, who became the chief architect of the pro-Tito policy in the West, recognized it also. Despite Mihailovich's patriotic record and strongly nationalistic background, his wisdom, sincerity and stamina became matters of dispute as the war progressed. Tito called him a collaborator with Nedich, who collaborated with both the Italians and the Nazis. The spirit in which Tito regarded Mihailovich's movement is shown by his description of the Chetniks as "the last remnants of the armed forces of the old, rotten, bourgeois order," who took up the patriotic fight so as "to preserve that old social bourgeois order from the people who were fighting to build up their own authority parallel to their struggle against the invader." [1]

Except for the adjectives, Mihailovich would probably have accepted the description. He was as anti-Communist as he was anti-Nazi; he accepted appointment as Minister of War in the Royal Jugoslav Government-in-exile; and he looked solely to the West for support in the war and salvation after the war. There is no doubt that he mistrusted and disliked Tito just as much as Tito mistrusted and disliked him, or that Chetniks and Partisans engaged first in rival manœuvrings for position and then in pitched battles. There is

[1] Political Report to the Fifth Congress of the Jugoslav Communist Party, Belgrade, July 21, 1948.

direct British and American testimony to the effect that many of
Mihailovich's lieutenants fell away from him in discouragement, that
in some areas they reached understandings with the enemy, especially the Italians, by which they secured arms to use in fighting the
Partisans, and that on the whole as the war went on Mihailovich's
tactics became passive and dilatory. There also is direct British and
American testimony to his personal fidelity to the Western allies and
to the continued resistance of loyal Chetnik bands, in discouraging
and tragic conditions, to the bitter end.

Personally, I do not believe that it lies well with Americans to con-
demn Mihailovich; it seems to me that we have sufficient reason to
fear that we ourselves may have contributed to his failings and his
fall. Our Government, like the British, fostered the spirit of resistance
in Belgrade in the spring of 1941, and when the Jugoslav patriots of
whom Mihailovich was one defied the Nazis we hailed it as an act of
outstanding courage, which undeniably it was. When the Jugoslav
armies had been defeated, we heard with joy that Mihailovich was
continuing to resist, and in due course we promised him help. I happen to have known something about the promises made when young
King Peter visited the United States at President Roosevelt's invita-
tion in June and July of 1942. Specifically, we undertook to drop
small arms, ammunition and condensed foods to Mihailovich by air-
plane. As a result of many factors—changes in strategic concepts,
conflicting reports about relative Partisan and Chetnik merits, pressing needs for matériel in other parts of the Mediterranean theatre,
and competing demands of various commanders for the air transport that would have been needed for Balkan missions—we actually
sent almost nothing. When I heard that one consignment via Egypt
had been diverted to Malta I wondered what the hard-pressed
Maltese would make of the encouraging messages in the Cyrillic
alphabet, signed Franklin D. Roosevelt, which came wrapped around
some of their food packages.

On October 6, 1943, four "Liberators" were presented in person
by President Roosevelt at Bolling Field to 42 Jugoslav aviators who
had volunteered to fight for the Royal Government-in-exile and had
now completed their training in the United States. Tito protested
this action as a "gift to a government which has nothing in common

with our fight for liberation." Three of the "Liberators" were afterwards shot down over Germany and Bulgaria during long-range
bombing missions with the 15th American Air Force, and the other
carried out 50 long-range fighting missions.[2] They proved to be the
only substantial "gift" to the Jugoslav Government by the United
States. They fought the common enemy; but they did not operate
under Mihailovich's command or (as he had hoped) transport supplies to his Chetniks in the mountains. I have not seen precise
accounts of the aid which Britain furnished to the Partisans in this
period. According to one Partisan authority, however, Tito informed
Stalin on July 20, 1943, in connection with the desperate but vain
appeals which he was then making for Soviet help, that the Partisans
to date had received "seven aeroplanes with various matériel" from
England.[3] Not very substantial, but more than reached Mihailovich.
Mihailovich's failure to get expected ammunition and food from the
West damaged his morale, and his inability to make good on his
promises that supplies were coming lessened his prestige with local
Chetnik leaders and his ability to control them.

There were several attempts at the start to reconcile the Communist and anti-Communist leaders. They seem actually to have met
two or three times, first in September 1941, last at Braichi on October 27. Their efforts to form a joint military command, plan joint
operations or even lay the basis for a permanent truce ended in
failure. Each accused the other of insincerity. Separate agreements
reached between local commanders were violated by one side or the
other, and ensuing bitter feelings and recriminations made further
meetings of the resistance chiefs impossible.

Mihailovich attributed Tito's failure to coöperate with him to
ulterior Communist motives which did not envisage the establishment of a really free Jugoslavia after the war. To justify this fear he
pointed to Tito's action in calling together delegates of his Anti-
Fascist Council of National Liberation (AVNOJ) in a frankly
political assembly at Bihac in November 1942 and a second time at
Jajce in November 1943. On the first occasion, when Tito was

[2] "The War We Lost," by Constantin Fotich (Jugoslav Ambassador to the
United States during the war). New York: Viking, 1948, pp. 211–216.
[3] Mosha Pijade, *Borba,* Belgrade, March 23, 1950.

making a particular effort to broaden his movement to include non-Communists, the manifesto adopted was fairly cautious. It attacked the invaders, the Chetniks and the Ustashi impartially, but promised the people true democratic rights after the liberation and specifically "the inviolability of private property and the provision of every possibility for individual initiative in industry, commerce and agriculture." At the 1943 meeting the AVNOJ transformed itself into a legislature, adopted a constitution, forbade King Peter to return to the country unless formally invited and gave Tito the title of Marshal of Jugoslavia. Simultaneously, Tito's National Committee of Liberation became a provisional government with Tito as its head. Mihailovich said that these actions proved that the Communist leader did not intend to let the Jugoslav people choose their own form of government freely after the invaders had been expelled.

Tito in turn accused Mihailovich of Serb nationalist tendencies which caused him to place special Serb interests above general Jugoslav interests. He stressed the fact that as Mihailovich was an officer in the Royal Jugoslav Army and Minister of Defense in the exiled Government in London he must necessarily be conservative and monarchist and would go to any lengths to forestall a republican or Communist victory. Just as the Partisans accused the Chetniks of betrayals and atrocities, so the latter accused the Partisans of accepting notorious Ustashi criminals as partners and asserted that they behaved more ruthlessly than even the Nazis toward prisoners and the families of Chetniks. The opportunities for double agents and agents-provocateurs to incite these resentments and snare the rival resistance groups into conflict were of course limitless. Some of the stories of treason which each side sincerely believed about the other doubtless originated in such sources.

As early as 1942 Tito was complaining not only that the Chetniks were fighting the Partisans but that they were not really fighting the Germans and Italians. In reply, Mihailovich pointed to Chetnik operations against Nazi lines of communication, which, he said, though less showy than the pitched battles of the Partisans, were really more useful; and he cited directives of the Western military commanders urging him to conserve manpower and build up his underground organization against the day when Allied troops might land in the Balkans. His services to the Allied cause were officially recognized as late as the beginning of 1943.[4]

Early in that year, however, Mihailovich lost favor in England. Churchill was miffed by his bitter criticism of the failure of British help to materialize. The incident was cleared up; but when Eden on May 7 informed the Jugoslav Government-in-exile that the British Government hoped "shortly" to be able to send Mihailovich material support "on a more considerable scale than in the past" he thought necessary to add a stipulation that the Chetnik leader must "definitely cease all collaboration with the Italians and General Nedich." That autumn Eden stopped in Cairo on his way home from his meeting in Moscow with Hull and Molotov. There he received a report from Brigadier Maclean that the Partisan movement was of "infinitely greater importance than was generally realized outside Jugoslavia" and that its effectiveness "could be considerably increased by Allied help." [5] On December 8, Richard Law, Minister of State, informed the House of Commons that henceforth Tito was to be favored, "for the simple reason that the Partisans' resistance to the Germans is very much greater."

In this period Stalin was not sure which of the Jugoslav rivals would come out on top and he also desired to avoid giving the Western Powers occasion to criticize him for staking out a future zone of Communist influence in the Balkans. He therefore refrained from openly supporting Tito's effort to assert a clear primacy over Mihailovich and he gave the military operations of the Partisans no direct help. Tito was chagrined and disillusioned by this attitude of expediency. Indeed, his wartime experience in some degree explains his attitude toward Stalin later. Perhaps, too, Tito's attitude toward Stalin in those hard days—pleading, complaining, even demanding —explains in part why Stalin was ready to disown him in 1948.

[4] A telegram from Admiral Sir Henry Harwood, General Sir Claude Auchinleck and Air Marshal Tedder on behalf of the British command in the Mediterranean and the Middle East, dated August 16, 1942, thanked Mihailovich and his Chetnik bands for cutting German lines of communication with Salonika and thereby curtailing German operations against the Allies in Libya and Egypt. At New Year's 1943, General Eisenhower telegraphed Mihailovich congratulations. Hitler repeatedly complained about the persistent guerrilla warfare in Serbia and impartially offered rewards for the capture of either Mihailovich or Tito. (For a full presentation of the Mihailovich case, see Fotich, *op. cit.*)

[5] Maclean, *op. cit.*, p. 390.

There now is reason to believe that in 1942 and 1943 Stalin not only did not credit Tito's stories against Mihailovich but actually pressed him to come to an understanding with the Chetnik leader. Evidence to this effect has been supplied by Mosha Pijade in two remarkable articles published in *Borba,* the leading Communist daily in Belgrade, March 22 and 23, 1950. In them Pijade quotes freely from letters and telegrams exchanged between Tito and Stalin during the war and from his own contemporary correspondence with Tito. Pijade had been sent to Montenegro in February 1942 to arrange for the reception of promised Russian planes. They failed to arrive, like the arms and equipment for which Tito made anguished appeals during the next two years.

Tito's letters to Pijade refer to Stalin as "Grandfather." On March 5, 1942, Grandfather telegraphed Tito asking why he had considered it necessary to organize purely proletarian brigades and whether he really was doing everything possible "to create a united national front." Tito told Pijade that in his answer he had tried to disabuse Grandfather of the idea that the Partisans consisted solely of Communists and fellow-travellers who were "fighting for Sovietization." He said he had indicated to him that the Moscow picture of what was going on in the country was very erroneous.

Grandfather nevertheless insisted on explaining to Tito the larger political interests which were at stake:

The defeat of the Fascist bandits and liberation from the occupier is now the basic task and is above all other tasks. Take into consideration that the Soviet Union has treaty obligations with the Jugoslav King and Government and that any open actions against these would create new difficulties in the common war efforts in relations between the Soviet Union and England and America. Do not consider your struggle only from your own national point of view but from the international point of view, from the point of view of the English-Soviet-American coalition. Strengthen your positions in the People's Liberation struggle and at the same time show more elasticity and ability to manœuvre. . . .

Writing about this to Pijade (March 26), Tito simply said: "I did not give too many explanations to Grandfather." Instead, he argued that if Grandfather wanted to create "a national liberation front" the best way would be to send the Partisans weapons. Grandfather always pleaded "technical difficulties," however. Replying to an urgent telegram sent by Tito on April 23, asking whether planes with munitions could be expected to arrive soon, he replied that the Partisans should not count on this. To sugar the pill he gave Tito permission to "unmask the traitorous actions by the Chetniks;" but what he gave with one hand he took back with the other, for he added that "at present it would be a better policy to do this by a general appeal to the Jugoslav Government" for support for all patriotic fighters. Tito considered this to be appeasement. On top of these disillusioning experiences he had to endure a heavy blow in the summer of 1942 when the Soviet Government raised the Royal Jugoslav Legation in Moscow to the rank of an Embassy. Tito telegraphed Grandfather (August 11) that this "made our liberation struggle more difficult," and he asked almost defiantly: "Can nothing be done so that the Soviet Government be better informed of the treacherous rôle of the Jugoslav Government and of the superhuman sacrifices of our people? Do you not believe what we tell you every day? . . . We emphasize: the Jugoslav Government is openly collaborating with the Italians and, under cover, with the Germans." Stalin was not accustomed to hearing talk like this from a subordinate and it probably left resentments. In any case, he remained unconvinced or considered it best to appear so for the present. In September he asked Tito for proofs of the accusations against the Chetniks, and indicated that he thought they might be based on enemy fabrications. Tito's reply was a suggestion that a joint commission representing all the Allies be sent to verify the true situation. This must have been definitely displeasing to Stalin and the suggestion was not taken up. "In 1943," says Pijade, "it was the same as in 1942"—Tito asked for arms and Moscow pleaded "technical difficulties."

It was to be expected that the Communism of one of the Jugoslav resistance leaders and the anti-Communism of the other would create complications in a war in which Soviet Russia was the partner of the Western democracies. Pijade's articles indicate, however, that at first the complications were greater between Tito and Grandfather than they were between Stalin and his Western allies. We are left with the impression that, at any rate in this period, Stalin felt less sure of

Russia's political and military position than Western observers assumed was the case.

Stalin's attitude was not made easier by the fact that by the end of 1943 Churchill had put all his money on Tito. In the First World War, Churchill had attempted to outflank the Central Powers by sending an expedition through the Dardanelles. That bold operation had failed by only a hair's breadth, and he was encouraged now to have another try of the same sort. He looked around for the "fightingest" ally on the spot. Charges of military inactivity and worse had already been made against Mihailovich, and Eden had brought back from Cairo Maclean's firsthand report as to the military capacities of the Partisans. Tito became Churchill's man. He referred to Jugoslavia with relish as "Titoland."

Stalin opposed the idea of a major Balkan invasion on the grounds that it would delay the opening of a front in Western Europe, which he counted on to relieve Nazi pressure on the Russian front. So did President Roosevelt and the American commanders. Like Stalin, they favored a mass invasion of Western Europe and opposed the strategy of an attack by the Balkan back door. At Teheran in December 1943 a definite decision was reached that the second front was to be in northern France. Churchill did not accept this as necessarily ruling out secondary operations in other theatres. Indeed, we know from General Eisenhower that until early August 1944 he clung to a revised version of his earlier project,[6] namely to force the Karst mountains at the top of the Adriatic and move thence into Austria by the Ljubljana gap. Doubtless he hoped to use Tito's strong Partisan bands in Slovenia to help with this undertaking and he may even have thought that he could wean Tito himself away from Communism. His tenacity in holding to specific projects on which he had set his heart was as remarkable as his devotion to the great lines of conduct that saved us all.

At Teheran, Stalin's attitude toward the situation in Jugoslavia was still unsettled. He naturally would have liked to strengthen the native Communist leader on the spot but apparently he was still afraid to put all his Jugoslav eggs in Tito's basket. I have been told

[6] Dwight D. Eisenhower, "Crusade in Europe." New York: Doubleday, 1948, Chapter 11.

by an American who was present that when Eden voiced disappoint-
ment over Mihailovich's recent rôle, Molotov reminded him that the
Chetnik leader represented the majority of the Serbian population
and could not be ignored. By this time, however, the Red armies
were on the offensive; they had forced the Nazis out of the Caucasus
and at some places behind the Dnieper, and were preparing for the
great drive that would carry them to Odessa and beyond, into
Rumania and Bulgaria. This made it desirable to plan for future
political moves in the Balkans, and here Stalin's need of Tito became
clear. The decisive meeting of the AVNOJ at Jajce had just ended,
having among other things given Tito the title of Marshal of Jugoslavia. Tito's star was plainly in the ascendant; nor was there any
reason for Stalin to hang back from supporting him lest he arouse
suspicions among the Western allies that he was aiming to build up
a Communist citadel in the Balkans. Churchill and Eden were
already in favor of helping Tito at the expense of Mihailovich and
would take over the job of persuading President Roosevelt. They
did so successfully. On his way home from Teheran, Churchill
stopped at Cairo. He told Maclean, who was there to meet him,
that he had "talked the Jugoslav problem over with Stalin and
Roosevelt" and that "as a result of these talks, it had been decided
to give all-out support to the Partisans." Maclean asked whether
there was any cause for concern in the fact that Tito's movement
was "avowedly Communist" and that the régime which he might
set up later would surely be "strongly oriented towards the Soviet
Union." Churchill told Maclean not to worry his head about Jugoslavia's future form of government. He was to be guided by one sole
consideration: which local leader was doing the Germans the most
direct harm? [7] We cannot say to what extent Roosevelt realized the
full implications of what was done about Jugoslavia at Teheran,
specifically whether he understood that it meant as a practical matter

[7] Maclean, *op. cit.*, pp. 402–403. Vladimir Dedijer, a Partisan Colonel and
later Director of Information in Tito's government, reports a conversation
between General Eisenhower and General Velebit, a representative of Tito in
London, just before the invasion of France, which shows that this was the prevailing reaction. Having told Velebit that "we are going to beat the hell out of
the Germans," Eisenhower said he was in favor of everyone who was fighting to
help beat them too. (Vladimir Dedijer, "Dnevnik," Volume 3. Belgrade: Jugoslovenska Knjiga, 1950.)

that no aid was to be available in future for Mihailovich. There were some in the State Department who when they heard of the decision regretted it.

Today, in their anxiety to damage Tito, Soviet propagandists assert that he was unfaithful to Stalin even during the war. To support the accusation they are incautious enough to mention Tito's repeated requests to the West for matériel and the fact that toward the end of the war he actually received some. This gives Tito the opportunity to recall that the only matériel which he did receive came from the West. Further, the Soviet charge ignores the fact that at Teheran the "Big Three" agreed that the Partisans "should be supported by supplies and equipment to the greatest extent possible, and also by commando raids." This knocks the props from under the whole accusation. Stalin himself placed no limits on the help that should go to Tito and specifically approved commando raids which obviously nobody but the British could possibly mount.

To prepare for the new situation when the Red Army would make contact with the Partisans, Stalin decided, soon after Teheran, to send a military mission to Tito. It reached Partisan headquarters in Bosnia in February 1944, and a Partisan mission under Milovan Djilas reached Moscow in April. The arrival of the Soviet mission after two and a half years of delay turned out to be something of an anticlimax. Individual British and American officers had been with Tito since May 1942; and Brigadier Maclean's mission, which had been there almost a year, now numbered several score officers, distributed in various parts of the country and connected with headquarters by radio. The Red Army lieutenant-general found himself in unfamiliar terrain in the Bosnian mountains; and Tito, for his part, being hard-pressed at the time, came to look on the belated arrivals as so much "excess baggage."

Shortly afterwards Tito was bombed out of his headquarters at Dvar by German *Stukas* and after some days of dodging about in the Bosnian woods was flown to the Adriatic island of Vis. He was carried in a Dakota plane, supplied to the Russians under lend-lease, based on Bari, flown by a Soviet pilot under British operational control. Tito has emphasized that the pilot was Russian in order to show that his action in leaving the mainland was approved by the Red

Army mission. Maclean has emphasized that the British made the arrangements which got Tito out of his tightest spot; and he adds, with justifiable pride, that in the week following the *Stuka* attack on Dvar "our planes flew over a thousand sorties in support of the Partisans." I have found no reference to this fact in Tito's speeches, though in his Fifth Party Congress report he admits that "some allied planes transported the wounded." The admirers of Mihailovich point out, meanwhile, that not in his moments of greatest desperation did the Chetnik chief ever have to quit the Jugoslav mainland. Partisans reply that this proves he must have been in cahoots with the enemy. The incident will serve as well as any to show the sort of verbal manœuvring which pervades most accounts of the Jugoslav resistance.

Having obtained Stalin's approval, Tito went from Vis to Italy to discuss strategy and supplies with General Sir Henry Maitland Wilson and strategy and politics with Prime Minister Churchill. In a book already mentioned, Stephen Clissold reports the conversation with Mr. Churchill, using quotation marks.[8] In this version Tito was closely questioned by Churchill as to whether he had any intention of "imposing" or "introducing" a Communist régime in Jugoslavia after the war, and categorically denied it. According to Tito, the only third person present at this talk was his personal interpreter, Olga Ninchich; and her memorandum of the conversation, corrected and approved by Tito, states that Churchill asked whether Tito intended to set up a Jugoslav régime on the Soviet pattern, and that Tito answered that while the Soviet experience would be helpful "we will also take into consideration our own conditions." Miss Ninchich's record states further that Churchill brought up the need of allowing the Serb people freedom to support Mihailovich if they wished to and to choose their own form of government eventually, but does not show that Tito made any reply to these representations.[9]

Neither account indicates that the Prime Minister said anything about the Soviet attitude toward Mihailovich. It will be interesting to see what Mr. Churchill himself has to say when his history of the

[8] "Whirlwind," p. 196. Mr. Clissold notes in his introduction that he has Mr. Churchill's permission to "reproduce" the conversation.

[9] Dedijer, *op. cit.*, p. 196.

war reaches this point; for if he indicated that Stalin and Molotov were still reluctant to abandon Mihailovich this would have increased Tito's wariness of Soviet policy.

Whatever satisfaction Churchill received from this talk was soon dissipated. In September, following Tito's return to the island of Vis, he unexpectedly vanished, or as Churchill put it "levanted." Later it became known that he had gone to Moscow to arrange for Soviet-Partisan military coöperation in view of the fact that Marshal Tolbukhin's armies had entered the Balkans.

This was the first time Tito had ever seen Stalin personally. The occasion was auspicious. Rumania had been overrun and had surrendered, and so had Bulgaria. Now the Red Army was approaching the Jugoslav frontiers. Tolbukhin politely "requested" permission to enter Jugoslavia and Tito graciously "granted" it. His troops made contact with the Partisans near the Danube and together the Russians and Jugoslavs engaged the Nazis in stiff fighting in the valleys below Avala where, in 1919, I had seen the shell-pitted fields and rusting barbed wire left by Mackensen's invading armies. Belgrade was captured October 20, 1944. Afterwards the Red Army moved up into the Hungarian plain in pursuit of more important objectives, ignoring the Nazi forces remaining in Bosnia and by-passing Zagreb, where Pavelich hung on until the final German capitulation. But the old capital on the bluffs where the Danube and Save meet was secure in the possession of Tito.

Looking back, however, we see that this was not the really decisive event for the future of Jugoslavia. That had been settled at Teheran. Once the main policy decision had been taken to make Tito the chosen instrument in Jugoslavia of all the Allies, his supremacy over Mihailovich and Communism's supremacy over democracy became inescapable. Hopes of establishing a new political equilibrium later were vain. No other authority or organized force remained inside the country to counterbalance him, negotiate with him on anything like an equal basis or exact enforcement of any undertakings which he had given or might give abroad regarding eventual free elections. Mihailovich—isolated, frustrated, confused and embittered—was condemned to the heartbreak of seeing his lieutenants compromise with the enemy, his main groups scatter and his political hopes fall to the ground. He himself and some of his followers held out to the end, and beyond. After the war, at the trial in Belgrade where he was condemned to death, he said: "I wanted much, I started much. But the wind of the world carried me and my work away."

Tito spread his wings to that wind and rode it beyond reach of any challenge.

# IV

## WHO, WHOM?

> There is to me something profoundly
> affecting in large masses of men following
> the lead of those who do not believe in men.
> Walt Whitman

MOSHA PIJADE is a bright-eyed little man, plumpish and with a stubbly mustache, who gave up painting for politics and as a result spent 15 years in prison, where he translated Marx into Jugoslav and learnt Chinese. He is now the chief intellectual of the Jugoslav Communist Party and the chief strategist in its fight against the Bolsheviks. He is also the only Communist dialectician of this generation—or left alive from the last generation—who has a vivacious wit. Pijade recently remarked, with heavy sarcasm, that although of course it had been "a great help" to have the Red Army participate in the liberation of Belgrade, the gratitude of the Jugoslavs has since then been tempered by the discovery that in that same October when the Soviet and Partisan forces took the Jugoslav capital Stalin was arranging with Churchill in Moscow for the Russians and the British to share their interests in Jugoslavia on a 50–50 basis. Pijade recounts how he himself was in Moscow at the time of Churchill's visit and was invited to a reception given at the Kremlin in honor of the British Prime Minister. Molotov came up to him, he recalls, patted him on the shoulder and congratulated him on how excellently everything was going in Jugoslavia. Pijade added: "However, he did not say that it was excellent in regard to dividing our skin." [1]

This negotiation between Stalin and Churchill caused Secretary Hull one of his greatest heartaches. When Lord Halifax first sug-

[1] *Borba*, Belgrade, March 22, 1950.

gested to him in May 1944 that it might be well to allow the Russians a controlling influence in Rumania if Britain in return could secure a controlling influence in Greece, Mr. Hull spoke against the idea out of hand. As he notes in his memoirs,[2] he was "flatly opposed to any division of Europe or sections of Europe into spheres of influence." In subsequent correspondence between Prime Minister Churchill and President Roosevelt, about which Mr. Hull knew nothing until afterwards, the President accepted the proposal for a three months' trial period and Russia and Britain completed their arrangement in June. Later it developed that Bulgaria and Jugoslavia were involved also, and that the future of all four Balkan countries was being discussed directly between London and Moscow. Mr. Hull's position was, and remained, that the whole concept of spheres of influence had been definitely rejected at the Moscow Conference the preceding October in favor of a broad system of general security in which all countries would have their part. Mr. Hull writes:

When Prime Minister Churchill and Foreign Minister Eden went to Moscow in October, 1944, to see Stalin and Molotov, they extended the agreement still further, even reducing to percentages the relative degree of influence which Britain and Russia individually should have in specified Balkan countries. Cables from our Embassies in Moscow and Ankara mentioned that Russia would have a 75/25 predominance in Bulgaria, Hungary, and Rumania, while Britain and Russia would share influence in Yugoslavia 50/50. Later the Russians took it for granted that by the agreement of June, 1944, Britain and the United States had assigned them a certain portion of the Balkans including Rumania and Bulgaria, as a sphere of influence. This assumption had its untoward effect at the Yalta Conference in February, 1945.

Had we made such a determined fight against the Anglo-Russian agreement as we had made successfully against the proposed territorial clauses of the Anglo-Russian alliance in May, 1942, [involving the Baltic States and portions of Finland, Poland and Rumania] it is possible that some of our later difficulties in the Balkans might not have arisen.[3]

It is a nice question whether Mosha Pijade or Cordell Hull is the more surprised today to find himself on the same side as the other, in

[2] *Op. cit.*, Vol. II, p. 1451.
[3] *Op. cit.*, Vol. II, p. 1458.

this or any matter. Certainly Mr. Hull took his stand on unassailable ground both morally and politically. As a matter of pure procedure it is difficult to imagine how the Russian and British statesmen planned to administer a country on a percentage basis. Pijade could have told Churchill and Eden exactly what Stalin's proposal meant; but even if he had known about it in time he would not have done so. Mr. Hull's message to him today, if he were to send one, would probably be merely "Better late than never."

Stalin's hesitation about letting the Partisan movement become frankly and solely Communist was, as we have seen, disillusioning to Tito. So was Stalin's failure to find any way of sending him military supplies. So was Stalin's acceptance, even if only as a stratagem, of the Karageorgevich dynasty. So was Stalin's agreement to divide influence in Jugoslavia 50–50 with the British, even though Stalin of course had his tongue in his cheek when he made it. But we must ask ourselves whether Tito, although he was a believing and disciplined Communist and as such recognized the superior wisdom of the higher command and accepted its orders, had not been forced even earlier than this to suppress vague feelings of disquiet, or perhaps worse.

Tito's Communist faith went back to the First World War. He was born Josip Broz on May 25, 1892, in a Croatian village when Croatia was a Hapsburg province. Many tales are now told, of course, about his childhood, and these give some idea either of what his salient characteristics were then or of which characteristics are so prominent today that people invent stories to show that they always existed. Until Josip Broz reached the age of 12 (an old associate of his has told me), he was a good Catholic and served as an acolyte in the village church. Then one day he fumbled in trying to hook up a cassock or robe on the back of a stout priest. The priest cuffed him; Josip walked out, and never set foot in church again. Another story from the same source indicates the same quick temper and independence. Josip was apprenticed to a locksmith. His master accused him of some irregularity, and he left. Later the master found out that Josip was not to blame; but he refused to return. Soon afterwards he was conscripted into the Austro-Hungarian Army to fight in the First World War. He was captured by the Russians, converted to Communism and joined the Red Army. Back from Russia after the war,

he became Secretary of the Metal Workers' Union in Zagreb and
was active in organizing Communist cells. He was popular with the
workers—"not too theoretical," says one man who knew him in these
days, "but on the other hand much more than just a man of action."
In 1928, he was arrested for illegal activity and sent to jail for five
years. There he met Mosha Pijade, who strengthened his understanding of Marxism. He also formed other close political and intellectual
associations—King Alexander's jails seem to have offered greater
opportunities for comradeship and cultural development than Communist jails do today. After his release he returned to Moscow for a
refresher course at the Lenin School, and then was sent as a Party
agent to Western Europe. He worked in Paris as a liaison officer for
the Communists who went to Spain from all over Europe to take
part in the Civil War; but unlike other East European Communists who have since been disgraced for showing too much independence he did not actually engage in the fighting. In 1937 he was
put in charge of the underground movement in his native Jugoslavia.

The Jugoslav Communist Party, which had been outlawed for
years, was by this time nearly defunct. Tito's predecessor, Gorkich,
had engaged in internecine disputes with other leaders; some were
Right deviationists, some were Left deviationists, some even were
agents of the régime. In 1929 the membership of the Party was only
about 3,500 and the leadership had fled to Vienna to escape the
oppressive measures of the Zhivkovich Government. Tito brought the
headquarters of the Party back into the country and set about building up a following. At once the elements for a later ideological disagreement with Moscow presented themselves, for he saw that in
order to give the Party country-wide vitality he would have to take
as the base of operations the vast majority of the population who
were peasants. It was most unlikely that he would ever gain their
active support, but he must at least avoid making them feel, as Stalin
was making the Russian peasants feel, that they were a principal
Communist enemy. Tito's supporters today claim that the wisdom of
his course became plain during the war when the Jugoslav peasantry
proved to be the main source of Partisan recruitment, and they contrast this with the fact that during the Russian Revolution the
Russian peasantry remained outside of, if not opposed to, Com-

munist revolutionary activity. They also assert that already in 1937 and 1938 Tito's domestic policies raised difficulties between him and the Comintern. One reads the long historical résumé given by Tito at the Fifth Party Congress in the summer of 1948, after the break between Belgrade and Moscow, without finding specific support for this view. The Party proclamations and directives which he quotes, and his comments on them, speak of "going to the masses" but not of "going to the peasants." Nevertheless, in a country where the peasants are the masses the meaning is clear enough to lend some credit to the idea that already before the war Tito may have met difficulties in carrying out Moscow's orders in conditions different from those in Russia.

On nationalist grounds, too, Tito might have suffered some pangs, if not of conscience at least of heart.

In 1938 Hitler annexed Austria and brought the Nazi war machine to the crest of the Karawanken Mountains and the edge of the Maribor plain. This, and Mussolini's tightening of the Italian grip on Albania, made Jugoslavia's strategic position most difficult. When Hitler annihilated the independence of Czechoslovakia the following year he gave as his excuse the need of "Lebensraum"—an ominous portent for other small Slav states. The Nazi and Fascist net was closing in, and although Communists are taught that war provides the ultimate opportunities for revolution it is doubtful whether Tito would have liked either the prospect of Hitler's and Mussolini's domination of his country or the alternative of war against them under hopeless conditions. Soviet Russia was not to blame for these events, but neither had she been able to halt them. Thanks to the resourcefulness of Litvinov, the last of the Soviet statesmen to have any understanding of Western mentality or any skill in propaganda, the Soviets had emerged from the Munich crisis with a good case "for the record." British prestige and influence had meanwhile been so undermined by Neville Chamberlain and Sir Horace Wilson that even when the British Prime Minister gave Poland his pledged word Hitler thought it meant nothing. Nor had Daladier, hindered by Georges Bonnet, done much better in his efforts to extricate France from her engagements to Czechoslovakia with something like honor and to assert France's continued right to be heard on such matters as the life or death of Poland. Then in August 1939 Stalin struck hands with Hitler. This act freed the Nazi dictator to launch his armor into Poland. Having secured a share of Poland, Stalin appropriated the Baltic States, denounced the 1932 Soviet-Finnish nonaggression pact, began what President Roosevelt termed "the rape of Finland" and seized Bessarabia and northern Bukovina.

As Tito watched Hitler overwhelm one nation after another, and then saw Stalin scavenge the débris, he may have realized how little the independence or security of any other country meant to either of the two mighty and unprincipled forces now working in alliance.

By 1941, when the time came to organize the Partisan resistance, Tito had built up the membership of the Jugoslav Communist Party to about 12,000. Not more than a quarter of these were to survive the guerrilla fighting. As the Party membership reached something over 470,000 by 1948, we see that the proportion of these who could at that time claim the prestige of being "old" members was a fraction of one percent. The fact that almost none of Tito's present followers have known any leader but him is an important fact which Stalin was to overlook. More than any Communist Party in the world the Jugoslav Party is the creation of one man. Its members are thorough Communists; but they look first to Tito and only through him to Stalin.

In the domestic arena, following the capture of Belgrade in October 1944, things fell out for Tito better than he could have planned in his cleverest stratagems. Early that spring the British Foreign Office, looking around for a possible middleman between young King Peter in England and Tito in Belgrade, had hit on Dr. Ivan Shubashich, former Ban of Croatia, at that time living in the United States. Shubashich was a trifling and ambitious man, but he was well thought of in certain American circles which agreed with the British policy toward Tito and supposed like the British Foreign Office that when the war was won things could be patched up between the different Jugoslav elements and a constitutional régime established. On the advice of his American friends in the O.S.S., Dr. Shubashich accepted the British proposal to serve as deus ex machina and flew to London. There he found, however, that King Peter was reluctant to empower him to conduct negotiations with such an arrogant and firm antagonist. In pressing the King to agree, Churchill and Eden undoubtedly felt that they were acting in the interests of Jugoslavia as a whole and even of the dynasty. And indeed, if anything were to be saved in Jugoslavia on the basis of the policy which they had adopted in 1943 this was the logical next step. On June 1, 1944, King Peter at last yielded to what came very close to being political blackmail, appointed Shubashich as Prime Minister and sent him off to see Tito.

Tito was then on the island of Vis, and there on June 16 he and Dr. Shubashich agreed on a rather ambiguous formula for coöperation. Tito has since stated [4] that the meeting was forced on him by the Western Allies, who "wanted by all means to save the old order in Jugoslavia—at least partly in the beginning, and later on completely if possible." The situation, in his words, called for "great watchfulness and elasticity" on his part. Evidently his talents were equal to the occasion. The agreement stated that the Government-in-exile would be reformed to ensure that it was composed of "progressive democratic elements," and it assigned the new government two chief duties, "to organize aid to the National Liberation Army" and "to see to the feeding of the population of Jugoslavia." A third duty would be "to coördinate the work of the representations abroad and that of the inter-Allied commissions with the protection of our people's rights, with the needs of the people and with the National Liberation struggle in the country." In return, Tito agreed that it was "unnecessary, for the time being, to emphasize and render acute the question of the king and the monarchy," since "both parties agreed that the people are to make a final decision regarding the state system after the liberation of the country." Dr. Shubashich also undertook to recognize "temporary administration of the country by the AVNOJ and the National Committee of Liberation as its executive organ." [5] His public declaration to that effect would "give full recognition to the fighting people's forces organized into the National Liberation Army under the command of the Marshal of Jugoslavia, Josip Broz-Tito." Tito's corresponding declaration was to contain

[4] Fifth Party Congress, July 21, 1948.
[5] This provision, readers of the preceding chapter know, will not have surprised Mihailovich when he read it in his retreat in the Serbian mountains.

only one promise: "not to raise the question of the final state system during the war." [6]

When Tito came to issue his declaration he attacked the preceding "émigré governments" for having remained "callously hostile" to the National Liberation Movement and for having helped the Chetniks wage "an armed struggle against their own people on the side of the invaders." However, he accepted the appointment of Shubashich as Prime Minister and the dismissal of Mihailovich as Minister of War (one of Shubashich's first acts) as the basis for future coöperation. He also included this statement:

The National Liberation Movement of Jugoslavia is in its essence an all-people's national and democratic one. We are, therefore, underlining once more that the leadership of the National Liberation Movement in Jugoslavia concerns itself with the only and most important aim—the struggle against the invader and his aids and creation of a democratic, federative Jugoslavia, and not establishment of Communism, as some of our enemies claim.

In quoting this passage in the course of his speech in July 1948, Tito interjected a significant remark: "This statement was, of course, a correct one at that time." One can only comment, both here and in connection with Tito's statements to Churchill as reported in the Clissold book, that the crux of the meaning of any such undertakings by a Communist is that the word "democracy" has an entirely different meaning in our vocabulary from what it has in the Communist's, where it is defined as a state organized to maintain the rule of the working class through the systematic use of force.

One more comment made by Tito in July 1948 referring to these historic events must be quoted, for it sheds further light on his intentions then and his actions since:

We had to consent to this agreement because the Western allies stubbornly insisted on it. They wanted, with all their might, to again impose

[6] Shubashich's declaration, in general on the lines promised, was issued in London on August 8, 1944. Tito issued his declaration August 17. The texts of both were quoted by Tito in his Political Report to the Fifth Party Congress, July 21, 1948. The texts of the June 16 agreement and of Tito's declaration of August 17 may also be found in the *United Nations Review,* New York, September 15, 1944, p. 240.

the king upon us, that is, the discredited monarchy and all the ballast around him, the worst reactionaries. The king would be a kind of Trojan horse, through which a return to the old way of life would be effected, and at best, the people would once more have to take arms to win what they once had. We therefore decided to make this agreement because we were aware of our strength, because we knew that a large majority of the people was with us and that they would always back us if needed. Besides, we had an armed force whose strength our adversaries could not even imagine, while the king and his government had nothing because Drazha Mihailovich was not only discredited as a collaborator with the invader but was defeated by our units. We, therefore, had nothing to be afraid of and we consented to this agreement which could be of no detriment but only benefit—if we worked correctly. And that is what happened later.

I have already mentioned Churchill's visit to Stalin in October 1944 when Jugoslavia's future became the joint and equal responsibility of British and Russian statesmanship. Soon thereafter, on November 1, Tito and Shubashich concluded a further more detailed and "final" agreement. By its terms a regency would be appointed to act in the king's name until the future of the monarchy had been determined by a popular plebiscite. The political assembly created by the AVNOJ during the war was to be enlarged to include members of the last prewar parliament who had not been compromised by collaboration with the enemy. The acts of this new legislative body were to be ratified later by a Constituent Assembly. This "final" agreement came before the "Big Three" at Yalta, and on February 11, 1945, they recommended that it "immediately be put into effect." Again King Peter was given no choice. Stettinius has written that Churchill said Peter "had been persuaded, or even forced, to agree to a regency." [7] On March 6 a provisional government was formed in Belgrade with Tito as Prime Minister, Shubashich as Foreign Minister, and a leader of the old Serbian Democratic Party, Milan Grol, as Vice-Premier.

The Yalta Conference approved the Tito-Shubashich Agreement as part of the general arrangement for compromising Communist and anti-Communist disputes and rivalries in Eastern Europe; and

[7] Edward R. Stettinius, Jr., "Roosevelt and the Russians: the Yalta Conference." New York: Doubleday, 1949, p. 217.

at least the two Western conferees, President Roosevelt and Prime
Minister Churchill, hoped that the results in Jugoslavia would be in
harmony with the high-sounding Declaration on Liberated Europe
which they and Stalin signed at this time. The Declaration promised
that the United States, Britain and Soviet Russia would assist the
liberated and former Axis satellite nations "to solve by democratic
means their pressing political and economic problems," cited the
Atlantic Charter on behalf of "the right of all peoples to choose the
form of government under which they will live," and looked forward
to joint action by the three signatory Powers and France to help the
peoples of Eastern Europe obtain broadly representative governments and hold free elections.[8] These hopes were not fulfilled in any
of the countries concerned.

In the case of Jugoslavia, specifically, the stage now was set for
the customary final act in the comedy of Communist and non-
Communist collaboration in a Communist-dominated "popular
front." Messrs. Shubashich and Grol found that they had no standing or influence whatsoever in the Government and that Tito paid
not the slightest attention to the promises which he had made in
order to secure their services as window-dressers. Tito has since told
us frankly about his purposes at this time: "Having created the
main pre-conditions during the war and having a clear perspective
for the establishment of a state of the new type to replace the old
one, we could not, during the period of joint government, make any
concessions to those elements in the government who actually represented the interests of the overthrown monarchy, the bourgeoisie and
their patron abroad, international reaction." And again: "This was
only a transition period in the development of the internal system
of new Jugoslavia. Even in this period our adversaries both in the
country and abroad had illusions about 'who would beat whom.'
But we had no such illusions, we knew how this whole thing would
end." [9]

[8] The authoritative account of the Crimea Conference is contained in Stettinius, *op. cit.* For an account of the general setting of the Conference and of
what happened eventually to the agreements there made see "The United States
in World Affairs," for 1945–47, 1947–48 and 1948–49, by John C. Campbell,
and for 1949 by Richard P. Stebbins (New York: Harper, published for the
Council on Foreign Relations).

[9] Fifth Party Congress, July 21, 1948.

When Shubashich and the others found that they were mere driftwood on the current carrying Jugoslavia toward complete Communization they turned to the Governments which had approved the agreement enumerating their supposed rights and safeguards. The British and the Americans found themselves in the humiliating position of being unable to do anything to obtain compliance with either the Declaration on Liberated Europe or the Tito-Shubashich Agreement. Grol resigned in protest against Tito's tactics on August 20, 1945, and Shubashich followed two months later. It was too late to establish any sort of equilibrium in Jugoslavia between democracy and "democracy." The scales had been tilted decisively at Teheran, and words did not bring them back into balance.

The finale was delayed only long enough to enable Tito to complete his preparations for the elections to the Constituent Assembly. When these were held in November they conformed to the pattern with which we have since become familiar in Communist-dominated countries. Candidates for a so-called "National Front" ticket were hand-picked, and persons not so picked were not allowed to stand as candidates. Legal and illegal opposition were equally impossible, for Tito controlled the police. About 40 representatives of the old prewar political parties had agreed to play a part in this farce. They accepted candidacies on the National Front ticket and were elected. The Communist Party elected 470 of its members. The political complexion of the Constituent Assembly having been assured, the next step was to abolish the monarchy. This was done at the first session on November 29, 1945, and the Federative People's Republic of Jugoslavia was proclaimed in its place. Shubashich and Grol were placed under house arrest, where they have remained ever since, though from time to time one or the other is reported to have been seen taking a walk in the street, shadowed by his police agent.

From November 29, 1945, there was no longer any shadow of doubt as to who was "who" and who was "whom." At the time the war ended Tito had ruled supreme in the Jugoslav Communist Party, in the National Committee of Liberation and in the Partisan army. Now he was equipped with a Government and a Parliament, both of which could pass for legal, at any rate in the new Communist world which was taking shape around the U.S.S.R. To this environment Tito's régime, Tito's Party and Tito himself appeared perfectly adjusted. Everything seemed comfortable and secure. Jugoslavia was an independent member of the Communist family of nations. The Jugoslav Communist Party had more prestige than any of its sister Parties except the Bolshevik Party itself. And in the Communist hierarchy, undisputed head of this Government and Party as well as of the powerful Jugoslav Army, Tito was accepted as "secundus inter pares." Or so it seemed.

# V

## STALIN AND TITO

> I would rather sit on a pumpkin and
> have it all to myself than be crowded on a
> velvet cushion.
>
> Henry David Thoreau, "Walden"

THE situation was so comfortable all
round that there seemed no reason why it should be disturbed. It
was not comfortable for the Jugoslav people, of course, who found
that they had been liberated into a dictatorship; but their comfort
was not a consideration. In April 1945 Tito again visited Grandfather in Moscow, and this time returned with a 20-year treaty of
friendship and mutual assistance. This was the zenith of their collaboration.

As time went by, Tito began to see that the assistance was not to
be mutual in just his meaning of the word. Stalin had been working
out the schedule of household chores to be performed by each member of the new Communist family, and his conception of family life
was different from that of some of his grandchildren. When he came
to assigning a rôle and a task to Jugoslavia, for example, he took
insufficient account, in Tito's eyes, of the circumstances which we
have been discussing. The numerous political, economic, military
and cultural missions which he sent to Belgrade after the war seemed
to vie with each other in bringing difficult or disagreeable instructions. No outward signs of the resulting discontent were permitted
to appear, of course; but it was there, and in time it became mutual.

Among Tito's discoveries was one that caused him particular
chagrin: apparently Stalin did not in fact, whatever might be his
pretensions, approve of Tito's determination to bring to Jugoslavia
swiftly and in great variety the blessings of industrialization which
always seem so especially great to those who know them not. This

has become the basis for some of Tito's most bitter comments about Soviet policy and one of his principal reasons explaining the eventual break with Moscow. Like all good Socialists, Tito was a planner, and he had made a Five Year Plan in 1947 and proudly affixed his name to it. Today he claims that although the Soviet press praised the Plan the Soviet Government was not pleased by the scope of his ambitions as there revealed, his energy in putting the Plan into operation or, above all, his independent manner of discussing it with the Soviet trade missions and his opposition to various exploitative aspects of the Soviet proposals. The Plan emphasized machine construction and metallurgy, and provided for increasing the means of production in Jugoslavia from 43 percent of the general industrial output in 1939 to 57 percent in 1951. Tito claims that Moscow hampered the fulfillment of these designs by discrimination, obstruction and delay in both financial and trade matters. He received the impression, as a result, that in the Soviet long-range scheme the new Jugoslavia was to remain principally a producer of agricultural and raw materials, which were to be exported to the Soviet Union and to such of the satellite states as in Moscow's opinion could use them to the best advantage, namely Czechoslovakia, which was already industrially advanced, and Hungary and Poland, where the industrial plant would be developed at forced draught. As time went by, then, he would have to set his own Plan aside or modify it out of all recognition and turn the energies of his people to fulfilling, instead, the Plan for the U.S.S.R.

Tito found also that critical decisions about the successive steps and tempo of the class struggle in Jugoslavia might soon pass out of his hands. Agrarian reform, a matter of surpassing moment in a country where from 70 to 80 percent of the people live on the land, was a case in point. If the methods used in collectivizing the land in the Soviet Union were transferred integrally to the Jugoslav scene they were certain to end in pitched battles between the peasants and the government agents and police. Grave economic difficulties would follow the consequent fall in food production, and Jugoslavia for a time might be uncomfortably dependent even for food on the over-all planners in Moscow.

Other seeds of discontent were being sown and soon grew and

blossomed. The Red Army had sent a number of its officers to Belgrade (at high salaries, paid from the Jugoslav treasury) to advise their country cousins. The Partisans were anxious to receive new weapons and learn how to handle them, but they thought they already knew something about fighting and did not feel that the Russians could tell them much about tactics in the Jugoslav terrain.

Soviet pedagogues also arrived to lecture the Jugoslav élite in Marxist theory, and especially in the interpretations which Stalin produced in support of the policies indicated above. Among other things, while publicly proclaiming the rule of the "toiling masses" they placed great emphasis, in their private instructions, on the Marxist doctrine that not peasants but industrial workers are the most progressive and revolutionary class and hence must play a predominant political rôle in all Communist societies. (In 1948 the emphasis would be put openly, as we shall see, on the special rôle of the industrial workers; but for the time being the true Russian aims in this respect were camouflaged in accordance with the general tactics of the moment.) Tito realized where this might end. He knew the oft-repeated maxim of Stalin's that Marxist-Leninism is not a fixed dogma but "leadership for action," and that the practical formula which that action takes "can change with every new turn of history." Incidentally, it seems that Communists can cite apparently contradictory directives from the body of Marxist-Leninist dogma to suit different purposes as readily as Christians do from the Bible. The visitors from Moscow were not deterred from urging Tito to take political power from the peasants and give it to the industrial workers by the practical consideration that the Jugoslav peasantry must vastly outnumber the urban proletariat into the indefinite future. These and other inconsistencies between the interests of the Jugoslav Party and the orders handed down from Moscow seemed to Tito almost deliberately designed to embarrass him both in his domestic politics and in the Communist world at large, where he naturally wished to cut a creditable figure.

He was not alone in his embarrassment, of course. The Communist leaders of all the People's Democracies of Eastern Europe were receiving directives for their respective countries. A detailed blueprint was emerging of the vast new mansion to be built for

Stalin, and a timetable for the pouring of each block of concrete, for the procurement of each timber and every nut and bolt and for the attachment of the red star to each cupola. Each member of the family had his stint to perform, not because he had volunteered for it in preference to others but because Stalin had assigned it. Nobody was asked whether he liked the design or whether he thought he would feel at home when the structure was completed. The plan was suited to Russia's convenience exclusively. Nor was there any indication that the relationship would change when the construction job was done. Quite the contrary. Having built Socialism, the satellites would be more than ever subject to the laws of Socialist planning, and everything pointed to these being interpreted towards one single end, the strengthening of Russia and the perpetuation of her predominance. The economy of each would produce for Russia first, and for itself—to the degree that it was admitted to have requirements of its own—second. What each had to produce and what each would be allowed to consume would be regulated by the simple means of allocating all raw materials centrally and dividing all the product centrally.

Just how rapidly all this dawned on Tito we do not know. We may be sure that when it did, however, he would not have felt any better about it because he was in the same boat with other satellite leaders whom he rather despised. In any case, he came eventually to realize that Jugoslavia's assignment in the over-all Soviet economic plan meant that she would remain what she had always been—poor, backward and therefore weak. We may think that Tito had quite erroneous ideas about how quickly he could bring a lopsided economy into better balance without creating bitter hardships for the people and doing many of them outrageous injustice—indeed, how quickly he could do it even if he ignored the fact that the price would be exorbitant. It was to be foreseen, also, that his plan to build up Jugoslav industry indiscriminately in almost all branches at once would run into difficulties. But Tito was not wondering about matters such as where Jugoslavia would sell a great new heavy industry's products once the domestic market had been filled. He thought in orthodox Marxist terms that industrialization was a necessary preliminary to socialization, and what struck him was that

Soviet obstruction was in effect forcing him to abandon or delay indefinitely the accomplishment of objectives which were essentially Socialist and which seemed to him quite feasible if only the Soviet Union would extend a brotherly Communist hand. If things continued as they had begun, in the Communist future as in the capitalist past the Jugoslav people would work with their hands in fields and mines. In time more tools and machines might be put in their hands; but these would come from abroad, and when and how they should come would be determined abroad. Jugoslavia would still be at the mercy of foreigners. Granted the foreigners would now be Russians, fellow-Communists. But if Grandfather was looking after Russia's interests so egotistically in this first period of building Socialism, might he not perpetuate his control, still in Russia's interest, until in the end it became indistinguishable from what the Jugoslavs had fought against all through history—foreign exploitation?

The situation confronting Tito had practical drawbacks, too, of a sort which bourgeois politicians will be able to recognize. He had promised the Jugoslav people after the war that under his Socialist program of industrialization, nationalization and collectivization—developed zealously and, as he liked to imagine, smoothly—factories and hydroelectric plants would spring up and begin humming, irrigation systems would bring water to arid regions and control age-old floodings, oil resources would be tapped and the product refined and a network of modern highways would spread out through the primitive countryside. Besides laying the foundations of a strong heavy industry, he would also stimulate the production of desperately needed consumer goods. Soap, combs, needles, razor blades, toothbrushes, scissors, thread—all the things that the Jugoslavs had hardly seen since before the war would again appear, this time on the shelves of his new nationalized shops. But if the necessary heavy equipment and financial assistance were not to be forthcoming from Soviet Russia all these plans would have to be abandoned or postponed. Raw materials which would have gone to feed native industries would be shipped instead to Russia or to satellite states chosen for an industrial rôle. Indiscriminate class warfare in the villages would reduce the food supplies available to support even the present industrial workers, let alone the increased number projected under the Five Year Plan. The commercial treaties which he had been negotiating with neighboring states, always with the requirements of his own Plan in mind, would have to be reinterpreted or rewritten so as to meet, instead, the requirements of the Soviet Plan. The other satellites would be required to procure from Jugoslavia what they needed to meet their requirements under the Soviet Plan; Jugoslavia would have to give them what they needed; and she would receive in return not what Tito and his planners thought would be most advantageous to the Jugoslav economy but what the Soviet planners calculated would best enable Jugoslavia to continue fulfilling her function as a producer of primary products.

Bukharin's prediction that economic competition would have no place in the international Communist society of the future seemed on the way to being fulfilled with a vengeance.

The political connotations of all this were plain to Tito. He would have to explain to the people how it was that he had come to over-estimate their need for smelting mills and dams and electrical de-velopment. Worse, he would have to tell them why it was better not to build factories to make buttons or matches or combs or needles, why pasteboard suitcases imported from Poland and bicycles im-ported from Czechoslovakia and bad-smelling soap imported from the U.S.S.R. were better than any that could have been manufac-tured in Jugoslavia from domestic hides and steel and fats. On top of this he was called on to give effect to orders that the leading politi-cal rôle belonged to the urban working class minority and that the peasant majority must be restricted to a secondary influence in both the Party and the government. The peasants were already restless and angry as a result of Tito's energetic collectivization program; and very energetic it was, whether or not it conformed to the Soviet prescription. Most of the Partisan fighters had been peasants. Some of his oldest and closest associates were of peasant origin. All of them would resent the enforcement of the Party line ordered from Mos-cow. There was an additional factor of a personal nature which would not have escaped his notice. The political discrimination ordered against the peasant class in Jugoslavia could hardly fail to carry over into the international arena. As representative of a peasant Jugoslavia he would wield less influence in Communist

councils than the representatives of more industrialized, more prole-
tarianized and therefore more politically mature peoples.

Tito paid another visit to Moscow from May 27 to June 10, 1946,
and came back with the announcement that the U.S.S.R. was going
to supply the Jugoslav Army with modern equipment. He felt con-
strained to interpret this as a triumph in order to offset a bitter
failure: Stalin had reproached him for asking that the Soviets go so
far as to make war to get Trieste for Jugoslavia, and had flatly
refused to entertain any such project. Actually, the Soviet offer to
rearm and reorganize the Jugoslav Army was in many respects a
blow which Tito did not know how to parry. The former Partisan
forces needed heavy equipment, but he did not relish the idea that by
deciding how the new Jugoslav Army was to be armed the Soviet
high command would settle its future character and rôle. He was
unwilling to permit the Soviet intelligence to operate in the Jugoslav
Army. He did not wish the Army to lose altogether its character as
a guerrilla force, suited to operations in the Jugoslav mountains, and
become in effect an auxiliary of the Red Army, part of a vast horde
of anonymous foot-soldiers. He found that this was just what some
of the Soviet advisers and technicians seemed to have in view, judging by the kind of equipment offered and the tables of organization
suggested. Jugoslavia was to train conscripts in yearly batches, but
not maintain any considerable standing army. She was not to build
a national armament industry. When I talked with Tito in the spring
of 1950 he told me that he also had sensed that the Red officers were
jealous of the fame of the Partisans, resented that they had performed their feats without benefit of Soviet guidance and wished to
obliterate their traits of nationalism and self-reliance. Altogether, we
are justified in believing that questions of the nature, rôle and command of the new Jugoslav Army became a prime reason for Tito's
growing restlessness.

Rumors of his discontent reached Moscow. The rulers in the
Kremlin heard that unkind things were said in Belgrade about the
demands of the Soviet trade delegates, about the behavior of Red
Army officers, about the way the Soviet intelligence was recruiting
Jugoslav citizens and about similar Soviet activities. Sometimes
members of the Soviet missions found that they no longer could im-

mediately get any and every fact about the Jugoslav internal situation which would make it easy for them to supervise the life of the country and exploit its resources. And there was a suspicion that some of the talks which Tito carried on with officials in neighboring countries, Bulgaria and Hungary for instance, aimed at coöperative satellite action to offset Soviet pressure.

This development did not follow a clear pattern on either side, and it would be a mistake to think of it in isolation from the general course of events in Eastern Europe. During and just after the war Moscow had permitted and encouraged local Communist leaders to adopt expedients which in time, as the Soviet hold on the area became more secure, were no longer considered necessary. While the Communist Parties in the various satellite states were busy consolidating their position they had found it advisable to respect and even pay tribute to national traditions and ambitions. The Kremlin encouraged them in this, and also gave them the impression that they would be allowed to attain the Socialist goal by roads of their own choice. That the new régimes constituted "proletarian dictatorships," or that they might be expected to develop into such dictatorships in the future, was carefully denied in Communist pronouncements. Instead, the new order was euphemistically described as "the rule of the toiling people" and no unnecessary emphasis was placed on the fact that in it peasants and intellectuals would play subordinate political rôles. Similarly, agrarian reforms helped to placate the peasantry, who did not foresee fully that distribution of the lands formerly held by large estates, the Church and prosperous peasants was, in Communist thinking, only a necessary first step toward inevitable collectivization. Attention was of course given to evading genuine mass participation in political decisions; but appearances were maintained by allowing non-Communist groups to coöperate with the predominant Communist Party in coalition "fronts," and by bringing together sections of the population in Communist-dominated trade unions and "mass organizations" of youth, women, consumers and so on.

The friction which was developing between the Soviet missions and the Jugoslav Communist régime showed Stalin where this sort of temporizing would inevitably lead. Not only was the policy of expediency no longer necessary; evidently it had become actually dangerous. Stalin decided not simply to discard it. He would blame Communist leaders in Poland, Czechoslovakia and elsewhere who had been taken in by it of having invented it. Those who had been contented with half-goals or half-measures would gradually find themselves criticized as deviationists from orthodox Marxism. They could abandon the practices complained of, accept blame for having trusted in them, suffer chastisement of a suitable sort and, if it seemed likely that they would be as useful in the new order as they had been in the old, might look forward to continuing in service. In the case of Jugoslavia, however, socialization really had been pushed energetically. Charges of an opposite nature, therefore, would be laid against Tito quite barefacedly. Since his collectivization measures and his program for wiping out "all remnants of capitalism in trade and industry" (published early in 1948) could not be denounced as Right deviationism they would be attacked as inept and hasty, smacking of Trotskyite Left deviationism.

In the new dispensation, fewer concessions would be made to national sentiment and traditions, independent initiative would be curtailed and the true goals of Communism would be set forth in their real light, with no pretense that anything less would be satisfactory for long or that excuses for not attaining them would be accepted indefinitely. The final goal was thoroughgoing Sovietization. The approved methods for reaching it included whatever degree of force and violence might be necessary. Thus collectivization of the land was to be complete, in line with Lenin's warning that the most dangerous seeds of capitalism live on in the peasantry. Proletarian dictatorship was to be absolute, in line with Lenin's dictum that the working class does not share power with other classes. The political expedients of the recent past—allowing popular front organizations to represent the masses and letting the scourings of old liberal non-Communist parties coöperate with the Communist élite—were to be stopped. "Bourgeois" political parties were to be liquidated. Social Democratic Parties, after undergoing a thorough purification, were to be absorbed into the Communist Parties. And the Communist Parties themselves, grown large and less completely reliable, were to be purged in line with Lenin's advice that the

limited-membership and strictly disciplined Communist Party is the
most important instrument for enforcing the transition to Socialism
and ultimately Communism.

The switch would not take place all at once, of course, and the
full ideological justification for it would not be laid out in one inte-
grated argument. There was no idea of creating friction for its own
sake, except perhaps here and there so that resisters could suffer
exemplary punishment. And indeed no new ideology was in fact
required. It would be sufficient to revive in its awful integrity, for
the benefit of Stalin's servants in the new Soviet realm, the concept
and practices which had become orthodox before the policy of expediency had been adopted, first to suit the exigencies of the "Great
Patriotic War," and then to smooth the path along which a whole
new aggregation of peoples was to be enticed, prodded and manœuvred into accepting Soviet rule. The postwar "zag" would merely
go back to being the prewar "zig." [1]

Since it was the Jugoslav situation which had revealed the necessity for revising Soviet procedure, naturally that was the first to be
taken in hand. Whether Stalin decided at the start to make an example of Tito or whether the necessity for this became evident only
as the discussion with him progressed is not certain. What we do
know is that early in 1948 the Politburo of the Bolshevik Party
opened consultations with selected members of the Central Committees of other Communist Parties belonging to the Cominform
about what should be done to curb the excessive independence of
the Jugoslav Party leadership.

One need for acting cautiously disappeared with the successful
Communist coup d'état in Czechoslovakia in February of that year.
The other Eastern European nations had already shed their popular
front governments and become Communist dictatorships, vassals of
Moscow. But so far Beneš and the younger Masaryk had saved a
remnant of democracy for the Czech and Slovak peoples and a sem-
blance of independence for the Czechoslovak Republic. Now this
weak point on the Russian front was filled in. Masaryk died on the
stones outside the Czernin Palais, and Beneš resigned—soon to be

---

[1] A penetrating analysis of the switch in the Stalinist line is given in an
article by Ruth Amende Rosa in *World Politics*, New Haven, Conn., July 1949.

dead, too, with a broken heart in a body hardly less broken than Masaryk's. With the disappearance of the last independent republic there was no further need to minimize or disguise the fact that the final result for all the People's Democracies was to be the same, *Gleichschaltung* with the Soviet empire.

There is no evidence to show whether the initiative which was begun through the Cominform at this time was approved unanimously in the Bolshevik Politburo, and specifically whether it was approved by Andrei Zhdanov, Secretary General of the Cominform and then commonly rated as the most influential member of the Politburo after Stalin himself. Zhdanov had been given the job of organizing the Cominform in circumstances suggesting that he had lost Stalin's patronage, which earlier had been almost fatherly. During the war he had been the Party boss of Leningrad and had conducted its defense with success and great glory. Did the glory become a little too great? Did the fact that he began to be spoken of as No. 2 become irksome to No. 1? In January 1945 Kalinin visited the former capital to decorate it for its heroic resistance. Two days before his arrival Zhdanov was replaced and his name was mentioned only perfunctorily in the course of the two-day ceremonies. The probabilities are that Stalin ordered him transferred to some field of activity where he would have more limited contacts within the top Communist leadership. After serving as Commissar to Finland he was assigned to set up the Cominform and then became its Secretary General. Hardly had he gotten the new organization functioning before the Tito affair developed and threatened to split it from top to bottom.

Those who suspect that Zhdanov and Stalin disagreed at this point are themselves in disagreement as to which of them favored strong action against Tito and which wanted to play the situation along without precipitating a showdown.

The merits of the case really turned on the relative importance to be attributed to Communist international objectives and Russian national objectives. According to the formula often repeated with tongue in cheek, the cause of world Socialism and the interests of the Socialist Fatherland were indistinguishable. But here was a concrete case where this was not necessarily so. Were the nations which had recently been added to the Soviet realm to be considered of greater importance because of their possible services to the cause of world revolution? Or because of their possible contributions toward strengthening Russian national power? If the former, they should be built up as independent Communist units, advance propaganda bases in the westward march of Communism. They should not be milked too barefacedly for the benefit of the Soviet economic Plan. Their local Communist leaderships should not be bossed about too openly or weakened by requiring that they emphasize unpopular things like the dictatorship of the proletariat and the collectivization of agriculture. Infiltration of their army commands should be by degrees. If the latter concept were accepted, however, the satellite states should be assimilated as rapidly and completely as possible into the Soviet political, economic and military system, perhaps with incorporation into the Soviet Union as the eventual goal. Estimates should be made of their resources individually and as a group and plans laid to channel the product into the Soviet hopper. The two programs, obviously, were not mutually exclusive; the difference lay in which should have precedence.

On the face of it, Stalin would seem likely to have been on the side of Russian power and Russian nationalism and no other. One would suppose, too, that Zhdanov would normally have wished to preserve the integrity of the organization which he had just created. He exercised great power in it, and this would compensate for his loss of influence at home. He would have realized that the success of the Cominform must be built on the willing collaboration of strong national Communist Parties, under Soviet leadership but not as mere lackeys of the Kremlin. This interpretation is supported by the reaction which certain competent foreign observers detected among the top officials of the Cominform Bureau in Belgrade late in 1947 after Tito had made a rather aggressive speech on September 27 criticizing the heads of other Communist Parties for timidity and going so far as to assert that some of them permitted "reactionary treacherous leaderships" to remain in power in their respective People's Fronts. One reporter is on record as having observed (some months before the first hint of a possible Stalin-Tito split) that certain Cominform officials in Zhdanov's confidence seemed to welcome

Tito's appearance as an aggressive junior partner in the work—long overdue in their view—of revitalizing the various People's Fronts, and as leader of a crusade to make international Communism more militant.

It is fairly well established, too, that several of the principal Communists who had collaborated with Zhdanov in creating the Cominform were perturbed at the idea of acting against Tito harshly and openly. Dimitrov, the Bulgarian Prime Minister, was one; and he was not only head of the Bulgarian Communist Party but a figure of world-wide prominence as hero of the Reichstag fire trial and for many years Secretary-General of the old Comintern (thus in a way Zhdanov's predecessor). Gheorghiu-Dej, the Rumanian Vice-Premier, Secretary-General of the Rumanian Workers' Party (Communist), was another. He made the mistake of telephoning his views to the Jugoslav Ambassador in Bucharest—a grievous mistake because the Ambassador was the only important member of the Jugoslav diplomatic service who promptly went over to the Cominform and, of course, informed on his informant. To save his neck, Gheorghiu-Dej became one of Tito's most impassioned vilifiers. Thorez of France and Togliatti of Italy favored efforts to bring Tito around gradually. Gomulka, the Polish Communist who had been a founding member of the Cominform, was opposed to disciplinary action against Tito and the Jugoslav Party. He had strong views as to the function of the Cominform, the relationship among Communist Parties and the relationship between the Communist states of Eastern Europe and the Soviet Union. He knew that if the Kremlin had its way this would be the end of all independence, either Party or governmental, in satellite capitals. His arguments were so persuasive that the Polish Party was ordered not to send him as its representative to the critical Cominform sessions where final action was taken. All the opponents were overruled. If it is true that Zhdanov was among them, he was overruled also. He conveniently died soon after, on August 21, 1948.

The mere fact that so many of the Communist leaders had ventured to question the wisdom of the Kremlin's judgment became, of course, an urgent reason to enforce it. At just what moment the Jugoslavs discovered what was going on is not certain, but it prob-

ably was early in March 1948, soon after the return from Moscow
of a mission under Vice-Premier Kardelj which had tried without
success to persuade the Soviet authorities to speed up trade between
the two countries and start the flow of Soviet industrial equipment
necessary to the progress of Tito's Five Year Plan. On March 18
formal notification reached Belgrade that the Soviet Government
had decided to withdraw all military advisers and instructors on the
grounds that they were "surrounded by hostility;" and the next
day the Soviet Chargé in Belgrade told Tito that all civilian missions
would be withdrawn also because of the "lack of hospitality and lack
of confidence" shown toward them. After two days of consideration,
on March 20, Tito decided to bring things to a head and asked
Moscow for an explanation. He was sure there was some misunderstanding. "We are amazed," he wrote to Molotov, "we cannot understand, we are deeply hurt." He asked to be informed of "the true
reason" for the Soviet action. Would not the U.S.S.R. "openly inform us what the trouble is?"

The U.S.S.R. would and did. Its communication, dated March
27, fell in Belgrade like a bombshell, dispersing any idea that the
reasons for Stalin's displeasure were minor or resulted from any sort
of misunderstanding. Stalin knew precisely what he wanted to do,
even though he miscalculated his capacities for doing it.

# VI

## TITO AND STALIN

What lies they told, and worse still, what
scandalous truths!
Winston Churchill, "Great Contemporaries," 1937

THE extraordinary correspondence thus
begun between Moscow and Belgrade in March 1948 throws more
light on the innards of the Communist political system than we have
had from any other source. Certainly it would not have been made
public if that could have been avoided. But each side was forced,
when the irretrievable split occurred on June 28, to publish its share
of the correspondence in order to justify its stand and shift to the
other the responsibility for the ensuing battles among the Communist
brethren.[1]

From the opening gun on March 27, when the Bolsheviks replied
to Tito's innocent request for "information," the tone of every Soviet
communication was coolly insulting. That first letter left no doubt
in Tito's mind that the deliberate aim was to replace him by a more
amenable leader. The other members of the Jugoslav Communist
Party's Central Committee (the Soviet communications were addressed to Tito and his colleagues collectively) realized that they
were slated for extinction also unless they could get rid of the
Titoist label. Two tried. Andrija Hebrang and Sretan Zhujovich
were found to be confirmed "fractionalists." They were said to have

[1] Translations of nine letters and documents are conveniently assembled in a
booklet, "The Soviet-Yugoslav Dispute," published by the Royal Institute of
International Affairs, London, 1948. There were preliminary communications
before March 18, which have not been published; and a Jugoslav letter dated
May 20 has been withheld for some reason also.

sabotaged Socialist planning and to have retailed gossip and slander to Moscow. They were expelled from the Central Committee and put in jail (where they still remain).[2] The other Committee members, including all the principal members of the Party and government, held with Tito. Some were specifically named in the Soviet bill of complaints; the rest shared his views or were personally loyal to him, or both.

Although the first communication from Moscow concerned itself mainly with specific acts of Communist leaders it included one or two portentous remarks about their general attitude and the theories on which it seemed to be based. One passage especially presaged what was to come. Trotsky, the letter recalled, had started out by criticizing the Bolshevik Party as "suffering from the limitations inherent in the narrow nationalism of great powers," though of course he "camouflaged all this with left slogans about world revolution." But it was Trotsky himself who was "degenerate," and who "when he was exposed, crossed over into the camp of sworn enemies of the CPSU and the Soviet Union." The concluding sentence showed what the Soviet line of main attack was to be: "We think that the political career of Trotsky is quite instructive."

The Bolshevik Politburo laughed at the suggestion that Tito was "deeply hurt" by the withdrawal of Soviet military advisers and trade delegates. He had asked for them to be sent, and then his people had insulted them and hidden information from them. Jugoslav officers had been heard to remark that "the rules of the Soviet Army were hidebound, stereotyped and without value to the Jugoslav Army, and that there was no point in paying the Soviet advisers since there was no benefit to be derived from them." One of Tito's closest associates, Milovan Djilas, had gone further. He had made the "insulting statement" that "the Soviet officers were, from a moral standpoint, inferior to the officers of the British Army." "This pitiful Marxist" seemed to be ignorant of "the main differences between the Socialist Soviet Army, which liberated the peoples of Europe, and the bourgeois English Army, whose function is to

[2] The decision in the Hebrang-Zhujovich case, dated May 8, 1948, is contained in "Statement of the Central Committee of the Communist Party of Yugoslavia." Belgrade: Jugoslovenska Knjiga, 1948.

oppress and not liberate the peoples of the world." The civilian missions had been withdrawn (continued the letter) because a Jugoslav decree had been adopted "forbidding the state organs to give economic information to anyone at all" without the approval of "the state security organs." This was intolerable, for it meant that "the Jugoslav security organs controlled and supervised the Soviet representatives in Jugoslavia." In the background, anti-Soviet rumors circulated "among the leading comrades in Jugoslavia," such as that "the CPSU is degenerate," "great-power chauvinism is rampant in the USSR," "the USSR is trying to dominate Jugoslavia economically" and "the Cominform is a means of controlling the other Parties by the CPSU." The letter admitted that every Communist Party is entitled to criticize; but Jugoslav criticism had degenerated into "slander."

As the controversy broadened and deepened, the historical background of the dispute became clearer. The first event of which Moscow complained had occurred in 1945. As already noted, there had been things even earlier which might have led Tito to place something less than perfect trust in Stalin's sincerity, but there is no reason to think that his Communist discipline weakened. And if he had had earlier misgivings of any sort he probably dismissed them when he visited Moscow in the spring of 1945. The pact signed at that time promised Jugoslavia 20 years of Soviet friendship and assistance. Tito, tongue in check, had just formed his "transitional" government with Shubashich. He must have talked over the success of that operation with Stalin and Molotov and doubtless secured promises of Soviet support against the inevitable protests that would come from the Western Powers when they found where the transition was leading. Stalin would naturally have approved the proposal to hold elections as soon as Tito was sure they would end the farce of "democracy of the Western type" in Jugoslavia. But he would not have been able to devote much time personally to details of Balkan policy. The war was not yet over in the Far East, the future of Germany was still under discussion and he would have been preoccupied with global strategy. If Tito showed signs of developing into a prima donna, Stalin would have felt that there was time to cut him down to size later on.

Former Secretary of State Stettinius has related an anecdote which shows, however, that Stalin was not unaware in 1945 that Tito could be difficult. At the Yalta Conference, a couple of months before Tito's visit to Moscow, Prime Minister Churchill suggested that "two words" from Marshal Stalin would do the trick in securing Tito's acceptance of a desired amendment to the Tito-Shubashich agreement. Stettinius writes: "Stalin replied that Tito was a proud man, and that now that he was a popular head of a régime he might resent advice. The Prime Minister answered that he felt Marshal Stalin could risk this. Stalin observed that he was not afraid to advise Tito." [3] Even if Stalin felt that he had no cause just then to complain of Tito the remark is a bit dry. But certainly it would never have crossed his mind that however precocious and cocky the schoolboy might be he could ever reject the master's teachings, let alone presume to give him lessons.

Something of the sort seemed to happen, nevertheless, in the course of a speech which Tito delivered in May 1945, not long after his return from Moscow. This is the first occasion that we know of definitely when he aroused Stalin's wrath.

One of Tito's primary postwar aims was to annex Trieste and the surrounding territory, parts of which are predominantly Slovene. Speaking in Ljubljana, the Slovene capital, he announced:

It is said that this is a just war, and we have considered it such. However, we also seek a just end. We demand that everyone shall be master in his own house. We do not want to pay other people's bills. We do not want to be used as a bribe in international bargaining. We do not want to get involved in a policy of spheres of influence.

Stalin's reaction to the suggestion that Jugoslavia had interests of her own which might not be used as small change in Soviet bargaining was violent. In the first place, Tito's statement raised difficulties in Italy, where Togliatti, the Italian Communist leader, knew that if he abandoned the Italian claim to Trieste he would lose a great part of his following. Stalin naturally wished therefore to avoid bringing the issue to a head. In the second place, it looked to Stalin as though Tito were publicly warning him—blackmailing him in

[3] Stettinius, *op. cit.*, p. 217.

fact. He instructed the Soviet Ambassador in Belgrade to state that this sort of thing "could not be tolerated." He was particularly incensed, he said, by Tito's failure to differentiate specifically between U.S.S.R. policies and those of "the imperialist states." On June 5, the Soviet Ambassador delivered this formal admonition to the Jugoslav Foreign Office: "Tell Comrade Tito that if he should once again permit such an attack on the Soviet Union we shall be forced to reply with open criticism in the press and disavow him."

The first threat of excommunication!

Tito was flabbergasted. He has assured me (in the course of a talk in the spring of 1950) that he meant his warning exclusively for the Western Powers. He found the Soviet reaction was very instructive. It informed him that Stalin had a bad conscience, that he was playing a double game over Trieste. It also made him wonder what the Soviet attitude might be in other outstanding territorial disputes between Jugoslavia and her neighbors. There was the question of Macedonia, always a bone of contention between the Jugoslavs and Bulgars, and there was also the question of Carinthia, an Austrian province inhabited partly by Slovenes.

The Ljubljana speech marked a definite turning point in the relations of the two men. Stalin felt that his subordinate had been insubordinate, had even threatened him; in the Soviet Ambassador's words, that was intolerable. Tito saw that the national interests of Jugoslavia might differ greatly from those of Russia, and that when they did there would be no question in Stalin's mind of anything like compromise.

On the heels of this came the disagreeable Djilas incident. Even if Djilas were innocent of uttering the obnoxious remark quoted above, many former Partisan fighters could certainly have been heard saying much the same thing—complaining about the high salaries paid the Red Army missions and gossiping among themselves about certain Red Army characteristics observed when Tolbukhin's troops entered Belgrade as though it were an enemy stronghold. Tito made strenuous efforts to explain away the Djilas affair, both orally and by letter to Stalin. Stalin finally said he was satisfied; but the fact that he raised the matter again in 1948 shows that he was not. His way of raising it, too, was ominous. The Soviet note said there was no doubt "that the Jugoslav Party masses would disown this anti-Soviet criticism as alien and hostile if they knew about it." The threat to appeal over Tito's head to the Party was unmistakable.

Tito mentioned two other events of that period in the conversation which I had with him in 1950, and though they do not figure in the Cominform correspondence they fit into our present chronology. The first arose in connection with the peace conference where treaties were to be made between the Allied Powers on the one hand and Italy and the lesser ex-Axis states on the other. Jugoslav interests were directly involved, and Tito expected that his representatives would be invited to participate in the deliberations of the Allied foreign ministers in advance of the conference. Soviet Russia, however, agreed with the Western Powers that the lesser Allied states should not be represented. Jugoslavia therefore had no part in those decisive negotiations, and simply was heard regarding details when the conference finally opened in Paris on July 29, 1946.

The second event seems to have particularly strengthened Tito's feeling that Stalin was not to be trusted to treat him fairly. Without warning, the Partisan units which had occupied parts of Carinthia and Styria received orders from the Soviet military command to withdraw behind the prewar Jugoslav frontiers. This portended that Stalin's support for the Jugoslav claim to part of these territories might be less than adamant. Even less palatable was the manner in which the manœuvre was executed. Moscow did not send a request for the withdrawal, explaining why it was necessary, but a curt military order. It was obeyed as such—and bitterly resented.

Further friction was caused by Tito's speech on September 27, 1947, mentioned in the preceding chapter. His call for a more militant international Communist program and his criticism of the leadership of other Communist Parties—particularly, by implication, the French and Italian—may have pleased the leaders of the newly founded Cominform but it seemed to Stalin most presumptuous. For one thing, the principles of organization and action which Tito advocated were about to be discarded. But what was really unforgivable was Tito's assumption that he had an international rôle to play in addition to his domestic duties. Probably it was at this point that the

Bolshevik Politburo began in earnest to canvass ways and means of getting rid of him.

The desirability of such action was emphasized by the negotiations then in progress for bringing Jugoslavia and Bulgaria together in a South Slav federation. The original plan had been approved by Stalin, although for various reasons he had not allowed it to materialize.[4] However, when Prime Minister Dimitrov of Bulgaria visited Tito at Bled in the summer of 1947 the project threatened to develop into something more ambitious, perhaps a federation that might eventually include most of the Communist states of Eastern Europe. This kind of broad association would of course be wholly unacceptable to the Soviets, since it could develop a dangerous will and strength of its own. Moscow called Dimitrov to order, and he was forced to issue a disclaimer and apology through *Izvestia* and *Pravda*. Tito believes the reason he was not "invited" to do likewise was that Moscow understood he was in a mood to refuse. To which might be added that the Soviet rulers probably had already made up their minds that the situation in Jugoslavia was intolerable and were planning to handle it much more definitively.

In the autumn of 1947 the world heard of the formation of the Cominform, a reincarnation of the old Comintern in a form to suit the new international situation. The Jugoslav Communists participated, naturally, and derived considerable satisfaction from the fact that the organization fixed on Belgrade for its headquarters. Pijade and others have since suggested that perhaps one reason for creating the Cominform just then was to provide the Kremlin with a convenient instrument for dealing with Tito and other satellite leaders who might show signs of insubordination. Obviously there would be advantages in masking autocratic Bolshevik measures behind a façade of inter-Party coöperation. Perhaps Moscow may simply have realized, after plans for the Cominform had already been made, that if Belgrade became the headquarters the international Communist luminaries assembled there might help quiet the membership of the Jugoslav Party while the Tito clique was being purged.

A final point to round out our chronology. Early in 1948 a general feeling spread through Europe that by spring or summer the

4 *Cf.* Chapter XVII.

cold war between East and West might become hot. As it turned out, the Soviet bid was made in Berlin, and it failed. The blockade began June 24; the Americans and British replied with the airlift; and its extraordinary success ended Russian hopes of making the Western Powers suffer such a loss of face that they would remain passive before even more open acts of aggression. Before the showdown, a principal Soviet objective was to make sure that the road would be open for an advance by the Soviet Army and satellite troops from Rumania and Hungary through Jugoslavia to Trieste, and thence to the plains of northern Italy and on into southern France. The Jugoslav Army was of course assigned a key rôle in this operation, which would turn the flank of Allied forces in Central and Western Europe while the main Russian columns pushed across Germany to the Channel. Tito was not satisfied, however, to see the Jugoslav Army become a mere auxiliary of Russian armored divisions sweeping westward. As already noted, he wanted his principal body of troops trained in familiar guerrilla tactics so that they could remain and fight in Jugoslavia under his own command throughout the war; and whatever Moscow might say, he knew that a new war would be a long one. His refusal to subordinate himself to the Soviet Army command was an added reason to replace him without delay.[5]

The Soviet-Jugoslav correspondence also reveals difficulties in the commercial relations between the two countries, though without stressing them as prominently as the facts would have warranted. The Jugoslavs complained (in their letter of April 13) that a trade delegation had been ready to leave for Moscow when word came that no protocol could be negotiated for the further exchange of goods during 1948, and that the question would be taken up only at the end of the year. This was a blow to Tito. UNRRA supplies were used up; imports had dropped; and the resulting slow-down in the Five Year Plan had been noticeable to foreign observers since late

[5] There was a clash of personalities also. One of the leading Partisan commanders, Tito's own wartime chief-of-staff, General Arso Jovanovich, went to Moscow after the war for a course at the Soviet military academy and returned to Belgrade converted to the Soviet strategy. As a result, he was not offered what was in his view a proper military command. After the break with the Cominform, Jovanovich tried to escape into Rumania and was shot by frontier guards. Presumably his intention was to set up a Jugoslav "government-in-exile" in Bucharest, the new Cominform capital.

in 1947. In the hope of persuading Soviet authorities to supply needed machinery Tito sent Vice-Premier Kardelj to Moscow in February, but he was put off with vague answers and finally returned empty-handed early in March. One of the Jugoslav complaints was that Kardelj was in Moscow just when the Bolsheviks began circulating their accusations against the Jugoslav Party to other Cominform members, yet said no word to him about them.

The refusal to help Tito proceed with his Five Year Plan was only a new demonstration that the Soviets were prepared to use their economic whip hand for political ends. They also used it for financial profit. They discriminated against Jugoslavia by deciding arbitrarily which of her products they would buy and which of the Soviet and satellite products she might buy, thus determining the structure of her national economy. They also discriminated in the prices paid for Jugoslav products and the prices charged for Soviet products.

Striking details of how the system worked were revealed in the Economic and Financial Committee of the U.N. General Assembly in the autumn of 1949. It seems that two joint Jugoslav-Soviet companies had been set up to create and operate Jugoslav shipping and air services—named, respectively, "Juspad" and "Justa." The two Governments were to contribute capital equally and share equally in the management. During the discussions at Lake Success, the Jugoslav delegate, Dr. Josef Vilfan, asserted that in the case of "Juspad" the Soviet partner paid in only 9.83 percent of its share in 1948 while the Jugoslav partner paid in 76.25 percent of its share. The Russian delegate, A. A. Arutiunian, replied angrily that this was a "slander," for the Soviet Government had been prevented from contributing its full share by the Jugoslav refusal to receive equipment on capital account or allow the construction of certain essential factories.[6] In the case of "Justa," the Soviet Government claimed to have paid in 41.2 percent of its share while the Jugoslav Government paid in only 5.9 percent of its share. The Jugoslav retort was that the Soviet figure was reached by including the transportation costs of Russian goods sold to Jugoslavia and of

[6] Provisional Summary Record of the Economic and Financial Committee of the U.N. General Assembly, A/C. 2/SR 93 and 94.

Jugoslav goods sent to Russia; further, that the managing director was a Soviet appointee who ignored his Jugoslav assistant and fixed schedules in accordance with which Jugoslavia paid 52 percent more for her shipments than the Soviets paid for theirs, and 30 percent more than was paid by other countries. Tito mentioned the matter to me. It was not the financial discrimination which made him angriest, but the fact that the actual flying arrangements were not on a basis of national equality. Soviet planes could come freely into Jugoslavia, but Jugoslav planes were not allowed to fly into the Soviet Union. The Soviet unwillingness to grant reciprocal flying privileges showed an insulting lack of confidence in Jugoslav pilots.

There was another Soviet transaction with Jugoslavia—a highly publicized Russian "gift" of 500,000 tons of wheat just after the war—which remains an unending subject for impolite jibes in Belgrade. I was told there that the amount actually received was only 50,000 tons and that this had been stolen from Jugoslavia by the Nazis in the first place, then captured by the Red Army and in the end shipped back to its rightful owners. The Russians were said to have admitted this quite frankly at the time, but to have suggested that it would be nice in the interests of Soviet-Jugoslav amity to call the wheat a gift and, while one was about it, to pretend that the volume was tenfold larger. True or made up, the story shows what Jugoslavs think today of Soviet benevolence.

Even the first of the capital equipment which had been promised from Soviet Russia—paid for in advance or due in return payment for Jugoslav goods already shipped—did not arrive. The matériel which came for the Jugoslav Army significantly was not accompanied by spare parts, which left the Jugoslav units so equipped dependent on the Soviet Army (a fact which today creates a serious weakness in the Jugoslav military position). The statement has also been made that it was not up to specifications.[7] Meanwhile, copper, manganese, lead and other minerals poured forth from the Jugoslav mines and were shipped to factories in the Soviet Union

[7] Lieutenant General Otmar Kreachich, head of the Political Department of the Jugoslav Army, has said that the artillery purchased from Russia after the war was not new, as represented, but "old repainted equipment," and that the explosives "turned out to be useless and most had to be thrown away." (The *New York Herald Tribune* and *The New York Times*, December 22, 1949.)

and the other satellite states. "A thousand carloads of Jugoslav iron ore would go to Czechoslovakia," one Jugoslav official complained to me in Belgrade, "and what do you think would come back?—machinery as promised, so that we could start constructing our own truck factory?—no, a carload of trucks!" Behind these disappointments loomed the fundamental cause for complaint already mentioned. The Jugoslavs considered that it was most unfair of the Soviet Union to figure its trade with Jugoslavia (and the same applied to its trade with the other satellites, of course) in world prices, which in the Marxist view are determined by the big monopolies in highly developed countries. When these were applied to trade between a socialized state having a high labor productivity, *i.e.* the Soviet Union, and one with a low productivity, *i.e.* Jugoslavia, there was no equality of competition, for the former could and did force the latter to export selected products and thus could and did exercise a controlling influence over her national economy. *Borba*, the Belgrade organ of the Communist Party, gave an example in its issue of March 31, 1949. Molybdenum, an essential ingredient of steel, cost 500,000 dinars a ton to produce in Jugoslavia; Soviet Russia monopolized the entire product and paid for it at world prices, which meant, said *Borba*, that the Jugoslav Government suffered a loss of 455,000 dinars on every ton delivered.

Under such circumstances the Jugoslav Communists could see little difference between Soviet economic policy and the policy of the capitalist and imperialist countries about which they used to complain before they won "Socialism and freedom." In each case they called it exploitation.

# VII

## HERESY

> The world is full of conscript minds, only
> they are in different armies, and nobody is
> fighting to be free, but each to make his
> own conscription universal.
>
> George Santayana, "The Last Puritan"

THE acrimonious charges and counter-
charges about specific acts, speeches or gossipings were as nothing
compared to the bitterness of the grand battle that was joined on
ideological grounds. Complaints in the Bolshevik letter of March 27
about Tito's independence (insubordination) and nationalism
(chauvinism) were supported with all the weight of the Kremlin's
claim to infallibility in matters of Communist faith and morals. In
insulting language, and with pointed references to the fate of former
enemies and traitors from the Mensheviks and Trotsky to Bukharin
and other deviationists of the thirties, the theme was developed that
Tito had led the Jugoslav Communists into errors which could be
redeemed only by his removal and the formation of a new leadership
wholly devoted to Stalin and the Soviet Union.

The first ideological attack centered on the lack of "democracy"
in the Jugoslav Central Committee and the damaging effects of this
on the class struggle in Jugoslavia. "Criticism and self-criticism"
(the letter said) did not exist in the Central Committee. Marxist
theory required that the Party control all the organs of the state,
but in Jugoslavia it was the other way around: the Minister of the
Interior controlled the Party, which explained why the "initiative of
the Party masses was not on the required level." The majority of the
Central Committee were not elected (as would have been the case
if a regular Party Congress had been held) but merely coöpted. "We
cannot consider such an organization of a Communist Party as

Marxist-Leninist, Bolshevik." [1] In view of this, it was not surprising
that the spirit of the class struggle was lacking. "The increase in the
capitalist elements in the villages and cities is in full swing." Then
followed this insulting comparison: the Jugoslav Party "is being
hoodwinked by the degenerate and opportunist theory of the peaceful absorption of capitalist elements by a Socialist system, borrowed
from Bernstein, Vollmar and Bukharin." [2]

The positive conclusion was as follows:

According to the theory of Marxism-Leninism the Party is considered
as the leading force in the country, which has its specific program and
which cannot merge with the non-party masses. In Jugoslavia, on the
contrary, the People's Front is considered the chief leading force and
there was an attempt to get the Party submerged within the Front. In
his speech at the Second Congress of the People's Front, Comrade Tito
said: "Does the CPY have any program but that of the People's Front?
No, the CPY has no other program. The program of the People's Front
is its program." . . .

In Russia forty years ago the Mensheviks proposed that the Marxist
Party be dissolved into a non-party mass organization of workers and
peasants, with the latter again supplanting the former. As is known,
Lenin described these Mensheviks as malicious opportunists and liqui-
dators of the Party.

This was rough talk, meant of course to scare Tito and fellow
"opportunists" who held the same "degenerate and opportunist theory" into such an advanced state of "self-criticism" that they would
either bow down to the Bolshevik oracle or flee from the presence
and leave worthier men to serve the sacred flame according to the
true Stalinist rite. Tito was not contrite, however, and was not over-
awed. Thus the stage was set for one of those great ideological duels
in which Communists delight to engage when they have really important practical business in hand, such as the destruction of an
opponent or a change in the Party line.

Perhaps, as Tito said in his reply of April 13, he really was "terri-

[1] The All-Union Party Congress of the Soviet Party is supposed to be held
every three years, but actually none had been held since 1939. Pijade trained his
guns on this point later to prove the difference between Soviet practice and
Soviet precepts for others (cf. Chapter IX).

[2] Eduard Bernstein and Georg Vollmar were leaders of the German Social-
Democratic Party.

bly surprised" by the tone and content of the Bolshevik onslaught.
At any rate, in order to gain time he thought best to assume that
his accusers were, as he told them, acting on insufficient, second-
hand and erroneous information. Why were the sources of this information not named, so that they could be investigated in a
brotherly manner in the open? The covert threat that the masses
might become angry was dismissed with the sententious remark:
"To oppose the leadership to the masses is incorrect." It opened the
way, too, for Tito to get in a dig of his own. The idea seemed to
prevail among "many Soviet people," he said, that the Jugoslav
masses spontaneously sympathized with the Soviets "on the basis of
some traditions which go back to the time of Tsarist Russia." This
was a mistake: "love for the U.S.S.R. did not come of itself" but
had been "stubbornly inculcated" by "the present leaders of the new
Jugoslavia."

The Jugoslav reply then turned to the criticism of the Jugoslav
Party organization. Did the Bolsheviks' "completely incorrect information" come from the Soviet Ambassador? If so, he ought to
be attending to government rather than Party affairs. "That is not
his business." If the Bolshevik Central Committee wanted information about Party matters let them ask the Jugoslav Central Committee. In any case, free criticism and self-criticism did exist in the
Jugoslav Party. A Party Congress was in process of organization.[3]
As for the statement that the class struggle was languishing, "the
entire world" knows that nowhere else had there been "such firm,
consistent social changes." For the Bolsheviks to criticize the People's
Front was especially strange in view of the fact that its quality was
superior even to that of many Communist Parties—superior in organization and superior in activity. In some countries, Bulgaria and
Poland for example, the Communist Parties had not only changed
their methods but had even lost their names by merging with other
parties—"yet no one tells these Parties that they will dissolve into
the masses." Moscow could stop worrying lest the Jugoslav Party
might be swallowed up in the People's Front; the program of the
Front was the program of the Party, and all "important decisions,

[3] This Congress, the Fifth Party Congress, mentioned in preceding chapters,
was actually held in July.

from those of the Federal Government down, regarding all questions
of social and state life, are either decisions of the Party or made on
the initiative of the Party."

He was making these explanations, Tito protested in conclusion,
solely "to eliminate every doubt and disbelief in the comradely and
brotherly feeling of loyalty" of the Jugoslav Party. But he prefaced
this with two remarkable statements which he must have known
would infuriate Stalin and which therefore show that he already
understood the duel was to be to the death and that he too was beginning to manœuvre for position. One pointed out how important
it was to the U.S.S.R. *in its own interest* to have Jugoslavia as an
ally against the capitalist world, which endangered not Jugoslavia
alone but "other countries of people's democracy and even the development of the U.S.S.R." The thought that Jugoslavia could help
mighty Russia against capitalist aggression would certainly have
seemed most presumptuous to Stalin and Molotov.[4] Equally so must
have been Tito's other statement, that many aspects of the Jugoslav
social experiment "can be of benefit to the revolutionary development in other countries, and already are being used." He continued
on this theme in an almost condescending tone:

This does not mean that we place the rôle of the Communist Party
of the Soviet Union and the social system of the U.S.S.R. in the background. On the contrary, we study and take as an example the Soviet
system, but we are developing Socialism in our country in somewhat
different forms. In the given period under the specific conditions which
exist in our country, in consideration of the international conditions
which were created after the war of liberation, we are attempting to
apply the best forms of work in the realization of Socialism. We do not
do this in order to prove that our road is better than that taken by the
Soviet Union, that we are inventing something new, but because this is
forced upon us by our daily life.

The Bolshevik Party spent over two weeks in consulting the other
Cominform members and preparing its rejoinder, which bore the

---

[4] The Jugoslav communications were signed either by Tito alone or jointly
by him and Kardelj, Vice-Premier and later Minister for Foreign Affairs. They
were addressed personally to Molotov or to Stalin and Molotov jointly. The
replies were signed impersonally "CC of the CPSU" (Central Committee of the
Communist Party of the Soviet Union).

date of May 4. It stigmatized Tito's effusion as "exaggeratedly ambitious," "childish" and "laughable." For the most part it summarized Jugoslav errors with which the reader is now familiar, but
in doing so added some most interesting reflections.

The Jugoslavs, for instance, had said that the Soviet Ambassador
should mind his proper business. Moscow's comment on this sheds a
flood of light on what a Soviet Ambassador's proper business in a
satellite state really is and on how the Soviet Government grades
diplomats representing Communist and non-Communist states. It
was "incorrect and anti-Soviet," said the Bolshevik note, to confuse
the Soviet Ambassador, "a responsible Communist who represents
the Communist Government of the U.S.S.R.," with "an ordinary
bourgeois ambassador, a simple official of a bourgeois state." How
could Tito and Kardelj "sink so low?" Their attitude must come
from an inability to differentiate between the foreign policy of imperialist and anti-imperialist states, a fatal tendency to "put the
foreign policy of the U.S.S.R. on a par with the foreign policy of
the English and the Americans." The Jugoslavs should remember
that "retaining this attitude means depriving themselves of the right
to demand material and any other assistance from the Soviet Union,
because the Soviet Union can only offer aid to its friends."

The unwillingness of the Jugoslav leaders to admit their errors
(continued Moscow) showed "unbounded arrogance." Other Parties had performed services to the revolution, but their leaders "behave modestly and do not boast about their successes" as do the
Jugoslavs, "who have pierced everyone's ears with their unlimited
self-praises." The French and Italian Parties had achieved less
positive success, but this was not due to any special Jugoslav qualities. At this point the Bolshevik note contains a sentence which is
most interesting, and which would be taken up and made much
of by Pijade and others in later debates. The Jugoslav success, it
said, was due to the fact that "the Soviet Army came to the aid of
the Jugoslav people, crushed the invader, liberated Belgrade *and in
this way created the conditions which were necessary for the Communist Party of Jugoslavia to achieve power*" (italics mine). "Unfortunately" the Soviet Army had not been able to render similar
assistance to the Communists in France and Italy. If Tito and

Kardelj would remember these facts (the Bolshevik note commented) they might "behave with greater propriety and modesty."

In their remarks on the respective rôles of the People's Front and
the Jugoslav Communist Party the Bolsheviks wasted no time in
explaining why they themselves had utilized the device of popular
fronts in the past or why they were now discarding it. Tito's willingness to share power with non-Communists was simply the old Menshevik error and he must have fallen into it because he was "afraid
openly to acclaim the Party and its decisions before the entire people
so that the people may know that the leading force is the Party."
In this he blatantly disregarded Lenin's dictum that the Party is
the most important weapon in the hands of the working class and
that the task of Party leaders is "to keep this weapon in constant
readiness." He was "blunting this weapon, diminishing the rôle of
the Party and disarming the working class." Nothing was said, of
course, about the fact that the same sort of methods had served the
Soviets in coaxing the peoples of Eastern Europe to accept Communist-dominated governments as transitional steps to the establishment of outright Communist dictatorships.

The theory that the class struggle could proceed in accordance
with special Jugoslav conditions was described in the Bolshevik note
as the rankest sort of opportunism. Tito's attitude toward the class
struggle in the villages, it blandly observed, was based on "the opportunist contentions that, in the transition period between capitalism
and Socialism, the class struggle does not become sharper, as taught
by Marxism-Leninism, but dies out, as averred by opportunists of
the type of Bukharin, who postulated a decadent theory of the peaceful absorption of the capitalist elements into the social structure."
Tito did not differentiate between classes in the villages, but considered the peasantry "an organic whole." He had admitted this
(the note went on) when he remarked: "We do not tell the peasants
that they are the strongest pillar of our state in order that, eventually,
we may get their votes, but because we know that that is what they
are, and because they should be aware of what they are" (*Borba*,
November 2, 1946). A statement of this sort was "in complete contradiction to Marxist-Leninism," which taught that "the working
class and not the peasantry is the most progressive, the most revo-

lutionary class," and that even though the poor and middle peasants can be in a union with the working class "the leading rôle in this union still belongs to the working class." Tito's attitude, said the Bolsheviks, was that of "petty-bourgeois politicians."

To conclude with the matter, the note from Moscow said there was no necessity for sending investigators, as Tito suggested, to learn the truth on the spot. The need was not to verify facts; what was at stake was "differences of principle." The proper place to discuss these was in the Cominform. Tito knew what this meant. An obedient and unanimous vote would be available there for whatever measures Stalin might propose—and in this case Stalin would certainly propose Tito's trial for heresy and his punishment by one of the methods usual with Communist heretics. In the case of Trotsky the method had been exile and murder with an axe; in the case of Bukharin and other purgees of the thirties it had been recantation and shooting.

The choices before Tito were only two: abdicate or fight. He decided to fight. On May 17 he declined to have the issues decided by the Cominform. He pointed out that even before the Jugoslav Party had been informed of the charges brought against it the other nine Cominform members had received instructions from Moscow and had taken their stand in Party resolutions. In making known his decision he stressed that what had happened (and what evidently was about to happen) would not affect his Communist faith. "We will resolutely construct Socialism and remain loyal to the Soviet Union; remain loyal to the doctrine of Marx, Engels, Lenin and Stalin."

No sentimental sops of this sort could assuage Stalin's wrath or weaken his will. The Central Committee of the Jugoslav Party (said a final Bolshevik note of May 22) had "gone a step further" in aggravating its "crude mistakes of principle." Was the Committee "deep in its soul" aware of how serious its mistakes had been and simply attempting to wriggle out of responsibility by declaring that the mistakes did not exist? Or did it really not understand how far it was deviating from Marxist-Leninism? No matter. In neither case could any "verbal assurances" that it would remain true in future to Communist teachings from Marx to Stalin carry the slightest weight. The refusal to appear before the "fraternal Communist Parties" was a tacit admission of guilt. The Jugoslav Party had "taken the path of cutting itself off from the united Socialist people's front of People's Democracies headed by the Soviet Union" and was preparing for a "betrayal of the united front of the people's democracies and the U.S.S.R."

Nothing remained for the accused to do but give formal notification that he refused to put in an appearance to receive the predetermined judgment. This was done on June 20 in a statement to the Cominform Conference then already in session in Bucharest. The Central Committee of the Jugoslav Party added its greetings to "the brotherly Communist Parties" and declared that no disagreements would prevent it from "remaining true to its policy of solidarity." On June 28 came the news that it had been expelled from membership.

The charges which the Cominform chose to emphasize as a basis for its action foreshadowed the propaganda line to be followed in the months ahead, not only in Jugoslavia but in all the satellite states. Under conditions like those in Jugoslavia, it stated, "where individual peasant farming predominates, where the land is not nationalized, where there is private property in land, where land can be bought and sold, where much of the land is concentrated in the hands of *kulaks,* and where hired labor is employed," the Communist Party is disarmed. By affirming that the peasantry were "the most stable foundation of the Jugoslav state," the Jugoslav leaders were "departing from the Marxist-Leninist path" and taking the path of a "populist, *kulak* party" in violation of Lenin's dictum that the proletariat "must be the leader." They were revising his teaching that the Party is "the highest form of organization," the "most important weapon of the working class," which must never "dissolve itself among the non-Party masses." The sectarian-bureaucratic nature of the Party exposed it to the risks of "military methods of leadership" like those advocated in his day by Trotsky. Its nationalist line could "only lead to Jugoslavia's degeneration into an ordinary bourgeois republic, to the loss of its independence and to its transformation into a colony of the imperialist countries." There were more of the old reproaches, sometimes embellished with new adjec-

tives, oftener with the old ones. The Jugoslavs were not only *kulaks,*
Mensheviks and Trotskyites; they were boastful, empty and dema-
gogic and their régime was disgraceful, purely Turkish and terroristic. When they were not deviating to the Right they were making
mistakes in a belated effort to follow a Leftist policy.

Tito thus was ready for anathema. An image had been created
and set up so that it might be pulled down, broken and obliterated.
With a heavy heart, foreseeing their own fate, delegates to the
Cominform who had fancied that they might be left to pursue a
fairly independent course within reasonable limits of Communist
discipline put their shoulders to the pedestal of the false god and
toppled it over. This was the decision:

> The Information Bureau unanimously concludes that by their anti-
> Party and anti-Soviet views, incompatible with Marxist-Leninism, by
> their whole attitude and their refusal to attend the meeting of the
> Information Bureau, the leaders of the Communist Party have placed
> themselves in opposition to the Communist Parties affiliated to the
> Information Bureau, have taken the path of seceding from the unified
> Socialist front against imperialism, have taken the path of betraying the
> cause of international solidarity of the working people, and have taken
> up a position of nationalism.

Thereby, concluded the Resolution, the Jugoslav Party was deemed
to have placed itself "outside the family of the fraternal Communist
Parties, outside the Communist front and consequently outside the
ranks of the Information Bureau."

As one reads even such a brief summary of the Stalinist case
as has been given here one must pause often to notice its implications both for states which possess a Communist régime and
also for non-Communist states which are called upon to maintain
relations with them. Speaking for one of the former, Tito and
Kardelj wrote in their letter of April 13 to Moscow: "No matter
how much each of us loves the land of Socialism, the U.S.S.R., he
can, in no case, love his country less." This was the central position
which Stalin had to challenge, and which he did challenge and
continues to challenge on every ground. probable or improbable.
He might not care much about love as such, but he did care about
the readiness to obey which it betokened. How highly he rated

obedience was stated clearly in the Cominform journal, *For a Lasting Peace, for a People's Democracy!*, on December 5, 1948, only five months after the expulsion of the Jugoslavs from the organization. Such progress had already been made by then in rallying Cominform members to the new concept of their duties that their mouthpiece could say without fear of awakening revolt: "The attitude toward the Soviet Union is now the test of devotion to the cause of proletarian internationalism."

These words announced to Communist governments and to all Communists that proletarian internationalism as it had previously existed had been destroyed. They were important also for non-Communist governments, for they informed them that all relations with Communist governments except the Soviet Government were unreal, that letters sent to them were sent to the wrong address, that letters from them bore signatures with false titles. The claim that they were governments, in fact, was a hoax. These things had been brought about, however, not, as Stalin claimed, by Tito's nationalism, but by the refusal of Stalin to admit that any nationalism except Russia's was any longer permissible for Communists. The reversal of Bukharin's "law of impossibility" was formal.

# VIII

## ECHOES OF OLD WARS

> Besides two arms and two legs for oratory, gesticulation and movement, Socialism has two heads and two hearts which are always at war with one another.
>
> J. M. Keynes, *The Political Quarterly*,
> April–June 1932

GRADUALLY the lines of ideological combat were enlarged and sharpened. At the start Stalin may not have meant his thrusts, or Tito his ripostes, as much more than glittering tributes to the traditions of Communist combat. While the swordsmen were displaying their virtuosity the gunmen would do their work. But when Tito made the duel a test of Stalin's moral rights (if one may use the term) as well as his physical powers, he forced him to begin manœuvring into position for the long propaganda campaign which would be necessary to establish them beyond all later question. Seeing this, Tito realized that his decision to fight, originally motivated perhaps by nothing more admirable than a determination to protect his own interests, had given him an importance transcending that of a local nuisance. His course assumed general significance in the evolution of Communism and might actually affect the Kremlin's ability to claim unique and universal authority. At once he and his colleagues set to work to develop their new articles of faith—or rather, as they called it, the old, true faith—in the form to do Stalin the utmost possible harm. Their efforts were conducted with resourcefulness and skill.

There is something reminiscent in all this of the great controversies which divided the Bolsheviks in earlier days. Now as then there was disagreement between those who were international revolutionaries and those who were determined to build Socialism in one country first. In the terms in which Zhdanov was presented in an earlier chapter he might be taken to represent those who aimed to create an international Communist community, under Soviet leadership, of course, but animated more by international revolutionary fervor than by fear of Russia or a spirit of servility to Stalin. On the other hand, Stalin, if we appraise his motives correctly, aimed to create a secure base at home before risking war to carry revolution abroad; to this end, adjacent lands were to be sucked directly into the Soviet economic, political and military system and their resources exploited mercilessly to make Russia self-contained and impregnable. When this goal had been achieved, or when Russia's progress toward it began to be threatened in a relative sense by the countermeasures of other Powers, then would come a moment of decision—to wage preventive war, or to continue strengthening the national base, against lengthening odds, while talking peace and peaceful coexistence?

In earlier ideological clashes in Russia Stalin had taken a position on various other issues which now reappeared in his conflict with Tito. In those days also there had been disagreement as to the rôle of private enterprise and the relations of urban workers and peasants. It was this which in 1927 had separated Stalin and Bukharin, who until then had seemed in general agreement. Bukharin had sided with Stalin against Trotsky in 1925 in the "Socialism in one country" debate; and in return Stalin had seemed to acquiesce in Bukharin's theory of the relationship of Socialism and private enterprise in the national economy. Bukharin stressed that there must be harmonious collaboration between the two sectors, and in particular that the peasants must be prosperous in order to supply more food to the towns. Zinoviev and Kamenev, on the contrary, pressed for more rapid socialization and especially for more emphasis on the change from private to collective farming. At first Stalin indicated tolerance for Bukharin's views. But in December 1927 Trotsky was successfully expelled from the Party and a month later deported safely to Alma Ata (to be exiled in 1929); and Zinoviev and Kamenev also were soon disgraced and deprived of power (to be tried eventually, and shot). Stalin now was free to turn on Bukharin. He disowned his policy of "alliance with the peasantry" and launched out furi-

ously on collectivization, spreading terror and turmoil through the
countryside and leading to the great famine of 1932–33. By 1929
Stalin was denouncing Bukharin publicly as leader of the Rightist
opposition. Bukharin recanted, and survived physically for nine
years. Already in Stalin's mind, however, he must have been allotted
the place before the firing squad which he occupied at last in 1938.[1]

It may be asked why Stalin chose to make an issue of Tito's
agrarian policy when the fact was that Tito had carried collectivization further than had been done so far by any other Communist
leader in Eastern Europe. Probably the reason was that to stigmatize
anyone as a Right-wing deviationist in agrarian policy has become
the accepted method of disgracing him. Almost every Communist
leader who has become troublesome in the last 20 years has had
that label attached to him; and the whole Communist world knows
that when it happens the victim is guilty by definition and has been
condemned in advance. Stalin sought to minimize the undoubted
progress which Tito had made in bringing the Jugoslav peasantry
into collective farms by asserting that he was proceeding on the
right principles but without adequate preparation. In other words,
he was a Left deviationist. Since his methods were wrong the results
must be wrong also, regardless of surface indications to the contrary.
The standard by which he measured Tito's principles was the one
which he had established in Russia in 1929 when he started stamp-
ing down peasant opposition by wholesale deportations, massacres
and starvation.

When Stalin made up his mind at that time to beat the Russian
peasants into insensibility, over 12 years had elapsed since the Revolution. In the intervening period there had been more than enough
vacillations, temporizations and retreats in agrarian policy to show
that the Russian leaders considered a direct and final assault on
independent peasant agriculture an extremely hazardous undertaking which they sought to avoid. But when Stalin called on Tito
to adopt the same policy in 1948 the Jugoslav situation was much
less like what it had been in Russia in 1929 than it was like the
one existing there in the early years following the Civil War,

[1] The events of 1925–1930 are related well in "Stalin: A Political Biography,"
by Isaac Deutscher (New York: Oxford University Press, 1949).

and especially in 1921 and 1922 when Lenin resorted to the N.E.P. and showed great leniency toward peasant individualists. In other words, Stalin was blaming Tito for not doing in 1948 what the Bolsheviks themselves had not dared to do at a comparable stage in the Russian Revolution.

Furthermore, the basic situations in the two countries were entirely dissimilar. The Russian colossus had been able to absorb the immense waste of 1929 and 1930; even the untold misery of 1932 and 1933 had been forgotten. But in Jugoslavia land was limited and labor was not expendable. Even had Tito been prepared to go relatively as far as Stalin he would have been prevented by the fact that the nation could not have survived such bloodletting. Further, although the Jugoslav peasants are primitive by many Western standards they were far ahead of the Russian *muzhiks* in political experience and literacy. Most Serbian farmers had been landowners either individually or under the family *zadruga* system since the end of the Turkish rule, protected by law from losing their houses, ploughs or a minimum of their land or cattle for debt; and in Croatia many farmers who had not owned land previously had acquired it in the reforms following the First World War. These landowning peasants were accustomed to being regarded as the foundation of the political system and were not to be trifled with too far at this stage.

At any rate Tito wanted to be left to determine how far. He did not want to narrow arbitrarily the limits of what he could achieve gradually by nicely calculated turns of the screw. The full and terrible compulsions of Moscow's doctrinaire approach might come later, or they might not. He was clear that it was impossible, without unbearable turmoil and loss, to force the peasants at one leap into a servitude which neither they nor their fathers had in most cases ever known; and he realized that the difficulties would be multiplied if in addition he had to tell them suddenly that they were to abdicate their accustomed political rôle in favor of mistrusted city workers, the urban proletariat which the Kremlin held to be the only reliable political class.

Something must have gone badly wrong with the Soviet espionage system in Jugoslavia, although it could hardly have been operating under more favorable circumstances. Shoals of Soviet diplomats, army officers, engineers and spies had been swarming through the country ever since the war. In the months when the dispute with Tito was coming to the boil the chief organ of Communist international intrigue, the Cominform, was located in Belgrade itself. Were all the Soviet agents so imbued with the doctrine of Russian omnipotence that they could not recognize realities under their noses if these differed from what they had expected? Or were they too stupid to understand them? Or too frightened of Moscow's displeasure to report them? Or was Stalin contemptuous of warnings? In his late sixties had he lost some of his uncanny political sensitivity and—what had once stood him in such good stead—his ability to postpone and manœuvre until the moment came to press his sword home in an adversary's vitals? He had purged every variety of traitor (using the word in its exact sense of unsuccessful rival). Had he become overconfident? Formerly he had been willing to use all the time necessary to work through his tortuous plans to the psychological moment when they could not go wrong. At last the stage would be set to perfection, when fractious or ambitious colleagues would have no choice but to make their final public appearance in the proper mood of repentance, offering their miserable carcasses as inadequate reparation for the sins they had committed against the Light of Marxist-Leninist doctrine held aloft in his sole hand, shaded in this direction or that by his sole whim and interest. Presented for the last time to the public gaze, they would no longer possess (Stalin would have made sure) will or strength to protest or even capacity to hope.

This time Stalin seemed to ignore the difference between Tito's position and that of a Bukharin. This time he was not dealing with a rival Communist theoretician who belonged to his own Politburo and was physically in his power, but with a rival Communist national leader who was the head of a Politburo of his own and physically outside the reach of the N.K.V.D. When his orders and reprimands brought arguments and reproaches instead of compliance and apologies, Stalin ordered the Cominform to issue the writ of excommunication. With whatever misgivings, and even though Zhdanov may have whispered to hold back, the members of the Cominform complied. Most of them, representing states adjoining the Soviet Union and occupied by Soviet troops, felt they had no choice. But further Stalin could not go without invading Jugoslavia and deposing Tito by an act of physical aggression. That entailed the possibility of a general war, and for this he was not at the time prepared.

Stalin erred as he had not done since he sent Trotsky out of the Soviet Union alive—and the results on this occasion were even more momentous. He struck at his antagonist and failed to kill him. The Cominform could bring in only one sentence—the "Guilty!" that Stalin told it to pronounce. But Stalin had failed to make sure that Tito would not and could not throw it back in his face. To his amazement, this Jugoslav's psychology proved as primitive as his own, his aims as concrete, his methods as crude, his hand as steady in aiming at the heart of a comradely foe.

# IX

## ISOLATION

> When and where in history had there
> been such defective saints?
>
> Arthur Koestler, "Darkness at Noon"

In dictatorial governments the hidden
strains and pressures are so enormous that what on the surface seem
trifling events may reflect shifts of weight or changes of direction
at the very seat of power. Perhaps outsiders might have been more
alert, while the great events just described were in the making, to the
possibility that the smooth surface of Communist discipline and the
synchronized voices of Communist propaganda concealed cracks and
discord. In Moscow, foreign diplomats apparently did not suspect
that Stalin's relations with Tito were near the breaking point in the
spring of 1948 or that the Kremlin was in correspondence with
trusted members of the Cominform looking to his dismissal and
destruction. In Belgrade, however, the American Embassy got wind
of the fact that something was wrong and reported its suspicions to
the State Department on June 18.

The alert American observers who predicted what would happen
two weeks before the news became public worked from stray facts
and keen "hunches." [1] They noted, for instance, that on May 25 Tito
failed to receive the congratulatory birthday message which had
come from Stalin in previous years. They watched a difference of

[1] Several members of the Embassy staff contributed to the report, which was
prepared by R. Borden Reams, chargé d'affaires, in the absence of Ambassador
Cavendish Cannon. Among them were Norman C. Stines, Alex N. Dragnich and
Charles G. Stefan. Details given here do not come from the persons directly
involved.

opinion develop between the Soviet and Jugoslav Governments as to where the Danube Conference was to be held in the summer. Originally Belgrade had been scheduled to act as host, but at the end of May Moscow decided that some other site would be more suitable. The Jugoslav Foreign Minister, Mr. Simich, reluctantly agreed, and so informed the foreign diplomats. However, he was peremptorily overruled by his superiors, already feuding secretly with Moscow, and had to call back the Americans and others with whom he had talked to tell them that his government now insisted that the Soviets stick to the original plan. The issue might not seem tremendously important, although to abandon Belgrade for some other city "with better facilities" would have been a blow to Jugoslav pride. The way in which the Jugoslav position was altered, nevertheless, indicated that the decision to oppose Moscow came from the top. Another straw in the wind was the fact that the Soviet press had lately begun to give less full and less eulogistic coverage to Jugoslav affairs. Further, an article by Pijade in *Borba* on June 12 defended the relationship of the Communist Party and the People's Front so vigorously as to suggest that it must have been subjected to severe criticism somewhere—and where but in Moscow? The issue of the Cominform journal for June 15 provided further grounds for speculation, for the leading article on page one delivered a sharp attack against any Communist "who persists in refusing to recognize his mistakes and who in the fog of eulogy and exaggerated self-praise fails to see serious shortcomings in the work." Since the French and Italian Communist leaders were pointedly excepted, this could be read to indicate that something spectacular was impending in Party circles in Eastern Europe. Who, in that area, could be objects of Stalin's displeasure? Probably only Tito or Dimitrov, or both. The Pijade article had suggested that Party tactics were being debated, but the Cominform article opened up the possibility that the subject was much more substantial when it said: "A non-Marxist attitude toward criticism and self-criticism is often the outcome of conceit and at times of a non-understanding of the rôle of self-criticism as a vital method in Party work, [and of] the desire to restrict criticism, to stifle it, to take measures against those who make serious critical remarks." Two of Tito's former ministers, Hebrang and Zhujovich, had been in jail since April.[2] Were they the critics whose criticisms were being stifled? As if to confirm suspicions that some showdown might be impending, Tito proceeded to overhaul Party organs and consolidate his hold on the foreign office and above all on the army.

These accumulated reasons for supposing that real and serious differences of opinion had arisen between Tito and the Kremlin were laughed off by the American Embassy in Moscow, where, naturally enough, the sense of Russian omnipotence was so strong that the idea of one of Stalin's satraps daring to defy him seemed ridiculous. Nor does the State Department seem to have been impressed by the cable from Belgrade. It nevertheless remains, I think, a model of diplomatic reporting. It assembled bits of information the significance of which would have escaped notice if considered separately, and on the basis of the collective evidence ventured predictions which in the event were justified at every point.

The world was amazed when news of the rift in the Cominform leaked out in Prague on June 28. Some declared the whole thing a hoax, others predicted that Tito's resistance, even if genuine, could not last a week. Nevertheless, the observers who were in the closest touch with Jugoslav as distinct from Russian affairs asserted that the breach was genuine, that it could not be closed by any conceivable compromise and that Tito would survive. So it proved. The moral is that it is well to examine the object of policy as closely as one does the subject, the anvil as well as the hammer.

Even after the schism became known the American and other non-Communist diplomats in Belgrade received no direct information about it and were not kept informed of later developments; nor was their advice solicited, much less their help. The Jugoslav Government treated the affair as a strictly Party matter of no interest or concern outside Communist circles. The same attitude was maintained in the Belgrade press, whose comments usually were made by Pijade and Djilas, experts in Party propaganda and political warfare, while Tito himself and Vice-Premier Kardelj remained silent. The Jugoslavs also took advantage of the fact that Moscow had

[2] The full story about Andrija Hebrang and Sretan Zhujovich is still not known, since they have never been brought to trial. In September 1950 several other leading Croat members of the Communist Party were deprived of their government posts on suspicion of being pro-Cominform.

acted behind the façade of the Cominform to blame that organization rather than Soviet Russia for what had happened, and as the Cominform offensive developed they replied more acrimoniously to charges in the satellite capitals than to those emanating from Moscow. No word derogatory to Stalin was uttered.

At the start, Stalin fell in with Tito's inclination to fight the war by proxy. The mere fact that the first blasts of the Cominform press and radio campaign came from Albania, however, was proof that it was centrally controlled; for the Albanian Prime Minister, Enver Hoxha, besides being indebted to Tito personally, was too puny to have dared attack his large neighbor on his own responsibility. The Albanian radio announced on July 1 that the Albanian Communist Party had "always" been in conflict with the Jugoslav Communist Party, which had "tried to impose on Albania its own treacherous hostile Trotskyism." The Bulgarian press and radio jumped to follow the cue given from Tirana, and soon all the satellite capitals were echoing with attacks on Jugoslavia as a hotbed of nationalism and reaction. But a dictator and his press can no more be disassociated than any other master and employee. Almost at once the Cominform had to drop the pretense that the press could attack Party figures in Jugoslavia without damaging relations with them as government officials. Belgrade, however, held to the theory that the satellite Parties were different from and independent of the master Party in Moscow and that disputes among the Parties did not necessarily involve the governments. A reader of the Jugoslav papers would have gathered that if Stalin so much as knew about the dispute going on inside his official family he was badly informed about its merits but would soon get the facts straight and intervene to set things right.

This was the attitude maintained in the draft program for the Fifth Party Congress, published June 30. It reaffirmed each of the policies attacked in the Cominform correspondence, but did not suggest that relations with the Soviet Government had become quite different from heretofore. Similarly, when Foreign Office officials talked with non-Communist diplomats they did not admit that the country's basic orientation had shifted abruptly. If Communist Party matters did not properly concern even the Soviet Ambassador how could they possibly concern the representatives of Washington, London and Paris? The same polite fiction was maintained during the Danube Conference in August. Nothing was altered in the relations of the Jugoslav, Soviet and satellite governments; only the respective Communist Parties were at odds, and this had no international significance. Tito stayed away from the capital during the Conference and thus had no occasion to encounter Vyshinsky.

The Party Congress, which the Bolsheviks had berated Tito for not holding sooner, took place in July. Tito's political report on this important occasion maintained the same rather anomalous position. "Monstrous accusations" had been levelled against the Party leaders, he said. They were supposed to have ceased being internationalists, to have renounced "the science of Marxist-Leninism." But the proofs of their "faithfulness and solidarity with the Soviet Union and other countries of people's democracy" would be found not in their words but in their deeds. Had not Jugoslavia entered into pacts of friendship and economic collaboration with not only the great Soviet Union but also with the smaller Communist states which needed her help, and had she not given them that help unreservedly? Now the very nations she had most befriended attacked her the most viciously. He and his colleagues were accused of being proud. As he watched the behavior of these others he wondered why Jugoslavs should not be proud—proud of their sacrifices in the war, proud of their workers, their youth, their People's Front, proud "of everything that all honest people marvel at." If this is nationalism, he said in effect, let those who define it as such make the most of it. And if, going beyond specific criticisms, they tried to teach him the ABC's of Marxist-Leninism, quoting Communist theoreticians to support their views, "they are knocking at an open door," for "we have been using and are using those quotations in practice." Had Trotskyist principles inspired the Jugoslav Communists to enter "the life and death struggle on the side of the Soviet Union in 1941?" Had false doctrines strengthened them to fight and win and found Socialism in Jugoslavia? Such charges were false on their face, and the theoretical reasoning which purported to support them was mistaken. Tito carefully admitted that everyone, Jugoslavs of course included, can make mistakes, but he added this for his detractors:

"There is no party, no man, who works without making mistakes."
Then followed an *amende honorable:* "We shall work with all
our might" to end the rift, still hoping that the Bolsheviks will
agree to testing the truth of the Cominform allegations "here, on
the spot."

Thus Tito successfully avoided taking up the theme on the international level where his former satellite comrades were furiously
debating it. He did not dignify the claim of the Albanians that he
had given them food and help because he wanted to make them
vassals or counted on annexing Albanian territory. He did not criticize Bulgaria for seizing on the dispute between Jugoslavia and the
U.S.S.R. to reopen her own claim to parts of Jugoslav Macedonia.
He said nothing about Hungary's having raised the minority question. He made plain that he retained the right to criticize the Bolshevik Party, but he still voiced friendship for the Soviet Union and
devotion to Stalin, still protested that he belonged to the anti-
imperialist camp and still expressed hope that what he implied
were misunderstandings could be removed. The official transcript of
his discourse, which lasted over five hours, records that towards the
end, "All rise amid hails of 'Stalin-Tito!' "

All in all, there was not much in this to aid or comfort the Bolsheviks, and the fact that the Jugoslav Party had now actually held
a Congress gave its spokesmen a chance to ask awkward questions
as to why the Bolshevik Party had not held a Congress since March
1939, although Article 29 of its statutes orders that one be held
at least once in three years. Was the reason, inquired Pijade sar-
castically,[3] that it was difficult to organize a Congress in wartime?
The Bolsheviks criticized the Jugoslavs for not holding a Congress
as early as 1944, when the war was still on and Nazi troops still held
part of the country. But the territory of the U.S.S.R. had been fully
liberated at that time. Might a Congress not have been organized
more easily there? In any case, the war now had been over for four
years and four months, and the Jugoslav Party had held a Congress
and the Bolsheviks had not. Could it be that the Russian leaders
had nothing to report or explain to their members as to what had
happened in the ten years since they last condescended to appear

[3] *Borba,* Belgrade, October 6, 1949.

before them? Might the members not like to hear, for example, how it had come to pass that Jugoslavia "was transferred from a Socialist country into a Fascist-Gestapo country, from a friend and ally into an 'enemy and foe'?" Might they not like an explanation of why the Balkan countries now were engaged in "a conflict such as never before, not even when there was not a single Socialist country in the world?" And why the concept of Great Russian patriotism had been substituted for internationalism? And why many strange phenomena had appeared in Soviet internal life, such as "personal tendencies" in the *kolkhozes* and chaos in legal literature and in philosophy? With so much to place on an agenda, the only possible reason a Congress had not been held in the U.S.S.R, concluded Pijade, was that "the entire new line" of the Bolshevik Party had ended in failure. "Many friends have been lost, and the sympathy which the Soviet Union gained in the world during the war has been ruined." Small wonder that the Bolshevik leaders were unwilling to face their members as the Jugoslav leaders had just faced theirs.

This article by Pijade was one of a series [4] propounding in a masterly way the fundamentals of the Jugoslav theory and practice of Marxism as against what emerges under his deft strokes as the Stalinist heresy. One point on which he was particularly effective is the claim, first put forward by the Bolsheviks in May 1948, that by sending the Red Army into Jugoslavia to smash the Nazis they had "created the vital conditions for the arrival of the Communist Party to power." Pijade dismissed in a few sentences the insult to the Partisans in "belittling and twisting" their rôle in the national liberation and in exaggerating that of the Red Army as the true saviors. What was really important, he said, was the assertion that Communism was able to gain power in Jugoslavia because the Red troops had created the necessary conditions there, whereas "unfortunately" it was not able to do so in France and Italy because of the lack of similar military assistance. Pijade pointed out that if this concept were accepted it would mean that there was "no possibility for the victory of a proletarian revolution except with the aid of the weapons of the Soviet Army, and that the proletarians of the entire world should have no illusions that they can win their liberation by their own

[4] *Borba*, Belgrade, September 22, 26 and 29 and October 5 and 6, 1949.

strength but must await the arrival of the Soviet Army, the liberator." In propounding this concept, he continued, the Soviet Union gave notice that it no longer pretended to aid the proletarians of all countries in their struggles for freedom in the true Leninist sense. He said that this was as thoroughly Menshevik and Trotskyite an idea as its twin, to wit that it is impossible to build Socialism in a country without the aid of the Soviet Union—an idea much stressed in Cominform anti-Jugoslav propaganda despite its incompatibility with the Leninist-Stalinist doctrine of the possibility of a single country's constructing Socialism independently. By such ideological deviations, Pijade maintained, the Bolsheviks excused their transformation of proletarian internationalism into Great Russian chauvinism and thence proceeded with "masterly hypocrisy" to try to destroy Jugoslav independence. The Tsar's ministers, he concluded, had been accustomed to boast that the Russians, by God's will, were the leading cultured nation in the world; the same petty conceit now obsessed their successors.

Another of Pijade's articles in the same series deals with less fundamental issues but throws interesting light on Tito's mood at the beginning of the Cominform crisis. The first Bolshevik letter, says Pijade, took the Jugoslav leaders completely by surprise. They had not liked the behavior of Russian missions in the country and had been disappointed by many aspects of Soviet policy, but they ascribed such things, in Pijade's words, "to the psychosis of a victorious Power which sees only its own sacrifices and does not understand the sufferings of others." This philosophical attitude of the misunderstood child was rudely shattered, however, by the suggestion in the first Bolshevik note that the Jugoslavs were in fact anti-Soviet and Trotskyite. When that happened, said Pijade, "nobody had to explain what it meant."

If they instantly understood "what it meant" why did the Jugoslavs leave the initiative to Stalin? Why, having defied him, did they allow him to set the bounds and define the character of the ensuing public debate? Because, it seems to me, Tito had decided that he must place on Stalin the full responsibility for converting what on the surface appeared to be a Party fracas, and hence should easily have been adjusted, into the life-and-death struggle which he foresaw it must become. He had not attempted to do more than establish his place as head of an independent Communist Party and state; but when he understood what wide principles were involved in the denial of his prerogatives he realized that his game was to leave to Stalin the initiative and with it the blame. As each successive measure to bring the Jugoslav Party to heel proved inadequate Stalin would pass to others still more autocratic and shocking to Communists and fellow-travellers everywhere, and to ideological excuses still more farfetched and unconvincing. Tito foresaw, I think, that the Bolsheviks would consider it absolutely necessary that he be disgraced before he was destroyed. They would have to demonstrate that he was not a simple defender of Jugoslav rights but an enemy of Communism. Only then would it be safe to eliminate him by assassination, a guerrilla uprising or outright invasion. A dead enemy of Communism would be one thing, a martyred national hero quite another. Whether or not Tito foresaw that this would be Stalin's strategy, his own strategy was well calculated to make it recoil in Stalin's face.

The drawback to such a policy, evidently, was that it left Tito's followers bewildered as to where they stood and where they were going. A great battle was plainly in progress, and they were on one side of it and the Bolshevik Party was on the other. Yet they still were shouting Stalin's name and Tito's in the same breath, just as if Stalin were not the Bolshevik chief. Tito nevertheless stuck to his Fabian strategy as long as possible. Stalin's name was not mentioned in the slightest derogatory manner until October, when his infallibility was questioned for the first time in an article in *Borba,* probably written either by Tito himself or under his direction by Djilas. This article, published October 4, 1948, contained this passage:

Until now we have not said anything of Stalin in our press. This was not because we have any illusions regarding his attitude in this entire conflict but because we felt that it would not be fitting on our part to use his name more than he does himself, and in any event the entire Party membership was acquainted with his attitude. Stalin is, and rightfully, the greatest living authority not only in the international worker's movement but in the entire democratic world. However, in the dispute between the CCCPY and the CCCPSU(b) right does not lie on his side but on the side of the CCCPY.

Tito knew that in Stalin's eyes even this mild declaration would be an irrevocable act, but it was the least that he could do to clarify his position in the eyes of his followers. A barrage of vilification for him followed in the Soviet and satellite press. He did not allow personal vilification of Stalin in return. As late as April 9, 1949, he was able to tell the members of the People's Front that "our press has not attacked Comrade Stalin, nor could it do such a thing."

I was in Belgrade not long afterwards and had the fatiguing privilege of watching the great six-and-a-half hour May Day parade. Pictures of Stalin were still carried in it along with those of Marx, Engels and Lenin. As I watched the endless squads of workers, peasants, students, government employees and shopkeepers file by I tried to imagine what might be in their minds. Many of them, I knew, were there by compulsion, and the banners they carried were inscribed with slogans which they either cared nothing about, disbelieved in or hated. But what were the others thinking, the real devotees marching exultantly in the front row or two of each group? The bulk of the marchers as they approached the grandstand applauded Tito cheerfully enough, but perfunctorily. These real enthusiasts, however, stretched out their hands toward him ecstatically and shouted the slogans called for by the cheer-leaders as though their lives depended on it (perhaps they did). What at heart did they think about the situation in which Tito and his régime and they themselves were now placed?

As good Communists, presumably, they would have studied the May Day proclamation of the Central Committee of the Party. They would have read there that "attacks on Jugoslavia coming from the U.S.S.R. and the countries of people's democracy" were "monstrous" and "slanderous;" that the rights of small peoples were "being trampled upon;" that the principle of nonintervention in a country's internal affairs had been abandoned; and that there no longer was equality between Socialist states. And what was the conclusion drawn from all this? Here was the proclamation's answer: "Long live the U.S.S.R., the first land of Socialism! Long live the countries of people's democracy!" If as good Communists they also had read that morning's *Borba* their bewilderment would not have been assuaged by the speech by Mosha Pijade there reproduced. Pijade denounced the "lies" and "dirty slogans" of the Cominform press and accused the Cominform states of "narrow nationalism" and "bossy imperialism"—epithets which a year before everyone belonging to the Cominform had reserved exclusively for denouncing Churchill and Truman.

As group after group passed by, the faithful in the front ranks would take up the chant, "Tito, Tito, Tito!" (while back from the Pariser Platz and the Piazza Venezia came dead echoes: "Hitler, Hitler, Hitler!" and "Duce, Duce, Duce!"). Yet there in their hands were the banners of Stalin which Tito's strategy demanded they still must carry. From the grandstand, Tito himself watched with the rest of us as that inscrutable visage went bobbing along in the company of the other major Communist prophets.

Actually, the May Day parade of 1949 marked the end of Tito's war with Stalin by proxy. The number of Stalin's pictures figuring in it was comparatively small, I was told, measured by the profusion of them on display the year before, while the fact that they were grouped exclusively with dead heroes of the past showed that he was receiving recognition as an historical figure only. As a living force, as a patron and ally, he had already been eliminated, and soon Tito would find it possible, even necessary, to deprive him of his historical rôle also. Before I left the country the last portraits of Stalin in railway stations and *kavanas* were being taken down by the police. And when the time came for the May Day parade of 1950 he had become an open enemy in his own right.

As I watched Tito standing there on the reviewing stand, smiling and apparently confident, surrounded by his uniformed generals and high Party and government officials, I thought of a cartoon a few days earlier in the humorous Belgrade weekly, *Jezh*. It showed a lighthouse, marked "KPJ," signifying the Communist Party of Jugoslavia, enveloped in mists and assaulted by waves from all directions yet flashing steady beams of light East and West. The waves were named impartially "Imperialism," "German Fascism," "Cominform Resolution," "Rumors" and "Lies." This was how the Jugoslav Communists still saw themselves a year after their expulsion from the Cominform—the beacon light of pure Communist idealism, equally menaced by Western capitalism and Stalin's corruption of Marxist-Leninism. They still laid emphasis on the word "equally." The old propaganda cocoon had been torn but they could not as yet face a flight into the light of full reality. The established church to which they belonged had excommunicated them; other members in good standing had been forbidden to have more than the bare necessity of intercourse with them; Moscow had launched a campaign of invective against them and inaugurated a systematic economic program aimed to strangle and destroy them. Yet though they retorted to the jibes and insults in kind they never omitted to point out simultaneously the evils of the capitalist West.

They needed its help badly. Without it they could hardly hope to survive the Cominform blockade. Much that they as Communists had always believed would be the world's greatest good would now, quite evidently, be their own greatest evil. If, for instance, Italy and with it the Adriatic should pass into Communist control almost their last window to the West would be closed and all hope for independent survival would disappear. But what hope was there that the catastrophe of a Togliatti victory in Italy could be avoided? Only the possibility that the democratic Western nations—in particular the archetype of capitalist greed, Uncle Sam—might save the Italian economy and give native Italian forces of regeneration time to assert themselves. And even if hopes on this score came true, even if the window to the West were not closed, where could Jugoslavia find the markets, materials, technological help and credits which Tito had always expected would be available behind the iron curtain? Nowhere except in America and the other Western nations.

The shattering truth became harder and harder to ignore. Behind Tito's calm, behind his defiant speeches and the telling articles of Pijade, Djilas and the rest, there was a terrible sense of isolation.

# X

## IMPASSE

> The puppy is feeling so good it barks at
> the elephant.
>
> Soviet note to the Jugoslav Government,
> August 30, 1949

EARLY in 1949 Moscow changed its line
of attack. Until then it had concentrated its fire on Tito as a nationalist—a deviationist from the orthodox faith, a Communist gone
wrong. The accusation had backfired. It had won Tito some open
friends and many secret ones.

At heart many Communists everywhere considered Tito's nationalist Communism to be nothing worse than what he himself described it, a simple assertion of independence for Communist Parties
and Communist states. When he said, "Socialism does not require us
to renounce our love for our country, a Socialist country," [1] they
agreed. When Soviet propagandists attacked him for paying Stalin
insufficient homage many of them disagreed. Like Tito they regarded Stalin as a Communist hero, but like him they fell short of
adoring him as a god. They would have to come around to this—as
the Albanian People's Assembly showed when they voted in January
1950 to erect a statue of "the deity, Joseph Vissarionovich Stalin"—
but many of them resented it. More than one satellite leader would
be accused of sharing Tito's nationalist and independent views and
of plotting to put them into effect in his own country. Some so
accused may have been innocent; but certainly many, many more
than were accused were guilty in their secret thoughts.

At home, Tito was strengthened more among the non-Communist

[1] Speech at meeting of the Slovene Academy of Arts and Sciences, Ljubljana,
November 16, 1948.

majority by being called a nationalist than he was weakened among the Communist minority. Even those who hated him most bitterly could not help taking secret and reluctant pride in the fact that their local tyrant had successfully defied the supreme tyrant in Moscow, the fountainhead of their sufferings. In Tito's own Party there was one category which was not disturbed at hearing him called a nationalist and one which was pleased by it. The first included most of his friends and colleagues in the Party hierarchy. To them, however freely they might engage in doctrinal exegesis, the conflict with Moscow was for power. It had begun as that, and so it remained despite the high-sounding phrases used on both sides. If they had to suffer being called nationalists in the course of their fight for independent power, so be it. The second category included rank-and-file members and younger leaders who had come to Communism by nationalist roads, either having joined the Party before the war in the hope that the triumph of Socialism might free their country from "foreign exploitation" or having entered the Partisan ranks as patriots to fight the invader.

A talk which I had with one of these younger Communists at this time, in the spring of 1949, showed how nationalist they could be in the very sense that Tito was termed a nationalist. This young man could hardly restrain his overflowing resentment as he thought back to how he had been, in his words, "fooled by Stalin." "In those days," he said, meaning the time of Partisan struggle and the period after the victory, "we were childish. We were too idealistic to doubt the perfection of the Soviet Union. Stalin—he was the true Communist, the ideal Communist! He would never dream of treating other Communists unfairly!" When had his first doubts about this arisen, I asked? After the establishment of the Cominform, he said, when it began to appear that the Jugoslavs were not to be allowed to run their own country. "All through history Serbs and Croats have worked for others—well, we were as good as told that we were to continue to do just that. We were to dig our coal and ores, but not build plants to smelt our iron and make it into steel and make the steel into the machinery we needed. We were not to build power stations to give our peasants electric light and milk separators and radios to listen to in the evenings. We were not to build concrete highways and the trucks to run on them or drill for our own oil to run the trucks. No, we were to send our wealth abroad, raw, just as always—we were to be exploited, we were to be a colony, just as always. After the struggles in the old times against the Turks and Austrians and Magyars, after our own fights with the Nazis and Italians, we were to keep our muddy roads, walk on them in our peasant *opanke* and step aside when the Russian engineers rode past in their motorcars just as Serbs used to do when the Turks rode by on their mules!"

Here, I thought, was a secret the clever men in the Kremlin had missed. No wonder their accusation of nationalism had strengthened Tito even with many Jugoslav Communists and no wonder it had disillusioned so many Communists in other nations in Eastern Europe.

This having become clear at last, the Soviets decided to improve their tactics. A gradual evolution in their propaganda line was noticeable during several months and became unmistakable in June of 1949 when Moscow answered a Jugoslav protest against the activities of Jugoslav émigrés in Russia, and especially against the support given by the Soviet Government to the anti-Tito organ which they published in Moscow, *For a Socialist Jugoslavia*.[2] The Soviet reply said that the émigrés were not traitors, as asserted by Belgrade, but "genuine Socialists and democrats, true sons of Jugoslavia," and then proceeded to make the formidable declaration that Tito's "terrorist and anti-Communist" régime had "slid over into the camp of the enemies of the Soviet Union." This went beyond anything heretofore charged by the Soviet Government or even by the Soviet press. *Pravda* in September 1948 had declared that Tito had joined "a common camp with the imperialists," and the Soviet magazine *Slavyanye* on February 2, 1949, had recalled and confirmed this statement and enlarged it as follows: "The Tito group has now finally moved into the camp of the imperialists, and has become a tool in the hands of the imperialist circles of the U.S.A. and England, which are struggling against the mighty democratic

---

[2] Moscow also subsidized Jugoslav émigré groups to publish anti-Tito papers in most of the satellite capitals: in Prague, *The New Fight*; in Sofia, *Forward*; in Bucharest, *Under the Banner of Internationalism*; in Warsaw, *For Victory*.

group and its guiding force—the Soviet Union." [3] Now the Soviet
Government in an official note designated the members of that camp
as "the enemies of the Soviet Union" and placed Tito and his régime
among them. An enemy of the Soviet Union! Was some climax at
hand?

There were various indications that this might be so. Czechoslovakia, Hungary and Poland in rapid succession denounced their
trade treaties with Jugoslavia. At the meeting of the Council of
Foreign Ministers in Paris, in June, Vyshinsky announced that the
Soviet Union no longer supported Jugoslavia's territorial claims in
Austrian Carinthia. This was a new departure in Soviet policy.
Members of the Soviet bloc had attacked Jugoslavia freely but had
tacitly at least included her in the united front which they presented
to the outside world. That front was now broken. In retaliation, the
Jugoslav Government closed the Greek-Jugoslav frontier against the
Cominform-supported Greek rebels; its own support of the Greek
rebels had ceased earlier, but until now it had not taken any formal
action which might seem to help the Western Powers bring the Greek
struggle to an end. Evidences of strain inside the Cominform world
appeared also. Purges were in progress in Bulgaria and Hungary in-
volving very high Communist personages—in Sofia, Acting Prime
Minister Traicho Kostov, and in Budapest, Foreign Minister Laszlo
Rajk. In Albania, a possible rival to Prime Minister Enver Hoxha
was disposed of summarily. This campaign of terror might have been
staged mainly for local purposes. Equally well it might be a prelude
to active intervention to end the Tito nuisance in Jugoslavia.

Four of Jugoslavia's neighbors—Hungary, Rumania, Bulgaria
and Albania—were now open enemies of Tito's régime and again,
following a brief experience in the Communist international brother-
hood, of the Jugoslav nation. Across all four frontiers came desultory
but persistent forays, as though to remind Tito that the polemics of
the press and radio and the sneers and jibes of his former Cominform
comrades might at any moment be translated into bullets and
bombs. Apparently inspired rumors were constantly cropping up of
Soviet troop concentrations in Rumania and Hungary; and there

[3] *Soviet Press Translations*, published by the Far Eastern and Russian Institute of the University of Washington, Seattle, June 15, 1949.

were reports of Bulgarian activities that might betoken a Cominform-sponsored rising in Jugoslav Macedonia. In April Tito had asserted that the inspiration for these rumors came from "warmongering" circles in the West; but he did so no longer.

Soviet manœuvres nevertheless had not broken Tito's determination to seem and if possible be "neutral" in the struggle between East and West, which had been increasing in intensity during the negotiations leading up to the signature of the Atlantic Pact in April. Shortly before that event, a representative of *Le Monde*, of Paris, had inquired among "responsible statesmen" in Belgrade whether Jugoslavia would resist "any" aggressor and had been told that they "preferred not to answer." Early in April, while Tito was vacationing in Brioni, he was reported as saying to a group of local delegations that "lies and propaganda slanders" were being spread against the new Jugoslavia "both by the Western capitalists and by the Eastern Socialist states." There was a subtle differentiation here between unofficial and official slanderers and warmongers. Was it deliberate? On April 9, back in Belgrade, he told the Third People's Front Congress that "no intimidation from the West or East can divert us from our principles as determined followers of Marxist-Leninism or from our own road to Socialism." Specifically, he noted the "hysterical cries" of capitalist Western newspapers that Jugoslavia cannot "hang in midair" but "must soon join the Western capitalist bloc." However, he devoted even more time to denouncing the "intensive propaganda disseminated in the countries of people's democracy to the effect that Jugoslavia was going over to the imperialist camp, that capitalism was to be revived in our country, and similar nonsense." And he added defiantly that Jugoslavia would of course trade with the West on a quid pro quo basis, Jugoslav goods for Western machines and money. Anything else would be "a crime against our Socialist country." The pose of neutrality nevertheless was hard to maintain, what with the hail of insults from the Cominform states and the fact that his struggle for independence was viewed sympathetically by the Western Governments and reported open-mindedly in the important Western newspapers. On May 15 the Cominform journal cartooned Tito as a mongrel dog sitting up on his hind legs to catch dollars dropped by Uncle Sam;

called Rankovich, the Minister of the Interior, a killer; and described Pijade as a miserable pygmy and (mixing its metaphors) "a jester in the Tito menagerie." Approximately half the space of this six-page issue was devoted to abuse of Tito, a measure of his importance as Cominform Enemy No. 1.

The Soviet Union's formal denunciation of the Jugoslav leaders as enemies seemed to release them from their set strategy. They did not shade their principles in the direction of Western democracy, although they emphasized that these were different from the precepts of Stalin; and they did begin definitely looking westward for life-saving loans and trade. The principal change was in their attitude toward Stalin himself. It was he, they now said, who was the real deviationist, the real traitor to the struggle to build a true and pure international Communist society. Tito in April had called the Cominform appeal "an attempt to provoke civil war in our country." Now he suggested a revolt inside the Cominform world. On the first anniversary of the Cominform Resolution, *Borba*, the Party organ, prophesied that more and more Communists would heed Tito's call to return to the true Marxist path. "The truth about the fight between the Cominform and Jugoslavia," it wrote, "and about the principles for which our Party is fighting, is growing daily in the international worker's movement, and there is no reason why it should not triumph." Tito himself expressed similiar confidence. Addressing Party and army leaders at Skoplje early in August, he said that he was determined to resist any invasion, and for the first time made clear that this specifically included one by the Soviet Army. He dwelt on the strength of the Jugoslav armed forces and their readiness for instant action. Then he remarked: "It might look at first sight as though we stood alone, but this is not true. A majority of the peoples of the East and the progressive peoples of the entire world are with us. An honest world cannot forget what Jugoslavia contributed in the great historic struggle against Fascism and against the enslavers of our people and of other peoples."

This had three results. It notified Soviet Russia that an attack, direct or by her satellites, would produce an armed conflict, and that he was ready for it. It appealed again for the support of "progressive peoples" everywhere in his struggle as a "genuine" Communist against the Stalinist Cominform. And it reminded the Jugoslav people that although the danger of war was always present there were forces abroad which might count eventually on their side. He was careful to claim that he had the support only of "progressive peoples," but the reference to what "an honest world" would have to think of a national struggle for self-preservation had definitely wider connotations.

Soviet pressure was screwed up another notch later in the same month. In a note recording that it had no further interest in supporting Jugoslav claims in Carinthia, the Soviet Government on August 11 told Tito that since he evidently preferred "imperialist" company to its own he could look to his new friends to support his case. Then, passing beyond the earlier assertion that his régime had slid over into the camp of its enemies, the Soviet note ended with this formal statement: "Let the peoples of Jugoslavia know that the Soviet Government regards the present Government of Jugoslavia not as a friend and ally, but as a foe and enemy of the Soviet Union." [4] Shortly afterwards (August 20), in the course of an exchange of notes regarding the treatment of Soviet citizens in Jugoslavia, the Soviet Government threatened to resort to "other more effective measures" if the "inhuman methods" of Tito's "Fascist Gestapo régime" did not cease. Having called the kettle black, the note went on to state that in Soviet eyes "the leadership of the Jugoslav Communist Party is at war with the Communist Parties of the whole world." The Jugoslav Government replied sharply that it was independent and sovereign and that "no pressure from outside had so far had any effect on its internal policy nor will it in the future." Nevertheless, it offered to settle all disputed questions with the U.S.S.R. in the spirit of the mutual obligations of the two governments. Some observers jumped to the conclusion that this was an olive branch, an offer to call quits. They quite misinterpreted the nature of the struggle, and *Borba* quickly set them right. The threat of Soviet attack, it said on August 25, was not to be taken seriously; what was serious was that the Soviets were worsening relations with Jugoslavia deliberately and depicting her as an "undemocratic and non-Socialist state" in order to damage her with "democratic"

[4] Supplement to *New Times*, Moscow, August 17, 1949.

elements abroad. During the first year after the Cominform split,
continued the Party organ, the satellites had led the attack on Jugoslavia, but without success. Now the Soviet Government was forced
to assume open leadership of the anti-Jugoslav campaign. As if to
italicize these statements, three divisions of the Soviet Army were
reported to have entered Hungary from Rumania and to have de-
ployed near the Jugoslav border.

Moscow's fury was increased by the failure of its commercial
pressure and its threats, verbal and military, to produce any discern-
ible effect—though it is not clear just what effect they were supposed to produce on a leader who had already staked his life on resistance. A new note to Belgrade on August 30,[5] broadcast over the
Moscow radio, called Tito "a malicious deserter" and his associates
"mad Fascists." *Borba* asked how it happened, if the Jugoslav
régime were "Gestapo" and "Fascist" and the Soviet régime were
"democratic," that the Jugoslav press published the notes from the
Soviet Union but the Soviet press did not publish the Jugoslav notes?
Going back a year, why had the Soviet Government never given its
people the reply of the Jugoslav Communist Party to the Cominform Resolution? Was it going to publish the Jugoslav reply now
being sent to the latest Soviet note? Pijade added the thought a day
or so later that Stalin's attitude toward Jugoslavia was comparable
only to Hitler's "racist" attitude toward smaller countries.

Not long afterwards the Jugoslav Government decided that the
gravity of the international situation should be more fully revealed
to its people, and simultaneously thought wise to let them know that
they were not completely isolated. The readers of *Borba* on September 4 were therefore provided for the first time with extensive
comments, filling a whole page, by Secretary of State Acheson, the
British Minister of State, Hector McNeil, and a large number of
Western newspapers, revealing that there was in fact a risk of war
and that there was strong support in the West for Marshal Tito's
efforts and preparations to maintain and defend Jugoslav independence.[6]

[5] This note was part of the interchange of charges and counter-charges of
bad faith regarding the Soviet refusal to support Jugoslav claims in Carinthia.
For details see "The United States in World Affairs, 1949," *op. cit.*, Chapter 7.

[6] M. S. Handler, *The New York Times*, September 5, 1949.

Soviet polemics were reënforced by further hostile acts, but not, as had been feared, in the military field. Evidently Moscow decided that it had best end its formal engagements with such a recalcitrant government and minimize its verbal exchanges with antagonists who knew the language of vituperation as well as Foreign Minister Vyshinsky himself. September was the month of the spectacular trial in Budapest of Laszlo Rajk, the former Hungarian Minister of the Interior and Minister of Foreign Affairs, the story of which will be related later.[7] Rajk was charged with having plotted with Tito to overthrow the pro-Cominform leadership of the Hungarian Communist régime. His trial became a propaganda vehicle for accusing Tito of having taken part in a widespread conspiracy against Moscow dating back to the years before the war and of having served during the war as an agent and spy of Moscow's imperialist "enemies" (then allies) in the West. The charge presumed that Tito foresaw the war, foresaw the Nazi invasion of Jugoslavia, foresaw the Soviet rôle in the war, foresaw his own formation of a Partisan army, foresaw that he would be victorious both in the struggle against the Nazis and in his effort to establish a Communist régime in Jugoslavia, foresaw that this would lead him into opposition with Moscow, and, foreseeing all these things, laid a plan in advance to sell out to the Western Powers (which, he foresaw, would break with the Soviets) and meanwhile acted as their undercover agent.

No evidence remotely credible was of course available to substantiate such a grotesque charge. The Soviet Government nevertheless took advantage of it—on the theory propounded by Rykov in 1926, perhaps, that suspicion is the equivalent of guilt—to abrogate the Soviet-Jugoslav Treaty of Friendship, Mutual Assistance and Postwar Coöperation signed by Tito when he visited Moscow in April 1945. The announcement was made on September 29, 1949. The satellites dutifully followed suit and denounced their respective treaties with Belgrade. Poland and Hungary acted on September 30, Bulgaria and Rumania on October 1. In abrogating the Bulgar-Jugoslav treaty of friendship the Bulgarian Government charged that the Jugoslav leaders were "formulating insolent pretensions for grabbing Bulgarian territories." The Czechoslovak denunciation

[7] *Cf.* Chapter XXI.

came on October 4. In connection with it, *Rude Pravo*, the Czech
Communist organ, devoted a full page to the charge that Tito and
members of his government had been in league with the Germans
during the war.

These synchronized actions emphasizing Jugoslavia's extreme isolation, and Marshal Tito's defiant reply that he would not be cowed
by threats, did not, according to one excellent observer at least, have
any adverse effect on Jugoslav opinion. M. S. Handler reported from
Belgrade, in a dispatch to *The New York Times* dated October 4,
that Tito seemed to have been successful in conditioning the minds
of opponents and supporters alike to the possible consequences of his
policy; and he added these reflections, which must have been read
sourly in Moscow: "Regardless of their economic or social origins,
the mass of the people of Jugoslavia are agreed on one point—that
they are being led by a determined group of men who have manœuvred well against the Soviet Government and who know what
they are doing. Even the harshest critics of the régime's internal
policy have been silenced by the spectacle of the leadership of a
country of only 15,000,000 people doing battle with a bloc of
Powers totalling more than 250,000,000 and hitting harder every
day."

The Soviets had not been able to intimidate Tito and there did
not seem to be much more that they could do to harm him short of
sending armies into his country and attempting to dispose of him
physically. In their frenzy they had passed far beyond calling him
a traitor out of weakness or through ignorance or error: he was a
traitor by malice aforethought. He was not a heretic but a scoundrel
who had deserted his allies, knifed his benefactor in the back, betrayed the revolution and sold out his country. His battle with the
Nazis had been a pretense. From the start he had been a hidden
Fascist, a spy for Western reactionaries. The trials which were held
in various satellite capitals of Tito's supposed fellow-conspirators
resulted in convictions, of course, but they were convincing to nobody who could read the full evidence and compare it with established fact. The charges that he himself had long been and still was
the agent of the enemies of the Soviet Union fell flat. What next?

Of hard fact, as it turned out, very little. In November the Cominform met for the first time since it had expelled the Jugoslav comrades a year and a half before and passed three resolutions, one of them devoted exclusively to Tito. Its tenor may be imagined from the title of the address which preceded its adoption—"The Jugoslav Communist Party in the Power of Murderers and Spies," by the chief Rumanian delegate, Gheorghiu-Dej. To those who counted on finding novel charges or even a fresh batch of adjectives to describe the old ones the resolution was disappointing. There was nothing new in it, and it therefore needs no elaboration here (although the temptation to quote it on the evils of a swollen military and police apparatus is very great). The chief purpose seemed to be to encourage Communists everywhere to "do their duty" in helping the Jugoslav workers and peasants "return" their country to the camp of democracy and Socialism. It expressed the Cominform's conviction that they would be successful in this; and on that note it stopped. Words had run out, and deeds of daring still lacked.

# XI

## TITO ON THE TIGHTROPE

> The ghosts I have summoned I can
> never shake off.     Goethe

How long would Stalin refrain from further deeds—daring and direct, or cautious, through a hired hand? After the attack of the North Korean Communists on the Republic of Korea the second hypothesis of course became the subject of particular study in Belgrade. Stalin so far had placed his East European satellites in the forefront of his operations against Tito. Would he continue the same tactics if he decided that the time had arrived to overcome Tito by force? Would he order the satellite armies to move against the Jugoslav Army in the same way that he had intervened to overthrow the Korean Republic, without engaging his own prestige directly and without incurring responsibility for the outcome until he saw whether it was going to be satisfactory?

Whatever crisis lay ahead, Tito was unable or unwilling to face it otherwise than as a Communist and a dictator. But although he could not or would not alter the essential nature of his régime he did seem anxious to ameliorate its practices. Stalin provided a reason. What Stalin did was wrong; and as Stalin functioned by intimidation, persuasion must be better. Experiments with persuasion were begun in 1950.

Early in the new year observers reported from Belgrade that a distinct effort was being made to reform the presentation of foreign news in the Jugoslav press. They felt that the coverage was wider, the selection of items more balanced and that there was a tendency to drop the habit of interlarding dispatches from abroad with comments designed to neutralize information and ideas which were objectionable from a Party view. For the first time since before the war, the Jugoslav people had a reasonably fair chance to judge their own national position and to understand the policies of other countries toward them. This was taken as a sign that Tito considered his domestic position more secure and was glad to be able to show it.

The first concrete development raised hopes which proved to be false. On January 21 an electoral law was adopted to enable candidates who were not named by the régime to run for Parliament in the elections scheduled for the spring. The new law permitted a candidate not belonging to the People's Front to stand in any constituency where he could secure the signatures of 100 voters. This modified the former impossible provision which authorized non-régime candidates only if they ran on a nation-wide ticket. Vice-Premier and Foreign Minister Kardelj praised the measure as a step that would develop true Socialism in Jugoslavia and prevent the re-creation of secret counter-revolutionary organizations. The aim here, again, might well have been to show that the régime was strong enough to tolerate a certain amount of open opposition, even though on conditions which insured that it would be innocuous. Either the the move was discovered to be too ambitious or its meaning was misread from the start. In the course of the campaign Marshal Tito announced that there was no room for two political programs in Jugoslavia, that opponents of Socialism would not be permitted to stand for election and that there was to be no revival of the old prewar bourgeois parties.[1] The election was held on these terms on March 26 and the results as announced showed more than 90 percent of the voters supporting the unopposed candidates of the People's Front.

During the campaign Tito promised the peasants to ameliorate the harshness of certain Communist measures, especially governing the forcible collection of produce. The compulsory delivery of a hog, for example, could be replaced with the delivery of 22 pounds of lard. This would not strike an American owner of two pigs as a great favor, but it was received as one by the Jugoslav farmer who was accustomed not only to having to deliver arbitrary numbers of livestock and amounts of produce at fixed prices but also to having frequently to go into the free market to buy corn or fats (at much higher

[1] M. S. Handler, *The New York Times*, January 22 and March 13, 1950.

prices) to make up his required quota. Tito also promised that unfair local functionaries would be punished. Finally, he announced that fats and wheat would no longer be exported, a concession intended to improve domestic living conditions. The drought which soon was parching the fields of Jugoslavia put an end to food exports in any case. It also defeated Tito's plan to revise peasant quotas downward (except in the case of bread grain).

Another effort to modify established practice was made in the industrial field. Mr. Kardelj told me while he was in New York for the 1949 U.N. General Assembly that he was working on plans for decentralizing the control of heavy industry in a manner to broaden the responsibilities of state governments and local plant managements and to increase group and individual initiative. I was particularly impressed, I recall, by his repetition of the word "individual initiative," which had been missing from most of the Communist statements that I had ever read. When the Jugoslav Parliament convened on January 20, 1950, the Kardelj plan was introduced and adopted, and on February 7 was embodied in three decrees of the Presidium. These decrees decentralized control of heavy industries; abolished the Ministries of Mines and Electro-Economy; proposed that six committees be set up to supervise the decentralized industries, two to act as coördinating committees on a national basis, the others to deal specifically with the four principal branches of heavy industry; and transferred responsibility for industries having only regional importance to the governments of the six republics constituting the Jugoslav Federation. In addition, a workers' council was to be set up in each factory and mine to share in running the enterprise with the government-appointed manager.

When the Chairman of the State Planning Commission, Boris Kidrich, reported this plan to the Presidium he admitted that it would be "naïve" to suppose that so long as the struggle for Socialism was in progress it would be possible "to liquidate the tendency to bureaucracy by directives." He nevertheless did claim that the new procedure would produce two important results at once: it would increase production by increasing the independent initiative of those familiar with local conditions; and, most important, it would demonstrate that the Jugoslav Government was firmly opposed to the Stalinist concept of a centralized and bureaucratic dictatorship and was moving away from it. As an offset to exaggerated hopes in this connection one must note that the six state governments are of course tied closely in with the central government and are responsible to it, while the highly centralized organization of the Communist Party ensures that policies will be carried out on a unified basis throughout the governmental structure. Further, experiments with workers' councils in the Soviet Union do not justify the belief that they can of themselves alter the management of individual concerns. Nevertheless, the purposes, within the limitations of Communist thinking, seemed sound. As Mr. Kardelj explained them to me, I remember he drew two vertical lines with his hands, parallel and close together, to indicate the restrictive control exercised by the central Soviet planning and administrative apparatus over the whole Soviet economy; and then he drew two other lines, sloping out to a broad base, to indicate the Jugoslav intention of giving industrial enterprises wide latitude in adapting the general economic directives received from the central government to their particular local conditions.

The Jugoslav Government also made some tentative concessions to the religious feelings of its people and incidentally to the conscience of mankind. It returned certain important properties to the Serb Orthodox Church, including the famous Patriarchal Palace and theological seminary at Sremski Karlovci, and indicated that it might take a more lenient attitude toward religious instruction in primary schools. Skeptical observers waited to see whether this intention would be put into practice. To emphasize the better relationship which was developing, Marshal Tito was reported by the Associated Press to have paid a call on September 26, 1950, on Patriarch Vikentije, recently chosen to head the Serb Orthodox Church after a long tug-of-war between anti-Communist bishops and those who wanted to make peace with the régime. The government also returned several Lutheran churches to their pastors and congregations. Its somewhat relaxed attitude toward the Roman Catholic Church was indicated by the fact that the first of the nine consecrations in view to fill vacant Sees finally took place at Pazin, a diocese in Istria. In October, the Bishop of Mostar, imprisoned as a wartime collaborator, was released. As for Archbishop Stepinatz of Zagreb, the régime had offered informally in 1949 to release him if he would leave the country or retire to a monastery; and in November, 1950, Tito revived the offer in a talk with C. L. Sulzberger.

Probably the outstanding sign of Tito's new desire to win support for the régime by persuasion rather than force was the announcement on October 15, 1950, that the many special privileges in food and housing enjoyed by Party and government officials and by army officers and others of the ruling hierarchy were abolished as of November 1. The ostensible cause was the great drought of the preceding summer and the grim prospect of near starvation in the winter ahead. Promises of American relief had been made, but even with large imports of food there would be iron rations for the many and Tito realized how unpopular it would be if while the masses were suffering intensely the few were known to be eating better, living in better heated houses and able to move about the country in cars supplied with government gasoline. The new decree stated that nobody in Jugoslavia should in future receive more than the basic food ration for workers entitled to the maximum allowance, that is, miners and forestry and railroad workers. The farms organized for the particular purpose of supplying food to the "special shops" for officials were to be turned back to ordinary uses; the shops themselves were to be closed; so were the special rest houses and hotels, except those used by unions for vacations for workers; free gasoline for anything but official use was to be ended; entertainments, except those given officially by the state, were forbidden; and as an economy measure further decoration or furnishing of government buildings was suspended.

As a propaganda move, if nothing more, this was a master stroke. But actually it did seem to be more. No Communist régime had ever until now practised equality between the rulers and the ruled. If the decree of October 15 was lived up to, Tito would have set a standard for the ruling hierarchies of the Soviet Union and the satellite states that would embarrass them no end. He had appealed dramatically from the practice of Stalin to the theory of Lenin. In substance as well as in propaganda effect this was a true "revolutionary" act.

Almost as important from a propaganda view, and even more important in indicating what might be the eventual character of the Jugoslav régime, was the announcement that the criminal code was to be redrafted and the whole system of administering justice reorganized. Soviet justice does not recognize what we in the West call due process of law. The police secretly arrest, detain and punish persons for certain categories of offenses under a procedure known as "administrative punishment." The proposed reform would transfer judicial powers exclusively to the courts and in proceedings there the public prosecutor would be given less authority and the defense counsel more. We may keep our fingers crossed while waiting for the proposal to be enacted into law. If this is done it will test the extent to which personal rights of citizens are compatible with the requirements of a Communist régime.

In 1950 the Jugoslav Communists even developed that most un-Communist trait, a sense of proportion, one manifestation of which is a sense of humor. The press became almost lighthearted as it poked fun at Soviet claims that Moscow was the center of the universe and that Russians had led the way in every human enterprise from time immemorial. If God had actually picked Russia as Paradise, as the Soviet propagandists wrote, then Eve must have tricked Adam in one of the Moscow city parks, commented an irreverent Belgrade columnist, and the next thing would be for them to claim that Christ had been a Russian. Serious political subjects also were viewed in better perspective. Writers dared to compare the "black reactionaries" of the West with Soviet "warmongers" to the latter's disadvantage. The reactionaries were powerful but they did not *necessarily* control governments, whereas two-faced hypocrites like Vyshinsky, preaching peace and preparing war, *were* governments.

Officials seemed to me to be less dogmatic, too, than they had been in the first flush of Communist enthusiasm. When they talked about what is called voluntary labor service, for instance, they no longer touted its advantages without admitting that it might have drawbacks. I found several who admitted that although the labor brigades have contributed much useful heavy work—particularly in building roads, digging irrigation and drainage projects and clearing up war damage—their performance is slow, uneconomic and wasteful compared to what can be accomplished by properly trained and paid labor. The verve and energy of many Jugoslav workers must strike any visitor from the West. Even the youth brigades, which are at least quasi-compulsory, boil with enthusiasm. I cannot say as much, naturally, for the "class enemies" in labor camps, which are a hideous blot on all the Communist countries of Eastern Europe, Jugoslavia included. But in Belgrade (as in Warsaw) it is the youth brigades that are on exhibition. Those with the best morale are chosen for the exhibition, of course. Even knowing this, the visitor can hardly fail to be impressed.

At six o'clock on every morning while I was in Belgrade a brigade of boys and girls marched into an area of rubble and half-wrecked buildings on the Terazia, opposite my hotel. They arrived with flags, singing, lined up like athletes ready for a hundred-yard dash, and at a given signal rushed at a tottering wall or a pile of broken concrete and began dismembering it with their bare hands. There were a few pickaxes to topple over the solid walls. But for the most part these 'teen-age boys and girls clawed at the masonry, pulled it apart, and either shouldered chunks or passed them in endless chains from hand to hand. They did this for ten hours, until four o'clock, and were back the next morning at six, singing. The theme song was not "Boy meets girl," but "Boy meets pickax and girl meets wheel-barrow." I asked an acquaintance in one of the ministries how there could be such unflagging energy for such heavy work. He said: "Because they are Jugoslavs, and Jugoslavs know they have to work." He added: "They know they have to work even harder since Stalin began trying to ruin us for not taking his path to Socialism." The ideology was an afterthought. The other explanation was the true one.

But although the youth brigades sing as they march to (and even from) work there is something infinitely pathetic about them. Lately the government has begun to realize not merely that they are not really efficient for serious construction work but that they are paying a toll in health that will be very expensive for the nation in the future. The tuberculosis rate in Jugoslavia is higher than in almost any other civilized country in the world. This is not entirely new, and therefore cannot be attributed to putting children at heavy work before they have attained their growth; but I was assured by a competent doctor that so long as the practice continues the tuberculosis problem is insoluble. The youth brigades are supposed to be "voluntary," but if boys or girls are ambitious to secure higher education and preferment later on they know that it is more important to have served their term in them than to have obtained good marks in school. This may change; indeed it had changed to some extent in the interval between my visits in 1949 and 1950. The disadvantage of giving a higher education to certain children simply because they have worked well with their hands is at last being recognized. But work of some sort, if only after office or school hours, will probably be required indefinitely to establish the "right" national attitude and qualify young people for any rôle in life except labor in fields or factories.

The sad thing about the energy and diligence of the average Jugoslav workers is that they do not receive a greater return in ordinary creature comforts or, in less favored occupations, even enough food to keep them in good working trim. There are rewards for some. The industrial workers, the pampered section of the population, have an advantage in rationing and also priority in getting what their ration cards call for. The higher Party and government officials (usually if a man is one he is the other also) live in the villas that the merchants, bankers and other "profiteers" of the old régime built in Topchider and Dedinje, and ride in American cars. Their way of living, even with all the privileges that were legal before November 1, 1950, was nothing to cause envy in an ordinary middle-class household in the suburb of any fair-sized American town; but measured against the comforts or pleasures known to the Jugoslav masses the contrast has been rather formidable. It has been less in the smaller towns than in Belgrade, where the numerous government employees, dispossessed shopkeepers, merchants and other remnants of the old bourgeoisie are considered drones and get only subsistence rations.

Almost everything is rationed, and ration cards are issued to all except the peasantry (and to some of them who are too poor to feed themselves). About 5,400,000 persons out of a population of something over 15 million hold ration cards. Any of these can supplement what is allowed on his card by purchases on the free market, provided he has the money and the goods are available. The price

of an article on the free market may be as much as 15 times the price
for the identical article purchased on the ration. For example, an
ordinary pair of women's shoes, of a sandal type, in white or brown
suede, roughly finished inside, costs 280 dinars, or $5.80 at the official
rate of exchange, on the ration, and 4,000 dinars, or $80, on the
free market. The catch is, of course, that the ration is not sufficient
by any standard of decent living; and those whose ration cards call
for the minimum quantities, the city "drones," are gradually being
reduced to rags and never get a satisfying meal.[2] Many items are (or
were in the spring of 1950) unprocurable, from needles and thread
to combs and soap—the most ordinary things distinguishing the
habits of a man from those of an animal. Prices should be measured,
finally, against the average wage for an employee or clerk in a Belgrade government office or shop—from 3,000 to 4,000 dinars a
month, or $60 to $80 at the official rate of exchange.

Both the best eating and the greatest misery are in the villages—
the former in rich districts in years of good harvest, the latter in many
poor districts every year. Visitors are told with pride that peasants
who before the war had sugar only a few times a year now receive
it regularly, and *The Economist* [3] worked out a table to show that
more wheat was being consumed per person in an ordinary year than
before the war, and that the peasants themselves were using a larger
proportion of it. Both statements are open to question even for
periods when there has not been a drought. There is not really
any dispute, however, about the fact that there is widespread discontent among the peasants, even those who have been transported
from barren areas in the south and settled on lands vacated by
German expellees in the Voivodina and other rich districts north
of the Save and the Danube. They complain of everything—from
high taxes and forced government buy-ups of their produce at low
prices to the lack of commodity goods in the market towns and the
high prices of those that are available. In 1950 many of them had

[2] Here are sample prices that confront a man and his wife if they turn to the
free market to supplement their rations (I give actual prices noted in shops in
Belgrade in the spring of 1950): men's low shoes, brown or black, rough finish
inside, $116 a pair (including laces—not a negligible item, for they are hard to
come by); rough grey wool blankets, unfinished at the ends, $94 apiece; coffee,
$16 per pound; butter, $7 per pound; eggs, three for a dollar.

[3] London, June 24, 1950.

before their eyes the spectre of near starvation. And continuously in their thoughts, day and night, is the hated Communist program for the collectivization of their farms. Collectives are not called that in Jugoslavia, but *radna zadruga,* or "working coöperatives," to recall the traditional and familiar family *zadruga* system of the Serbian peasantry. The authorities make much of the fact that a peasant's application to join a working coöperative is "voluntary." It is true in a literal sense, for no order is issued to him to join and no gendarme arrives at his cottage to enforce it. But conditions are so arranged that for him not to join becomes difficult, painful, costly and in the end almost impossible. In the spring of 1950 the number of working coöperatives in operation in Jugoslavia was given as about 6,500 [4] and the proportion of the arable land of the country thus brought into the "socialized sector" of the national economy was between 20 and 25 percent.

The government's pressure on the peasants originates in the double desire to extract the maximum amount of produce from them so that the industrial and urban population may be fed, and to complete the Socialist task of abolishing private ownership of land. When a peasant enters a government farm he may retain title to his land, but that is a technicality. He does not necessarily or even probably work on it. He is put into a neighborhood working brigade and assigned to tasks according to his aptitude or the pleasure of the boss—as ditch digger, say, or poultryman or ploughman. He is paid for his hours of work, punched "in" and "out" morning and evening on his work card as though he were a factory hand. In fact he is a factory hand, employed in a great outdoors government factory. He no longer is a free man who works as he wishes and receives a price for the product. This is repugnant to Serb and Croat peasants whose families have tended the same ancestral farms for centuries. They resist. The government does not succeed in convincing them that they would be better off as hired hands than they used to be fending for themselves at the mercy of the climate and of city and foreign

---

[4] The rate of development may be judged from the fact that the number of working coöperatives was stated to be 3,046 in the spring of 1949; and a dispatch to *The New York Times,* October 8, 1949, quoted *Borba* as putting the number at about 5,000 at that time. The *Economist* article already quoted says the number in 1948 was 1,318.

"exploiters." It therefore has had to find ways to make them conscious of how much worse off they now are and will continue to be so long as they remain individualists.

The ways of accomplishing this are many. Government agents set very high quotas—often impossible ones—for the compulsory government buy-up. The peasant who is unable to fill his quota goes into the free market to make up the difference and avoid the fines which he cannot pay except out of savings (if he has savings). Sometimes the free-market prices are so high that rather than pay them (supposing he can find what he needs, which is not always the case) he cuts his own food reserves and he and his family go on short rations. Taxes are high. Tools, clothes and family necessities of all sorts are not always procurable, and when they are he considers the prices exorbitant. Finally, threadbare, harassed and behindhand in every respect, he signs up to enter a working coöperative—voluntarily.

I spent a day in the houses of several peasant families in a smiling district south of Belgrade. In the big cities, Belgrade especially, the police are watchful of contacts between foreigners and the local population. But apparently they recognize that what a peasant can tell a foreigner is already common knowledge and cannot have any conspiratorial implications. It is just a sad tale, often told—but still told, I found, with wit and spirit.

It was a Sunday, so that both the men and women were at home, the latter dressed up to some extent in remnants of their peasant finery. One farm had a bit of vineyard, so that the owner was able to give us a little thin but not bad pink wine, and one of the innumerable older women brought out some dry cakes. We sat on a sort of side porch, or alcove, giving onto the farmyard, where there were two pigs, a goose and a couple of beehives, and beyond which was visible a slope of pasture. The air smelt of spring and hummed with its special noises. The head of the house was in his late sixties, I suppose, very gnarled but very sturdy and very sharp. He told me that he had about 20 acres of land, which would make him a *kulak*. In all, eight or ten persons lived and worked on the farm, all of them members of his immediate family, including the wife of one son who was doing his service in the army. He himself had fought in the

Balkan wars and in the First World War. I asked him what his politics were and he said "farming." The taxes on his 20 acres last year
and the year before had been 62,000 dinars, and the same rate had
been set for the present year. At the official exchange rate, this is
$1,240 a year, or a total for the three years of $3,720. When I asked
him how he could pay that sum he said out of savings. He added
that he had to supply a fixed quota of wine to the state—I forget how
much—and was allowed to keep the remainder. But last year there
not only had been no remainder (the wine he gave us was the vin-
tage of two years before), he had not been able to supply the government quota and had to purchase the difference for about $150. In
addition, he was taxed on the part of the wine crop which he would
have been allowed to keep if there had been any. These sums, added
to his taxes, gave a total cash payment to the state in three years of
nearly $4,000. I asked him how long he could continue at this rate.
"This year is the last," he replied, and continued without waiting for
me to ask the next question: "No, I will never join a working co-
operative. I know how to farm well. My father taught me. I have
taught my sons. We work hard. Our farm is in good shape, one of the
best here. We never will put ourselves under ignorant people who
know nothing about farming or about this farm, and I won't share
my produce with farmers who have not looked after their land as
well as we have, don't work as hard as we do and just want to live
off us." So what, I asked? He shrugged his shoulders. Was he not
afraid of the police, I said? He replied with another question,
"Why?" And continued, "They are not bad. The trouble is with the
orders they receive. We are not afraid of them in this village. At the
elections the other day the old woman who lives there (pointing
across the road) went to the voting place and said: 'Show me which
is the hole where I put my ballot for the people who took my lard.'
And did she put her vote in that hole? I ask you! And with the police
standing all about, too! They said this village voted about seven
out of eight for the government. Well, I don't know anyone who
voted for the government, and I know everybody hereabouts."

Since he was more prosperous than the average farmer the government agents evidently were deliberately bleeding him of his savings in the hope of bringing him to his knees. When we said goodbye

I had a feeling that somehow they would fail, but I could not see how.

The great drought of 1950 made the lot of the average peasants harder in two ways: it ruined any chance that they could meet their quotas and it made it hard for the authorities to relax the effort to extract every possible bushel of wheat and pound of fat from them. In March, when the weather still was propitious, a venturesome group of peasants in the Shumadia sent a petition of grievances to Tito. He asked them to appear before him, told them their complaints were justified, and ordered certain officials supposedly responsible to be dismissed. It was a futile gesture. The officials may have erred, but it was the system—his system—that was responsible. For although he has freed himself from what he considers to be Stalin's distortions of the Marxist system he still keeps his doctrinaire belief in its ability to provide a good life for the masses and in his ability to operate it to that end. He still feels competent, whether or not he feels confident. In the case of those miserable peasants, he was the only person to whom they could appeal; and like the French Monarch he was the only person who could save them from his servants. He was less able than ever to do so (within the limitations of his Marxist thinking) after the drought had done its worst.[5] Already he had looked abroad for help to keep his program of industrial development going. The drought forced him to look abroad also for food supplies and means to finance their purchase.

From the start, the Soviet's most substantial weapon of attack on Jugoslavia short of war had been the commercial blockade. The economic arrangement under which Soviet-Jugoslav trade had been conducted before the split was negotiated in Moscow on July 25, 1947. Under it, the Soviets were to deliver "whole enterprises" to Jugoslavia on credit, along with technical assistance, and be repaid in Jugoslav raw materials and hard currencies beginning in 1950 and continuing over a seven-year period. Boris Kidrich, Minister of Heavy Industry, gave details on December 28, 1948, of how the Soviet Union and the satellites who had signed commercial treaties

---

[5] The dispatches of Gaston Coblentz from Belgrade in the late summer and autumn of 1950 told of heartbreaking experiences of peasant families and even of peasant riots in Belgrade itself. (*New York Herald Tribune*, August 1, 10 and 23, and September 9 and 17, 1950.)

with Jugoslavia had failed to meet their commitments. Two days later *Tass,* the official Soviet news agency, announced that in the new year Soviet-Jugoslav trade would be reduced by seven-eighths, "in view of the unfriendly policy of the Jugoslav Government." Tito could not meet the resulting situation successfully by courage and skill alone. He must display those qualities and also gain access to non-Cominform cash and non-Cominform markets.

His main political preoccupation, of course, was that whatever credits or loans he might get in the West should not entail any loss of independence or self-respect. He had already risked everything to preserve these against Soviet encroachment, and he had not put his life and the safety of his country in jeopardy in order to "sell out" in the end to Western capitalists. The policy of the Western Powers, fortunately, was to help him as much as possible without asking impossible returns, political or social. Since there were obvious difficulties in supplying public funds to a Communist state, even though the political and military justifications were sound, the United States Government suggested that Tito turn to the international financial agencies with headquarters in Washington. As a preliminary, in February 1949, it paved the way for a resumption of more general trade than was permitted with the Soviet bloc of states. The National Security Council revised American commercial policy so as to permit American concerns to sell Jugoslavia whatever was necessary to maintain a "peacetime economy." Several trade missions arrived in Belgrade—British, French and Italian, among others —to discuss agreements for the exchange of goods and materials; and it was obvious that various Jugoslav products, notably metals and other strategic materials, would find a market in the United States, thus producing some dollars to finance Jugoslav imports of machinery, etc.[6] But the hole in the Jugoslav economy could not be filled by such methods alone. Tito had already been forced to make adjustments in the operation of his Five Year Plan, and the lack of the most elementary consumer goods was, as we have seen, only short of disastrous. Cash was needed.

[6] As an example, the Jugoslav freighter *Gorica* arrived in Brooklyn in August 1949 with a cargo of metals, mainly lead and copper, valued at $1,800,000 (*The New York Times,* August 31, 1949).

At the time the International Bank sent its first mission to Jugoslavia in August 1949 the thought seems to have been that it would
recommend a loan of about $25,000,000 to increase the productivity
of Jugoslav agriculture, mining, transport, forestry and hydroelectric
power, roughly in that order of importance. More than a year later
it had not yet granted any loan of such proportions. At about the
same time the Export-Import Bank was approached for a loan,
largely to purchase machinery for developing Jugoslav copper, lead
and zinc mines. The news that it would supply $20,000,000 reached
Belgrade in September as an exhilarating offset to the hostile actions
being taken just then by the Soviet bloc. In October the International Monetary Fund followed with a currency loan of $3,000,000
and the International Bank supplied $2,300,000 to finance a timber-
ing equipment project sponsored by the United Nations. These were
most welcome in Belgrade, of course, though they seemed small in
comparison to what was needed and what had been hoped; and the
Cominform press shouted gleefully that the "American imperialists"
knew that Jugoslavia could be bought cheap. The Warsaw radio
broadcast in Serbo-Croat on October 19 that Tito was "transform-
ing Jugoslavia into a semi-colony of the imperialists" in return for
"scraps from the master's table." It was not restrained, apparently,
by fears that this talk would sound strange in the ears of any Pole
who remembered that Poland had received a $40,000,000 loan from
the Export-Import Bank in 1946, and had wanted more. If $20,-
000,000 was treason to Communism, what was twice that sum? But
the broadcast was in Serbo-Croat, and beamed at any Jugoslavs who
might be unhappy at the prospect of receiving a loan free from
political strings.

In agreement with Britain and other interested Powers, the United
States in November 1949 modified its ban on shipment of "war potential" materials to Jugoslavia to the extent of permitting the export of aircraft gasoline and lubricants and "reasonable quantities"
of civil aircraft, used motors and spare parts. Negotiations were
begun, also, for reciprocal rights for American and Jugoslav commercial aircraft—note the word reciprocal, which was vital to Tito
after his experience with the joint Jugoslav-Soviet aviation company.
A provisional pact was signed December 24. In December the British

and Jugoslav Governments signed a trade agreement providing
Jugoslavia with a credit of 8,000,000 pounds sterling, repayable in
five years, to facilitate purchases in Britain. Two further Export-
Import loans followed, one for $20,000,000, the other for $15,000,-
000, to enable Jugoslavia to purchase a wide variety of American
products, including capital equipment, spare parts and such. In
neither case were there political or economic conditions which could
in any way be construed as interference with the independence of the
Jugoslav Government either in home or foreign affairs. With additional sums provided by the International Monetary Fund, the total
made available to the Tito régime by the middle of 1950 (including
the British credit) amounted to about $89,100,000.

I was told in Belgrade that among the chief products for export,
lead ore was being produced currently at the rate of 600,000 tons
a year and copper ore at 700,000 tons, besides timber, silver, maize,
etc. Exports to the United States in 1948 had been to the value of
about $5,000,000; in 1949 to the value of about $17,600,000; and
the hope was that in 1950 they might reach a value of over $30,-
000,000. No arms had been bought so far in America or Britain
by virtue of the international loans; none had been asked, and
none were offered. Tito would have found difficulty in buying arms
in other countries (*e.g.* from Bofors, in Sweden) due to the fact that
payment would have been required in dollars.

Toward the end of 1949 a Jugoslav official had spoken to me of
what he described as Tito's "realistic" attitude toward East and
West. He did not say that because Tito was disillusioned with Stalin
he had become convinced of the merits of Western capitalism and
democracy; that would have been untrue. He simply meant, I
think, that Tito had understood one important aspect of Stalin's
manœuvre against him and was determined not to be taken in by it.
Stalin had not intensified his pressure on Jugoslavia solely in the
hope of breaking Jugoslav economy and with it the Tito régime;
and not solely in the expectation of forcing Tito into some desperate
act of defiance of the East or surrender to the West. His design had
been, in addition, to frighten him off if possible from the dealings
with the West which could save his régime from collapse. Fortunately the policy of the Washington and London Governments was

sincere and astute enough not to demand a return from Tito which
as a Communist and as an enemy of foreign interference he could
not have paid. This part of Stalin's manœuvre therefore failed also,
at least in 1949 and down to the autumn of 1950.

Tito's conception of his rôle between East and West was expressed
very well in a speech made by Foreign Minister Edvard Kardelj before the General Assembly of the United Nations on September 26,
1949. Kardelj affirmed his belief that different social systems could
exist side by side, "on the principle of every nation's right to self-
determination and of every state being able to define its own way of
life." The danger of war, he continued, does not arise from differences between social systems but from "imperialistic and anti-democratic tendencies in international relations, from the violation of the
principle of equality, from the economic exploitation of other nations
and from interference in the internal affairs of other countries."
When I saw Tito some months later I referred to this speech. It
obviously had been good tactics. Did it indicate that he sincerely believed in the peaceful coexistence of states representing different,
even opposite, social concepts? His reply was that different systems
had existed alongside each other in the past without coming into
conflict. Where conflicts occurred they had been due not to the differences in systems but to the ambitions of individual leaders. Conflict was not inevitable and was not desirable. But competition was
desirable, for the most progressive system would win. With this latter
idea I had no quarrel, and left the subject. A dictator learns to con-
ceal his thoughts behind a straight face. I hoped that in this instance
the earnestness of Tito's manner might be matched by earnestness at
heart.

We do not have to attribute Tito's "realism" or that of his Foreign
Minister either to good motives exclusively or to bad motives exclusively. Their experiences with "Grandfather" rudely revised their
primitive conception that Communist international life would be
rosy, and their dealings with Washington and London revealed
that capitalism need not always be exploitative and therefore was
not uniformly evil. They did not on this account alter their basic
attitudes. Speaking before the U.N. General Assembly a year later,
on September 25, 1950, Dr. Kardelj indicated that his government's

objections to international financing in accordance with traditional capitalistic principles would continue even though its exploitative characteristics might often be absent. The Jugoslav Government, he said, could not approve a system which permits the determining factor in foreign investment to be "solely the economic interest of those who provided the means, rather than the interest of those whose productive forces the means were supposed to promote;" and his government would maintain this general position even though specific deals were conducted in a "civilized form." His reason was that while this system prevails, "a small country, pursuing an independent policy, cannot—despite the existence of the United Nations —obtain adequate economic support in the majority of cases" against the economic aggression to which it is exposed. The United Nations, he said, would have to sponsor a new approach to international financing in order to deprive "aggressive Powers" of the favored position they now enjoy on this account.

Perhaps Dr. Kardelj was speaking under the influence of a new situation which threatened to undo some of the reassuring effects of the American Government's consistently friendly policy toward the Jugoslavs and its avoidance of anything like interference in their domestic affairs. In the summer of 1950 reports circulated that Jugoslavia might find additional openings for trade in Central Europe. In September the Allied High Commission in Germany was ready to approve a plan of the Bonn Government to loan $35,000,000 to Jugoslavia in connection with a bilateral trade agreement. But apparently the German loan was involved in the continuing negotiations for a substantial loan to Jugoslavia by the International Bank. The Bank's difficulty was that it can make loans only where there is reasonable expectation of repayment, and its officials apparently did not feel that it should be responsible for what in their view was an uneconomic over-extension of Jugoslav heavy industry at the expense of light industry. This presented almost insoluble difficulties for Tito. He would look on any drastic shift in the emphasis of his Five Year Plan as a blow to his standing with his followers and a comfort to his foreign enemies, and he was reluctant to consider a loan in such circumstances.

Up to this point the Jugoslav leaders must have felt that, all things considered, they had received fairly good treatment from the capitalist world. They knew that the West was being quite realistic in its dealings with them, as they were with it. They had not reversed their hostility to capitalism, though they denied the Stalinist assertion that the conflict must or should end in armed conflict. They did not reiterate the statements of many Moscow oracles that Communists may suit their words and acts to the tactical considerations of the moment; but as believing and practising Communists they could hardly be surprised that in the light of such statements in the past their relations with Western nations could not at once become completely trustful. The money received from the West had not met their full needs, and the theories on which it had been supplied may have seemed, from their viewpoint, old-fashioned, not "progressive." But it had saved the Jugoslav economy from collapse—so far—and the dealings which had produced it had been, as Kardelj said, "civilized." No Jugoslav would say that Stalin's dealings with or about Jugoslavia had been that.

At the start of this book I spoke of the signals sent out by the Jugoslav Communists to the Communists of other lands since the actual occurrence of the "impossible split." Subsequent pages have recounted how the split became a chasm, across which the Soviet Union and its satellites shouted imprecations at their former comrades, first calling them heretics and then traitors, enemies and agents of the enemies of all true Communists. They have also told how by pressure and threats of physical violence the Soviets have emphasized the possibility that their polemics momentarily might be carried over into the field of action. The time now comes to see what effect these developments have had on both the Communist leaderships of the satellite states of Eastern Europe and on the non-Communist masses over whom they have established their rule. Judging by nothing more than the hysterical Soviet reactions, Tito's rebellion and the continued existence of his independent Communist régime have awakened spectacular hopes and anxieties wherever the Soviet word is (once again to use an incongruous term) law.

# XII

## STRONGHOLDS OF POLISH INDEPENDENCE

> Poland is a public road on which foreign
> armies constantly jostle one another.
>
> von Clausewitz

POLAND is the largest and richest of the Soviet satellites, and she also is the most determinedly herself. This makes both Soviet opportunities and Soviet problems greater there than in any other part of Eastern Europe. Soviet efforts to capitalize on the opportunities and eradicate the problems have met with some success but also with setbacks and frustrations. Poland still is not Sovietized. Even the Polish Communist hierarchy contained elements which resisted Stalin's assertion of absolute authority in 1948; and there is evidence that this resistance has not yet been wholly eliminated. But let us begin by looking at the special conditions which would limit Soviet operations in Poland even if no Communist leader there had ever had a dangerous thought.

The Poles are used to a hard life. In modern times their country has been partitioned oftener than it has been united. They are accustomed to wars, destruction, inefficient government and the failure of hopes. They are used to compensating for all the ills which they do not know how to avoid by working harder than ever. As a result, nowhere in Eastern Europe except Jugoslavia do you find such a passionate determination to rebuild the ruins of this war and lay the physical basis for a new life. The determination does not originate, I believe, in any Communist policy, in anything the Communists promise or forbid, create or destroy. It seems to be, as in Jugoslavia, something native and irrepressible, an almost blind upsurge of a strong people who find themselves after long struggles still caught in the mud. Their first aim is to reach a footing of some sort on which they can resume their national existence. Once they have achieved this, they seem to say, it will be time to settle accounts with anyone who may plan to force them back or keep them under. Now it is enough to stand erect in the ruins, to work, to survive.

The instinct for survival is universal, but the point about it in Poland is that it seems to be unbeatable even though nowhere else in Europe did the war leave it under greater handicaps. To begin with, no capital city was devastated more methodically and completely than Warsaw. The ruin of Warsaw has often been described but the reality is in fact indescribable. When you walked through Berlin in 1946 and 1947 you saw mostly caverns left by high explosives and mounds of brick and twisted iron, and even today, though the façade of Unter den Linden has been propped up by the Russians, it still is essentially false. Nevertheless in some districts of Berlin rows of villas stand unharmed, some business structures are comparatively intact and there are even great apartment houses that suffered only minor damage. In London, old Georgian house-fronts on quiet streets often shield empty spaces where weeds grow and birds nest, and the empty neighborhoods of the Temple and St. Paul's are sickening reminders of the Blitzes, buzz-bombs and V-2s. But London never ceased to live, breathe and work. In Warsaw after the war even the skeletons of buildings were rare, a smokestack still standing was an object to be noted and the structures left intact (because they had served some Nazi military purpose) could be counted on a man's fingers. Even today you ask your way of a passerby and discover you are standing at the crossing of two main avenues, near the archway where you used to enter the Foreign Office. No familiar trace remains. Hitler directed that Warsaw be reduced to a name in history books, and to execute his orders his troops methodically blasted block after block level with the ground. Many districts, the Ghetto particularly, are nothing but undulating expanses of gray dust and crumbled brick, without form and void.

From these beginnings, the reconstruction accomplished in the first years since the war is formidable. When I was in Warsaw early in the summer of 1949 I spoke despairingly about the desolation to a friend who had been there for nearly four years. "Why," he said in honest wonder, "haven't you noticed all those new buildings?" It is hard for a newcomer to notice them, or to pay proper attention to important recent constructions like the Vistula bridge and the tunnel traversing one corner of the old city to accommodate the new East-West railway trunkline which is being built to suit the needs of Soviet strategy probably more than those of Polish commerce.

Visitors are not allowed to miss the activities of the youth brigades, one or two of which always manage to pass your hotel daily. They looked to me just like the boys and girls who had arrived every morning to demolish the bombed-out buildings across from my hotel in Belgrade, except that these were a little better dressed and seemed a little more mature. They went by with the same swing in the same clumsy boots and singing the same sort of broken marching refrains —echoes from a dim past when their Slavic forebears marched in the ranks of the mediæval *Landesknechte* along with the Teutonic forebears of the *Hitlerjugend*. The reasons they are there in uniform instead of at school are the same as those which make the Jugoslav boys and girls "volunteer." But somehow in both cases the effect conveyed is that since they have to be there they are ready to exhaust their energies on whatever work is at hand, not because they are Communists but because they are young. Incidentally, there are no signs of similar work among the ruins of Budapest.

Outside Warsaw the picture of activity is only slightly different, and not so much because of any difference in the willingness of the people to work as because of differences in the objective conditions of work. People in an individualistic old city like Cracow go their former ways more than they do in Warsaw under the watchful eye of the central secret police. Police controls do not have to be so severe in industrial towns where labor receives favorable rationing treatment. In the villages they are still embryonic; collectivization of farms has begun, but though there are many threats and some punishments the Communists still do not push it to extremes. All but about two percent of Polish farming is still done on privately owned and individually worked land.

So far neither the collectivization program nor the nationalization of industry and business—from the great Silesian coal mines to the individual kiosks which sell papers and speckled cakes on the sidewalks of provincial towns—has killed the hopes, energies and speculative enterprise of the Polish people. While I was in Warsaw a newspaper published statistics of the private businesses closed or taken over by the government in that city during the month of April 1949. The total was 176. Yet in the same period, with undiscouraged energy, 42 private citizens of Warsaw started *new* businesses. Some of these probably calculated that when their new shops were seized they might secure appointment as government managers, but others must have hoped against hope that they might somehow survive on their own feet. As late as the middle of 1950 private trade in Poland as a whole still accounted for nearly a third of the total retail turnover. However, as the proportion would be smaller in Warsaw than in remote localities we have no way of estimating what happened to those 42 desperate but enterprising individualists.

The same vitality is evident in everything Polish. The Polish people pour out children as generously as the wide Polish plains yield potatoes, rye, oats and wheat. Their pastures produce meat and animal fats and their forests lumber. In Silesia their coal and their growing industries of iron, steel, textiles and machinery create a potential eastern Ruhr. Though in many respects Poland's economy is primitive it is developing as rapidly as Communist social objectives and Soviet demands permit, and the variety of her natural resources makes her more nearly self-contained than any of the other satellites. In consequence, her leaders sometimes have actually been able to bargain a bit with the Kremlin about the standard of living to be maintained in the country. Two underlying principles of Soviet commercial policy were that duplication of industrial plant should be avoided and needs of each member met within the satellite sphere.[1] Despite this, Hilary Minc, Vice-Premier and Chairman of the Economic Planning Commission, has continued to obtain in Western Europe some of the capital goods and raw materials not available in the satellite bloc and to ship enough agricultural prod-

[1] The Council for Mutual Economic Assistance was formed in 1949 to facilitate Soviet control over the commercial policies of the East European states. It is still not clear whether CMEA is much more than a name. If it exists as a working organization it is only a façade for Soviet manipulation.

ucts in return to pay for them. Poland probably is permitted this economic independence only while a heavy Polish contribution of meats, fats and potatoes is needed to help feed the Soviet Army in Eastern Germany and to supplement the food supply in Czechoslovakia and Hungary, where the former balance between agriculture and industry has been destroyed. When I was in Poland meat was so short due to exports that it was being rationed—in this land of pigs and cattle. After agriculture and industry have been nationalized in the whole satellite area, Poland theoretically will no longer need any Western products and the industrial proletariat of the whole area will be fed from inside. Soviet living standards will prevail in all the satellite states and trade with the West can cease.

Poland's geographical position makes her even more important to Russia strategically than economically. Whether the dominant ideologies in Russia and Germany happen at a given moment to run parallel or conflict, the two nations cannot plot either together or against each other without taking into account the 24 million people inhabiting the river valleys, plains, marshlands and forests that lie between. The Polish war potential is a factor in all Russian or German plans of aggression or defense. Today it is in Russian hands as never before, and Russia is determined that it shall still be when the Germans are again strong. Poland is the greatest prize won by the Red Army and Stalin's diplomacy.

Two principal elements in Polish life make it unlikely that the Polish people will change their old ways rapidly. One is the Roman Catholic Church, a bulwark of conservative traditions and national settlement. Practically all Poles are *ipso facto* Catholics.[2] The second is the peasantry. Over half the population live on the land. The thorough agrarian reform which the former régimes stupidly withheld the Communists executed at once. But now the peasants have got their land they are determined not to lose it, even by a finagle which is politely called "voluntary association in producer coöperatives."

[2] Before the war, 64.8 percent of Polish nationals were Roman Catholic. Of the remainder, the Jewish population was largely eliminated during the war and most of the Orthodox population lived in the eastern regions since annexed by the Soviets. Today, 95 to 98 percent of the population are Catholic. (*Cf.* "Eastern Europe Between the Wars," by R. W. Seton-Watson. Cambridge, England: University Press, 1946.)

Thus the Polish peasantry have two reasons to be anti-Communist: they are Catholic and they do not want their land to be collectivized.

A third influence in Polish national life, impalpable but powerful, gives it unusual continuity even in a time of revolution. The Polish élite—intellectuals, military leaders and politicians—hold themselves in quite exceptional self-esteem. It was natural for Poles to be proud when they were fighting oppression. Pride salved the spirit while bodies were being bruised under the horse-hoofs of Cossacks or Teutonic knights. But natural and right as Polish pride then was, it became an obstacle to political and military collaboration with other countries when Poland was free, and in particular it prevented her from showing necessary moderation and caution toward her two great neighbors. Experience has also made the Poles suspicious. In 1945 the people of Warsaw did not know whether to hail the departure of the hated Nazis with more joy or the arrival of the hated Russians with more foreboding. Both represented histories of oppression and both will continue to be mistrusted and rejected by Poles for a long time to come.

The Communists have weakened the physical power of the Roman Catholic Church in Poland and thus inevitably to some degree its hold over the masses of the people. They have confiscated church properties, suspended religious newspapers, seized "Caritas" (the major Catholic charitable organization), arrested recalcitrant priests and bishops and propagandized ceaselessly about the alleged immorality and insincerity of the clergy in general. Nevertheless religion is still a formidable enemy of Communism's materialistic philosophy and a barrier to the success of its political ambitions. The people turn to their parish churches not only for the customary sacraments from birth to death; they also find there the only centers of national and community life which the Communists have not been able to appropriate. Universities, schools, trade unions, agricultural cooperatives, newspapers, theaters, courts—all belong to the Communists and are exploited for Communist purposes. Only the churches remain where Poles who are not Communists can gather in communion and fellowship.

In the battered old Church of the Holy Ghost, in Warsaw, I realized how much this means. The people flocking to the almost con-

tinuous series of services are not like the congregations one often sees
in churches in Latin countries, bent old women and rheumatic men
scattered here and there in an echoing darkness. They are of all ages
and they enter eagerly a warm interior of lights, music and movement. Particularly prominent are the young men and women who
stop in on their way to and from work and the 'teen-age boys and
girls who arrive singly or in groups to join their families at a designated spot—perhaps the pillar with the tablet telling that Chopin's
heart is buried below. The roof is new and ugly, the walls are
patched, the stone pavement rough. The crowds kneel together, sing
the old hymns together, momentarily feel safe together. In this warm
proximity they find fulfillment of the universal human yearning to
"belong."

On a Saturday afternoon in a Polish village I realized again the
powerful attraction of continuity, and the ability of the Church to
provide it. It was a small village, a dozen kilometers of rutted muddy
road from a main highway. The sun was warm, the whole countryside smelt of spring earth and lilacs. In the churchyard maybe 30 or
40 small boys stood about or played quiet games while waiting their
turn to make their Saturday confessions. All were dressed in reasonably presentable clothes, including shoes and caps. Inside, a crowd
of little girls, most of them with tight pigtails and in clean cotton
dresses, sat in silence around the sides of the church while one of their
number, about ten years old, pink-faced with the intensity of her
effort to describe her sins, confessed to a priest through a small
wickerwork square which he held up between them. I came away
feeling that if the children of most Polish villages were similarly
occupied on a sunny spring afternoon it would be another generation
at least before even the most hostile government could drive the
Church entirely out of the national life.

The government is unscrupulous as well as hostile. The Church
was too powerful in Poland to be tackled head on and at once, but
the preliminary positions are being prepared for the eventual assault.
Continuous propaganda is carried on in the press and by radio
against the Vatican on both political and doctrinal grounds. Local
priests are accused of all sorts of crimes, moral and political, and

members of the hierarchy who oppose Communist decrees are denounced as black marketers or Nazi collaborators. Pressure is exerted
on individual priests to repudiate the control of their bishops and
thus make sure of receiving jobs in the "national church" of the
future. A principal target, of course, must be the Primate of Poland,
Archbishop Wyszynski. He presents a real difficulty for the Communists, however, since it is impossible to make out a case against
him like that constructed in Jugoslavia against Archbishop Stepinatz
on the basis of his wartime record, or even like that manufactured in
Hungary against Cardinal Mindszenty. The Polish Primate is a
serious student of labor problems and a confirmed liberal; he has
been at extraordinary pains to avoid interfering in political affairs
and maintains a blanket refusal to consort with westerners, visiting
or resident. Though this makes him nearly impregnable it also leaves
him on the defensive. Some observers feel that the Church will have
growing difficulty in holding its flock together by such cautious
tactics.

On the other hand, too sharp opposition to Communist policies
calls down punishment on helpless heads. This was seen when the
Holy Office issued a finding in June 1949 that no Roman Catholic
could "show favor to the Communist Party" or read a Communist
newspaper and continue to receive the sacraments. Doubtless the
thought in issuing this decree was principally to safeguard members
of the Church in non-Communist countries, but until it was given
a lenient interpretation it threatened to place communicants in
Communist-dominated countries in a dilemma. How is even the
most anxious and devout member of the Church to avoid direct collaboration with the persons who offer or withhold work, staff government offices, preside over courts and supervise sports? Communist newspapers can hardly be avoided, since laws and regulations
are printed there; in any case, all but the Communist newspapers are
being suppressed. Martyrdom calls for a particular form of heroism.
Men who can be heroes in battle may not be capable of prolonged
individual defiance of authority. Too sharp a juxtaposition of Heaven
and daily bread, of Rome's spiritual command and the orders of
the secret police, can actually weaken the influence of the Church

and facilitate the Communist campaign to depict it as a social anachronism in "progressive" societies.[3]

Like the effort of the Communists to destroy the Church, their effort to put an end to the private ownership of land is producing results very slowly. Hard as they try they cannot make the peasant willingly give up control of his own land. The peasant coöperatives which they have set up are of three sorts. The "weakest" and most common is the one where the peasant puts in nothing except his share of the joint tilling and harvesting. A member of a group of this sort remains the owner of the land and its product, both cereal and animal. The second is a compromise form, usually known as the "Bulgarian system," in which the peasant puts in part of his land but reserves part for his own use. Here he gets a share in the joint product proportionate to the acreage put in and his man-hours of work. The third and so far the least common is the true Soviet-type *kolkhoz,* though that name is never used, in which the peasant puts in his land and livestock, except perhaps a cow and some chickens for family use and a bit of back yard for vegetables. In these cases the total yield is divided according to the labor of the participants.

The government claims that no direct police force is used to make peasants enter any form of collective farm but admits that it applies both "indirect" inducements and pressures. The distinction is growing more and more fine. For example, those who join pay less for fertilizers and the use of farm machinery than those who remain outside, and also have priority in obtaining them. Obviously a farmer can be ruined by discrimination at a vital planting or harvesting season. Equally important, credit is given or withheld by the village councils, which also set the credit rates for the recipients. These councils have been or are being reorganized as rapidly as practicable to insure that they reflect the "reliable" political viewpoint. The

[3] A modus vivendi between the Church and the government seemed to be reached in April 1950 when the Polish Bishops agreed to various concessions, political as well as administrative. The Vatican did not ratify it, and even the attitude of Archbishop Wyszynski and Cardinal Sapieha of Cracow toward it was never quite clear. It broke down after about six months, largely over the reluctance of the Church to set up permanent Polish dioceses in the former German territories. The government said the delay encouraged revisionism, and it launched a new anti-Church campaign.

peasants fight each step of a procedure which they foresee is meant to end with their again having no land of their own in any real sense, regardless of who owns the title to it technically. To become chattels of an impersonal state run by Warsaw bureaucrats seems to them no improvement over their former lot as tenant farmers or hired laborers of private landlords.

Progress toward collectivization has been slow for the additional reason that the authorities must take outside factors into account in regulating their pressure on the peasants. One limiting factor is the industrialization program. Industry must supply the increased amounts of machinery and fertilizer required to operate state farms and newly organized collectives. A second limitation is the need to maintain production in the face of declines due to the decreased work performed by collectivized peasants and peasants fearful of collectivization, in order that the export of farm products to the West can continue. If Poland should cease to export to Britain under the existing commercial treaty, she would not receive in return the cotton, rubber, wool and other Empire products needed to fulfill the industrial schedules of the Six Year Plan inaugurated in January 1950. A third factor is the relationship of labor supply and demand as between agriculture and industry. The surplus of agricultural labor in Poland today is estimated at four million; and with the progress of collectivization agricultural employment will further decrease. Industry cannot absorb this surplus now but must do so eventually. The Six Year Plan aims to increase non-agricultural employment by a million or more and agricultural production by 35-45 percent. It is at least dubious whether a great program of industrialization can succeed when living standards in the countryside are being reduced instead of raised.

Hilary Minc, the leading Polish planner, must have had his doubts about it from the start. He did not state them clearly in his report to the First Congress of the United Workers' Party on December 19, 1948, but his promise at that relatively late date that "farm producers' coöperatives will be systematically developed on a completely voluntary basis" indicated that he was reluctant to face the difficulties of enforcing rigid collectivization based on doctrinaire reasoning.[4] In the same report he made another remark which could be considered fairly daring in view of what had happened to Tito for advocating a special Jugoslav road to Socialism. Although Stalinist theory prior to the denunciation of Tito had admitted variations to suit different local conditions, it often had been Stalinist practice since then to punish them. Minc took pains to extol the basic lessons of the Soviet experience for all countries, but he went on to say that "we understand and applied in practice the Leninist principle of concretely taking into consideration differences in historical and economic development." It was just at this time, incidentally, that Premier Dimitrov of Bulgaria was indicating the need for class war in the Bulgarian villages, and shortly afterwards Minc's chief, President Bierut, echoed the same refrain. These and other similar statements by Minc were responsible for periodic rumors that he was about to be purged. But his outstanding abilities made him indispensable, and after a period of comparative inactivity, during which he perhaps received fresh indoctrination, he again appeared in the summer of 1950 as the guiding influence in Polish economy. It was noticed that he no longer voiced reservations about Socialist measures either in industry or agriculture.

I was told in Warsaw in May 1949 that the number of collectives of the *kolkhoz* type was then something under 200, while all three types together accounted for just under one percent of all arable land in the country. The figures were given to me as representing actual achievements. However, they may merely have been 1949 targets. At about the same time Roman Zambrowski, Secretary of the Central Committee of the United Polish Workers' Party, admitted that the 1949 plan was to collectivize not more than 45,000 hectares, which would account for approximately 7,350 individual small holdings. As there are some 3,140,000 individual farms in Poland, we can deduce from Zambrowski's figures that not much more than two-tenths of one percent of all individual holdings would be collectivized in 1949 under this program.

If official Polish reports are credited, the Three Year Plan of 1947 was completed two months early, that is, in November 1949. One

[4] Hilary Minc, "Poland's Economy, Present and Future." New York: Polish Research and Information Service, 1949.

of the major achievements claimed was that the proportion of persons employed in agriculture had dropped from 64.5 to 51.6 percent while the number of salaried workers and wage earners had increased from 18.2 to 35.9 percent. However, the base selected for making the comparison was not when the Plan began, but 1938; this renders the statement almost meaningless. In July 1950, Minc announced that the goals of the new Six Year Plan had been revised upwards.[5] By 1955, industrial production is to rise 158.3 percent above 1949 levels instead of 85–95 percent, and agricultural output by 50 percent instead of 35–45 percent. Virtually all industry and trade are to be completely socialized by the terminal date. The number of workers in socialized sectors of the economy is to rise to 5,700,000 from the 3,600,000 so employed in 1949. At this point, said Minc, "Poland will be more than half-way toward the level of industrialization in the United States and will eliminate the capitalist elements in the towns as well as in the countryside."

How this will be managed seems highly uncertain. "Class war" has been proclaimed for the villages a number of times, and still all the available evidence goes to show that the slow progress of collectivization admitted by Zambrowski in April 1949 has not so far been altered in an important degree. An analysis in *Polska Zbrojna* in March [6] said that since the first of the year 406 "producer coöperatives" had been established, compared with the 243 that had been organized in the preceding two years. This would mean a total of 649, and while it would treble the number of existing organizations it would not greatly increase the figure for the percentage of individual holdings collectivized throughout the country. The figure is close enough to the one mentioned by Zambrowski at about the same time (590 "producer coöperatives" of all sorts) for us to accept it as representing what the government claims to have achieved as of the spring of 1950.[7] Zambrowski put forward what is probably the Polish alibi for this comparatively poor showing when he said that "a serious mistake" had been committed in overstressing the formation of a large number of collectives rather than in seeing that those

[5] *For a Lasting Peace, for a People's Democracy!*, Bucharest, July 28, 1950.
[6] Warsaw, March 13, 1950. Reported by Edward A. Morrow, *The New York Times*, March 14.
[7] *For a Lasting Peace, for a People's Democracy!*, Bucharest, March 10, 1950.

formed were of proper quality. This is the answer of local Communists everywhere to Soviet pressure for speed. He claimed as usual that "in the flames of the sharpening class struggle in the countryside there grows and becomes ideologically stronger the Party's active nucleus," but added a significant qualification. "A section of the working people are hesitating," he said. "They want to convince themselves of the correctness of this idea of producer coöperatives, therefore they wait to see concrete economic results from existing coöperatives and depend on this before taking a decision." If a high Party official admits that the peasants are "hesitating" we can be sure that they in fact are fighting desperately with all their resources, active and passive.

Though Minc now professes confidence in the collectivization program he apparently realizes that peasant opposition to it will continue and that complete success is still far off. Thus he stated in July 1950 that when the Six Year Plan is realized in 1955 there will exist a total of 850 tractor stations possessing 35,890 machines, and that by then Polish agriculture will have been provided with 61,000 tractors. The figures contain an important admission. If only slightly more than half the total production of tractors is to go to the socialized sector of agriculture, evidently individual peasant ownership of land and individual peasant farming will still exist in Poland on a very extensive scale.[8] Minc seems to be reconciled to the fact that in 1955 half the arable land of the country will still be privately owned and privately worked. Whether Moscow will also be reconciled remains to be seen.

The slow tempo brings the Polish Government some advantages. It permits the continuation of some trade with the West, and so postpones the date when Poland must be absolutely subservient to Moscow. It allows the régime an occasional flash of popularity in the countryside, as when word spreads that Minc must after all really be fooling his Soviet masters; this idea gives enemies of the government grim satisfaction, just as Tito's defiance of Moscow pleased even violent anti-Communist elements in Jugoslavia. Occasional concessions to the peasants bring in more than a fair return. For instance, in the summer of 1949 the authorities set a rate of about $5 a

[8] *Cf.* analysis by Harry Schwartz, *The New York Times*, August 14, 1950.

bushel for wheat (figuring the zloty at 400 to the dollar). Such a good rate was taken to signify that the government had been forced to confess defeat on the collectivization front, with the result that autumn sowings were increased; after which the rate was lowered. In order to satisfy Moscow, however, the authorities some day will have to push the class struggle in the villages in earnest, and when they do the full strength of the peasant's rôle in the national economy will become plain.

Wherever Stalin looks in Eastern Europe he sees that the independent peasantry are strongholds of what he considers bourgeois reaction. One by one he is breaking them down. He has good reason for leaving the Polish stronghold to the last.

# XIII

## A POLISH TITO

It is clear that where there is suppression
there must also be violence, and there cannot be liberty or democracy.

Lenin, "The State and Revolution"

THE first Titoist outside of Jugoslavia
was Wladyslaw Gomulka, Deputy Prime Minister of Poland and
Secretary-General of the Polish Workers' Party (Communist)—
government and Party posts which in other countries as well have
offered Communist leaders the opportunity to act with dangerous
independence. Gomulka must have possessed a good deal of the traditional Polish pride and daring. At any rate, when the Russian
Bolsheviks brought the question of Tito's independent attitude before
the Cominform Parties he favored a policy of leniency toward the
Jugoslav leader. Even when the Cominform Resolution of June 1948
showed the perils of such a course, he openly upheld Tito's position on the peasantry and the right of individual countries to develop
Socialism in their own way. Like any believing Communist, he must
have accustomed himself long ago to the idea that Communist
dogma represents revealed truth, rigid and changeless through time
and experience; but he seems not to have been able to accept the
pretension that Communist methodology, as ordained by Stalin and
applied with such flexibility in Russia, is too sacred for discussion by
subordinates outside the precincts of the Kremlin. As I write,
Gomulka's insubordination has not yet cost him his life. Whether
it will do so in future will be settled by Communist convenience, and
Communist convenience knows no law. No Party member who is
physically within the grasp of the M.V.D. can say at a given moment
what his life is worth, if anything.

Other factors besides Gomulka's pride led him into error. One was the extent of his power. He often was called the strong man of Poland and certainly was one of the most prominent Communists in Europe. The whole evolution by which he had reached the top made it seem that he exercised power by right and not on sufferance. He had been a leader of the Polish underground during the war; when the Communist-dominated Lublin Committee announced itself as the Provisional Government of Poland he became Deputy Prime Minister in it; and since June 1945 he had served in addition as Minister of the Regained Territories. Such high government assignments were unimportant, however, beside the fact that he was Secretary-General of the Party, a post which put him at least on a par with Moscow's two most favored Polish agents, President Boleslaw Bierut and Jakub Berman. Indeed, with the individual threads of the country-wide organizational web converging in his hands, he seemed more strategically placed than any other Polish leader. On the international Communist stage his prestige was similarly high. He had been one of the founders of the Cominform in September 1947; and in the meetings of the organization he spoke as representative of the largest and strongest member state after the U.S.S.R. itself.[1]

One of the elements in Gomulka's career which he probably thought of as a strength was in fact a weakness. To have been in Poland through the long struggle against the Nazis, instead of in Moscow like most of the men in the Lublin Government, did not count against him in the first postwar years when Communist resistance leaders were getting rid of their former Social Democratic partners and preparing to establish one-party dictatorships. But when the Communists were tightly in the saddle there was less need for Moscow to humor those who had not served their apprenticeship in the Soviet Union; and the difficulty of managing Tito revealed that to do so might be positively dangerous. Soviet control over the

---

[1] The Communist Party of China is not a member of the Cominform. Neither is the Albanian. The largest and the smallest are both ruled out, for obvious if opposite reasons. Incidentally, it is interesting to note that Stalin has never considered it necessary to give representation in the Cominform to the Communist Parties of the Ukrainian and Byelorussian Soviet Socialist Republics. These remain merely administrative branches of the Bolshevik Party.

new satellites was no longer in danger from class enemies but might well be threatened by presumptuous individuals within the Communist élite itself. At this point Gomulka's services in Poland during and after the war began to be weighed against the risks of allowing a man with ideas of his own to control the Party machine in a key satellite state.

The first indications that Gomulka's career might end badly dated from September 1947. At the secret conclave of international Communist luminaries at which the Cominform was founded he made a statement which was to cause him trouble subsequently. He said: "We intend . . . in the future to base the power of the bloc of democratic parties on the alliance of workers and peasants [and] on coöperation with the progressive sections of the petty bourgeoisie. . . . The Peasant Party, as the party of the toiling peasantry which constitutes the bulk of the Polish people, is the most important element in the bloc." By the Stalinist specifications of only six months later this would be pure heresy. Reporting to the Central Committee of the Polish Workers' Party (Communist) about the founding of the Cominform he made another faux pas. He said: "It would not be proper to define the Polish Workers' Party as a Communist Party. . . . Despite membership in the Cominform, the Polish Workers' Party maintains its former ideological character intact." This reminds us of what Tito was to be saying the following spring about the separate character of the Jugoslav Communist Party. Both statements must have been taken very much amiss in Moscow. Such views had not yet been declared heretical, but the fact that Gomulka held them would have put the Kremlin on notice that the Secretary-General in Poland was someone to be watched.

Gomulka appeared before the Congress of the Polish Socialist Party in December 1947 and strongly urged that it unite with his own Polish Workers' Party. The Soviet leaders of course approved the merger, but not on the basis outlined by Gomulka, namely that room be made in the new party for Socialists who favored coöperation with the Soviet Union but believed as he did that Poland could follow a "third path" to Socialism. They would have seen, too, that there were risks to be guarded against inside the new monolithic party once it had been formed. Might Gomulka entertain the idea

that a right wing would emerge and that this might enable him to
manœuvre (as Stalin had done inside the Bolshevik Party) between
right and left? Was it possible even that he aimed to create eventually a "third Socialist society," perhaps with an organizational structure of its own, between Stalinism in the East and the traditional
Socialism of the West?

If Gomulka in fact held any of these notions seriously he forgot
that Stalin had succeeded in manœuvring between Bolshevik right
and Bolshevik left because there was no one above to observe and
thwart him. Soon after the Congress he was summoned to Moscow,
along with Cyrankiewicz, the head of the Polish Socialists, and
Hilary Minc, another Communist sometimes suspected of holding
individualistic views. There they were instructed that the Socialist
Party was to undergo a further cleansing of moderate elements—
specifically of all leaders brought up in contact with Western Socialism—before its union with the Polish Workers' Party could be permitted. The ensuing purge was so exemplary that only thoroughly
"easternized" Socialists were left to join the Communists when, a
year later, the merger finally went through.[2]

The delay was caused not only by the purge but by the rise of
"Titoism" as an issue inside Communist Parties everywhere. From
the start of the Jugoslav crisis, Gomulka refused to accept the view
that the Cominform should merely rubber-stamp Stalin's decision.
He could not understand why this attitude automatically barred him
—Poland's most experienced wartime leader, Secretary-General of
his Party and one of the founders of the Cominform—from participating in the Cominform debates and in decisions which would
vitally affect the future of Communism not merely in Jugoslavia but
in Poland and indeed everywhere. He was not permitted to attend
the meeting at Bucharest in June 1948 when the Jugoslav Party was
read out of the Cominform, and when he argued against that action
he was called before his Central Committee, censured for tendencies
toward bourgeois nationalism and told to recant. He was not alone
in the Central Committee, however, and indeed seems to have
had an important enough following for the Muscovite wing to consider it unwise to follow up the vote of censure with direct punish-

[2] See "The Fate of Polish Socialism," by R, *Foreign Affairs*, October 1949.

ment. Also, Tito's unexpected success with his declaration of independence made the advertisement of a second nationalist rebellion undesirable.

Gomulka's insolence in defending himself at the June plenum of the Central Committee was almost worse, in the Soviet view, than his original offense. Bierut said that for even the Secretary-General of the Party to speak without permission of the Central Committee was a breach of discipline. Further, he noted, Gomulka's speech "contained a false and anti-Leninist appraisal of the past of the Polish workers' movement," constituted "an actual ideological capitulation to the nationalistic traditions of the Polish Socialist Party" and disclosed a "negative attitude toward that portion of the [Cominform] Resolution which discussed the program and problems relating to the transition of agriculture to Socialism and how to combat the exploitation of the peasant working masses by the capitalistic rural elements." Even this did not cow Gomulka. He neither apologized nor resigned his posts; he simply withdrew or was suspended from active Party work. He was absent from the July meeting of the Central Committee and made no effort to come to terms with the Stalinist leadership or to heal the breach in the Party.

As the summer wore on and the stalemate continued the so-called Muscovite wing of the Party decided to face up openly to the fact that Tito had intellectual allies in Poland. During the plenum of the Central Committee, August 31 to September 3, Gomulka seems to have recanted in a formal sense. His enemies, however, denied that he had made a sufficiently "radical reconsideration of the essence of his incorrect position" and refused to accept his "self-criticism" as adequate. The Central Committee dismissed him as Secretary-General and appointed Bierut in his place. He was allowed to keep his seat in the Committee; but six other members were accused of sharing his views and were dropped altogether or reduced from full to alternate membership. Soon it was admitted that the crisis in the Party was connected with the disgraceful Jugoslav affair. On September 8, 1948, a front-page editorial in *Glos Ludu,* the leading Warsaw newspaper, announced: "The importance of the last plenum's resolutions in the battle to cleanse the Party ranks of the false concepts of Rightist opportunism and nationalism has already been emphasized many times—these are concepts which could have pushed our movement down the road of Tito, the road of actually relinquishing the construction of a Socialist state and of rupturing the united front of all the anti-imperialist forces." Specific admissions that Gomulka was a Titoist appeared in the Central Committee's official magazine, *Nowe Drogi,* and in *Pravda* of September 9. It was revealed that one of the resolutions passed at the plenum stated formally that Gomulka's attitude was not an "accidental mistake" or an "isolated occurrence;" the Jugoslav events had actually "constituted a stimulus for the attitude of Comrade Gomulka in June."

Even so, Gomulka apparently still retained too much influence in the Party for the Muscovites to be able to prevent him from addressing the Unification Congress of the Polish Workers' Party and the Polish Socialist Party when it met in December. His speech was at once denounced, however, as still exhibiting "his own peculiar brand of cosmopolitanism." Bierut, resorting to a kind of euphemism not always considered necessary in Communist debate, referred to it as "an ugly noise" that had been heard in the hall. Yet in the elections three days later for the Central Committee of the new United Polish Workers' Party (as the merger of parties was named), Gomulka was chosen as a member and even, according to report, received more votes than any other candidate except Bierut. Only in January 1949 did the Muscovites finally feel strong enough to move decisively. First they abolished Gomulka's office as Minister of the Regained Territories, then they "accepted" his resignation as Deputy Prime Minister. He was not arrested, but given an honorary position as vice-president of the Supreme State Control Chamber, a sort of fiscal accounting office, where he came under the watchful eye of Franciszek Jozwiak, one of Moscow's most reliable servants.

While I was in Warsaw I inquired several times about the possibility of meeting Gomulka. General Wiktor Grosz, the combative young man in charge of such matters at the Foreign Office—now Polish Ambassador in Prague—always put me off with the answer that "Gomulka's present assignment doesn't concern foreigners," or "he really is not an interesting person," or "his importance has been exaggerated." Of these the last was certainly the truest. Where everyone is expendable you overestimate the importance of this or that particular luminary as much as he may do himself. Past services and pride of place are no guarantee that he will not suddenly be hustled from his gilded office direct to prison and thence, perhaps after a pause for a spectacular demonstration of remorse, to the scaffold. Or if there seems no particular advantage in hanging him at the moment, he may be retained in the background, ready for utilization again in case the Party line doubles back and what had been his error becomes again respectable.

Whether I might have seen Gomulka under the general conditions prevailing in Poland in the early summer of 1949, even had he not been in such an anomalous personal position, is doubtful. The number of persons in any Communist government allowed to speak with foreigners is strictly limited, and even for these (except specified officials of the Foreign Office) a fresh dispensation has to be given in each case as it arises. Sometimes visitors in satellite capitals receive appointments to meet high Party or government officials whom the resident foreign diplomats seldom even see and with whom they never have a chance to talk. These officials are selected for the purpose by the competent Party authorities and the choice is approved by the secret police. I learnt how elaborate the arrangements to talk with an eminent Communist can be when I was in Moscow in 1928 and applied to be received by Bukharin. His letter in reply, sent after about two weeks, stated that if I could wait another two weeks a meeting might become possible; he could not say definitely, but it might. Bukharin's secret struggle with Stalin had already begun, and probably he was being exceptionally cautious. But officials at the Commissariat for Foreign Affairs explained to me that the reason he had acted so slowly and still was unable to say whether he could see me in the end was because as a member of the Politburo he was obliged to secure the consent, in writing, of every other Politburo member before making an appointment with a foreigner.[3]

Analogies with Bukharin and other stars of the great Russian purges of the thirties, or with Rajk, Kostov and other satellite Communists who have been liquidated since 1948, do not mean that Gomulka necessarily will be tried or if tried will be executed. That

---

[3] Actually I did not meet Bukharin until nearly eight years later, and then when he was visiting Paris incognito (*cf.* the Preface).

will depend on many factors of convenience and expediency. Presumably, however, the leaders in Moscow will have asked themselves frequently whether all the contaminated elements in the Polish Party hierarchy were discovered and eliminated when Gomulka was, and if they have any doubts about this they may decide that a trial would have a deterrent effect on anyone tempted to follow his example. In that case, whether or not Gomulka is sitting at the moment in his office in the Supreme State Control Chamber, he will calculate from the analogy of others in his predicament that his life expectancy is brief.

A particular moment of danger came for Gomulka at the end of 1949, as well as for a number of other formerly important Communist personages who by that time had joined him and the members of the original "Gomulka gang" on the list of "Titoist criminals."

We have seen in earlier chapters that early in the summer of 1949 the Bolshevik high command took stock of accomplishments in the satellite area as a whole and came to the conclusion that they did not match the over-all strategic needs of the Soviet Union. It was proving harder than expected to proletarianize the East European peoples from the roots up and even to complete the Sovietization of the native Party leaderships from the top down. Poland's economic and strategic importance made it particularly necessary that the situation there be made secure while these objectives were being accomplished; and the interval threatened to be particularly long due to the recalcitrance of the Polish peasants and the Catholic Church.

In the Russian view there was another flaw in the Polish situation and that was the independent spirit of the Polish Army. Although many Soviet officers had been sent to serve in the Polish Army as divisional and corps commanders they had not destroyed its nationalist traditions or altered its anti-Russian sentiments. Indeed, as with the Soviet instructors assigned to the Jugoslav Army, they often had created friction and jealousy. Polish officers, unlike the officers of satellite armies which had fought on the Axis side during the war, remained as aloof as possible from their Soviet Army colleagues and commanders. Professional pride had something to do with this, but tradition even more, for Polish military strategy has always been directed equally against possible Russian and German invasions, and many officers still on the active list remembered the great days of 1920 when the Red Army was turned back from the gates of Warsaw.

Soviet strategists decided that they could not wait for time, discipline and propaganda to rectify this unsatisfactory and perhaps dangerous situation. On November 7, 1949, it was announced that a Marshal of the Soviet Army, Konstantine K. Rokossovsky, had been appointed Commander-in-Chief of the Polish Army.[4] This marked the end of an era in Soviet-Polish relations, in fact in Soviet Russia's relations with all the states on her periphery from the Baltic to the Black Sea. From now on there would be no mistake as to why she had insisted that the government in every capital of Eastern Europe be Communist. The pretense that "friendly" régimes were required for defense purposes was dropped. The present step could not be explained on economic or social revolutionary grounds. The aim was plainly to make the Polish and other satellite armies adjuncts if not integral parts of the Soviet Army in whatever military operations the Soviet Union might have in view.

This must have been a period of particular danger for Gomulka and the other Polish Communists who by now were under suspicion of being nationalists, Titoists and Trotskyists. If there was ever to be some great cautionary spectacle would it not be staged when Polish feelings were being injured so deeply? Possibly in preparation for such a move Gomulka's place on the Central Committee of the Party was finally cancelled at the November plenum. His 18-month fight was over. To make certain that they would not be involved in his

[4] Until his appointment to head the Polish Army, there was no suggestion that Rokossovsky was anything but a Soviet citizen and an officer of the Soviet Army. A volume entitled "Information on Poland," issued by the Polish Ministry of Foreign Affairs, contains a chronology with the following entry: "August 5, 1945. Official visit to Warsaw of the U.S.S.R. Marshals George Zhukov and Konstantine Rokossovsky. Marshals Zhukov and Rokossovsky decorated with the highest Polish military awards." And again: "February 10, 1949. Marshal of the Soviet Union Konstantine Rokossovsky visited Warsaw on the occasion of the 31st anniversary of the Soviet Army." Where Rokossovsky was born is uncertain. Communists have recently claimed that he was born in Warsaw, but there is some evidence that his birthplace was a small town about 200 miles to the east, in territory of mixed Polish and Ukrainian population. In any case, no free Polish state existed at the time of his birth, so he cannot be, as is sometimes stated, "a Polish national by birth."

fate, all the Committee members who had ever been suspected of any sort of independence, and those who maybe felt guilty of having wronged their careers by merely thinking secret heretical thoughts, hurled the heaviest verbal stones they could lay hands on against their former colleague. Hilary Minc accused him of lacking faith in Russia's determination to guard the western frontiers of Poland against the Germans, and conversely of doubting that the German Communists would have the "courage" to refrain from demanding that those frontiers be revised. When Gomulka defended himself, his words were described as "hissing reptilian insinuations." [5]

As it turned out, however, a military rather than a civilian scapegoat was needed to explain the existence of such evils in the Polish Army that only a Soviet Marshal could be trusted to eliminate them. The same plenum that dismissed Gomulka also expelled another and highly important figure in the Central Committee, General Marian Spychalski. Like Gomulka, Spychalski had been a member of the Committee and a power in the Party from the earliest days of the régime. As Vice-Minister of Defense he had been chief assistant and as it were political custodian of Marshal Zymierski, Rokossovsky's predecessor as Polish Commander-in-Chief. The former American Ambassador to Poland, Arthur Bliss Lane, has written that "the real directing force within the Army came from General Spychalski," and he adds that "at political meetings of the armed forces it was he and not Zymierski who made the important address." [6] He describes him as "a lithe, quiet-spoken, nonmilitary-looking officer whose training had been in Russia." Another American who had frequent official contact with him tells me that he gave the impression of being fanatically devoted to Communism and that although courteous toward westerners he was always icily reserved. Spychalski's main job was to reëducate the Polish Army on Communist lines. Whether anyone could have succeeded better or faster than he in denationalizing one of the most nationalistic organizations in the

[5] For a report of the proceeding see a special supplement of *Nowe Drogi*, Warsaw, November 1949, summarized by Edward A. Morrow, *The New York Times*, December 11, 1949. See also excerpts from President Bierut's closing speech, printed in *For a Lasting Peace, for a People's Democracy!*, Bucharest, December 9, 1949.

[6] Arthur Bliss Lane, "I Saw Poland Betrayed." Indianapolis: Bobbs-Merrill, 1948, p. 154.

world seems open to question; but regardless of whether or not
failure was inevitable he automatically was marked as the scapegoat.
The specific accusations against him were ominous; it was said he
had known of foreign spying activities and had concealed them. His
successor was a "hatchet man"—Edward Ochab, a member of the
Politburo, essentially a M.V.D. agent, experienced in purging the
trades unions and coöperatives.

Others dismissed from their posts about the same time included
the Vice-Minister of Justice, Zenon Kliszko, also a member of the
Central Committee of the Party, accused of not having reformed his
earlier Rightist tendencies in spite of having had the Party line carefully explained to him; Dr. Stanislaw Kowalewski, Vice-Minister of
Agriculture, who was branded as a "hypocrite;" Ryszard Borowy,
Vice-Minister of Forests; and Tadeuez Kachanowicz, Vice-Minister
of Labor and Social Welfare. Former Minister of Food Supply
Lechowicz had been arrested some time earlier. None of these names
can be omitted from the list of candidates for a "Rajk trial." [7]

In 1937 the Soviets tried Marshal Tukhachevsky for conspiring
with Germany and executed him. "Plus ça change . . ." If General
Spychalski is tried it will be for conspiring with the United States or
Britain, and an item of the indictment doubtless will be that he was
doubtful whether Russian collaboration with Germany would work
out to Poland's advantage. That would link him and Gomulka together, but whether civilian deviationists would be included in a
military trial is unpredictable. Rajk's army "accomplices" were
tried with him.

It is worth emphasizing how mature Gomulka's nationalism seems
to have been even before Tito's heresy was brought into the open. In
1947 he urged political coöperation between the Communists and
progressive elements of the petty bourgeoisie and emphasized that
since the peasants formed the bulk of the Polish people they should
be favored politically ahead of any other element. He did not change
these views when Tito was denounced for holding them and called a
nationalist. We have no evidence to show that his mistrust of Russia

[7] Laszlo Rajk, Minister of Foreign Affairs of Hungary and former Minister
of the Interior, was convicted of treason and hanged October 15, 1949 (cf.
Chapter XXI).

went back to the period when Stalin and Hitler were allies, but if he was such a nationalist in 1947 and 1948 it is interesting to speculate what his feelings might have been in 1939 or in 1944. If the Ribbentrop-Molotov Pact disconcerted Tito, what effect would it have had on a Polish Communist who was also a nationalist? And if Tito minimized Jugoslavia's obligation to the Soviets for their aid in the liberation, what would a leader of the Polish underground have felt during the Warsaw insurrection of 1944 when Marshal Konstantine K. Rokossovsky's victorious Red Army halted just across the Vistula from the Polish capital and waited two months while the Nazis methodically annihilated the resistance fighters? General Bor, encouraged by the approach of the Red Army, had sprung the carefully prepared revolt of the Polish Home Army on August 1, 1944. Premier Mikolajczyk of the Polish Government-in-exile at once made desperate personal appeals to Stalin for help (he was in Moscow for several days beginning July 31, just as the insurrection was starting). Roosevelt and Churchill supported him with strong representations. But the Red troops remained motionless while the Nazis dealt with the Home Army, and did not stir during the three months following while the city was being depopulated and razed building by building. On January 5, 1945, the Soviet Government recognized the Communist-dominated Lublin Committee as the Provisional Government of Poland. Two weeks later it announced that the Red Army had crossed the Vistula and "liberated" the void where Warsaw formerly had stood. The fanatical patriots who might have caused the liberators trouble were buried under the rubble. What would Gomulka have been feeling at that moment? In intellectual terms, doubtless, he convinced himself that the destruction of General Bor's anti-Communist forces was a necessary step in creating the political vacuum in which Communism could come to power. But he might at the same time have been unable to suppress a fierce Polish pride in the Bor uprising, just as later he could not suppress his resentment at Stalin's pretension that Communist rule meant Soviet domination.

The suggestion that Gomulka was something more than an opportunist trapped by his rivals in a deviation from the Party line might seem farfetched were it not that nothing—literally nothing—is too

fanciful to be true of a professional revolutionary. Maybe the Gomulka case is merely routine—thieves fall out and the devil takes the
hindmost. Through all Polish history, however, there have been
quixotic characters willing to die for a Polish ideal—sometimes noble,
sometimes perverted. If Gomulka ever comes to trial, one of those
obscure Communist manœuvres which we observe but never understand may bring him to confess that instead of working for any
Polish ideal he was being paid all along to betray Poland with
American gold. Even so the suspicion will not quite down that like
other Poles he feared the Russians deep in his heart at least as much
as he hated the Germans, and that, hard-bitten Marxist as he was, he
had visions of a Polish state that would have its own Communist
identity and be an independent makeweight between East and West,
not just one more item on the Soviet menu.

For two principal reasons Gomulka's opposition to Stalin ended
differently from Tito's, despite the fact that Poland is fully as proud
and nationalistic as Jugoslavia and has a larger population and
greater economic resources for resistance. One was that Tito held a
position of unchallenged leadership in his Party and owned a fighting force with no immediate rivals, domestic or foreign. Geography
was even more compelling. On the east, Poland adjoins the Soviet
Union; on the west, she adjoins the Soviet zone of Germany; neither
of these frontiers is suited by nature to defense; and across her territory, rendering her still more helpless, are spread contingents of the
Soviet Army, called communications troops but not on that account
very different from occupation troops. There was a chance that if the
Jugoslav Communists acted daringly they might free themselves
from Soviet domination. Tito seized it. Gomulka had no such chance.

# XIV

## POLES, RUSSIANS AND
## GERMANS

> Poland of the Versailles Treaty will
> never rise again. This is guaranteed by two
> of the largest states in the world.
>
> Hitler, October 6, 1939

THE principal political agent of the
Soviets in Warsaw, Jakub Berman, admitted to me that the example
of Tito's successful rebellion in Jugoslavia had been influential in
Poland. It had stiffened the opposition in the Church and the peasantry and it had "confused" Communists whose indoctrination had
been "incomplete." But all this is unimportant, Berman said, because
Tito himself is a temporary phenomenon who soon will disappear,
leaving no trace of his heresies or his political successes. Berman said
he was sure of this not because Tito will be assassinated or because
Moscow will boycott him into submission, but for a more subtle
reason—Tito and his followers are suffering from a "psychological
dichotomy" which will split and destroy them (and here Berman
used a strange word) "spiritually." The internal strains to which
they are subject will be too much for them both as individuals and as
a party. "It is only a matter of time," he said, "a short time."

Berman conceals his authority under a mild demeanor and the
minor title of Under Secretary of State at the Presidium of the
Council of Ministers. He is a carefully dressed man, in his late forties
I should say, with a mobile face and delicate hands. When he joins
in the decisions which consign opponents to the firing squad he probably feels as the Bishop of Beauvais did when he sent Joan to the
stake—the political reasons for the action are excellent and his own
judgment has not been tainted by any feelings of personal rancor.

Polish Communists boast that "Berman can telephone to Stalin direct." Probably that is why he speaks to you in an ordinary conversational tone, which in itself prejudices you in his favor, for most Communists seem to feel it necessary to prove their orthodoxy by assaulting you angrily before they have heard your views. Berman take his orthodoxy for granted. This makes him a more interesting subject for a few words of personal comment than most of the other leaders whom I met in the satellite capitals. Also he was one of the few who did not seem to mind speaking for the record.

After disposing of Tito, Berman answered questions as to what sort of Germany he would like to see created. He said that Poland opposes a federal solution and opposes the division of Germany into eastern and western states. "We mistrust the sort of Germany which would develop in the first case," he said; and he expatiated on the reactionary forces at work in Bavaria and the possibility that they might secure control of a weak federal régime. He continued: "As for the second proposal, we think such a step could be taken only in a most fatalistic mood—the mood that conflict is inevitable." More important than the form of organization which Germany adopts, he said, is the *nature* of the new Germany. "We are interested in Germany's form of organization only as that determines Germany's nature." He admitted that the "nature" which he would like might be different from the "nature" an American would like, also that if we were to judge the German nature of the future solely by the one we have known in the past "we might be pessimistic." "But we must look ahead. No people remains what it has been." He added in more specific terms: "We want a Germany which recognizes not just in words but in its heart that our frontiers are final."

In view of what has since occurred Berman's reply to another of my questions is rather significant. I asked whether if Poland had only two choices she would prefer to see Germany unified under whatever régime the German people themselves freely elected or to see a Communist state established in East Germany. "The latter has short-run attractions," Berman said. "It would give us a guarantee from the start that no hostile régime could control the territories on our western frontiers. But the German question would remain in its essentials; the final settlement would have been merely postponed. No, we want a centralized and democratic Germany. We are sorry that the Western Powers no longer favor this solution but instead are seeking to utilize the elements in Western Germany which do not know they have lost the war for German supremacy for good—the people who still think *noch einmal*."

"The West will certainly argue," I objected, "that the kind of democracy you talk about, and which we see a sample of in the Eastern zone, is in fact an aggressive force, built on the Soviet pattern and for Soviet purposes. The French are at least as legitimately interested in Germany's future as you are. So are the British, and so are we and other nations which have had to deal with German aggression in the past. The Western nations see Russian power expanding westwards, towards them. Two stages in this expansion have been Poland and the Soviet zone of Germany. Aren't they entitled to be alarmed by this, just as what you say about their policies in the Western zones alarms you and the Russians?" Berman took refuge here in a somewhat lengthy explanation that if the Western Powers were afraid that Soviet methods in the Eastern zone concealed purposes of aggression they were entirely mistaken because the Soviet organization was based on the workers and the peasants, "who love peace and are not ambitious, nationalistically speaking."

Enough has been recorded, perhaps, to show that Berman (as I told him) looked at Germany in very limited terms—not as a subject of policy in her own right but only as an object of other people's policy. An indication has also been given of the difficulty of talking with Communists, even one so courteous and painstaking as Mr. Berman, with the idea of reaching any sort of conclusion understandable and agreed to on both sides. It is not possible to push a conversation to that point if words which have always had one sense are used in an opposite sense. Talk with a Communist also suffers in interest from the fact that nothing you say can possibly influence his way of thinking in the least. You may, of course, try to worry him. For instance, I suggested to Berman that it would be useful if the Poles would put their longer experience with Western peoples, their linguistic facility and their knowledge of Western habits of thought at the service of the U.S.S.R. They could, for instance, supplement the information reaching the Kremlin from Soviet diplomatic agents who are entirely ignorant of the West, never see or talk with any Westerners except their own paid agents and would be afraid in any case to report adverse turns of opinion in countries where they are stationed since they are responsible not merely for reporting on foreign opinion but for creating it. It is amusing—perhaps even useful—to make suggestions of this sort. But in general the best you can expect to get from talk with a Communist is some idea of what he thinks he ought to make you think he is thinking.

Even at the time I visited Warsaw there was sufficient indication that the Soviets were already committed to organizing their part of occupied Germany in a way that would make unification impossible except by the use of outside force. The first step had been to create military units and a para-military police force in Eastern Germany as a means of blackmailing the rest of Germany. Berman did not dare hint in any way that this made him unhappy. But even a Muscovite Pole, dependent on Stalin for preferment and dying if it should cease, must have fears for his country on the day Stalin renews the Hitler alliance in whatever form seems advantageous in the new situation. August 1939 tells in red letters what any Russian-German deal portends for Poland.

The Russians, having read Clausewitz's contemptuous description of Poland as a public road where foreign armies jostle each other, are converting it into a private road—one-way to Germany and beyond. They mean to keep it open to the Soviet Army and closed to any other, and to make sure that the Soviet Army will never be ambushed along it. The Polish challenge to these aims is indirect but even today not entirely ineffective.

Most Poles hear very little directly about what is happening in Soviet-occupied Germany. If they worry that it portends evil, that Russia someday may buy German coöperation at their expense, they figure not from specific knowledge but simply from past experience. They have no basis for a clear opinion of what the Communist régime in East Germany is like or what rôle it plays or will play in power politics. But anything they hear and all they imagine make them remain almost solidly anti-Russian and only somewhat less solidly anti-Communist. As for the Communists themselves, we have seen that defections have occurred in the highest ranks and that these were at least partly motivated by the fear of what Stalin's policy toward Germany might involve for Poland. The Muscovite leadership lives for Russia and by the Russian Army, but many of the rank-and-file Communists certainly favor neither the purpose nor the instrument. It takes a great deal of faith or a great deal of force to make a Pole even pretend to like a Russian.

The Rokossovsky appointment occurred when the success of the Marshall Plan had forced Russia to recognize that she had lost the great postwar struggle to win France, Germany and Italy to Communism by parliamentary tactics. Production in Western Europe was increasing and living conditions were improving. A start was about to be made, too, to restore the military potential of most of the West European democracies, and meanwhile a military guarantee was being given them under the Atlantic Pact. This did not mean that the United States could protect them from attack, but it did mean that there could no longer be any hope of snatching them one by one while the United States stood hesitating whether or not to throw itself into the struggle. A relatively stable régime had been established at Bonn. This and the failure to force the Western Allies to evacuate Berlin had compelled Russia to abandon hope for the time being of merging the Eastern zone with the Western zones in a united Germany which would be her partner or her tool.

Before these developments occurred, Soviet Russia had planned that the Oder and Neisse rivers should be the outer line of her defense and her potential *point d'appui,* but she felt that the new situation in Western Europe made this strategic concept inadequate. The Rokossovsky appointment pushed the line forward to Lubeck, the Elbe and Hersfeld. Now Poland proper would no longer be a forward area but a communications area between the U.S.S.R. zone of the interior and the westernmost bastion of the Soviet empire, the new East German Republic formed in October 1949 with Wilhelm Pieck as President. With Rokossovsky in command in Poland, Soviet military power would extend uninterruptedly to the Elbe. This would be true whether the Soviet Army itself remained indefinitely in Eastern Germany or was replaced there by Soviet-armed and Soviet-led forces, and whether the Polish Army remained a nominally autonomous force under its Red Marshal or eventually was amalgamated with the Soviet Army.

One Polish official told me that he thought Germany's shattering defeat had changed her superiority complex, and he professed confidence that the Communist leaders of Eastern Germany would easily induce their people to reconcile themselves to the new geography. "We faced problems similar to theirs," he said, "when we had to persuade our people to accept Poland's new eastern frontiers—and not pro forma but in their hearts. At first our people inclined to dwell on the loss of Lwow and Wilno. We had two courses open. We could tell them simply that it was a military fait accompli, that we regretted it as much as they did but could do nothing about it. That would have angered the Russians and kept a running national sore permanently open. Or we could tell them that it was the necessary price for settling a frontier dispute which for ages had been a cause of great national weakness to Poland and a continuous danger of war. We told them that, and said it was cheap at the price. Henceforward there would be no bone of contention between us and Russia. Her firm friendship would make up for our territorial losses many times over. Today the German leaders in the Eastern zone can use the same argument to persuade their people to forget the lands east of the Oder. If they are farsighted, they will interpret the loss not as a penalty for Germany's defeat in war but as a necessary testimony of German friendship for Poland and the Soviet Union and a guarantee of Polish and Russian friendship in return. Then the German people will regard the new territorial arrangement as a pledge of peace. They will realize that this will mean much more to them in the future than the lost lands themselves could ever mean."

Even before the Rokossovsky appointment an event had occurred which was upsetting to Polish Communists. A congratulatory message sent by Stalin to President Pieck in October 1949 contained this sentence: "The experience of the last war has shown that the German and Soviet peoples made the largest sacrifices in that war, that both these peoples have the largest potentialities in Europe to complete great actions of world significance." As Anne O'Hare McCormick pointed out, this frankly said that Stalin looks on the recent war as an unfortunate interruption in the German-Russian collaboration established in 1939. That collaboration was based on a new partitionment of Poland, planned in advance when Ribbentrop visited Moscow, August 23 and 24, 1939; and as soon as Poland lay dead, each took his allotted share of the body.

Whatever relative importance Stalin may assign to Poland and East Germany in his future plans, he tries for the present to keep either of them from becoming unnecessarily restive. After the congratulatory message to President Pieck in October 1949 and the appointment of Marshal Rokossovsky in November, both heavy blows to Polish pride, it was time to redress the balance. Permission was therefore given the Polish Government to make ready to incorporate the occupied territories east of the Oder and Neisse rivers into the Polish state. I say "occupied" because although at Potsdam the Western Powers accepted the Polish claim for compensation in the West for the territories annexed by Russia in the East, they did not agree to the cession of any particular areas and did not recognize that there had been any legal Polish annexation. The Soviets had established the Oder-Neisse line early in 1945 to mark the western border of the Polish occupation, and the Potsdam Agreement of August 1, 1945, sanctioned its continuance for that purpose. The final frontier was left for determination in the eventual peace treaty.[1] Secretary Byrnes held to this position in his Stuttgart address of September 6, 1946; in fact, he urged that in the meantime the boundary be moved to the east of the Oder-Neisse line. Secretary Marshall reminded the Council of Foreign Ministers in Moscow, April 9, 1947, that no "final delimitation" of the Polish-German frontier had yet been made, and hence the status of "about 40,000 square miles of Eastern German territory" which had been placed "under the administration of the Polish state" was still unsettled.

Nevertheless, early in March 1950 it became known that all Germans still living east of the Oder and Neisse rivers would be expelled. By this time these numbered about 125,000, all that were left of the former German population of between nine and ten mil-

---

[1] The relevant paragraph (VIII, B) of the Potsdam Agreement ended with this sentence: "The three Heads of Government reaffirm their opinion that the final delimitation of the western frontier of Poland should await the peace settlement."

lions. The United States and Britain protested to Warsaw that the step was illegal, but the protest was rejected and the expulsions began. On June 1 the Polish Government moved in even more direct violation of the Potsdam Agreement by dividing the occupied area into three provinces and incorporating these formally into the Polish state. Naturally Moscow must have sanctioned both measures in advance.

On June 6, 1950, Vice-Premier Walter Ulbricht of the East German "People's Republic" arrived in Warsaw at the head of a large delegation of political and economic officials. In greeting them, Hilary Minc said that the Oder-Neisse line was a "frontier of peace," not separating but uniting the two peoples; and Ulbricht replied that "across the Oder-Neisse frontier we stretch out our hands in eternal friendship with Poland." What was about to happen was plain, and it happened quickly. After a single day of "negotiations" an agreement was signed by which the East German régime accepted the Oder-Neisse frontier as final and dropped all claims to former German territories beyond. The Polish communiqué noted that the document implemented an East German declaration made by Premier Otto Grotewohl October 12, 1945. The East German Communists had taken four and a half years to bring themselves to the point of carrying out such a grievous intent. When the text was ratified in the East German "parliament" on June 28, Foreign Minister Dertinger preferred to say that it implemented an agreement made under Mr. Molotov's auspices in Warsaw in June 1948 by which Poland and Czechoslovakia accepted East Germany as a member of the Soviet economic and strategic bloc. And in fact Ulbricht was able to announce on July 22 that the East German Republic had been admitted to the Council of Mutual Economic Assistance. By autumn it had signed friendship and economic treaties with Poland, Czechoslovakia, Hungary, Rumania and Bulgaria and so established itself as a full-fledged satellite.

The Bonn Government and the West German and Berlin press called the whole negotiation with Poland treason. The cession of the lands beyond the Oder and Neisse must have been an especially bitter pill for the 18 million Germans living huddled in the Soviet zone.

Even German Communists have been made restless by the East German régime's subservience to Moscow.[2] Some who accepted high positions in the early days of the Soviet occupation have been censured or have simply disappeared, some have been tried and imprisoned. Even Pieck is accused of not playing Soviet power politics with enough devotion. *Die Neue Zeitung,* American-licensed Berlin daily, reported on April 18, 1950, that Ulbricht had just come back from Moscow and told the Central Committee of the S.E.D. that the Soviets were ready to discuss a separate peace treaty with the East German People's Republic if in return it would pay a further five billion dollars in reparations beyond the ten billion set at Potsdam. Pieck is supposed to have opposed this blackmail and to have rejected the sum as utterly beyond German capacities; he said he would go to Moscow the next day (as in fact he did) to maintain his position, "even if it meant that he would be called a Titoist." Stories of this type are frequent in the Berlin press; sometimes they are mere canards, sometimes they turn out to have been correct.

More accurate information is of course available about Communist changes of heart in the Western zones. One spectacular case was that of Kurt Mueller, deputy to Max Reimann, Chairman of the West German Communist Party, who was kidnapped in West Berlin, transported to the Soviet zone and sentenced to 25 years in prison as a Titoist. Titoist pamphlets, some of them printed in Jugoslavia, are in circulation among Communists in all zones. In Western Germany the Communist Party has been losing strength steadily. In the spring of 1950 Drew Middleton estimated that its membership was down to 125,000 or 130,000 compared with figures of 270,000 or 300,000 in 1947.[3] He attributed the loss mainly to the growing popularity of National Communism. Repeated purges and violent shifts in the Party line dictated from Moscow make the concept attractive, and Tito's continued success in pursuing an independent

[2] It was accentuated after the emergence of Ulbricht as the chief Kremlin agent in East Germany. He was appointed Secretary-General of the S.E.D. (Communist) Party on July 25, 1950. Pieck and Grotewohl were retained as joint Chairmen of the Central Committee, but Ulbricht was believed to be actually in charge.

[3] *The New York Times,* May 24, 1950.

policy in Jugoslavia make it seem more practicable than is really the case under present German conditions.

Publicly the Polish Communists take great satisfaction in the treaty with their East German brothers but in their hearts they know that in the long run they must look in the other direction for the guarantee that it will be observed. They realize that the majority of Germans in all zones are anti-Communist, anti-Russian and anti-Polish, and that no united Germany except one created and maintained by Russian force will ever renounce the German heritage beyond the Oder and Neisse. In view of this, the criterion of Polish satisfaction in a realistic sense must be Stalin's intention. He made the East German Republic and can unmake it by a nod. Will he keep the new Polish-German frontier permanently intact or is he prepared to bargain with the Germans about it at the proper time? He has in his hands a handsome bribe. There is no possibility, of course, that while Russia is able to prevent it the Silesian industrial basin will ever pass back into German hands. But other areas are of less military or industrial importance. Stettin, for instance, or the agricultural lands on the right bank of the lower Oder, would be valuable to Germany as outlets for trade or surplus population. If Stalin could make a cheap down-payment and secure German collaboration, might he not tell the Poles, seriously and sensibly, that German friendship will mean much more to them in the future than these particular possessions?

Polish Communists have cause for immediate worry in the news of developments inside East Germany—news that is not published, of course, in the Warsaw press. They will have expected that some of the results of "democratization" in the Soviet zone would be unpleasant for them, but they can hardly have been prepared for remilitarization there on the present scale and under the present leadership. Fairly accurate accounts of the program are now available in the West. On May 23, 1950, the United States, Britain and France protested to the Soviet Government that it was violating five international agreements in creating an East German police force with "the character of an army"—a mild description, since it was equipped with machine guns, howitzers, antiaircraft cannon, mortars and tanks. The State Department also revealed that this police

force included 39 "Bereitschaften" (alert units). In Berlin at about
that time I was told that officers for the "Bereitschaften" were being
supplied from 13 training schools, some of which had been in existence since August 1949; that the training period was one year;
that the number enrolled at each was about 1,000; and that at this
rate in the course of a year enough graduates would be turned out
to officer a military force of over 100,000 men. It was assumed that
this figure would have been passed before the end of 1950. The
additional 100,000 members of the regular People's Police would
raise the total strength of military and para-military units in East
Germany by that date to 200,000.

The history and character of the persons who are creating this
new German military force can be no more reassuring to Poles than
to Americans. The Inspector General, Vincenz Mueller, is a former
Nazi general, a corps commander in the 4th Army; and another of
the commanding officers is Arno von Lenski, also a former Nazi
general, commander of the 24th Panzer Division. Both were captured by the Russians, put through the "Antifaschool" in Moscow
and have found their niches in the new "New Order." In July 1950
their names figured among the signers of a formal call issued "to all
former members of the Nazi Party, officers and professional soldiers"
to line up "on the correct front" by signing the Communist-spon-
sored manifesto against the atomic bomb.[4] Twenty-one other spon-
sors listed the details of their former Nazi positions under their
signatures.

The Communist régime does not stop with utilizing individual
Nazi officers who have been "reoriented." Its search for wide support
among former Nazis and other enemies was disclosed by Premier
Otto Grotewohl during the Congress of the S.E.D. Party on July 21,
1950, where 4,000 delegates, including 75 foreign Communist
leaders from 25 countries, heard the following:

The National Front of Democratic Germany does not by any means
desire to limit coöperation to democratic forces. On the contrary, we
are ready to cöoperate with all patriots who have Germany's interests at

---

[4] *Die National Zeitung,* Soviet-licensed organ of the National Democratic
Party, the political organization of former Nazis in the Soviet zone, July 8, 1950,
reported by Joseph Newman, *New York Herald Tribune,* July 9, 1950.

heart. No patriot who is willing to fight for the justified national interests of the German people will be excluded from the German National
Democratic Front.

Joseph Newman, reporting the proceedings, wrote that the delegates heard this bid for a popular front "without batting an eyelash."
Had they already forgotten the scorn poured out by Stalin and
Molotov on Tito for his insistence on relying on the People's Front
in Jugoslavia, calling it a proof of the Jugoslav Communist Party's
feebleness and his bourgeois nationalism? The Poles would have
been worried for less abstract reasons. The Nazi officers and S.S.
veterans thus made welcome by the East German Prime Minister as
comrades in the new struggles ahead—the same struggles, perhaps,
that Stalin was thinking of when he wrote his congratulatory letter
to Pieck?—were the men who had attacked Poland in 1939, organized the mass atrocities of the occupation and ground Warsaw to
dust.

One Russian vulnerability in Poland has not been mentioned;
paradoxically, it is the fact that her strength there is so overwhelming. From border to border the country is physically at Stalin's
complete disposal and its leaders lie in the crook of his little finger.
If he cannot Sovietize Poland completely under these conditions,
what becomes of the materialistic conception that if you own men's
bodies you can do what you like with their souls? Under different
conditions a failure would not entail loss of face. If the voice of
Stalin fails to reach General Mao distinctly across the vastness of
Asia, or if the Russian rewards for exploiting Chinese resources seem
slow or scanty in comparison to the Russian investment of capital
and energy, a thousand alibis are available. But compared to Peking,
Warsaw is a Moscow suburb; Bierut and Berman sit in Stalin's
anteroom and the Soviet Army guards all doors. The satellite populations saw that Stalin's physical powers were not sufficient to control
Jugoslavia. If the spirit of Polish nationalism and individualism is
able to live along under the surface of the Soviet conquest, thwart-
ing Stalin's will in spite of his acknowledged omnipotence, that will
be a second failure, a fresh reason for other populations under Communist rule to hope that what Hitler could not do to them perma-

nently Stalin may not succeed in doing either. Poland thus becomes an exceptional test of Soviet prestige.

The West might make more, quite legitimately I think, of the propaganda opportunities thus offered. Poland is in a state of permanent revolution. We have every reason to make plain that we are confident the Soviet conquest will not last forever and that we intend, when it ends, to support legitimate Polish national interests. The United States Government might well take more positive steps in this direction, not only through the Voice of America but in giving the Voice of America something concrete to talk about. The State Department was correct, for instance, in protesting the Polish-East German boundary agreement of June 7 and declining to be bound by it. Might it not have used the same occasion to remind the Polish people that although we do not accept all the Polish claims in the West we also do not accept all the Soviet land-grab in the East?

The present Polish-Russian boundary was fixed by Ribbentrop and Molotov in a secret protocol to the so-called Pact of Non-aggression of August 23, 1939. While Poland lay lifeless the deal was carried into effect. These circumstances do not prejudice us in its favor. At Yalta, Stalin argued that the Ribbentrop-Molotov line was the same as the Curzon Line which had been acceptable to American, British and other experts at the Paris Peace Conference of 1919–1920. The part of the Yalta communiqué dealing with this question read as follows: "The three heads of government consider that the eastern frontier of Poland should follow the Curzon Line with digressions from it in some regions of five or eight kilometers in favor of Poland." The Soviet-dominated "Polish Provisional Government of National Unity" accepted this decision on August 16, 1945. It had no choice. But that was not the whole story.

The American delegation at Yalta may have forgotten that the Curzon Line as originally drawn and as accepted by the American experts in Paris in 1919 extended as far south only as the northern boundary of Eastern Galicia. In other words, the whole province of Eastern Galicia and its capital city of Lwow—which mean so much in Polish sentiment, and which never in history had belonged to Russia—were not affected. A British authority reported as follows on the attitude of the American and other delegations in 1919: "All the delegations, except the British, were, however, strongly in favor of assigning the whole territory [of Eastern Galicia] as a natural unit to Poland in some form or other, with such safeguards and limitations as might be thought necessary." [5] The chief American territorial expert at Paris, the late Dr. Isaiah Bowman, told me more than once that the American delegation was never enthusiastic about the Curzon Line in its original form and never sanctioned the later projection of it southward across Eastern Galicia to the Carpathians. Unfortunately, neither Dr. Bowman nor any American geographical or historical expert was present at Yalta to remind President Roosevelt and Secretary Stettinius that there were two "lines" bearing Curzon's name and that the American record regarding them was different. Stettinius states in his book on Yalta that there was discussion there of East Galicia, that Roosevelt urged Stalin to leave Lwow to Poland and that Stalin refused. The Yalta Agreement as signed simply referred to the Curzon Line without defining it.

At the same time that the State Department rejected the Oder-Neisse line in June 1950 it might well have noted, it seems to me, that the United States also reserves for future consideration the Russian annexation of Eastern Galicia. It might do so on some future occasion, and the Voice of America could tell the Poles all about it. By our protest in the Oder-Neisse matter we reminded the Germans that their hope of recovering part of their lost lands does not depend wholly on Stalin's favor, thus diminishing the value of any territorial bribes he may offer them. We might similarly remind the Poles that their lost lands may not be lost forever and that their claims may some day receive fair consideration on the basis of the Curzon Line which we considered equitable in 1919. We would give Polish nationalists new heart and a new reason to continue their resistance to Russian Sovietization. The Russians would be, of course, displeased. If there is any reason why that should worry us it is minor in comparison with our interest in seeing to it that Soviet manœuvres to dominate Poland and Germany are as difficult as possible. Perhaps in addition to our interest we have a duty. Poland was our ally, we promised to help her to freedom and she lies in chains.

[5] H. W. V. Temperley, "History of the Peace Conference of Paris, 1919–1920." London: Frowde, 1920–1924, Vol. VIII, p. 271.

# XV

## RELICS OF NATIONALISM
## IN THE LAND OF MASARYK

> The land is there, the men are there, but
> the nation has been lost.
>
> Stanislas Wyspianski, "The New Europe"

THE pain of visiting Prague for anyone
who remembers it in its time of hope and energy is almost physical.
The sun still slants across the Vltava in the evening, and swallows fly
in the mist off the river where Hradčany casts a cool shadow. But
from the castle on the hill to the Square of the Martyrs ghosts throng
in and push out the living so insistently that suddenly this seems a
city of the dead. They hover in the crooked streets of Mala Strana,
line the bridges, nudge you in the bustle of Vaclavske Namĕsti and
stand at your elbow as you look rememberingly up at Jan Masaryk's
window in the Czernin Palais. Of the venerable Masaryk the Liberator there is no more trace than of the Republic he founded. His
picture has vanished and the songs of the Legionnaires who circled
the globe in the fight for freedom may not be sung. Nowhere in the
new Soviet realm do the pictures of Stalin stare down on passersby
more incongruously than in this city of graceful baroque palaces and
bridges dotted with statues of old saints.

I was startled in 1949 by the changes that had taken place in the
two years since my last visit. In the crowded shop windows of 1947
the products of all the world were on display. Then Prague was an
oasis in the economic and cultural desert of Eastern Europe. Vienna
was still poverty-stricken and apathetic; Prague was bustling and
the windows were overflowing with clothes, food, medical supplies and books. Now the situations were reversed. "Marshallized"

[ 171

Vienna, after a bout with the voracious exploiters from America, was busy and prosperous; Prague windows were empty or contained dummy goods that were not for sale. The label on that pair of shoes, for instance, would indicate that it cost only seven or eight dollars; but if anyone tried to buy it (in the country of Bata) he was directed, even if he had the necessary coupons, to the "free market" where the price was seventy dollars. People queued up glumly outside the food shops; there were long gaps on the shelves of the bookstores, where books in all languages used to be on sale; and at the newspaper kiosks each newspaper was like the other and all were intolerably boring. The ban against foreign contacts has now become as complete as the police can make it. Letters from abroad are opened and delivered with a stamp stating that they were received in damaged condition and "had to be resealed." Anyone wishing to send a letter to a foreign country must take it to the post office and identify himself.

A city, a people, a life are gone.

As Czechoslovakia was the most advanced state in Eastern Europe, the most thoroughly bourgeois, Moscow prudently left it to be "processed" last. In contrast with the other satellites, it was still a political democracy at the start of 1948 under a four-party (including Communist) coalition government. The Communists had made ominous headway in establishing control over the trade unions, police and the new Soviet-type organs of local government set up after the war, and banks, insurance companies and heavy industry had been nationalized; but private enterprise still retained a relatively secure footing in both domestic and foreign trade.[1] Outside the urban centers, no radical redistribution of land had been attempted, as in the other "new democracies," and the organization of agricultural collectives, state farms and tractor stations had barely begun. Czechoslovakia still belonged to two worlds.

When early in 1948 the men in the Kremlin realized that the Jugoslav situation called for a drastic solution they decided as a necessary preliminary to consolidate their hold throughout the rest of Eastern

---

[1] Cf. "Czechoslovakia, Poland, Yugoslavia," by Philip E. Mosely, *Political Science Quarterly*, March 1948.

Europe. The Czechoslovak salient of bourgeois democracy would have to be sliced off sometime, and there were strong reasons for doing it now. An especially pressing reason appeared after the Bolshevik Party began circulating its secret bill of complaints against Tito to chosen members of the Cominform. The opposition to Communism in Czechoslovakia gathered about President Beneš and Foreign Minister Jan Masaryk. If the leaders of Czech democracy got wind of the rift developing inside the Cominform they would be encouraged to resist a Communist coup d'état, and there was more than an even chance that if they did the Army would support them. The danger both that they would resist and that they would receive powerful support would obviously increase once the Jugoslav crisis came to a head. The Soviet leaders thus saw that before they advanced further toward a showdown with Tito the Czechoslovak Republic must be brought into line with the other satellites, and they instructed the Czech Communists to take direct action to secure that result without delay.

Americans remember their sense of almost personal loss as they read the news of the sudden and successful Communist coup in Prague in February 1948. They admired the constitutional and liberal state which the elder Masaryk and Beneš had created and were proud of the fact that Woodrow Wilson had encouraged and helped them. Its destruction warned Americans that the Soviet program of indirect aggression was being speeded up and convinced them of the need of speeding up the Marshall Plan in reply. Moscow would have done well to leave the intimidation and defeat of Czechoslovak democracy until a little later. But the secret Jugoslav crisis was hurrying to a climax and the *Gleichschaltung* of Czechoslovakia could not be postponed.

Since the Czechs are methodical, deliberate and not highly imaginative they did not believe in the imminence of the Communist revolution until too late. They also are obstinate, so that now that it is too late they will not accept it. This, plus the fact that Czechoslovakia came last on the Moscow timetable, explains why more blood has been shed in Czechoslovakia recently than in any of the other Sovietized countries. The period of general hanging and shooting, reached in Rumania and Bulgaria soon after the "liberation" in 1945, and afterwards in the other satellite states as each local revolutionary situation matured, arrived in Czechoslovakia only in 1949.

This does not mean that there was no resentment against Soviet Russia at the time of the coup of February 1948. But Beneš himself, for all his brilliance of intellect, or perhaps because of it, always believed that things could be "managed." His failing health also deprived him of some of his accustomed sharpness. Perhaps, actually, he knew in 1948 that it was already too late to resist the Soviets, that he had taken his great gamble when he accepted Communists in key positions in his first postwar government as the price for being allowed to return at all to Prague; and that he had lost. At any rate, he did not call on the Army to oppose the coup. Shortly afterwards Masaryk met his shocking death.

The Communist strategists, having won their main objectives without a fight, spent a brief period in perfecting the Party apparatus for its new functions and in weeding out patriotic elements in the Army and police. Then they went to work in earnest. Foreign and domestic trade were nationalized; industry was further nationalized, with the result that by May 1948 over 93 percent of all enterprises employing more than 50 workers were in the socialized sector; and a new agrarian law was passed providing for the division of all holdings over 50 hectares. The Socialist Party was forced to merge with the Communist Party, with hardly any pretense that it wished to do so; single-list elections were held; and a new constitution of the standard Communist type made Czechoslovakia a regular people's democracy. With these events popular resentment hardened into resistance. Today the Government's continuous exhortations, rebukes and punishments reveal that the resistance is not limited to any one region, class or group. Slovak resistance shows itself not only in peasant uprisings in support of village priests but in the purges of Slovaks in the top leadership of the Communist Party. Rural jails are as full of recalcitrant farmers in Moravia as in Slovakia. Teachers and judges have received orientation courses and those who do not show "positive attitudes" have been sent to the uranium mines or to work on irrigation projects. The Roman Catholic Church, though it is not so entrenched here as in Poland, has put up a strong fight and so far has held the loyalty of most of its priests; but loyal or not, all had to undergo rigorous "lay schooling" under the appropriately violent atheist chosen by President Gottwald to be Minister for Church Affairs, his son-in-law, Dr. Alexi Čepička (later promoted to be Minister of Defense). Archbishop Beran of Prague was "detained" in his episcopal palace.

The faculty of Charles University, with one of the proudest and oldest traditions of learning in Europe, has been combed over carefully and scientists who doubt the Lysenko theories on the inheritance of acquired characteristics and professors of literature who see any merit in bourgeois writers join the ranks of forced labor also. Minister of Information Vaclav Kopecky stated in March 1950 that what out of habit he referred to as "cultural" activities were being reorganized; the press would become, "on the Soviet example," "an organization of the working classes" and books "a weapon of ideological purity." Thus intellectuals and artists who will not consent to be active servants of Communism are eliminated physically, since life in a labor camp, on starvation rations, without sanitary facilities, is no more bearable for anti-Communists than it was for anti-Nazis. People as cosmopolitan, literate and experienced as the Czechs find these crimes against the intelligence even more repulsive than crimes of direct violence.

Before the war, labor was particularly progressive and well-organized in the industrial regions of Bohemia. Under the Nazi occupation a large Communist minority developed. But now that the workers have the state as master, both Communists and non-Communists find that they do not enjoy it. To air a grievance is unpatriotic; and the government union, instead of protecting the man who protests an injustice, expels him and thereby ensures that he cannot again find a job, either in his own trade or in any other. Moreover, the workers resent being twice removed from the seat of power. The state which orders them about is not even their own, but only a subdivision of a larger state, which gives orders to those who give orders to them. The Prague bureaucracy is helpless to protect their standard of living even if it tried. Moscow permitted a slight economic rally in the first half of 1950 to offset the unpopularity of the moves being made against the Church, the independent farmers and the shop owners. But its hand is always on the faucet, nicely regulating the supply of consumer goods and determining the list and prices of rationed articles so as to fulfill immediate Soviet requirements without entirely destroying the incentive of the Czech workers. Moscow also controls Czechoslovakia's standard of living by controlling her so-called foreign trade. On the one hand, trade with the West in Bohemian specialties such as fine glass and china has all but disappeared. On the other hand, even the machinery, armaments and other products of Czech heavy industry which are now absorbed by Russia as fast as they are produced do not aid the national economy. The larger the Russian slice of Czech trade, the greater the net Czech loss, for Czech goods exported to Russia are credited on the Czechoslovak national account at less than world prices while the raw materials received in return for processing in Czech factories are charged for at higher than world prices. Nor is the loss only in bookkeeping. Russia pays particular attention to securing satellite products which can find a market outside the Soviet sphere. When these are resold the foreign exchange assists the Soviet state rather than the original producer. By such methods the Czech standard of living has been pushed down relentlessly since 1948. As the Czech standard before that was relatively high, and as the fall has been more rapid than in any of the other satellites, resentment has naturally been particularly acute.

Moscow's decision that all the satellites should suspend trade relations with Jugoslavia put Czech industry more than ever at the Soviet mercy. Jugoslavia was a good market for Czech manufactures and a source of needed lead, copper and iron ore. A trade treaty with Albania in March 1949 did not provide a satisfactory substitute, though it was advertised as opening up new outlets for Czech goods. Moscow directed that it be made primarily in order to compensate Albania for her loss of trade with Jugoslavia and thus help the Hoxha régime over a most trying economic crisis. The deal was in every respect most disadvantageous for the Czechs, but they apparently were considered well able to stand the losses involved. The basis of the deal was a Czech credit to Albania of about $3,000,000 to finance the import of Czech consumer goods, with repayment supposedly to begin in 1951 and to extend over a five-year period. As

Albania has never in history had a favorable trade balance the outlook for repayment was no better than for current profits.

The fall in the standard of living was smaller for Czech factory workers than for "city drones" and "anti-social elements" but it was enough to be unpopular, and production dropped. Communist exhortations have not raised it. Rudolph Slansky, Secretary-General of the Communist Party, told factory foremen in May 1949 that they must not be afraid of becoming disliked as a result of driving the workers too hard. Communists should be ready to work harder than non-Communists in order to prove the superiority of the Communist system. "Make them work," he instructed the foremen, "make them produce!" When the situation remained unsatisfactory, another rebuke was delivered by Prime Minister Antonin Zapotocky, who denounced absenteeism, said shirking must "absolutely" stop and demanded that individual production quotas be raised. Absenteeism had increased 37.3 percent in the preceding two years, he said; in future, those indulging in days off would be "deprived of the right to enjoy the advantages of our achievement," i.e. the right to work (except, of course, at forced labor). To demonstrate that sufferings would be equalized, there were mass arrests of middle-class elements in the towns and cities. Professional men, business managers, shopkeepers and former government employees were rounded up and sent off to labor camps. That the purge extended far below the ranks of the "bourgeois leadership" was shown by estimates that in the first days of October no less than 10,000 persons were arrested, half of them in Prague alone.

No sign of National Communism appeared at first in the Czechoslovak Party leadership, but everyone knew that the taint must be there. One of the events that brought it to the surface was Moscow's order that Czech technicians and selected workers be sent to Poland to help build up Polish industry. Poland's industrial potentialities are very great but her techniques have been primitive by comparison with those used in Czechoslovakia. The unpopularity of sending Czech instructors to develop stronger competition in Poland was not lessened by the fact that the two countries now were sister Communist states. The discontent seemed to be equally great among Communist and non-Communist workers. Both foresaw that they would have to work harder for a smaller return once neighboring Polish resources were better exploited; and both took pride in Czech standards of workmanship and in the preëminence of famous Czech establishments like Skoda. Such fears are unreasonable and such conceits are foolish according to the Bukharins; but there they were.

The Czechoslovaks have also been apprehensive that the integration of Czech and Polish industries, as favored by Moscow, will involve them too directly in Polish disputes with Germany. Having gotten rid of all but a small proportion of their Sudeten German population they see no reason for friction with Germany in the future and do not wish to be tied too closely to a country which has annexed former German territories. This uneasiness is aggravated by a proposal, said to originate in Moscow, that a certain number of German expellees be brought back to work at their old jobs in the Bohemian glass, ceramic and other industries, releasing less skilled Czech workers for labor in the Soviet uranium mines near Jachimov. Also, so long as the old dispute with Poland over Teschen remains unsettled there are sure to be rumors that Czechoslovakia may be forced to give the Poles compensation in that region for their loss of East Galicia to Russia. In Slovakia, the Czechoslovak Government carried out the Soviet order to settle the problem of the Hungarian minority on Hungary's terms. This was much resented inside the régime itself. And the picture of a régime which had been on the winning side in the war being unable to protect its interests against one which had been on the losing side has certainly not added to its prestige or popularity. Such considerations are not important while the foreign relations of all the countries concerned—the East German Republic, Poland and Hungary, as well, of course, as Czechoslovakia—are being run from Moscow. But the Czechoslovaks have lived through periods of foreign domination before, and even the Communists are not all convinced that subservience to Russia is a necessary part of the new social order or that it is bound to last forever.

At first no Party officials higher in rank than regional secretary laid themselves open to the accusation of being better Czechs than Communists. It is an old Czech tradition to wear out and absorb "the conquerors," to "live through" rather than take to the barricades. The first official admission that there was Titoism in Czechoslovakia came on May 21, 1949, when the Party secretary for the Karlovy Vary area and a number of other local officials were purged "for the same acts that led to the expulsion of Tito from the Cominform." By autumn rumors were spreading that much more important personages were involved, in particular Foreign Minister Vladimir Clementis.

During the meeting of the U. N. General Assembly in the fall of 1949 Clementis remained aloof from Western journalists and obediently voted the Soviet line, but even when he was being photographed with Vyshinsky striding in or out of meetings he wore a sombre look, and it was said in the Jugoslav delegation that he was debating whether to return to Prague at the end of the session or seek sanctuary in the United States. The Jugoslavs were not unprejudiced observers; and their contact with former intimates in other satellite delegations was now limited to knowing glances when they met in corridors or friendly nudges when they brushed against each other in the privacy of washrooms. In this case, however, they were right. Clementis did go home, but on March 14, 1950, he presented his resignation to President Gottwald and it was accepted without thanks.

Omens of a major purge had been accumulating for several weeks. On February 28, Gottwald warned the Central Committee of the Czechoslovak Communist Party that "Titoists" had been plotting to put the country "into the imperialist camp." The same day it was announced that Vilem Novy, former editor of *Rude Pravo,* the leading Party organ, and Chairman of the Foreign Affairs Committee of Parliament, was being expelled from the Central Committee and from the Party. Novy had disappeared from his desk the previous October, about the time the rumors about Clementis began circulating in New York. Ladislav Kopriva, a member of the Central Committee, supplied details about Novy as well as others in the alleged plot. It seems that a certain foreigner had helped Novy to flee via Poland to England at the beginning of the war, and after the war Novy twice helped this man, who was in fact a "foreign agent," to come to Czechoslovakia "without the Party's knowledge" and had given him information. Dana Adams Schmidt, correspondent of *The New York Times* in Prague, reported that this foreigner might be Noel Field, an American relief worker in Poland who helped many Jewish, Czech and Polish refugees to escape from the Nazis. Field was known to be a friend of Novy's, as also of Dr. Evzen Klinger, head of the Press Department in the Foreign Office, who disappeared about the same time that Novy did.[2] Kopriva also disclosed that Prime Minister Antonin Zapotocky's *chef-de-cabinet*, Milan Reiman, who likewise had disappeared the previous autumn, actually had committed suicide after questioning; that Bohdan Benda, formerly in charge of military questions in the Prague headquarters of the Party, had "served Tito's agents" and had been purged; and that another "unmasked traitor" was Josef Stavincha, Secretary of the Communist Party in Olomuc, who had accepted bribes and protected enemies of the Republic. Seemingly referring to Evzen Loebl, formerly Deputy Minister of Foreign Trade, who also had disappeared in October, Kopriva said: "In our foreign trade organization a group of responsible functionaries were discovered who pursued a policy of directing foreign trade to the West in order to maintain Czech dependence on the West."

After these premonitory tremors the earth opened and engulfed Foreign Minister Clementis, who had been in charge of the Foreign Office since the Communist seizure of power and the death of Jan Masaryk. Clementis, a Slovak, 48 years old, a lawyer by training, is a man of considerable cultivation. He joined the Communist Party in the early thirties and was elected to Parliament in 1935. When the Nazis occupied Prague after Munich he escaped to Poland and then to Russia, but unlike many Czech and Slovak Communists did not stay in Moscow but went on to Paris. Later he seems to have been dropped from the Communist Party. When the war on the Continent ended he went to England and collaborated with the Beneš Government-in-Exile, first broadcasting in Slovak over the B.B.C. under the name Petr Hren, later becoming Under-Secretary for Foreign Affairs under Jan Masaryk. When the Red Army was liberating Slovakia (and annexing Sub-Carpatho Ruthenia), Beneš made his deal with Stalin in Moscow and set up a provisional government

[2] *The New York Times*, March 3, 1950. Noel Field disappeared in Prague in May 1949. His brother Hermann Field disappeared in August on a flight from Warsaw to Prague. Noel's wife, Herta, disappeared at the Prague airport where she had gone to meet Hermann. His daughter also has been reported missing.

at Kosice. It was part of the arrangement that Clementis should retain his No. 2 post in the Foreign Office. I once asked Masaryk whether he did not feel hampered by the fact that his assistant had loyalties to a foreign government. "On the contrary," he said, "as Russia is our nearest neighbor we must always take account of her wishes in foreign affairs. Having Clementis in the next room saves time and telegraph charges." And he added, "You know I almost like the bastard. He lies to me only when he has to."

Various statements by Clementis can be cited to indicate that although he was a good Marxist he had an independent turn of mind, which means that Moscow must have employed him only because there were few outstanding Communists available to represent strongly Catholic and conservative Slovakia in the early postwar governments. Forecasts of the line of thought which got him into trouble later can be found in a book which he published in London in 1943, "Panslavism, Past and Present," as well as in several articles in the *Central European Observer*. In his book he predicted that after the war there would be coöperation among the Slav nations, "all of them possessing independence and equal rights of their own, and developing in accordance with their respective spiritual traditions." [3] It was "*a priori* out of the question," he said in another place, "that there should be any revival of the tendencies to Russify the Slav nations." In one of his articles he spoke of the wartime Slovak underground as "nationalistic and patriotic." These ideas, which were common-form among Polish and Czechoslovak Communists at the time, have now become reprehensible, and the phraseology, natural enough in the London wartime atmosphere, is now used by Tito and is heretical.

The reasons for the abrupt dismissal of Clementis were given for the first time by his successor, Viliam Siroky, in an address to the Congress of the Slovak Communist Party at Bratislava on May 24, 1950. Clementis, he said, was a "bourgeois nationalist." He had been dropped from the Party in 1939 because he had "become a class enemy," as demonstrated by the fact that he opposed the Molotov-Ribbentrop Pact during the period when (as Siroky phrased it)

[3] Cited by Paul Dorian in "Behind the Czech Purge," *The New Leader*, May 27, 1950.

"western Ukraine and western White Russia were being liberated by
the Soviet Army." Another reason for purging him was that in London during the war he allegedly was an ally of the "bourgeois
émigrés around President Eduard Beneš and developed a bourgeois
ideology in his B.B.C. broadcasts." Siroky could emphasize this
safely because although like Clementis he had escaped to Paris after
Munich, he went on from there to Moscow instead of to London.
He maintained further that Clementis continued after the war the
same line he had followed in London. Further, he pointed out his
connections with two recently deposed Slovak leaders, Gustav Husak,
former Chairman of the Board of Slovak Commissioners, and Ladislav Novomesky, a Slovak poet, former Commissioner of Education
in Slovakia. Both were members of a cultural group called "Hro-
mada," of which Clementis was the head, and all three had "fallen
under the influence of the nationalist Slovak bourgeoisie" and had
tried to "isolate Slovakia from the Czech working class." They did
not understand "liberation" in the Leninist and Stalinist sense but
in the bourgeois, democratic, nationalist sense.

President Gottwald and Rudolf Slansky supported the charge in a
joint letter to the Congress. Clementis and the others had failed, they
wrote, to "appreciate the decisive rôle of the Soviet Union and the
fraternal help of the Czech working class." Such failures were among
"the most insidious weapons of the enemy in the period of transition
from capitalism to Socialism." Husak and Novomesky thereupon
confessed to "bourgeois nationalist deviationism," giving as their
excuse that they had been so anxious to protect Slovak autonomy
against Beneš and the Czech bourgeoisie that they had made the error
of mistrusting the Czech working class as well. Husak admitted that
by joining forces with the Slovak bourgeoisie he had helped it rally
"the backward sections of the population and then pass to an attack
on all the achievements of the people's democratic order." This was
a welcome confession because (as the correspondent of *The New
York Times* noted) it provided an explanation for the poor Communist showing in the 1946 elections in Slovakia, the peasant riots
in defense of the Roman Catholic clergy and the resistance to collectivization—or, as Husak put it, "why Slovakia was for a long time
a weak spot of the Republic." The explanation might be acceptable

to Marxist theorists, but the one usually given in the West is that during the long history of the Slovak people as part of Hungary they had missed the Hussite reformation of the Czechs and remained apart, strongly Catholic, agricultural, conservative and separatist.

Clementis did not appear at the Congress. Foreign Minister Siroky announced that his predecessor's self-criticism had not been accepted because he "still did not understand the gravity of his mistakes and shortcomings." In July Clementis was reported to have been given a post in the State Bank. But in view of the fact that his confession was not accepted he must still expect that at the right moment he may be made a scapegoat for some Communist failure. Whether he is tried, and if so whether besides being called a Titoist he is accused of being an agent of Western imperialism, will depend on whether this course promises to make more or fewer admirers for him than if he is left in disgrace and obscurity (as Gomulka so far has been left in Poland), reappearing occasionally to repeat an unavailing *mea culpa*. Unquestionably his root sin is nationalism. It showed itself in his negotiations with Hungary over the rights of Slovak and Hungarian minorities and with the East German Republic over the Sudeten question,[4] and probably it also made him a stumbling block when Czechoslovak trade was being rechanneled to suit Soviet requirements and plans were being laid for the assimilation of the Czechoslovak Army with the Soviet Army. His desire to benefit from the Marshall Plan could hardly be held against him, for practically all the satellite leaders were similarly tempted. If he comes to trial the essential charge against him will be that he is so thoroughly Slovak. As the Siroky speech showed, Slovak nationalist and separatist feeling can be made a useful alibi to explain the embarrassingly strong resistance of the Slovak people to the new Communist régime in Prague.

To strangers Clementis was a reserved, moody man, who often puffed silently at his pipe instead of replying to a question. His ex-

[4] Pijade states (*Borba*, Belgrade, September 26, 1950) that Clementis in June 1946 requested the Jugoslavs to support his demand for the expulsion of the Hungarian population from Slovakia. He adds that at this time all the Czechoslovak Communist leaders took the same attitude. He also says that as late as October 1947 the Czechoslovak Ambassador in Belgrade stated that Czechoslovak-Hungarian relations were strained and would probably worsen because of his Government's position in this matter.

perience with Westerners had taught him, however, that even when he was unable to give a satisfactory reply to some question he had better assume that the problem under discussion actually existed rather than attempt to dismiss it in dialectical terms as impossible of existence. When I talked with him he never uttered a word to suggest even remotely that he was anything but an uncompromising Communist and a hard, shrewd servant of the Czechoslovak Government, and the same impression is held by those who negotiated with him at international meetings. It is true that he was not (how quickly we learn to speak of Communists in the past tense!) one of the new barbarians; his speech was not limited to one social dialect. His failure was in not recognizing the complete supremacy of the Soviet Government and Party, the omniscience of Stalin living as against Lenin dead. This ended his career and may end his life. If he acted in error, if he merely miscalculated the strength of rival forces in the struggle for power, we can take some satisfaction in the thought that thieves again have fallen out. If he chose his way by a deliberate act of national conscience we can be pleased that although the Republic of Masaryk the Liberator has been extinguished, one of the goals for which he worked—national self-determination—still appeals to lesser men. Masaryk first made his name in the world by travelling to Zagreb to aid in the defense of a Croat patriot falsely accused of treason in a Hapsburg court. In his twisted way, Tito sends back to the Czechs and Slovaks, through a servant of Communism who was not wholly a servant of the Kremlin, if not Masaryk's supreme message of personal freedom at least his call to national independence.

# XVI

## MACEDONIA: OLD STRUGGLES
## IN NEW DISGUISES

A new period of embittered nationalist
agitation, national hate, and national-
bourgeois wars threatens the Balkan and
Danube peoples. Only the Proletariat can,
through its victory, avert a new catastrophe.

G. Zinoviev, 1920

CASTING about for means to damage
Tito, the men in the Kremlin must have thought often and long
about Macedonia, the meeting-place of three rival nationalities—
Jugoslav, Bulgar and Greek. The first two merge to some extent,
and to the extent that they do—a violently debated point—another
nationality is formed, the Macedonian. Those inhabitants who feel
themselves more Macedonian than Jugoslav, Bulgar or Greek further
complicate the picture of national rivalries by demanding a separate
state of their own. Since in addition nature made Macedonia a poor
land, and since men and governments have kept it so, any régime
in any part of the area is bound to have many enemies. One would
have expected the Soviets to capitalize on this situation by staging
revolts against Tito in the Macedonian districts which constitute the
Jugoslav Macedonian People's Republic. But thus far they have been
foiled by the difficulty of bringing nationalist and Communist cur-
rents into a single stream of action.

Russia, whether Tsarist or Soviet, has always been tempted to take
a hand in the struggle over Macedonia, hoping that by picking the
winner she might secure control of a land bridge to the Aegean and
thus to the Mediterranean. Usually she has taken Bulgaria as her
protégé, and usually Bulgaria has welcomed the rôle. Tsarist min-

isters manœuvred to get as much of the debatable territory as possible for Bulgaria, and when the prospects for this seemed poor, advocated the creation of an autonomous Macedonian state which eventually might come under Bulgarian sway. After the Revolution, the Kremlin tried to devise a policy which would serve traditional Russian designs and also the interests of international revolutionary Communism. Unlike the former strategists of St. Petersburg, those of Moscow had two barrels to their gun and wanted to be free to fire whichever seemed most likely to bring down the quarry. But they never could quite make up their mind to pull either the nationalist or the revolutionary trigger; and they are unable to do so today.

For a time the Kremlin came close to adopting a policy for Macedonia based, like that of the Tsars, on nationalism. The Fifth Plenum of the Comintern in the spring of 1924 encouraged the Balkan Communist Parties to make common cause with the I.M.R.O. (Internal Macedonian Revolutionary Organization) and other Macedonian nationalist groups, and to that end proclaimed "the right of oppressed nationalities to self-determination, up to political secession." [1] This suited Bulgarian aspirations. Bulgaria had been on the wrong side in both the Second Balkan War and the First World War and therefore had little to lose by any possible "secession," but she had hopes that a new Macedonian national state created at the expense of Jugoslavia and Greece might someday become part of a Greater Bulgaria. The Jugoslav and Greek Communist Parties immediately complained loudly; the I.M.R.O. held back from the alliance with Bulgaria; several of its rival leaders were murdered in quick succession; and the whole manœuvre foundered in the usual Macedonian welter of discord, treachery and blood.

Later, Nazi Germany's espousal of revisionism and racism made these unsuitable themes for Communist propaganda, and from the time of the Comintern Congress of 1935 prevailing Communist tactics were based on "popular fronts" with Social Democrats. The Comintern did not abandon its reliance on national Communist parties for the long revolutionary pull; but as a tactical manœuvre

[1] For a convenient summary of events through 1949 see "Macedonia: Its Place in Balkan Politics," by Elizabeth Barker. London and New York: Royal Institute of International Affairs, 1949.

in the period of extreme Nazi peril it played down nationalism as a revolutionary weapon, minimized the revolutionary rôle of the Red Army and emphasized Marxism's reformist aspects. After the Nazi attack, Stalin revived the emphasis on nationalism with a bang; and the successful progress and outcome of the Great Patriotic War prepared the way for the reappearance of nationalism in international Communist tactics.

When the Nazi armies overran Jugoslavia and Greece, Hitler placed most of Macedonia in charge of his Bulgarian allies, who tried with usual Balkan violence and lack of success to convince its inhabitants that they were all Bulgars. One reason why Tito developed the political organ of the Partisan movement, the AVNOJ, described in an earlier chapter, was in order that there might exist some national body to protest enemy annexations and occupations— Italian and Hungarian as well as Bulgarian—and stake out Jugoslavia's counterclaims in debatable areas. Thus at a meeting at Jajce in November 1943 the AVNOJ adopted a resolution setting forth Jugoslav territorial claims against Italy, which had just collapsed, and another calling for the future organization of Jugoslavia on a federal basis and naming Macedonia as one of the six component units. The borders of Macedonia were not specified. In other words, no indication was given whether Tito would be content with the part of Macedonia which had formed part of the national territory before the war or would try to enlarge Jugoslav holdings at Bulgaria's expense. Tito asked for Stalin's approval of the Jajce program, and secured it.

But although Stalin approved the Jajce declaration he was not ready to relinquish the Bulgarian card entirely, as was presently shown by the fact that the Bulgarian Communists continued to espouse a contrary solution for the Macedonian question, joining with other anti-Nazi Bulgarian elements in proclaiming that the only way to dispose permanently of the "apple of discord" would be to merge the three segments—Jugoslav, Greek and Bulgarian—in "an integral, free and independent Macedonia." Nor did he forbid them to indicate which nation was entitled to be the "apple's" custodian: their proclamation described Macedonia as "the cradle of the Bulgarian nation for which a river of blood has been given."

In other words, the Bulgarian Communist Party appealed again to the "right of secession," approved by the Comintern 20 years earlier, as the basis for a new Macedonian deal following the war.

Stalin simply aimed to keep the situation fluid, of course, so that he could impose whatever final solution best suited Russian interests. Hitler had allowed the Bulgars to occupy Jugoslav Macedonia but not formally to annex it. Stalin hedged in the same manner. He approved the plan to make Jugoslav Macedonia one of the units of the future Jugoslav Republic, but permitted the Bulgarian Communists to continue hoping that all parts of Macedonia might be brought together in an independent state. Possibly there might even be advantages in allowing the Jugoslavs and Bulgars to fulfill the dreams of idealists in time past by joining hands to form a South Slav state, thus offsetting Italy on one side and Turkey on the other and incidentally overshadowing and overawing Greece. As to this he would wait and see. Conceivably he might confound both Jugoslavia and Bulgaria by creating a Macedonian state and incorporating it directly into the Soviet Union. For the present, however, he encouraged both nationalism and Communism, and drove them in double harness.

The Jugoslav and Bulgarian Communists remained on bad terms until Marshal Tolbukhin's armies entered the Balkans in the autumn of 1944. Then political power in Sofia passed to the Fatherland Front, composed of Agrarians, Socialists, Communists and other anti-Nazi elements; Bulgaria left the Axis; and the Bulgarian Army switched from its rôle as an occupying force in Jugoslav and Greek Macedonia and joined the Jugoslav Partisans in attacking the retreating Germans.

Towards the end of the year Tito sent his leading foreign policy adviser, Edvard Kardelj, to Sofia to see whether the time had not come to solve the Macedonian problem within the framework of a Jugoslav-Bulgarian federation. Soviet successes were at a high tide from the Baltic to the Aegean. Rumania and Bulgaria were "in the bag," with Communists in key government posts and Soviet troops backing them up. Marshal Rokossovsky waited watchfully outside Warsaw while the Nazis finished mopping up General Bor's Polish patriots, and made ready to move in for the kill. Belgrade had been captured in October, and Marshal Tolbukhin was pressing on into Hungary. The ELAS revolt had given the Communist-led forces control of most of Greece outside parts of Athens and the Piraeus.[2] While Tito was in Moscow in September he had realized that the speed of events made it wise to cash in at once on the fact that he had been Stalin's steadfast ally while the Bulgars had been Hitler's. The Bulgars of course saw this too and played for delay. Kardelj wrote Tito disgustedly from Sofia on December 23, 1944, that Traicho Kostov, the Bulgarian Communist leader with whom he was principally negotiating, wanted "far from what we proposed," indeed was willing to agree to no more than a "defensive alliance."

The main points of difference were whether Bulgaria should have equality in the proposed federation with each of the six Jugoslav republics or with Jugoslavia as one unit; what should be the new Bulgar-Jugoslav frontier, especially which nation should have the debatable Pirin district; and whether Bulgaria as an enemy country had the right to enter into an international agreement before a peace treaty had been signed. These and other controversial issues were to be fought and refought without decision for the next three years.

Real progress toward a Jugoslav-Bulgar rapprochement seemed to be registered when Prime Minister Georgi Dimitrov visited Marshal Tito at Bled in August 1947 and announcement was made that a treaty of friendship and a customs union were in prospect. Nothing was said publicly about the future of Macedonia; the ancient "apple of discord" still dangled tantalizingly between the two countries. Tito indicated that he still hoped federation might be the solution when he visited Sofia in November to sign the treaty. Bulgaria and Jugoslavia were being bound together so closely, he said, that "federation will be a mere formality." His optimism did not turn out to be justified. Tentative agreement was reached on specific phases of the Macedonian problem, such as the future of the

---

[2] As a hedge against the possibility that Greece would end up in the Western camp, Stalin in September 1944 instructed Ambassador Gusev, Soviet representative on the European Advisory Commission, to see whether the Bulgarians might not be left in possession of the parts of Western Thrace assigned to them by Hitler. But this was overplaying the Russian hand, and when Philip E. Mosely, the American deputy, replied that it would be intolerable to leave an ex-enemy in possession of an ally's territory, the proposal was dropped.

Pirin district; but it was most unsatisfactory to Sofia, and the whole controversial question was in fact still open when the Cominform resolution of June 1948 ended all prospect of friendship, let alone of federation. The discussion of the proposal for federation actually contributed, as we shall see in the next chapter, to Moscow's growing mistrust of Tito and hence to the final break.

Even after Stalin had lost Tito as an ally he found difficulty in exploiting the Macedonian question profitably in Soviet propaganda. The natural course would have been to come out openly for transferring control over Jugoslav Macedonia from the new enemies in Belgrade to the eager sycophants in Sofia. But to indicate that Tito's fall would produce this result would have strengthened his régime and ended the hope of Cominform forces overturning it from within. The best that Moscow could do was to permit the revival of Bulgarian propaganda for the creation of a separate Macedonian republic, in the name of Macedonian nationalism, but to take no part in it officially.

Even this limited Bulgarian propaganda complicated things for the Greek Communists. The Greek people suspected one wing of the Greek Communist Party of being willing to contribute Greek territory to bring a separate Macedonian state into existence. The suspicion had been strengthened by a story that one of the old-line Greek Communists, Yannis Ioannides, had agreed in July 1943 with a Bulgarian Communist named Dushan Daskalov to carve a Macedonian state out of Greek, Bulgarian and Jugoslav territory after the war and incorporate it directly into the Soviet Union. The plan as reported was grandiose; apparently Turkey was to be deprived of Istanbul, which was to be included in the Macedonian Soviet Socialist Republic along with Salonika. Russia would at last control the Straits and dominate the Aegean. When the American intelligence first got wind of the story it assumed that it had been planted by Nazi propagandists; but then it learnt that Ioannides had visited Moscow just before his meeting with Daskalov, and other bits of corroborative evidence indicated the probability that the Soviets actually were setting up an alternative design for use in the event that Tito proved troublesome or Bulgaria in some manner escaped the Soviet net. True or not, the story aided the Greek anti-Communists by raising popular fears that a Soviet-dominated régime might partition Greece.

To add one more convolution to the involved situation, a strong element among the Greek Communists had always hoped to bring Communist Greece into a federation of East European Communist states—precisely the sort of federation which Russia was determined never to tolerate lest it limit her own control of the area.[3] By something more than a coincidence, the announcement that a "Free Greek Government" was to be established by the Greek Communists had occurred at about the same time that Tito and Dimitrov were meeting at Bled; and it also is significant that when such a government actually was set up in December 1947, with General Markos Vafiades as a principal leader, it was not accorded recognition by the Soviet Union or any of the satellites. Whether other satellite leaders were involved in the project, Gomulka in Poland, for example, or Clementis in Czechoslovakia, is not known. But the signs that Markos was suspect in Moscow from then on are unmistakable.

Tito's expulsion from the Cominform faced Soviet policy-makers with a hard choice in Greece. Tito had been an indispensable middleman in transporting Soviet help to the Greek rebels and their most active supporter on his own account. Soviet military equipment and arms went to the rebel bands over Jugoslav railways and Jugoslav food and uniforms nourished and clothed them. When the mountain fighters found themselves in a tight corner the Jugoslav frontiers always were open to them, their wounded were succored and cared for in Jugoslav hospitals, reënforcements were trained in Jugoslav camps and the Greek children whom they evacuated (or kidnapped) on their retreats found homes in Jugoslav institutions. Neither of Greece's other satellite neighbors, Bulgaria and Albania, was so well situated geographically to provide this help. Besides, all Greeks, including Communists, had hateful memories of wartime experiences in Albania and under the Bulgarian occupation of Greek Macedonia; and these memories would not down despite the ideological affinities existing between the Greek guerrillas and the Com-

---

[3] *Pravda* in January 1948 condemned the idea of a "Balkan or Danubian federation including Poland, Czechoslovakia *and Greece*" (my italics) and forced Dimitrov to disown it (*cf.* Chapter XVII).

munist régimes now installed in Sofia and Tirana. No such memories troubled the relations of Greek and Jugoslav Communists. But now the Jugoslav Partisan leader who had been extolled among Greek Communists not only for his outstanding Communist zeal but as the closest and most helpful of allies was suddenly declared an enemy of all true Communists and the Greek rebel bands were ordered to cease traffic with him.

The conflict between the call of warfare in the Greek mountains as heard by the guerrillas directly and the call of international revolutionary tactics as relayed from Moscow split the Greek Communists. In the ensuing confusion the Greek guerrilla chieftain, General Markos Vafiades, disappeared from view. After his absence had been noted for some time both in Greece and abroad, the Greek rebel radio simply announced, early in February 1949, that he had been superseded. But soon afterwards it admitted that the Greek Communist Party had been purging itself of "opportunists" and "national deviationists" and was now being reorganized on stricter "monolithic" lines. Evidently Titoism had an appeal for some of the Greek mountain fighters, and evidently Markos was one of them.

The man chosen to succeed him was the same Ioannides who reportedly had been ready to sacrifice Salonika and the rest of Greek Macedonia in 1943. Markos and other nationalistically inclined Rightists having been purged or cowed, and with Moscow's unquestioning servants in charge, the "People's Liberation Front" adopted a propaganda line like the Bulgarian and called for "the union of Macedonia as an independent equal state in a confederation of Balkan peoples" (February 27, 1949). In March, Nicolas Zachariades, the Secretary-General of the Party, and Constantin Karageorgis, commanding the guerrillas in the Peloponnesos, attended a meeting in the mountains of northwest Greece described by the rebel radio as concerned principally with building a "Front of Macedonian National Liberation." All Macedonians—Greek, Jugoslav, Bulgar, Albanian and Turk—were to be brought into an "autonomous" state under Cominform auspices. The composition of the new rebel "government" announced in April confirmed the trend: it contained two non-Greeks described as "Slav-Macedonians."

Jugoslavia reacted strongly. Lazar Kolishevski, Premier of the Macedonian People's Republic in Jugoslavia, charged that the Cominform was manœuvring to break up the Jugoslav state by reviving the propaganda for Macedonian independence. It did not mind breaking the unity of the Greek "democratic" movement, he said, provided it thought it could damage Tito at the same time. Acts followed words. On July 23, 1949, Foreign Minister Kardelj announced that since the Greek Communist Party had entered into a conspiracy with the Cominform at Jugoslavia's expense his Government was closing the Greek frontier to the guerrillas and withdrawing all support from them. This was merely formal acknowledgment of a state of affairs that had existed for some months, but it marked an important stage in the reorientation of Jugoslav foreign policy toward better relations with the West. Simultaneously, propaganda emanating from Belgrade began to emphasize that the Macedonian People's Republic of Jugoslavia offered a natural rallying ground "for all Macedonians who lack a national home"—for the Macedonians, that is, of Greece and Bulgaria. Tito was setting up his own Macedonian Piedmont.

All through the Greek civil war Jugoslavia had refused to participate in the attempts of the United Nations to bring it to an end. The Belgrade Government religiously followed the Soviet line that the General Assembly had no right to send a commission to see whether foreign aid were reaching the rebel bands from the north, and, like the Bulgarian and Albanian Governments, it refused to coöperate with the commission and denied the veracity of its reports. Today it no longer makes any bones about having helped Markos. Indeed, it boasts of the magnitude of its effort,[4] emphasizing that without it he could never have fought so successfully and so long as he did and that it was when Moscow ordered Jugoslavia expelled from the Communist family, cutting off the Greek revolutionaries from their main source of supplies, that he was finally defeated and disgraced. Even after the rift in the Cominform, the Jugoslavs con-

---

[4] According to *Borba*, Belgrade, November 7, 1949, Jugoslavia cared for 6,317 Greek rebel wounded at a cost of about $1,600,000 and sheltered some 11,000 Greek children at a cost of about $1,320,000.

tinued for a time to provide asylum for Markos' men and care for his wounded, and when the rebel radio was forced out of Greece they allowed it to function temporarily near Belgrade. A report of the United Nations Special Committee on the Balkans, published August 25, 1949, covering the period October 1948-July 1949, confirmed the fact of this Jugoslav help to the guerrillas and noted that direction-finder tests had established the eventual transfer of the rebel radio from Belgrade to the vicinity of Bucharest. According to M. S. Handler, the well-informed correspondent of *The New York Times* in Belgrade, all forms of Jugoslav assistance actually ceased as early as November 1948, only four months after Jugoslavia's expulsion from the Cominform. If so, this would indicate that Tito had already heard that Markos was supplanted and would be the scapegoat for the rebel débâcle now in the cards.

The next Soviet move was to try to place the blame for this débâcle on Jugoslavia by attributing it to the cessation of Jugoslav aid and by attributing that, in turn, not to the Cominform attack on Jugoslavia, in which the new Communist leadership in Greece was participating, but to Jugoslavia's alleged shift to "the Western imperialist camp" and hence into secret alliance with the "Monarcho-Fascist" Greek Government. Tito retaliated by telling a Macedonian audience on August 2, 1949, that the Greek people's struggle for "social and national liberation, for the creation of a better, more progressive democratic Greece," had been stifled and defeated, not by their enemies abroad but by their own leaders in the Greek Communist Party, whose only interest was to make out that the responsibility for their colossal failure did not rest on the Soviets, where it belonged, but on Jugoslavia.

By 1950 Tito was ready to normalize relations with the constitutional government of Greece. The opportunity for doing so without loss of face seemed to come when the Greek elections resulted in the formation of a Center coalition government under General Plastiras. Constantin Tsaldaris, the man always cited in Jugoslavia as the incarnation of Greek "Monarcho-Fascism," was not included. A Jugoslav ambassador was dispatched to Athens in May, but the Greek Government kept him waiting to present his credentials, and soon an argument arose as to the treatment of the non-Greeks in Greek Macedonia. According to the Jugoslav press they were being subjected to a policy of "nationalization," meaning apparently that they were not allowed to use the Macedonian Slav dialect but only Greek. The Greek reply was that this was an exclusively internal Greek affair, all inhabitants of Greek Macedonia being Greek citizens since the exchange of populations with Bulgaria following the First World War. The Jugoslav Ambassador-designate thereupon returned to Belgrade. In a dispatch datelined Belgrade, June 24, 1950, Gaston Coblentz, Balkan correspondent of the *New York Herald Tribune,* pointed out that Tito was having trouble keeping his Macedonian population as happy as a dictator's subjects are supposed to be, and that advocacy of minority rights in Greek Macedonia was designed to fortify the loyalty of his own Macedonians and encourage them to resist Cominform propaganda.

Western diplomats hoped that the failure to establish normal relations between Athens and Belgrade might be only temporary. The fall of the Plastiras cabinet and the formation in September 1950 of a government under Sophocles Venizelos, supported by Tsaldaris, did not strengthen the hope; neither did the Jugoslav vote in the Security Council in favor of a Soviet motion to investigate "increasing terrorism" in Greece. On the other hand, one main issue between the two nations, the return of Greek children who (as the Greeks put it) had been abducted by the Greek guerrillas and detained in Jugoslavia, or who (as the Jugoslavs put it) were given a refuge in Jugoslavia from their Fascist persecutors, seemed to advance a step toward settlement with word that Tito was willing to send back all children whose families asked it. Shortly afterwards Prime Minister Venizelos made a conciliatory move by announcing that emergency shipments of supplies to alleviate the Jugoslav drought would be permitted to pass through the port of Salonika. The next step would be to repair and reopen the Belgrade-Salonika railway, closed since the war. In their own selfish interests the two governments should make urgent efforts to reach at least a modus vivendi. Only Moscow profits from the continuance of a situation in which if Soviet armies enter the Balkans the Jugoslavs would not have a back door through which to receive Western war materials and the Greeks would be as exposed to the new invaders as they were to the Nazis.

It was a bitter decision for the Russians to end the Greek civil war, but they saw the risks of any other course. One factor was the growing strength of the Greek Army. Following accepted international practice, the United States had supplied the legal Greek Government with arms. As a result, the armies taking the field in 1949 were well equipped and had good morale. Another influential factor was that the United Nations Commission had kept world opinion posted about the aid reaching the rebels from Communist sources abroad. Thirdly, now that Jugoslav railways could no longer be used, the best overland line for Soviet shipments via Bulgaria was cut. In future, Russian help could not be so easily disguised, would involve Soviet prestige directly and hence if supplied at all would have to be supplied on a scale to be decisive. This would amount to open intervention and involved the risk of general war.

In the spring of 1949 the Communist and fellow-traveller press of the world had still been talking bravely of certain victory for the Greek "democrats." "The Monarchists could never repeat the scale of their offensive in Grammos last summer," and "this year will mark the turning point in the task of liberating Greece." [5] But after General Papagos's victories at Vitsi and Grammos that summer the Russian decision to liquidate the civil war became final. On October 9 the Central Committee of the Greek Communist Party accepted defeat. It held that the hopes of the year before had been correct, "under the conditions when the Tito clique had not yet openly gone over to the imperialist camp and pretended to be a friend of the Greek democratic movement." Now, however, the Jugoslavs had "stabbed the Democratic Army in the back" and the military struggle had to cease. [6] The rebel radio broadcast the news on November 4, summarizing the reasons as follows: "Tito's treachery; the exploitation of this treachery by the Americans; the latter's growing determination to hold their bridgehead in Greece;

[5] *The New Central European Observer*, London, April 30, 1949.
[6] *For a Lasting Peace, for a People's Democracy!*, Bucharest, November 18, 1949.

increased U.S. aid to Monarcho-Fascism; and so forth." The Party line, the radio added, was formally changed. Henceforth the emphasis would be on "the organization and leadership of the political and economic struggles of all the strata of the working people—above all, the working class and employees, the displaced peasants, the hundreds of thousands of wounded, the war victims, the women and the youth."

The admission that Greek nationalism had won a military victory and that Greek Communism must try to regain its hold on the masses by returning to the first principles of social action did not mean, of course, that propaganda warfare or even terroristic acts had to cease. Soon Nicolas Zachariades was writing in the Cominform journal that the American aim of creating a "Belgrade-Athens axis" must be fought "concretely, daily, constantly and tirelessly." As an example of what he meant he suggested sabotage of Jugoslav railway lines. But nothing could hide the fact that once again the feud with Belgrade had damaged Soviet Russia. It had drawn attention to the difference between her interests and those of her satellites. It had split the Greek Communist forces. It had helped the Truman Doctrine achieve its purpose sooner than might otherwise have happened.

In the autumn of 1950 as so often in the past Russia faced the old dilemma that if she favored one Balkan nation too openly she would outrage the others. The Soviet leaders now were aware, too, that when they spoke of a nation they could not exclude the Communists in it: Tito had added a complication to the Soviet game instead of simplifying it. The temptation to set the Bulgars loose against Tito must nevertheless have been very strong. The Bulgarian Army was newly equipped with Russian arms and had been reorganized by the new Minister of Defense, Lieutenant-General Peter Panchevsky, a former Soviet Army officer. Another former Soviet officer, General Novikov, was in command at the key center of Plovdiv. The size of the Bulgarian Army was not known precisely—certainly it was in excess of the 55,000 permitted by the peace treaty—but in any case, though growing, it was still smaller than the Jugoslav Army and inferior to it also in training and morale. Nevertheless Korea had shown that Soviet tanks could do much to stiffen a satellite army, and Western military men could not be sure how many tanks Moscow had sent to Bulgaria and how many more would arrive in an emergency.

By anyone's reckoning the outcome of an invasion of Jugoslavia was uncertain. Nor could anyone reckon how wide the reaction against an open act of aggression might be. So Moscow hesitated, fingering both the nationalist and Marxist triggers, not seeing how to pull one without losing the chance to pull the other.

# XVII

## BULGARIA CONTAMINATED

> Great are your achievements, Comrade
> Kostov, as the builder of the Party, as the
> teacher and instructor of the Party mem-
> bers. Under your leadership and inspired
> by your heroic life, thousands of Com-
> munists were educated into unquestionable
> loyalty to the Party.
>
> Declaration by the Central Committee of the
> Bulgarian Communist Party on Traicho Kostov's
> 50th birthday in 1947

ONLY a month after the Greek rebel
radio announced that Markos had been liquidated, victim of a fatal
inability to forget that he was a Greek as well as a Communist, the
Bulgarian Communist Party was forced to admit that nationalist
symptoms had appeared in its ranks also. The sufferer was the
Deputy Premier of Bulgaria, Traicho Kostov, Secretary-General of
the Party since 1944. On March 27, 1949, he was deprived of his
office and dismissed from the Politburo. We have been supplied with
a full Stalinist diagnosis of his case.

Kostov had been a member of the Party since 1919, had spent
fourteen years in Bulgarian prisons, had been Bulgaria's leading
Communist organizer and would have seemed as immune to criticism on the score of discipline and orthodoxy as Georgi Dimitrov
himself, chief Bulgarian émigré in Moscow, hero of the Reichstag
fire trial and former Secretary-General of the Comintern. It was to
Dimitrov that Kostov relinquished control in 1945 when Dimitrov
returned to Sofia in the wake of the Red Army; and Dimitrov made
him one of his trusted lieutenants, as Deputy Prime Minister and
chairman of the economic and financial planning committee. Kostov

[ 199

wrote the Constitution of 1947, the Party pamphlets and the Five
Year Plan. As things turned out, the most risky of his functions was
planning and administering the national economy, for it involved
making Bulgaria a service station for the Soviet economic machine.
But this danger was not apparent at first. Kostov's long years of
hazardous service in the underground, the intensity of his Communist faith and Dimitrov's affection and favor combined to make
him the Number 2 man in the régime, and when Dimitrov became
ill his mantle fell naturally enough on Kostov as Acting Prime
Minister.

It was from this pinnacle of power that Kostov was toppled in
March 1949. The grounds for his expulsion from the Politburo
and his removal as Acting Prime Minister were "gross political and
Party errors," "insincere and unfriendly policy regarding the Soviet
Union" and "nationalistic deviations." On April 15, the news
leaked out that Dimitrov had been sent to Russia "on leave" to
repair his health. The Prime Minister's illness had evidently inaugurated a struggle for his succession. At the right moment the
Kremlin issued its orders. Kostov, leader of the wing of the Party
that had been more closely identified with the revolutionary struggle
inside the country than with the international headquarters in Moscow, was dismissed and disgraced, and Vassil Kolarov, an elderly
man of 73 who had spent most of the time since the 'twenties in
Moscow, part of it as an official of the Comintern, became Acting
Prime Minister in his place. Subsequently, Kostov was removed
from the Central Committee of the Party, then from his position as
a deputy in Parliament, and finally from the Party itself. On July 20
Parliament voted to have him indicted and tried for "economic
sabotage."

Kolarov explained that his predecessor's crimes were particularly
atrocious since they were not haphazard but formed "a system of
political mistakes based on a glaringly expressed nationalist deviationism and anti-Bolshevik attitude towards the methods of Party
leadership." Specifically, during the time that Kostov was acting
as Prime Minister he had broadened the law against divulging state
secrets and had applied it to the officials dealing with the Soviet
trade representatives in Bulgaria; as a result, the Soviet agents had

not been able to find out at what prices Bulgaria was selling her products to capitalist countries. In this way Kostov revealed his mistrust of the U.S.S.R. and went counter to the accepted rule that "secrets and commercialism" do not figure in Bulgarian-Soviet relations. A man's attitude toward the Soviet Union, Kolarov explained, defines his whole ideological orientation; anti-Sovietism is "the most heinous form of national deviation." [1]

The reader will recall that when opposition to the Soviets appeared in Poland it was dealt with at first quite circumspectly. Gomulka's connection with Tito was carefully concealed. Nothing of the sort was attempted in Kostov's case. By now the Cominform acknowledged that Titoism was not peculiar to Jugoslavia but was an infectious disease menacing the whole Stalinist empire.

The events which awakened Kostov's resistance were like those which had antagonized other satellite leaders. In 1948 the Bulgarian tobacco crop amounted to about 20 million kilos, of which the Soviets bought between 18 and 19 million kilos at arbitrarily fixed prices. When the time came for Bulgaria to market what remained of her crop, after the Soviets had taken the lion's share and after she had provided for her own domestic consumption, she found that she was competing in Italy, Egypt and New York with her own Bulgarian tobacco, offered by the Soviets at less than prevailing world prices. The Soviets profited in the same way with attar of roses, of which Bulgaria possesses almost a world monopoly. The Soviet purchasing agents in Sofia bought up the entire 1948 crop and resold it at higher prices in New York.[2] Later they laid hands on the store of this valuable essence accumulated during the war by the Bulgarian National Bank and disposed of it at whatever prices the world market would stand. Kostov apparently could not bear to see his country cheated in this way. In one sense it does not matter that the sums which the Soviet Government credits to the Bulgarian Government for its purchases in Bulgaria bear no relationship to the prices at which it later resells those same products abroad; it is all a matter of bookkeeping anyway, and Bulgaria cannot win. What does matter is that as the Soviet Government resells in hard-cur-

---

[1] *For a Lasting Peace, for a People's Democracy!*, Bucharest, May 15, 1949.
[2] *The Economist*, London, July 16, 1949.

rency areas, the dollars which it gets from the sale of Bulgarian products go to finance imports not into Bulgaria but into the Soviet Union. That ends the last vestige of Bulgaria's freedom of economic manœuvre.

Bukharin might have called this sort of finagle the absence of "selfish competition," just as Kolarov called it the absence of "secrets and commercialism." Kostov decided that it was good old-fashioned exploitation, the sort of thing which he had always heard denounced as a mean capitalist trick. When he tried to tighten up the government agencies which dealt with the Soviet purchasing agents, however, he found that he was a "nationalist deviationist."

The Sofia morning papers of November 30, 1949, carried the text of the formal indictment against Kostov,[3] based on a 32,000-word statement purporting to have been signed by him in prison and on similar statements by ten codefendants, all of them high government and Party officials. Kostov is described as a consistent supporter of "Left-sectarian," Trotskyite policies. While an émigré in Moscow in 1933–34 he supposedly formed contacts with many other Trotskyites, including Bela Kun and Tito; plotted to replace Dimitrov and Kolarov as leaders of the Bulgarian Communist Party; and, as an official of the Balkan Secretariat of Communist Parties, recommended Tito for political work in Jugoslavia. All this seems vague and farfetched, no reason being given why with such a consistently bad record he was allowed to continue as Secretary-General of the Central Committee of the Party and was promoted to be acting head of the government.

The indictment goes on to make the bland statement that when Germany's "final defeat" had been sealed on the Soviet front as far back as 1942 (*sic*), the British and American intelligence services, faced with this apparently unwelcome fact, and seeing how Soviet prestige was growing in Southeastern Europe, began to smuggle their agents into the underground Communist Party. Among those allegedly recruited besides Kostov was a former Minister of Finance, Stefanov, who was accused of having given the British information on the budget and on military expenditures in 1946 and 1947, and

---

[3] A translation in English is to be found in a supplement to the *New Times*, Moscow, December 7, 1949.

Nikola Pavlov, former administrative secretary of the Politburo and Deputy Minister of Construction. These three were accused of having formed a "conspiratorial center" aimed at "overthrowing the lawful government of the country and replacing it by a criminal government headed by Kostov." The indictment also asserted that they had "endeavored to disrupt business, commercial and other economic ties between Bulgaria and the other People's Democracies headed by the Soviet Union, in order to deprive our country of the generous and disinterested aid of the U.S.S.R."

Of special interest is the further charge that Kostov "entered into secret criminal connections with Jugoslav leaders" with the intention of "depriving Bulgaria of her national sovereignty, territorial integrity and independence by joining her to Jugoslavia." The "plot" for a federation is supposed to have begun when Kardelj, as already recounted, visited Sofia towards the end of 1944. Dimitrov was still in Moscow, Kostov was the undisputed leader on the spot and it was with him that Kardelj discussed the pros and cons of the project. The indictment admits that Kostov made no secret of this; he "informed the leadership of the Bulgarian Communist Party, which he headed in 1944, that Kardelj had been in the country and had suggested a federation between Bulgaria and Jugoslavia," as well as that the Jugoslavs would submit a written proposal to this effect shortly. What he failed to tell his colleagues, says the indictment, was that the arrangement "was directed against the U.S.S.R." According to the indictment, Kardelj told Kostov that "the British and Americans had supplied the Jugoslav guerrillas with arms and ammunition on condition that, when the war was over, Tito would keep Jugoslavia away from the U.S.S.R.;" that in Tito's view Jugoslavia should "not definitely tie herself with the U.S.S.R., but should pursue a policy of her own and maintain and develop ties with the Western states;" that he would request withdrawal of Russian troops as soon as the war was over; that Soviet troops should leave Bulgaria too; and that the best means of bringing this about would be for Bulgaria to join Jugoslavia immediately, for then she would no longer be regarded as an enemy but as part of an Allied state, which would make the presence of Soviet troops on her soil "superfluous and entirely unjustified." Kostov contended that he had expressed doubts about all this, giving among other reasons his opinion that the Allies might oppose the idea of federation; and in fact the British Government did issue a formal warning that Bulgaria could not take any independent action until after there had been a treaty of peace. On this point the indictment merely mentions Kardelj's comment that if Allied protests were made they would be window-dressing. The project failed in the end, the indictment concludes, because of a warning sent by Dimitrov from Moscow.

In the summer of 1946, Kostov was sent on a formal visit of friendship to Belgrade on behalf of the Bulgarian Communist Party and is supposed to have used the opportunity to continue his sub-versive work. Alexander Rankovich, Jugoslav Minister of the Interior, is alleged to have talked with him about Tito's plan to create "a great comity of Southeastern European countries," while Tito himself spoke approvingly of the idea of a federation which "would dictate its will in the Balkans, and would represent a serious factor in international politics." The plot supposedly was carried further when Tito came to Sofia in November 1947 to sign the treaty of friendship. On this occasion, it was alleged, he urged Kostov to reorganize the Bulgarian Communist Party, form a new government and proclaim the union with Jugoslavia. If he found he needed help, Tito is supposed to have said, the Jugoslav Army stood ready to supply it, and since the help would be "within the framework of the federation," it would be a domestic affair and "no one could qualify it as an act of aggression."

Such, said the indictment, was the "criminal conspiracy against the state of Bulgaria, plotted and headed by Kostov." Before examining the evidence we might note that on their face some of the Bulgarian Government's contentions seemed improbable. Kardelj had reported that Kostov was very reserved on the federation question, indeed much more reserved about it than Dimitrov and the others. And Tito has asserted that he always distrusted Kostov as the most anti-Jugoslav of all the Bulgarian leaders. This would indicate that although Kostov's complaint against Moscow was similar to Tito's, he did not support Tito in the Cominform dispute. In September 1948, in fact, he strongly attacked Tito and his colleagues; but of course he may simply have been endeavoring to offset criticisms being voiced against him by Party colleagues.

The trial was held in December 1949 in accordance with a new law, passed for the purpose, before a new court, set up for the purpose and from which there was no appeal. The sensation of the trial, and something new for Communist judges, was that Kostov in open court repudiated the confession which he was alleged to have signed in prison. The whole case against him was based on that confession and on the similar confessions of the other defendants. These did not revoke what they had said in jail but instead fell over themselves to confirm the worst of it and to find new grounds to inculpate both Kostov and themselves. While Kostov did not hide the fact that he had opposed Dimitrov in ideological and Party matters, or that he had miscalculated the strength of *kulaks* and other Bulgarian reactionary elements, he did categorically deny that he had ever been a spy or foreign agent, that he had had anything to do with sending Tito to Jugoslavia in 1934 or that he had been Tito's stooge in the negotiations for a Jugoslav-Bulgarian federation.

The judges at first could not believe their ears, and when Kostov insisted on repudiating his "confession" in spite of hoots from the audience and rebukes by his own counsel, they hastily adjourned court for half an hour to enable him to "rest" and "refresh his memory." After the rest period he still stuck to his guns. For two days the Communist press maintained a stunned silence. Then *Pravda* commented that Kostov had a "soft and oily voice" and the "cunning eyes of a thief," details which his colleagues might have noticed in the last twenty or thirty years, and a "bent back," which *Pravda* did not bother to explain he had acquired in 1924 when he jumped from a window in attempting to escape torture by the Sofia police.[4]

The account of the negotiations for a Bulgarian-Jugoslav federation produced at the Kostov trial omits many well known facts and runs contrary to many others. Nothing is said about the active and

---

[4] *Cf. The Economist*, London, December 24, 1949; for details of the trial see also *The New York Times*, December 8 and successive days.

continuous part taken by Soviet officials in the negotiations. No hint is given that Kostov had been in favor of simply a defensive alliance. No reference is made to *Pravda's* criticism of Dimitrov in January 1948 for saying that the ultimate goal was a federation of all the East European peoples. In fact, one would gather from reading the Kostov indictment that Moscow knew little about the project for federation and consistently opposed it; that among the Bulgarian Communist leaders Kostov was the one who particularly favored it; that Dimitrov had never agreed to federation, and had not figured in the negotiations except to warn against it; and that the obnoxious suggestion for including other Balkan and Danubian countries originated entirely with Tito and his stooge, Kostov. Evidently Soviet apologists felt it necessary to rewrite a chapter of history that had become embarrassing.

The pretense that Moscow had no part in the negotiations has been demolished by Mosha Pijade.[5] It seems that when Kardelj left Sofia in December 1944 it was agreed that Bulgarian and Jugoslav representatives should reconvene in Belgrade the next month. But the Kremlin disapproved and the negotiations were transferred to Moscow. Not a word was said at the Kostov trial about this. Actually Kostov was not even present in Moscow; Dimitrov was still there to advise the Bulgarian delegation, and Kostov probably was needed at home. The chief negotiators were Vyshinsky and Zorin for the Soviet Union, Prime Minister Georgiev and Minister of the Interior Yugov for Bulgaria and Pijade for Jugoslavia. Although he could not go to Moscow, Kostov had prepared in advance the Bulgarian draft of a treaty (a copy of it exists in the Jugoslav archives, says Pijade, annotated and corrected in Kostov's hand). Whereas the Jugoslav draft proposed a definitive declaration that the two countries "are uniting" in a federal state, the Kostov draft was more preliminary, for the two governments would merely "declare that they are proceeding to a union," with such joint institutions as might be finally determined in an eventual constitution.

As things turned out, neither draft was formally discussed, for Vyshinsky indicated that the Soviet Union had decided that the first step should be a treaty of political, economic and military coöpera-

[5] *Yugoslav Fortnightly*, Belgrade, January 27, 1950.

tion (as Kostov had favored in his first talk with Kardelj). Vyshinsky asked Pijade to draw up a text; and using that as a basis Vyshinsky then prepared a draft of his own. On January 27, 1945, the three delegations agreed on the final text.[6] A day earlier the Bulgarians received word from Sofia that the British Government had just presented a démarche against federation. Pijade tells how letters thereupon were prepared for Georgiev and Tito to exchange when the treaty was ratified, reaffirming their intention of realizing "a federation of the South Slav peoples in the shortest possible time." This indicated that the federation was being merely deferred until Britain could no longer object on legal grounds. Obviously the Soviet representatives must have approved.

Bulgarian and Jugoslav aims conflicted from the start, says Pijade, in detail as well as in the general objective. Most notably, Bulgaria demanded equal status with the six Jugoslav republics as a single unit, whereas the Jugoslavs wanted a federation in which Bulgaria would have equality with each of the Jugoslav republics. He says that the first time the two delegations called on Stalin, Dimitrov argued that because Bulgaria had been an independent state she could not merge her identity in a group of seven; to which Pijade replied that Serbia and Motenegro had longer records as sovereign states than Bulgaria, and that he supposed the Croats, who had been independent a thousand years ago, were at least equal to the Bulgarians in importance. A couple of days later, continues Pijade, the two delegations were again received by Stalin, this time at a state banquet. Stalin himself reopened the subject, and gave his opinion that Bulgaria ought to form one of the seven federal units. Pijade adds: "The Bulgarians said nothing, while I had nothing to say."

When the conferees left Moscow the intention was that the treaty and the accompanying letters should be signed at Belgrade in February. Before then, however, the Jugoslav Ambassador reported from Sofia that although the British had vetoed a Jugoslav-Bulgarian federation they did not close the door to the idea of a wider grouping

[6] Pijade notes that a copy of the Vyshinsky text exists in the Jugoslav archives, that he has his own manuscript copy of the final text and that the Jugoslav archives also contain a copy of it in Russian, initialled personally by Zorin, of the Soviet Foreign Office, as "seen," that is, approved.

including Albania and two pro-Western states, Greece and Turkey. The Russians seem to have decided that with so much talk of a broad federation in the air it would be best for the time being to postpone even the Bulgarian-Jugoslav treaty of friendship. This was done. Pijade's sarcastic comment is that the case made out against Kostov was very unjust to the British—for if Bulgaria would have lost her independence by joining a federation in which she was only one among seven, as the prosecution affirmed, then it was the British who saved it by their veto.

As for the implication that Dimitrov was not involved, it is easily refuted. The plan for a treaty of friendship, dropped in 1945, was revived when Dimitrov was in Bled in the summer of 1947 and a treaty was signed when Tito visited Sofia in November. Rankovich has asserted that the treaty was still looked on at that time as simply a step towards federation.[7] Dimitrov said during a visit to Bucharest that the goal was a federation of the East European peoples, plus Greece. He seems to have talked in the same way when Prime Minister Hoxha of Albania came to Sofia to sign a treaty of friendship and mutual aid on December 16. Kardelj implied that bigger things were in the making when he presented the text of the Bulgarian treaty for ratification in the Jugoslav Presidium on January 8, 1948; it was an augury, he stated, of "collaboration between the Balkan-Danubian peoples." Moscow decided to lose no time in scotching the idea that anything of the sort would be permitted. *Pravda* wrote angrily on January 28 that a "Balkan or Danubian federation including Poland, Czechoslovakia and Greece" was inadmissible; "these lands do not need a problematical or farfetched federation or confederation and customs union but the strengthening and the defense of their independence and sovereignty by way of mobilization and organization of internal popular democratic strength." Dimitrov accepted the rebuke, and crawled. Neither he nor any member of the Bulgarian Government, he announced, "thinks or has ever thought of the creation of an Eastern bloc under any form whatsoever," and he thanked *Pravda* for its "valuable and useful warning."

Tito, who did not seize the same opportunity for "self-criticism,"

[7] *Yugoslav Fortnightly,* Belgrade, February 1949.

has since told why.[8] In February and early March of 1948 Kardelj and Djilas were in Moscow trying to speed up Soviet economic aid. A Bulgarian delegation was there at the same time, headed by Dimitrov, Kolarov and Kostov. "In the presence of that delegation," asserts Tito, "Stalin himself imperatively demanded the immediate conclusion of an act of federation between Jugoslavia and Bulgaria, while on the other hand the Soviet was against a federation with Albania." But in view of the fact that Jugoslav relations with the Soviet Union "were already strained" Tito looked on this renewal of the old plan with a fishy eye. "We came to the conclusion," he continues, "that the demand was put forward in order to facilitate the overthrow and subjugation of Jugoslavia."

Speaking of this matter with me, Tito explained that the creation of a Jugoslav-Bulgarian federation would have brought many Bulgarian leaders to Belgrade. Some would have received high places in the new joint government, and as they would have been under Russian orders Moscow would in this way have received a direct voice in Jugoslav affairs. He already was subject to so many kinds of Soviet interference that he was unwilling to open new doors for it. In any case, he added, not he but Dimitrov had taken the initiative for a federation to include Rumania and perhaps even Czechoslovakia. Dimitrov was unhappy over Bulgaria's increasing dependence on the Soviet Union and hoped to reverse the process by finding a place for her in a strong grouping. To a question as to why Dimitrov had not realized that this would get him into difficulties in Moscow, Tito replied that Dimitrov had just been in Bucharest, where his head had been turned a bit by the enthusiastic reception which he received from the Rumanian Communists and by the discovery that they too were restive under the tight Soviet rein. As a result, said Tito, Dimitrov became a bit too daring. Whether Dimitrov suffered physical punishment will never be known. He died in Russia in the summer of 1949 and Stalin stood among the honor guard by his catafalque.

Of all these matters no word was said at Kostov's trial. On December 14, 1949, he was found guilty on all charges and sentenced to death. The ten other defendants had tearfully inculpated both

---

[8] Tito's speech at the opening of the Jugoslav National Assembly, April 26, 1950 (*Yugoslav Fortnightly*, Belgrade, May 5, 1950).

him and themselves in every imaginable sort of crime against the Bulgarian state, the Bulgarian Communist Party and, worst of all, the Soviet Union. They received prison sentences and fines. Kostov, according to witnesses, took the verdict calmly. It was the second time he had heard a death sentence pronounced against him, the first having been in 1942 when a royal Bulgarian military court ordered him shot for resistance to the Germans. This time the sentence was carried out. He was hanged on December 16, and the next day the Sofia press carried the text of a new "confession." There was of course no way of verifying it. It seems wildly improbable that after being sentenced Kostov would have recanted, even under torture, what he had previously maintained under torture and the threat of death.

A day after this show of Communist justice the electors of Bulgaria gathered in their polling places, decorated with pictures of Stalin, Bulgarian flags and doves of peace, to take part in national "elections." These had been scheduled for November but delayed to give time for the complete elimination of "Kostovism"—called "nothing but Titoism on Bulgarian soil" by Kostov's successor, Deputy Prime Minister Vulko Chervenkov (described to me by an American diplomat as "the most rigid and unintelligent of the Bulgarian Communists, with a neck like a bull and a face like a bullfrog"). As there was only a single list of candidates, the news that this list had been elected was not startling.

As good as any of the obituaries for Kostov was one inserted by Pijade in the speech already quoted: "If Traicho Kostov was hanged merely for wanting a federation with Jugoslavia, although he insisted on precisely the same form of federation, with Bulgarian hegemony, as all the other members of the Bulgarian Politburo, then, from their standpoint, from the standpoint of the indictment of that shocking trial, they have hanged an innocent man. But though they did hang a certain Kostov, the truth about the federation of the Southern Slavs cannot be hanged. Neither the hangman in Sofia nor his teachers are tall enough for that."

# XVIII

## PRESCRIPTION: FORCE

Faceless as water, naked as the dust.

Stephen Vincent Benét, "Litany for Dictatorship"

DICTATORS — and other demagogues when they are able—divert their publics from real miseries by denouncing foreign machinations, staging spectacular parades, sports shows, funerals and rallies, and starting witch hunts which always end in the conviction of an enemy, real or fictitious. We have no way of knowing how much this motive may have entered into the Kostov affair. He may have become genuinely troublesome to Moscow, and the decision to liquidate him may have been taken on grounds which are logical to a dictator and even to the victim, he having accepted the hazards of the game from the start. But even if Kostov was merely a scapegoat, he deserves and will receive no tears. His noose was made from the same rope that he had ordered used for so many others.

The terror started by the Bulgarian Communists against their rivals and opponents after the war was really ferocious, even for Communists and even by Balkan standards; and Kostov was in the lead in planning the hangings and shootings. Official Bulgarian reports state that by March 25, 1945, there had already been 131 political trials, at which over 10,000 persons had been found guilty, of whom over 2,000 had been executed.[1] Among them there certainly were Nazi collaborationists, but there also were anti-Communists of every stripe, including some who had been the bravest leaders of the anti-Nazi resistance and were the strongest surviving exponents of free and democratic government. In practice, collaborationists

[1] Statistics issued by G. Dimitrov, October 7, 1945, quoted by Albert A. Brandt, *Harper's Magazine*, December 1947.

usually fared better in the "People's Courts" than liberals; having compromised successfully with one dictatorial régime they knew how to compromise with another to save their skins.

The Agrarians, Socialists and others had joined with the Communists in forming the "Fatherland Front" to take over from the Nazis. It was a mistake—the same mistake being made by liberals in all countries of supposing that they could collaborate on fair terms with Communists. The Bulgarian democratic elements also erred in not recognizing that American and British policy in the Balkans was chaotic and could not be depended upon after the war to prevent the spread of Soviet power in Eastern Europe. The first to pay for these mistakes were the leaders of the old Agrarian Party founded by the peasant hero, Alexander Stambuliski. As they had always worked to raise peasant living standards within the framework of the general welfare, they were the most dangerous rivals of the Communists and became their first targets. The head of the Party, Dr. G. M. Dimitrov, ceded his place to Nikola Petkov under Soviet pressure in January 1945 and escaped abroad. Petkov, who had been one of the four signers of the 1944 armistice, still trusted the word of the Communists that the Fatherland Front would be a real coalition and that the Agrarians would be permitted to carry on independent political activity. He was executed September 23, 1947. The State Department protested that his trial was a "travesty on justice" and contrary to the rights guaranteed to Bulgarian citizens at Yalta. Kostov personally prepared the case against Petkov.

With the last of the powerful and avowed opponents of dictatorship out of the way, the Communists were free to proclaim Bulgaria a one-party state. They did so on February 4, 1948, securing for their country the honor of being the first satellite to abandon the pretense of a popular front. This was the period, one recalls, when Dimitrov was being rebuked by *Pravda* for favoring a Balkan or Danubian federation, and was issuing his denials, and when Moscow was beginning to talk secretly inside the Cominform about expelling Tito. The connection of these events is not to be missed.

Ordinarily Dimitrov might not have gotten off so lightly, but there were reasons for not sullying the name of such a great Communist luminary, the hero of the Reichstag fire trial, at the very moment when another Communist of world-wide repute was headed for disgrace. Some do not agree that Dimitrov was probably informed of Tito's impending fate and allowed to save himself by disavowing the policies to which Moscow objected. I have even heard it said that Dimitrov was Moscow's agent-provocateur, deliberately luring Tito to destruction. The official Jugoslav view, however, is that Dimitrov may have been weak but that he meant well. Mosha Pijade has written that Dimitrov was "the only man among the leaders of the Bulgarian Communist Party who sincerely wished for brotherly relations with Jugoslavia." [2] He also has told of an incident when Dimitrov was passing through Belgrade early in April 1948, that is, some little time before the Tito affair was finally thrashed out in the Cominform. Pijade says that Dimitrov "told us to 'remain steadfast.' " In Belgrade I heard some details of this meeting, which took place in the Bulgarian Prime Minister's sleeping car on a siding at Topchider, a Belgrade suburb. Dimitrov supposedly said to Djilas, the Jugoslav participant: "Tito must stand firm or we shall all be lost." Djilas referred to Dimitrov's weak behavior in the recent federation crisis and asked whether he would knuckle under again to Moscow on the question of the right of Communist nations to develop along their own lines. Would he "stand firm" for Tito while Tito was "standing firm" for the others? Though Dimitrov appears not to have made a direct answer to this, the current Jugoslav view is that if Dimitrov had been in good health he would have taken a stronger stand. The Jugoslavs assume as a matter of course that even if Dimitrov was not quietly liquidated while "regaining his health" in the Soviet Union his death certainly was hastened by the grilling he received there. Tito himself attributes Dimitrov's subservient attitude toward Moscow not only to his broken health but to the fact that Bulgaria's geographical and military position is so weak in comparison to Jugoslavia's.

Obviously the Jugoslavs have much to gain by making out that a Marxist theologian of Dimitrov's eminence was on their side, but their liking for him seems quite spontaneous—in contrast to their dislike of Kostov, at any rate, whom they always considered an enemy. To emphasize that Dimitrov remains a hero to all pure Com-

[2] *Borba*, Belgrade, September 29, 1949.

munists, meaning of course those who think like the true-blue Communists of Jugoslavia, and to show that he is not to be glorified only by Stalin and his lackeys, the Jugoslav Government has changed the name of a town in eastern Serbia from Tsaribrod to Dimitrovgrad.

Regardless of any trouble that Kostov's nationalism may really have made for the Soviets, marking him in any case for prompt liquidation, there was a so-to-speak impersonal reason for starting proceedings against him—namely, that a political *divertissement* of some sort was greatly needed at the moment and that he was eminent enough to draw everybody's attention as a prisoner in the box. What could be a more piquant warning to other Communists who might secretly share his views than the sight of their old Party mentor writhing under the prosecutor's relentless invective and of course in the end crumpling up in a helpless panic of self-inculpation? But a more general reason for staging a public spectacle was that the revolution was lagging in Bulgaria as in the other East European satellites, and Moscow had decreed a speed-up in socialization measures and a "cleansing" of Communist Parties.

The impact of the new line was especially severe in Bulgaria, which was the satellite state where Stalin was determined that full success should come first. Dimitrov indicated this in a speech on December 19, 1948, when he raised the sights of the Bulgarian revolutionary movement to a degree which possibly startled his hearers, Party leaders assembled from all over the country, for it was the first time that the Cominform program adopted in consequence of Tito's defection had been placed squarely before them. The speech, which in typewritten form fills nearly eighty pages, had as its theme the real meaning of a "people's democracy."

Just after the war, said Dimitrov, the Bulgarian revolution had been in a transitional phase. The "armed people's uprising" of September 1944 had succeeded, with "the decisive aid of the heroic Red Army," in wresting control from "the capitalist bourgeoisie and the Monarcho-Fascist minority of exploiters," but "the old bourgeois state machine was not completely smashed" and the Communists remained a minority in the new cabinet. The Nazis were still in the Balkans and nothing could be allowed to interfere with the task of expelling them. For this reason, "social transformations" had to be delayed, even to the point of working with "some anti-German elements of the bourgeoisie." Impatient Party members had to be restrained. Even after the Fatherland Front had been "consolidated," Dimitrov admitted, there was a "certain lag" in "revolutionary changes." "We continued," he said, "to speak of the possibility of coördinating the interests of private industrialists and merchants with the general interests of the state." But in the last year and a half fresh progress had been made—a new republican constitution had been adopted, industry nationalized and progress recorded in socializing agriculture. It had finally become possible, also, to let the last "vacillating and unstable" elements in the Fatherland Front "drop off"—or, if they did not do that, to "kick them out." Now at last there had emerged a "mass political organization" suited to the task of "constructing the foundations of Socialism via the people's democracy . . . under the leadership of the working class." Henceforth there was to be "a relentless class struggle against the capitalistic elements, and for their liquidation." Dimitrov did not assert that the end of the road had been reached. Bulgaria and the other new democracies, he simply said, were now "marching toward Socialism . . . creating the conditions necessary for the building of Socialism."

This boiled down to saying that Bulgarian Communism was still in a transitional stage, though a new one of relentless attack against all remaining capitalist elements. The second half of the proposition would have been the impressive point for Dimitrov's Bulgarian audience. It was the first half, however, that the Jugoslav Communists seized upon. What! they jibed, did the Bulgarian and other Cominform Parties still not dare proclaim the dictatorship of the proletariat? Could they still only say that they were "on the way?"

Even so, Dimitrov had talked very differently in more easygoing days. As recently as September 1946, for example, he had addressed a delegation of foreign trade union delegates as follows:

With great satisfaction we acknowledge Comrade Zilliacus' statement that the working class, the English working people represented by the

Labor Party, are on the way to Socialism and endeavoring to reach it in a peaceful way. . . . I should like to tell our English friend that we too feel that it is quite possible in Bulgaria, granted the work and necessary preparations, to pass on to Socialism some day without dictatorship of the proletariat, on the basis of democracy and a parliamentary régime.

Now, however, the British Labor Party had become a horde of imperialist hyenas, lackeys of Wall Street. Now Socialism was to be attained in Bulgaria not in a peaceful parliamentary way but by force. To make sure that his audience would swallow this strong meat Dimitrov threw in the ominous warning that the program had been developed under the guidance of Stalin himself; he "personally" had helped with advice and explanations so that any "mistakes" which were made could be "corrected quickly."

The Dimitrov talk, though derided in Jugoslavia as postponing indefinitely the advent of Socialism, nevertheless gave notice that the proletarian revolution would now be pushed in Bulgaria by all means and at all costs. Applied to the agrarian problem, it meant that the class war was to begin in earnest in the villages. Collectivization had not proved any more popular with Bulgarian peasants than it had in other agricultural countries. Even at their face value, the official figures of progress in forming collectives (more delicately called "working agricultural enterprises") were not impressive. And one hesitates to accord them face value because of the ample opportunity and great temptation to juggle statistics. Changes are made frequently in the rules for membership, the presidents of village councils (soviets) are desperately anxious to make a good showing in their reports to Sofia, and the Minister of Agriculture himself hopes to save his skin by reporting progress to Moscow.

At the end of 1948, according to a published Soviet source, 73,000 Bulgarian peasant households owning 300,000 hectares of land were joined in 1,000 agricultural coöperatives (collectives); and by August 1, 1949, the figures had become 146,583 households, owning 538,-458 hectares, in 1,594 coöperatives.[3] Writing in the official Cominform journal in November 1949, T. Chernokolev, a member of the

[3] N. Vorobyev, *New Times*, Moscow, September 7, 1949.

Bulgarian Politburo, reported that the number of peasant households had recently reached 147,000 (13.3 percent of all households), the amount of land involved was now 540,000 hectares (11.2 percent of all cultivated land), and the total of coöperatives was 1,600.[4] Soon after Vulko Chervenkov became Prime Minister [5] he revealed that at the end of the first quarter of 1950 the number of coöperative organizations had increased by only 33 over the figure given previously, and that the number of peasant families involved had grown by only about 28,000.[6]

This unsatisfactory organizational progress was matched by production failures. The government organ, *Otechestven Front,* complained on March 27, 1949, that spring sowing quotas which should already have been completed were fulfilled only 56 percent for wheat, 45 percent for rye, 55 percent for barley and 51 percent for oats. It called these figures "extremely disquieting." [7] The results were noticed in the failure of the peasants to meet their wheat and rye requisition quotas in the autumn. Quotas were fulfilled or overfilled in districts bordering the Black Sea or Rumania, *i.e.* where Soviet pressure was most direct, but in districts towards Jugoslavia they were fulfilled only from 20 to 27 percent and in the three districts of Bulgarian Macedonia 59, 54 and 20 percent respectively. The correspondent of *The Economist* (London, November 5, 1949) who reported these figures remarked that "clearly, the 'Tito influence' does exist in Bulgaria, and especially in Bulgarian Macedonia." In the spring of 1950 the same pattern was repeated. Gaston Coblentz gave quotations from *Rabotnichesko Delo* and other Sofia newspapers calling attention to "disastrous" failures in agricultural production, "disgraceful episodes" where village councils showed "open opposition" to the mechanization of agriculture (an indirect way of saying that they opposed the collective farms), and so on. The spring plowing, supposed to be completed by March 8, was

[4] *For a Lasting Peace, for a People's Democracy!,* Bucharest, November 18, 1949.

[5] On February 1, 1950, Chervenkov succeeded Vasil Kolarov, who had died January 23. Chervenkov, who was Dimitrov's brother-in-law, had spent many years in Moscow.

[6] Harry Schwartz, *The New York Times,* May 18, 1950.

[7] Quoted by Michael Padev, *Manchester Guardian,* August 16, 1949.

completed only 15 percent on time, and the spring sowing 10 percent.[8]

The amount of compulsory self-criticism ensuing on such events, and the number of purges and trials of officials and arrests and trials of *kulaks*, bourgeois "saboteurs" and other criminals, can be imagined. In the article already quoted, Mr. Chernokolev admitted that there had been "serious mistakes" even in administering the comparatively moderate Bulgarian collectivization program, with the result that many "injustices" had occurred. Party organizations had failed to gauge correctly what was technically possible, people who owned land without actually working it had been admitted to collectives, even *kulaks* had been taken in, and so on. When lands were exchanged so that practicable coöperative farms might be organized, peasant rights often were "grossly violated." *Kulak* elements "took advantage of this and in a number of cases tried hard to win to their side the disgruntled poor and medium peasants and endeavored to turn them against the coöperatives and the people's power." They not only tried, apparently, but succeeded, for in some villages, the writer records, they fomented "strife between coöperative members and individual peasants," which "created a certain danger for the alliance between the working class and the poor and medium peasants."

Since the Cominform journal is designed for an international audience these comments were more moderate than those made on the spot. In a speech before the Central Committee of the Party in June 1949, Kolarov spoke of "clearly unreasonable and unfair" measures taken against the peasants; of many peasants being forced to join collectives against their will; and of peasants being indifferent to whether crops were big or small, the quota to be sold to the state at a fixed price being much too high—in some cases even comprising the total harvest.[9]

Kolarov put the blame for all that had gone wrong in the countryside on Kostov. So did Chervenkov. So did the Bulgarian press. So did the Committee which investigated Kostov's activities for the Grand National Assembly. It reported that besides the crimes de-

---

[8] *New York Herald Tribune*, April 16, 1950.
[9] Quoted in *The Economist*, London, July 16, 1949.

scribed in the preceding chapter he had "carried out a policy leading
to the estrangement of the overwhelming mass of medium peasants
and of a great part of the small peasants from the Fatherland Front
and putting them under the influence of *kulaks* and the reaction,
thus destroying the union between workers and peasants." [10] This
was very convenient. At one stroke Kostov was linked with the crisis
in the countryside, and an excuse was provided for the existence of
the crisis. It was not a very good excuse, for the same difficulties with
the peasants continued after Kostov had been eliminated from any
share in the country's economic life. As for the expectation that the
trial would sober nationalist elements in the Party, that did not seem
to work out to Moscow's satisfaction either. One count of top-level
Communist officials purged in the six months beginning October
1949 showed a tally of nearly 50.

Class war in the villages, presaged by Dimitrov in December 1948,
did not materialize at once. The expectation may have been that
the simple threat would overcome peasant resistance, but when it
did not a new model statute for collective farms was brought up
"for discussion," *i.e.* to prepare the peasants for what the Party had
decided would now be imposed by force. Peasants who had come
into the collective system and those who had stayed out would both
be hit. A member's share in the profits of a coöperative (if there were
profits: another story) was henceforth going to be figured 30 percent on the amount of land he had put in and 70 percent on the
number of "work days" he contributed, instead of being compensated, as formerly, in direct proportion to the amount of land and
the number of "work days." In other words, he was becoming one-
third a landowner and two-thirds a state agricultural worker. If he
knew about what had happened to the Russian peasants in the final
step of the Soviet agrarian "reform" in 1937 he could foresee what
would become of the remaining one-third of Bulgarian land values.
Actually, of course, the distinction between "rent" for land and
"pay" for labor often was theoretical anyway. The product of a
collective is turned in to the state in amounts fixed in advance and
in return for payment at rates which in practice are confiscatory. A

[10] Report by the Bulgarian radio, Sofia, July 20, 1949, of the proceedings on
that date in the Bulgarian Grand National Assembly.

surplus may or may not remain to be divided among the peasants. Often, as Kolarov admitted, there is none. The rate at which it would have been divided if it had existed is then only of theoretical interest. There is no space here to indicate the punishments awaiting the peasants who infringe the new statute.[11] Even negligence is defined as "treason to the common good" and punished as—treason. But I must add one item contributed by a Bulgarian friend of mine, for it reveals clearly one of the important intentions of present Communist policy in Bulgaria. In this man's native village the coöperative contains both industrial and agricultural workers. The first group is scrupulously allotted the same number of ration cards as the second. Nothing could be fairer, except that the first group contains 14 persons and the latter about 500. "Recipe for horse and rabbit stew: one horse, one rabbit."

Membership in collectives is "voluntary," but the meaning of this is shown by Prime Minister Chervenkov's description of what is to happen to peasants who do not join. "All tractors and agricultural machines belonging to peasants outside the coöperative farms should be confiscated," he has warned, and in future "only peasants belonging to coöperative farms can use tractors and machines." After this gloss on the 1950 model statute there is no need to go into further details. Peasants who do not have the use of farm machinery cannot fulfill their government quotas, let alone have anything left over to feed themselves and their families. They will "volunteer" or starve.

We have seen repeatedly that Bulgaria is the satellite where extreme Soviet measures are given their tryout. She was the first to suppress religious freedom and the first to introduce the system of local government by soviets. She was also the first, as already mentioned, to become officially a one-party state, and Dimitrov was the first satellite leader to proclaim the advent of the dictatorship of the proletariat. Russia's reasons for pushing ahead in Bulgaria seem to be two. It is the country where, with the exception of Rumania, her physical domination comes closest to being absolute. But whereas Russians are contemptuous of Rumanians, and are hated in return, they feel close to Bulgarians in race and language and suppose that they will repay past favors by swinging naturally into their allotted

[11] Details are given in *The Economist*, London, May 27, 1950.

Soviet groove. Secondly, Bulgaria is highly important to Russia strategically. She flanks enemy Jugoslavia. She provides the only direct approach to Greece since Tito has closed the main route. She adjoins Turkey, on whom the Soviets desire to exert pressure from all directions. She is, as we have seen, Russia's chosen instrument of intervention in the Macedonian question. On every count she is the country which, more directly than any other except Poland, can be useful to Russia in the present line-up of European forces. It is not by chance that she and Poland had the honor of being the first to receive high officers of the Soviet Army as commanders-in-chief of their troops.

The sources of opposition are two. One is nationalism. It may be called Titoism or Kostovism, but it is always treason. Nationalists are dealt with as Petkov and Kostov were dealt with. These two, such poles apart, are simply conspicuous examples among tens of thousands who have suffered for opposing the Communization or Sovietization of their country. Any successors they may have, whether noble like Petkov or hateful like Kostov, will be put down with the same irresistible brutality.

The other source of opposition is the peasantry. The peasants resist being made into sharecroppers. They do not think that they are being forced into collectives so that a great social goal can be achieved but in order that a group of adventurers can exploit their hold on them and on the country more conveniently. The Communists are everything that peasants hate and fear—the city slicker, the government bureaucrat. These newcomers in the villages, wearing city clothes, often speaking with a foreign accent, urge the peasants to enter collectives for their own good. Those who do are only one degree better off than those who do not—they are allowed to live, while those who refuse starve. But they live as serfs. They will work for the rest of their lives, as they figure it, to support others who will not or cannot work so hard as they must do—other peasants who have let their lands run down and are glad to merge with those who have kept theirs up, and surplus townsfolk who will never learn to "pay their way." That there are other answers to such arguments than force does not matter. The answer has been given, and it is force.

Only if some external ally appears in the field—in a time of world crisis when all the would-be free see that they have a last chance to make common cause with those that still are free—can the two main sources of Bulgarian opposition to Communization and Sovietization generate power of their own.

# XIX

## FROM SUB-SATELLITE TO SATELLITE

> We are linked by unbreakable fraternity and unity with the heroic people of Tito's Jugoslavia, a guarantee of the freedom, the independence and the sovereignty of our— and all—democratic peoples in the Balkan peninsula. This fraternity and this unity ensured our country unselfish and fraternal aid during the war, and now make possible the all-round development of our new life.
>
> Prime Minister Enver Hoxha of Albania, New Year's Eve, 1948

THE diplomatic representatives of the Western nations are harassed in all the satellite states; and since any inquiry of even the most routine sort is called spying, and movement is restricted arbitrarily to specified areas, they occupy themselves mainly with reporting on the local press and complaining to the Foreign Office about the abuse they find heaped on them there. In Tirana, the tiny Albanian capital, they are especially isolated and feel especially frustrated. France and Italy are the only important Western Powers maintaining legations there, and their small staffs are under rigorous surveillance. The lack of official information about Albanian affairs is not compensated for by news in the press, local or foreign. Albanian newspapers are insignificant except as propaganda organs, and even so are few in number and more puerile if possible than those in satellite capitals with some traditions of cosmopolitanism. Foreign journalists, except Communists or fellow-travellers, have been banned from the country since soon after the war. Albania thus is the satellite about which we know the least; and much of what we think we know is rumor or conjecture.

Albanians are accustomed to having the world know little about their affairs, and are even accustomed to the rôle of satellite—though their national spirit, which exists in spite of the vivacity of their religious and tribal conflicts, forbids one from saying that they are reconciled to it. The last time I was in the country, a good many years ago, Italy and Jugoslavia were contending for predominance. Italy won, expelled King Zog and in 1939 annexed the country. Ciano has recorded the arrival in Rome of the sad-faced group of Albanians summoned to make obeisance to the Duce, lacking only the iron collars of the slaves that used to grace the old imperial triumphs. But after Mussolini was hung up by his heels and Tito was accepted as one of the Allied victors all this was rectified. The new Albanian dictator, Enver Hoxha (pronounced Hodzha), was a Communist guerrilla who had been in contact with the Jugoslav Partisans during the war. Indeed, an emissary from Tito, Miladin Popovich, is credited with having organized the Albanian Communists into a unified party in November 1941. Hoxha was an original member, and Tito's influence over him, dating from that time, endured until the Cominform row broke the Communist world front in 1948. Though Hoxha was never Tito's creature to the extent that the successors to Zog had been Mussolini's, he looked to Jugoslavia from the start for almost everything in the way of practical relief, technical assistance and even funds. From Moscow he received, apart from a small military mission, only remote ideological control and the prestige of enjoying at second hand the patronage which Stalin accorded Tito.

While Jugoslavia herself was an obedient satellite this seemed to be satisfactory to Moscow. Soviet enthusiasm for what was being done in Albania was reflected in the Moscow press. Take, for example, this report published in *Trud* in April 1948 from a special correspondent who had just visited the country:

In the Democratic Front, a political organization has been created that unites all the forces of the people. . . . Agrarian reform has been effected, putting an end to the feudal system of landownership. . . . Industrial enterprises, transportation, communications, etc., in the country have been nationalized. Coöperatives are developing successfully. State and coöperative property form the economic foundation of the New Albania. . . . Unemployment has disappeared. Wages are increasing.[1]

The Soviet visitor went on to record that Albania had "established especially close ties with Jugoslavia and Bulgaria," and added: "Even during the war of liberation against Fascism, a friendship took root between the peoples of Jugoslavia and Albania. Both nations are assisting one another to restore and develop their economy."

Here is an even more enthusiastic picture from one of the few Americans admitted to the country, a correspondent of *The Worker*:

Albania is so undeveloped industrially that its citizens regard Jugoslavia as the rich big brother who will always come to their rescue. The Jugoslavs—despite their own poverty—sent food down to save the Albanians last year when floods devastated most of their crops. Jugoslavia is providing the rails and locomotives for Albania's first and dearly cherished railway. Jugoslavia paid two-thirds of Albania's state budget. "Rroft [Long live] Tito" signs are almost as numerous as the "Rroft Enver" ones. Russia holds second place in the public esteem, though it is not too well known. Now that Hoxha, on his recent trip, signs agreements to send oil and tobacco to Russia in exchange for much-needed machinery, you can expect many more "Rroft Stalins" to crop up.[2]

These and other enthusiasts were wrong, of course. The lack of foresight shown by the reporter from *Trud* must have embarrassed him particularly, for only two months after his return to Moscow the Soviet newspapers began their campaign against Tito and soon were claiming that he had been exploiting his small neighbor all along.

At first, however, Moscow seemed to grant that Belgrade was so much closer to Tirana, so much better informed about local vendettas and feuds, had so much more stake in settling railway, irrigation and other regional problems, that Hoxha's dependence on Tito was natural. To a large extent it was. Albania is enclosed by Jugo-

---

[1] I. Golubnitchy, *Trud*, Moscow, April 25, 1948 (*Soviet Press Translations*, June 15, 1948).

[2] Helen Simon, writing from Tirana, in *The Worker*, New York, September 28, 1947.

slavia on two sides, and her only other land neighbor is Greece, a traditional enemy and at present particularly disliked by Communist Albanians because of her "Monarcho-Fascist" government. When Hoxha established his régime at Tirana in November 1944, the Jugoslav Government had been the first to recognize it and establish diplomatic relations. Albania's first and for a time only economic treaty was with Jugoslavia, a customs union was created between the two countries and the Albanian currency was tied to the Jugoslav dinar. Close and continuing political coöperation seemed assured by the pact of friendship which was arranged when Hoxha paid a state visit to Belgrade in June 1946. The reorganization of the Albanian Army was carried out with the help of a Jugoslav military mission. The study of the Serbo-Croat language became compulsory in Albanian schools, Jugoslav and Soviet flags flanked the Albanian flag in schoolrooms, and Tito's and Stalin's photographs flanked those of Hoxha in government offices. To complete the picture, Albania was allowed to play only a secondary rôle in international affairs. This was underscored by the fact that the Soviet Union did not grant her a treaty of guarantee like those made with the other satellites and that the Cominform failed to admit the Albanian Party to membership.

Nevertheless, when Tito's expulsion from the Cominform faced Hoxha with the choice between Belgrade and Moscow he did not hesitate. It was inconceivable to him—as to others—that Stalin would be unable to change the guard at Belgrade if he so desired. C. L. Sulzberger, chief foreign correspondent of *The New York Times,* a connoisseur of things Albanian, suggests that Hoxha may have foreseen how things were going as early as 1947 and that he arranged then to throw in his lot with Moscow.[3] It is true that he did complain in 1947 about the Jugoslav program for Albania to produce raw materials and buy Jugoslav goods in return—a piquant preview of what Tito would say later about Stalin's idea of proper relations between Communist states. Nevertheless, such murmurs of discontent seemed insignificant in comparison with the frequent messages of ebullient friendship that passed back and forth between the two heads of state. In June 1948, however, Hoxha rushed to be

[3] *The New York Times,* April 5, 1949.

in at the kill. Perhaps he had chafed secretly under the weight of so much kindness from Belgrade; more likely, his heart was not really in what he was doing and he wished to disarm suspicions by showing especial vehemence against his friend and benefactor. Whatever the reason, Albania was the first of the Communist states to attack Tito openly, and the Albanian press and radio led the way to each new level of intensity in the campaign of invective against him.

Even after Hoxha had seated himself as prominently as possible on the Moscow steamroller he did not feel secure. The technical, commercial and military agents of Tito's "reactionary" régime were gone, the customs union with Jugoslavia had been dissolved, railway and other communications had been cut, oil shipments to Jugoslavia had ceased and Jugoslav imports had been halted. The Russian military and civilian mission (which first arrived in February 1946) had been increased to something between two and five thousand; there was a major-general of the Soviet Army on hand to instruct the Albanian Army; and there was another high officer to supervise the police. But the Soviet Army itself was far away. Albania no longer had direct contact with any Cominform state. The only routes by which Soviet assistance could arrive were by plane from Hungary or Bulgaria over Jugoslav territory, by ship through the Dardanelles and the Aegean, by rail across Austria to the Allied-controlled port of Trieste and then by ship down the Adriatic, or (most roundabout of all, although actually sometimes used) by ship from the Baltic via Gibraltar. The economic situation of the country was deteriorating. There was not enough food. Grain and other supplies had been required from Jugoslavia in the past to tide over bad crops. Not merely were such shipments as now arrived at Durazzo and Valona in Soviet bottoms quite insufficient to fill similar needs but a good part of them were consigned to the Greek guerrillas. The war in Greece was not going well, and the strain of keeping up a good face about it was increased by the fact that the wounded and refugees who sought shelter in Albania were, of course, Greeks—Communist Greeks, yes, but not disliked much less on that account by the Albanians who had to look after them. Worst of all, Tito was not simply holding his own at home, he was counterattacking abroad with propaganda for the independence of all Communist governments and parties. Hoxha

wondered whether this might not appeal to certain of his followers
who had been indoctrinated originally by Jugoslav instructors or who
had joined the Party for national even more than social objectives.
Many younger member in particular had taken to Communism as a
*pis aller* when all other methods of protesting against the extinction
of Albanian independence seemed to be blocked.

The Russian stake in Albania was too great for the Kremlin to risk
letting her slip over into the Tito camp. For a second member of the
Communist family—even the least and meanest—to go whoring
after false gods would be intolerable. Furthermore, in this period the
Party line still described Tito as an isolated megalomaniac. If even a
minor figure like Hoxha joined him it would signify that he was the
head of something like an international movement.

But more than face was at stake. This pinpoint of barren land,
malarial swamps and snow-capped mountains could be serviceable
in the over-all strategy of even a colossus like Russia. Whenever Tito
decided to close the Greek-Jugoslav frontier—which it became certain he would do eventually, once the Greek Communist Party had
accepted the Cominform line [4]—Albania would offer the only remaining road for Soviet supplies to reach the Communist bands
operating in northwest Greece; while if the Greek war had to be
liquidated the only refuge for the guerrillas would be in Albania.

The value of Albania in Soviet strategy also extends far outside the
Balkans. In the event of war with the West the Russians would find
submarine bases beyond the Turkish-controlled Dardanelles im-
mensely valuable. They had shown that they were aware of this immediately after the war, when engineers of the Soviet mission took
over the Italian naval station on the island of Saseno, off the port of
Valona. Soviet submarines based on Saseno, which commands the
Strait of Otranto and is only 50 miles from the Italian coast, would
close off the Adriatic from the main body of Mediterranean waters.
This meant that so long as Jugoslavia belonged to the Cominform
bloc, Soviet and Jugoslav craft operating from the Jugoslav harbors
of Kotor and Split would be free to attack Bari, Ancona and other

---

[4] The Greek-Jugoslav frontier was closed formally by the Jugoslav Government July 23, 1949, but had been closed in fact some time earlier (*cf.* Chapter XVI).

Italian shipping centers, also Foggia, reputed to be a prospective bombing base for long-range American operations against the Soviet Union. Meanwhile, the eastern and central Mediterranean basin and much of North Africa, more important than ever in the latest British and American strategy, would be within bombing radius of Jugoslav and Albanian airfields. Tito's withdrawal from the Soviet camp made it necessary to rely solely on Albanian bases for carrying these plans into execution. Without Saseno and the Albanian airfields (of which there were about ten by latest report, half of them developed to the point where they could serve heavy planes), Soviet submarines would be barred from the Mediterranean and Soviet bombers would be pushed back to the Danube valley. We of course have no direct information about the extent of recent Soviet activity on Saseno. However, foreign intelligence services in contact with underground elements inside Albania believe that although newspaper stories about elaborate concrete submarine pens are exaggerated the scale of fortifications makes Saseno a formidable threat to naval movements in the Mediterranean in time of war as well as to military installations in Italy and North Africa.

With such valuable eggs in its little Albanian basket, the Kremlin naturally ordered Prime Minister Hoxha to show the utmost diligence in rooting out any dangerous nationalist sentiments that might appear in the Albanian Communist Party. There had been a nationalist movement of some promise in Albania during the war, but its leaders had lost standing for various reasons—some because they collaborated with the Communists, some because they collaborated with the Nazis when the latter replaced the Italians after the Italian capitulation, some because American and British propaganda tended to favor the Albanian Communists as a way of helping the Jugoslav Partisans, especially after the Allied landing in Italy made it seem possible that Churchill might succeed in having an Allied expedition sent into the Balkans. When Hoxha set up his government in Tirana in November 1944 he maintained the appearance of collaboration with such non-Communist resistance elements as still existed and were willing to join the new "Democratic Front," the organization which now replaced the openly Communist "National Liberation Front" of the war years. But the need for concessions to patriotic,

nationalist and democratic forces in the country diminished as the
Communist Party tightened its hold; and following the one-ticket
elections of December 2, 1945, it came to an end. The monarchy
was abolished in fact as well as in name, the People's Democratic
Republic of Albania was proclaimed and the non-Communists who
had been collaborating with Hoxha fled abroad or were shot. There
followed the agrarian "reforms," the nationalization (confiscation)
of such small industry as existed in the country, the elimination of
independent shopkeepers and the other measures which so much
pleased the Soviet commentator quoted earlier.

Among the strongest incentives to Albanian nationalistic feeling
are Albania's claim to the Kossovo area in Jugoslavia, where there is
an Albanian minority, and Greece's claim to the Northern Epirus
district in southern Albania, where there is a Greek minority. Propaganda in favor of one annexation and counter-propaganda against
the other are the habitual stock-in-trade of Albanian patriots.

Italy annexed Kossovo to Albania in 1941—one of Mussolini's
cheap rewards for the Nazi victory in Jugoslavia. The action
strengthened the Jugoslav resistance, notably on the part of the Serb
Chetniks, for the Kossovo plain holds a special place in Serb history
and in the hearts of Serb patriots. In the end the district went back to
Jugoslavia, after the Italians and later the Germans had been
expelled. One of the returns which Hoxha had to make for Tito's
material and moral support was to put an end to the former annex-
ationist propaganda in that direction.

Developments on the other front were more favorable to Hoxha.
Britain always had been a friend and protector of Greece, from
imperial interest as well as Byronic sentiment, and the United States
had taken over a share in that rôle under the Truman Doctrine.
Hoxha could point to the fact that the two Western Powers were
hostile to the Greek Communists as well as to his own Communist
régime, whereas the Soviet Union was friendly to both; and on this
basis he could argue that if the Greek Royal Government won it
would have British and perhaps American support in claiming
Northern Epirus, whereas if the Greek Communists won they would
be instructed by the Soviet Government to withdraw any claim on
another Communist country's territory. On balance, Communism

did not come out badly as a defender of Albanian interests, for the lands in jeopardy in the south constitute nearly a quarter of the entire territory of Albania and are much more important to the country's existence than the territory claimed from Jugoslavia. Recently, with Communist fortunes at a low ebb in Greece and with Jugoslav-Albanian relations as bad as possible, the situation has been reversed. Hoxha can still claim, however, that a Communist victory all around is the only guarantee of a safe solution of the quarrel with Greece, and he also is now free to attack the treatment received by the Albanians in Kossovo and to say that if only there were a "true" Communist régime in Belgrade it would do them favors which a "false" comrade like Tito refused.

Basically, however, Hoxha felt insecure, and not only for the reasons mentioned a few paragraphs back. He must constantly have wondered how he himself stood in the Kremlin. What was the Soviet estimate of his own fidelity? He had been Tito's friend, had protested countless times how much he loved him, how he would fight to the death for him. What could he do to demonstrate that he, Hoxha, who had gone back so easily on one ally, would remain faithful to the next?

Hoxha's second-in-command was Lieutenant General Koci Xoxe (pronounced Dzodze), Deputy Prime Minister, Minister of the Interior, organizing secretary of the Communist Party, an able theoretician and adept also at ruthless action. Like Hoxha he had been Tito's close collaborator, but he had not hesitated a fraction of a second longer than his chief in announcing his switch to the anti-Tito camp, and he vied with Hoxha in denouncing their old ally's ideological errors and political perfidy and in lauding Stalin as the fount of Communist wisdom and the Soviet Union as Albania's only protector. During the summer of 1948 as Minister of the Interior he conducted the purge of Titoist suspects in the government and Party.

What more convincing proof of his own fidelity could Hoxha offer Stalin than to be willing to sacrifice even this outstanding friend and colleague? To denounce Xoxe would be almost like denouncing himself, but preferable. He called the Central Committee of the Party to meet in Berat in September, and after it had listened to his account of how Xoxe, who had been purging Titoists, was himself a

Titoist, it voted that this was indeed so and that he in turn should be purged. Also implicated were Pandi Christo, former President of the Control Commission, Nosti Kerentyi, former President of the State Planning Commission, both like Xoxe members of the Politburo, and more than a dozen other influential officials and party members. As a first step, Xoxe was removed from his key post and nominated as Minister of Industry. Moscow-chosen and Moscow-trained Major-General Mehmet Shehu helped Hoxha direct this manœuvre and succeeded Xoxe as the Number 2 man of the régime. Xoxe's new post was announced by the Albanian radio October 2, 1948. Before the month was up he had been deprived of it, expelled from the Party and arrested with Christo and the others as "agents of Trotskyite Jugoslav agents." He was convicted as "chief bandit" of "the Trotskyite group of enemies of the people," [5] and shot on June 11, 1949.

Hoxha may have had other motives besides a desire to offer Stalin the most dramatic burnt-offering possible as proof of his own zeal and fidelity. He may have seized on the chance to get rid of his nearest rival. Nor must we rule out the possibility that Communists sometimes act for the reasons they allege. Hoxha may have told the truth about Xoxe. The Minister of the Interior may have purged a few minor Titoists in order to cover up the fact that he had left more important ones at large, and that with them he was plotting to take Albania into the anti-Cominform camp at the first opportunity.

A writer in the *New Times* of Moscow has given us a summary of Soviet opinion of Xoxe:

Koci Xoxe was a shifty little man who combined the brutality of a wolf with the cowardice of a jackal. He wormed his way into the Ministry of the Interior and the Central Committee of the Party. He flooded the country with sleuths of Tito, helped the latter to organize the economic invasion of Albania, violated the foreign trade monopoly and the sovereign rights of the Republic. Tito speculators made their way into the country and plundered Albania's commodity reserves, buying up with devaluated dinars cattle, grain, olive oil, fruit, wool, wine, tobacco, as well as valuable handicraft ware, the work of Albanian peasants. The goods were shipped by truck and boat to Jugoslavia, and

[5] Tirana radio, home service transmission, June 10, 1949.

were sold in the markets of Belgrade and in the profiteers' shops at a hundred times the price paid for them.[6]

For some months after Xoxe's death the Jugoslav Government took much abuse from the Albanian Government and press (though not without returning it), and accepted many rebuffs, probably on the theory that nationalist elements still existed in the Albanian Communist Party and might at any time stage an anti-Cominform coup. With some outside help a revolt might indeed have been precipitated. However, the risk that it might end up an anti-Communist revolution rather than a pro-Tito one deterred the Jugoslavs from giving indiscriminate help to anti-Hoxha elements, while the Western Powers were afraid that any incident in the Balkans might provide an excuse for Soviet intervention, particularly while the Greek civil war was still in progress. Italy, Albania's nearest influential neighbor to the west, was not at all anxious to see the Albanian question reopened, with the possibility that the country might be divided between Jugoslavia and Greece. As pointed out to me by Count Sforza in the spring of 1950 (when there were rumors that a concerted effort might be made to overthrow Hoxha), Italian interests are safer with a small nation rather than a large or middle-sized one occupying the opposite coast of the Strait of Otranto. He added: "Besides our political reasons for wishing Albania to remain united and independent we have a moral one. I always opposed the idea of making the Albanians into Italians by force. Any government in which I am Foreign Minister will oppose making them into Jugoslavs and Greeks."

Hoxha thus remained in office. Whether he was still Number 1 or had become a figurehead under Mehmet Shehu—or whether, as some say, Shehu had himself been liquidated at Moscow's orders—is not established. But although the chance of a successful revolt in Albania seemed to recede, the danger of an Albanian-Greek clash remained. The retreat of the Greek guerrillas into Northern Epirus provided many chances for incidents and there was even some fear lest the Soviets might instruct the Greek Communists to try if possible to

[6] "Albania: From a Writer's Travel Diary," by Arkadi Perventsev, in *New Times*, Moscow, November 23, 1949.

tempt the Government forces to pursue them across the Albanian frontier. A Greek invasion of Albania would place the Jugoslav Government in a dilemma—whether to support the Cominform enemy against the Greek "Monarcho-Fascists," or to renege and incur criticism as a secret ally of reaction? Tito feared that the Soviets might put him on this spot and use whatever action he took as a pretext for intervening themselves. Events elsewhere gave color to the idea that Moscow might be planning a coup. The autumn of 1949 saw the beginning of the great Budapest trial at which the Hungarian Government accused Laszlo Rajk, former Minister of the Interior, of plotting with Tito to overthrow the régime. In Belgrade, Mosha Pijade asserted that the Soviets were seeking an excuse for armed action against Jugoslavia. If they were unable to make the Rajk trial serve their purpose, he said, they would foment a Greek-Albanian war, accuse Tito of being in secret alliance with Athens and either go to Hoxha's assistance themselves against both Jugoslavia and Greece or send their satellite armies.

Tito's position was legally a complicated one, for in spite of everything that had happened the Jugoslav-Albanian pact of mutual assistance was still in force. Tito had so far avoided taking the initiative in abrogating an agreement with any of his former Cominform allies. The other six members of the Soviet bloc had one after another denounced their treaties with Jugoslavia. Albania only had held back, in order not to release Tito from his uncomfortable position. At last Tito felt that the risk of having to carry out his treaty obligations to Albania or of being accused of aiding and abetting the Athens Government and its Western backers was intolerable. On November 12, 1949, it was announced in Belgrade that the Albanian treaty had been cancelled.

The picture of Jugoslav-Albanian relations given by the Jugoslav note was the contrary, of course, of that painted by the *New Times* of Moscow in the excerpt quoted above, but rather recalled what the correspondent of *The Worker* and various Soviet reporters had been accustomed to write in the days before it occurred to anybody to deny Tito's benevolence toward Hoxha. According to the Belgrade story there was no phase of Albanian life which did not owe a debt to Jugoslav generosity. In 1946 the Jugoslav Government had sent

Albania 20,000 tons of wheat "without demand for any form of payment;" in 1947 it had granted 2,000 million dinars for Albanian development, a sum which "amounted to over half of the total Albanian budget;" and in 1948 it had made a new grant of 3,000 million dinars, which like the grant of the year before carried no conditions as to repayment. Thanks to these grants Albania had obtained Jugoslav locomotives, cars, trucks, ships and agricultural machines. When in addition she asked for an automatic telephone exchange for Tirana, a printing plant and a radio station, she had received them as outright gifts. She also had requested and received the loan of Jugoslav experts and workers in various fields, besides Jugoslav military instructors and teachers for her schools; and she had sent over 1,500 Albanian pupils to study in Jugoslavia on Jugoslav scholarships. This and much more the Jugoslavs had done, said the Jugoslav note, to give practical application to "the principle of true Socialist aid to a backward country, aid free of all exploitation, not conditioned by political concessions." It added: "For the first time a new Socialist form of economic coöperation came into being in the relations between two Socialist countries, that is to say, a coöperation freed of the capitalist features of the economically weaker being exploited by the economically stronger." Bukharin himself could not have argued the merits of the case more convincingly.

Heaping coals of fire on Hoxha's head, the Jugoslav note quoted expressions of everlasting gratitude and friendship voiced by Hoxha on the basis of all this support from "the brotherly peoples of Marshal Tito's Jugoslavia." Why, it inquired, had that gratitude failed and that friendship ceased? The answer was that Hoxha had allowed himself to become the tool of the very persons who wished to "eradicate" the Jugoslav-Albanian example of true Socialist coöperation. Those persons, *i.e.* the men in the Kremlin, were afraid of the impression caused by that coöperation, found it "hateful" and had determined not to permit it to continue.

Almost automatically, the man whom Hoxha had executed as an alleged tool of Jugoslavia, personifying nationalist and anti-Soviet errors, became in Belgrade eyes a true hero, a martyr to his determination to preserve Albanian national rights and combat Stalinist hegemony. A close confidant of Tito, Milovan Djilas, called Xoxe's execution "murder." It was ordered by the Cominform, he said, "to frighten all those in other Communist Parties who favor equality, morality, truth and justice among Communist Parties." Whether or not Xoxe deserved such eulogies, there is little doubt that his trial was part of a concerted move against "nationalist deviationism" all along the Cominform front. The June in which he was executed as a Titoist was the same month, the reader will remember, in which another secretary of a Communist Party, Traicho Kostov, was ousted from his government and Party posts in Bulgaria and arrested as a Titoist, preparatory to being tried and hanged. It also was the month (as we shall now see) in which another former Minister of the Interior, Laszlo Rajk, was dismissed from his government and Party posts in Hungary and arrested as a Titoist, preparatory to being tried and, inevitably, hanged.

# XX

## WARNING IN BUDAPEST

In revolutionary tactics under a bourgeois régime, reform naturally becomes an
instrument for disintegrating this régime,
an instrument for strengthening revolution.

Stalin, "Voprosy," 1945

BUDAPEST in the early summer of 1949
gave few signs of realizing that a new phase in the Hungarian revolution had begun. The man in the street would have heard nothing, of
course, of the first Kremlin directives that to be a People's Democracy
meant henceforth to be a proletarian dictatorship—if not immediately in the precise Soviet form, nevertheless with that as the goal.
However, when Josef Revai, ideologue-in-chief of the Hungarian
Workers' Party (Communist), made a programmatic speech in
March to the Party leadership it clearly reflected the new Moscow
line; and his ominous remarks were printed in one of the Party
organs for anyone interested to read. There had been preliminary
warnings also. As far back as the summer of 1948 the Deputy Prime
Minister, Matyas Rakosi, had said that individual farming could
not be tolerated in Hungary, and again, shortly before Revai went
into explicit detail, Rakosi had spoken about the need for giving
effect in Hungary to policies similar to those which his colleagues
Dimitrov and Bierut already had announced in Bulgaria and Poland.
Revai observed sharply that Rakosi's speech had not been "given
the attention by Party leaders which it deserved." The general public might therefore have been excused for skipping over such unpleasant matters also. But the Revai talk should have been an alert
to those outside the Party as well as to the faithful that the period of
camouflage revolution was over.

From now on, Revai said in effect, the revolution would aim directly and continuously towards establishing a Hungarian Communist dictatorship on the Soviet model. He admitted that contrary statements had often been made in the past. These had been merely useful tactical devices, however, to salve national pride and mollify moderate elements. He warned explicitly that he was not talking theory, "but about a really practical problem." The watchwords which he gave for the new offensive against surviving capitalism were "oppression and violence."

This sort of an offensive against the remnants of capitalism would mean more in practical terms in Budapest than in the other satellite capitals where similar warnings were being given. The everyday life of average people in Warsaw, Sofia or Bucharest, for example, would not be changed very drastically. In villages everywhere there would be resistance to Moscow's orders, and violence and perhaps starvation would follow. But in the three capitals mentioned the level of physical existence had already been reduced to about that in Russian provincial cities, and citizens who had not learnt to express their ideas about this or any other matter in language acceptable in a police state had already been put where their voices could not disturb the prevailing quiet. Changes could be only in degree, and a rather small one at that. In Prague the proletarianization process had been delayed, but was now under way with usual Czech thoroughness. In Budapest, however, the bourgeoisie had held on to their traditional easygoing manners under repeated blows and so far even found many of their accustomed surroundings and pursuits not unbearably altered. Among the Hungarian Communists themselves only the top leaders, Moscow's men of confidence, had understood how utterly the old life of the city was condemned to eventual destruction, as now disclosed by Revai, or how inevitably class warfare in the villages would ultimately utilize the full armory of terrible weapons that had converted the Russian peasantry into wage slaves of the state.

It was May, and all Budapest seemed to be enjoying the first really warm weather. Several of the graceful bridges across the river to Buda were still down, but the two or three in operation could accommodate the necessary tramcars by which all Budapest (outside the government) moves to work or pleasure. Gone were the glittering night clubs where giddy people from all over the world used to do their part in supporting the Hungarian currency, and the palatial hotels by the Danube lay in their untouched piles of rubble just as the departing Nazis and liberating Red Army had left them; but there still was night life of a sort for anyone who did not mind the political commissar sitting in the corner, checking up on those with too much money to spend. The artificial waves were still breaking over bathers on the artificial beach at the public pool on Margaret Island. The best pastry shop in Europe was still serving hot chocolate with *Schlagobers* and all the old varieties of little cakes. There still were silk stockings on some of the women shoppers, and silk pajamas in the windows of one or two haberdashers who had reopened their stores amidst the débris of their rivals. The Cardinal Primate of this heavily Roman Catholic country was in jail, but the churches were open and people flocked to them as usual—which meant less regularly in Budapest than in the villages, but nevertheless in numbers to justify the verb.[1] One Saturday night the headwaiter at my hotel on Margaret Island—luckily not quite monopolized by members of various Soviet purchasing commissions—told me that he had served over two thousand dinners to cheerful Budapest trippers out under the trees, and these guests looked to me no more underfed than the amply stomached visitors from Moscow.

I found one old-time liberal friend who was not afraid to talk with a foreigner, and asked him what he thought of the Revai speech. He was not interested. "What the Communists say is not sincere," he remarked, and from this incontrovertible premise arrived at the less accurate conclusion that what they say is not worth thinking about. He is far from being a typical Budapester, for he always held such extremely liberal views that even régimes less reactionary than

---

[1] The Hungarian Bench of Bishops was reported to have signed an agreement with the Hungarian Government August 30, 1950. By its terms the Bishops accepted the Constitution of the People's Republic, agreed to take steps against any ecclesiastical person who opposed the Government or its constructive work, condemned all subversive activities and specifically undertook to ask the clergy and their congregations to participate in forwarding the Five Year Plan and not to oppose the collectivization program. In return, the Government promised freedom of religion, undertook to allow the reopening of eight ecclesiastical schools and said that it would provide, on a sliding scale, for the financial needs of the Church. Within a few months each side was accusing the other of violating the pact.

Horthy's might have been tempted to label him, as Horthy's did, a
Communist. But not being in fact a Communist, and on the other
hand never having been enrolled as an "Awakening Magyar" and
never having collaborated with the Nazis, he was now in extreme
danger; the exact point at which he would be liquidated must
already have been noted in his dossier at the A.V.O., the police section of the Ministry of the Interior. He spoke to me in a matter-of-
fact way about how the A.V.O. operates in its headquarters, a rapidly lengthening row of buildings, all with pansies in window-boxes,
on Andrassy Utca. He gave no sign, however, of realizing that one
day he was bound to discover the exact truth of all the tales about
its system of interrogations and ingenious tortures. Bourgeois survivors in states well along on the road to being Communized seldom
let themselves realize the desperateness of their situation; they can
do nothing to change it, and so they avoid even thinking about it.
If such a man of the world as the friend I am speaking of gives way
to this instinct, how much more would the ordinary citizen who is
unaccustomed to noting subtle signs of change in the political climate and who inclines anyway to discount the influence that theory
exercises on action, Communist or otherwise? If my experienced
friend had not read the portents in Revai's speech, who were these
other thousands to stop at home and shudder?

Of several dozen persons with whom I had casual contact in shops,
streetcars, coffeehouses, hotels or in asking my way in the street,
only one or two failed to say some word of lament, when they found
that I was an American, for the old days. But they had been through
too much during and since the war to believe that the future could
really be worse than the past. Even the surviving Jews, who form
such an important sector of the Budapest middle class, hesitated to
draw the full conclusions from the fact that all Zionist organizations
had been dissolved in March and that legal Jewish emigration was
becoming impossible and clandestine emigration more and more
perilous. Some thought that the large numbers of Jews in the Hungarian Communist hierarchy would guarantee the security of the
Jewish community as a whole. So many Jews held office in the first
Communist-dominated cabinet that it was said that the one or two
so-called Christian members had been included in order to make sure

there might be someone to countersign decrees of execution on Saturdays. The Jewish cabinet members maintain, however, that all Hungarian Jews ought to embrace Communism in gratitude to the Soviet Union for having saved them from the Nazis. There are from 150,000 to 200,000 Jewish survivors still in Hungary, most of them shopkeepers or members of the professions and therefore anti-Communist. Probably as much as 75 percent of them would like to emigrate to Israel. Since that is forbidden they have settled down to a life as near to usual as possible.

The opinion in diplomatic circles was that Laszlo Rajk, the Minister of Foreign Affairs, was less powerful than he had been as Minister of the Interior and head of the secret police, his post until August 1948. His transfer was interpreted as a demotion, since foreign ministers of satellite states do not make their own policy but execute the policy of the Kremlin. As he was head of the Foreign Office, however, I asked to see him. His colleague in charge of the press and propaganda, an intelligent and cultivated Mr. Boldizsar, told me that to Mr. Rajk's great regret he was too busy in view of the coming elections to find time to receive me. I remarked that this must mean that the elections promised to be very close, to which Mr. Boldizsar replied with a look of studied blankness. A week or so later the elections were held, and the announced returns gave the government list—the only one permitted, of course—95.6 percent of the votes. The next step was to form a new cabinet. When the names were published, Mr. Rajk's was not among them, even in the innocuous post of Foreign Minister.

June of 1949 was a particularly trying period for Communist leaders everywhere in Eastern Europe. In Sofia the Kostov purge had begun and in Albania Koci Xoxe had ended his career before a firing squad. Might not leaders in other satellite countries be called on to make some sacrifice—accept the blame for Cominform plans gone wrong or bear witness to what could happen to a Communist who was nationalist enough to resist Moscow's policies? The question was answered for Hungary on June 15, 1949, with the announcement that Laszlo Rajk had been dismissed as Minister for Foreign Affairs and expelled from the Politburo and the Party as a "nationalist," "Titoist" and "Trotskyite."

These were the epithets that had been used against Kostov and Xoxe, and their use against a leading Hungarian Communist showed that Moscow's educational campaign was proceeding methodically among the faithful and not-quite-so-faithful in all the satellite states. Actually, the Rajk case was destined also to inaugurate a new phase in the Cominform's direct attack on Tito. It would provide evidence that he was not only a megalomaniac and heretic but that his heresy was simply a clever subterfuge behind which he was enabled to carry forward his traitorous work as an agent of the Western imperialists. But before we turn to this main theme let us learn a little more from Revai's speech about the policies that Moscow had decided to put into effect inside the individual states, in order to immunize local Communist Parties against any further spread of Titoism and strengthen the governments against new foreign risks. For it must have been realized that there was definitely a new risk in accusing Tito and the Western Powers of conspiring together to attack the Communist world, and in ordering the diplomatic and military measures which would naturally follow the making of such impudent charges.

Revai's first point was that a People's Democracy is "the dictatorship of the proletariat though not in the Soviet form," and his second was that the objective is to give it that form.[2] Coalitions of Communists with non-Communists are temporary tactical devices. Bourgeois parties are accepted in popular fronts merely in order to destroy them. Sometimes impulsive hotheads nearly spoil the game, as when the left-wing Socialists in Hungary after the war adopted the slogan "For a Red Budapest." The Communists had been more clever; they had avoided anything so frankly provocative, for their enemies outnumbered them and could still have saved themselves by taking resolute action. Thus Communists were careful not to mention, for instance, that the ultimate choice would be between any sort of private property and complete socialization, and they kept the public from worrying about such matters by talk about liqui-

---

[2] Revai's speech was delivered to leaders of the Hungarian Workers' Party (Communist) in March 1949 and published in the March-April issue of the Party magazine, *Tarsadalmi Szemle*. The text can be found in translation, with explanatory notes, in *Foreign Affairs*, New York, October 1949.

dating the old feudal system by progressive means, something on which almost everyone was agreed.[3]

Once the Communist Party secures control, continued Revai, it cannot and does not share that control with any other party, class or group. He explicitly named the "working peasantry" among the outsiders. True, the Party platform states that "Today in Hungary the working class and its ally the working peasantry are in power." But the dictatorship of the proletariat, as defined by Lenin and Stalin, means that power "is undivided in the hands of the proletariat and that the working class does not share its power with other classes." (He passed over in silence the fact that Lenin and Stalin had defined it, when opportunism so dictated, as an alliance of the proletariat with the poor and middle peasantry.) And he added specifically: "Therefore it does not share its power with the peasantry." The Party platform dealt with these matters "only in a disguised form" because various basic questions, including "the Socialist development of agriculture, its collectivization," cannot always be talked about "by their real name." Similarly, though persons who call themselves Smallholders and Peasants are still in the government, this is only a convenient formality. "*In fact*, Comrades, it is the working class which is alone in power, *in fact*, it is our Party alone which runs the state machine."

The reason it is so absolutely necessary that the peasantry be excluded from power, Revai explained, is that "even its working part" is "halfheartedly for private property and halfheartedly for the coöperatives." It "vacillates," and must be led, educated and assisted. Obviously it would be foolish to let the very elements which

[3] This part of the speech must be read with particular chagrin by ex-Premier Ferenc Nagy, whose Smallholders Party won a decisive majority of votes in the Hungarian elections of November 4, 1945. In compliance with a preëlection promise made under pressure of the Soviet Government and its troops of occupation, Nagy then formed a coalition government in which Communists as well as Socialists and National Peasant representatives were included. The Communists received, among other portfolios, that of the key Ministry of the Interior. The former American Minister to Hungary, H. F. Arthur Schoenfeld, has written (*Foreign Affairs*, New York, April 1948) that Nagy yielded on this point "only by peremptory Soviet orders." He might have done better to face a showdown then, for in May 1947 he was ousted by the Communists and their stoolpigeon deserters from the other parties, after a series of arrests of leading members of those parties. He decided not to return from a vacation in Switzerland to face arrest also.

vacillate participate in the work of indoctrination: "that is why power cannot be divided with the peasantry."

Revai's conclusion is that "the power in possession of the working class must, in the interest of the shaping of Socialism, the oppressing of class enemies and the defense against imperialism be still much more decidedly and severely exercised than it has been up to now. 'Dictatorship' also means the exercising of force in oppressing enemies." [4] He said he recognized that force is not the only weapon. This, however, "does not mean at all that the functions of oppression and violence also appertaining to the dictatorship of the proletariat should be overlooked as secondary." The appropriate organs of the state should be unified and made ready for periods when "the chief function of the dictatorship of the proletariat will consist of using force against enemies from within and without."

Our summary of all this can be brief. The Hungarian Communist Party relies on the Soviet Union for guidance and on the Soviet Army for support. It never coöperated with non-Communist progressive parties in good faith but only for tactical advantage. A People's Democracy is a dictatorship of the proletariat, and though not now in precisely the Soviet form it will steadily draw closer to it. A pressing task is collectivization of the land, by force if necessary. The peasants may coöperate with the workers, but the workers, represented solely by the Hungarian Workers' Party (Communist), will not share their leadership and power. Opponents will be liquidated by force.

The intellectual climate having been prepared, the next step was to bring home to each member of the Hungarian Communist Party that he personally faced not a theory but "a really practical problem." This was achieved for the rank-and-file by ousting about 200,000 persons from membership and the privilege of belonging to the ruling minority. For Party leaders the lesson would be more terrifyingly "practical." It would take the form of a laboratory demonstration on the living body of one of their number. The choice fell on Laszlo Rajk.

---

[4] Earlier in the speech Revai had assured his hearers that they need have no fear that resort to force may provoke civil war. The power of the Soviet Union ensures against this; and in Hungary, specifically, the Soviet Army is "always here" to "support us."

# XXI

## HIS OWN MEPHISTOPHELES

> Apart from the Soviet Union, no other
> country has shown us such friendship as
> Jugoslavia.
>
> "Szabad Nep," official Communist organ, Buda-
> pest, January 4, 1947

WHY Rajk? For two reasons.

First, for the primary reason that he was well suited to induce terror as a ceremonial sacrifice. To single out such an eminent personage in the Party and the government for punishment would demonstrate that none was immune to the workings of "the system." If he did not happen to be guilty the demonstration would be all the more awe-inspiring. The hardest slave-driver had no recourse when he came under the lash of the master.

As the Cominform strategists thought the situation over they saw, in addition, that Rajk was particularly fitted to fulfill a useful function in a wider framework by reason of having been first in control of the Hungarian secret police and then of Hungarian foreign relations. Before his legs dangled over the little doorway to eternity he could be made to strike a good blow at the enemy who was causing the Soviets to lose so much face in the world. Incidentally, he would provide them with an excuse for having failed to deal with that enemy effectively. In this plan, Rajk would be made to reveal that Tito was a puppet and accomplice of the reactionary Western Powers. He would also show that the reason Tito had not been disposed of was that he was being helped systematically by traitors within the Communist gates. Rajk would be presented as one of those traitors. He would be tried not as a heretic but as a spy, and he would confess and name his paymasters.

During the summer of 1949 the indictment was prepared in the

necessary terms and various codefendants were selected for their
ability to play supporting rôles in a well-rounded cast. By autumn
the play was ready, and on September 11 a full outline of the plot
and the names of the players were published in the Budapest newspapers.[1] Rajk had star billing, but some of the others were well-
known too—Lieutenant-General Gyorgy Palffy, Chief-of-Staff of the
Hungarian Army; Dr. Tibor Szonyi, head of Party enrollment and
appointments; and Pal Jusztusz, member of the National Assembly
and director of the Hungarian radio. To establish the link with Belgrade, Lazar Brankov was added. He was a former chargé d'affaires
of the Jugoslav Legation who had renounced his post and stayed in
Budapest at the time Tito was expelled from the Cominform, and
he was now to have a chance to demonstrate his allegiance to his
new masters by confessing publicly that he had betrayed them also.
Several minor characters were brought in to play bit parts.

Were the story unfolded by these characters true it should encourage opponents of Communism no end, for if such trusted chiefs of
an old and important Communist Party were free to practise every
sort of perfidy their responsible colleagues could not be described
except as naïve, careless and ignorant. There evidently was in addition a highly satisfactory degree of inefficiency and corruption in the
counter-intelligence and among the spies whom the Hungarian Communist leaders employed to watch each other.

Thus the indictment asserts that Rajk, who helped bring the
Communist régime to power in Hungary and from 1945 to 1948
controlled its chief organs of security, had become a police informer
against his fellow Communists as early as 1931, and that he had
continued as stool-pigeon and spy without interruption and without
arousing suspicion for 18 years. It describes how he first became an
agent of the Horthy police in return for being set at liberty after an
arrest for distributing Communist leaflets; how he organized Communist groups of university students in order to denounce them;
how he organized Communist strikes and denounced the participants; how he became a spy of the Horthy government in Czechoslovakia, and then enlisted in the Rakosi Battalion in the Spanish

[1] An English translation of the indictment of Rajk and his codefendants was
published in the *New Times*, Moscow, September 14, 1949.

Civil War in order to be able to start "undermining actions" among the other volunteers. When he was discovered (continues the indictment), he fled to France, was interned, and in certain specified camps met a number of "Jugoslav foreign intelligence agents," including Aleš Bebler, afterwards Jugoslav member of the U. N. Security Council, Karlo Mrazovich, afterwards Jugoslav Ambassador in Budapest, and other men who rose to top rank later on in Tito's Partisan army, besides many French, American and Gestapo agents. With these valuable new connections Rajk returned to Hungary to undertake espionage work on a larger scale. For appearance's sake he got himself arrested, but was let off lightly. If what was said about him were true he must have been in contact with more intelligence services than almost any other spy in Europe; yet he was so successful "in concealing his past," as the indictment puts it, that the Hungarian Communists received him back with innocent confidence, made him Secretary of the Party organization in Budapest, a member of the Politburo and a Member of Parliament. Then, still not recognizing him as a mortal enemy, they put him in charge of the Ministry of the Interior and the secret police. From that vantage point, and afterwards from the Foreign Office, he built up an espionage network throughout the government and recruited other conspirators to help execute his grand design. This was to assassinate his colleagues, seize power and sell out Hungary and Hungarian Communism to Marshal Tito and the American and other imperialists who were Tito's paymasters. His chief assistant was General Palffy, who was to see to the assassinations.

The substance of what might have been a common enough tale of the Communist underworld was thus spun into the scenario of a melodrama worthy of being played under the klieg lights and before the microphones of the Budapest People's Court, in the presence of 60 representatives of the world press. An inspired Soviet strategist saw that what had been planned as the sacrifice of a Communist official for the good of Party souls in heretical jeopardy could be lifted into the realm of international policy and perhaps made to bring Tito crashing down under the curses of his people. Convenient to this design, Rajk had been active before the war in Czechoslovakia, Spain and France, and later his high government posts had given him many opportunities to develop foreign contacts, secret and public. According to the Soviet story, Tito and his diplomats, knowing all that Rajk's own colleagues did not know about his past, entered into relations with him. They were able to do so without awakening Hungarian suspicions because, as the indictment put it, they "vilely exploited" the friendship felt by all Hungarians for the workers of Jugoslavia.

So far the story would not have caused much of a sensation outside of Hungary. Another spy, another scapegoat, another execution. But the action was destined to occupy a larger stage. After the defeat of the Nazis in Jugoslavia, it seems, the American intelligence enlisted a large number of the former Gestapo agents remaining in the country, as well as Jugoslav "agents-provocateurs and Trotskyites." They worked so well together that in a short time "Tito's immediate entourage consisted mainly of these spies," who "systematically ousted from the government" the honest and loyal Partisans who had fought in the war. Tito, it seems, had secretly gone over to the Americans as early as 1944. At any rate, in December of that year the American intelligence was able to recruit a band of "Hungarian Trotskyite émigrés" in Switzerland, get them provided with false Jugoslav papers and send them in an American army plane to Belgrade. From there (after receiving further instructions from the Jugoslav secret police) they were landed by the same plane in Hungary, "in the rear of the Soviet Army." Safely at home, they destroyed their Jugoslav papers, infiltrated into government posts and set to work as spies for Jugoslavia and the United States. In the summer of 1945 Tito and his Western bosses were ready to move into higher echelons. They took on Rajk as their chief agent and also engaged the Chief-of-Staff of the Hungarian Army, General Palffy, described in the indictment as "a Fascist officer of Horthy's army . . . who posed as a Communist." Apparently the Hungarian Communists were as innocent as the Russian Bolsheviks in picking their worst enemies to head their army and run their secret police—Palffy was the equivalent of Marshal Tukhachevsky and Rajk of OGPU chief Yagoda. Palffy went to work to help Rajk get "former Trotskyites, provocateurs and spies" into high posts. Among them were not merely Jugoslavs, but agents of Great Britain, the United States and France.

Lazar Brankov, the former Jugoslav diplomat who had gone over to the Cominform camp and now found himself accused of being a "double agent"—and who knows if he was not?—confessed that in the autumn of 1947, that is, before the Cominform dispute reached an acute stage, the Jugoslav Government considered the situation in Hungary ripe enough for them to proceed to overthrow the régime. Tito at about this time visited Budapest and signed the Jugoslav-Hungarian treaty of friendship which received such universal praise throughout the Communist world. The treaty was only an excuse, however. Rajk wanted to prepare the way for his *putsch* by "systematically endeavoring artificially to create popularity for Tito and diminish the great prestige enjoyed by the Soviet Union." When Tito left for home, accompanied by Rankovich, the Jugoslav Minister of the Interior, Rajk went with them as far as the frontier. Brankov, who acted as interpreter on this trip, states that Rankovich used the occasion to tell Rajk the full scope of Tito's plan: "to bring the People's Democracies into Jugoslavia's orbit, with its center at Belgrade." The action in Hungary thus was to be only the first step. Tito's instructions for carrying it out were that Rajk should "orient" himself "on the nationalist, chauvinist elements in the Army, the police and the government service, and on the petty-bourgeois forces in the cities, and especially in the countryside."

However, in the spring of 1948 the Cominform decided to act strongly against Tito. As Rajk was a member of the Politburo he naturally heard that the Cominform was aware of Tito's "treachery" and, according to the indictment, told Tito what was happening. Exact dates are not mentioned, but it will be recalled that in August, following the break between Tito and the Cominform, Rajk was "demoted" from Minister of the Interior to Minister of Foreign Affairs. Was he in fact a "nationalist" in the sense that Gomulka and others objected to arbitrary Soviet action in the Cominform? If so, there may have been others in the Party hierarchy in sympathy with his views. That would explain his being retained in the government and even placed where he would have frequent opportunity to consult with other satellite statesmen who might be sympathetic also.

Tito's expulsion from the Cominform made it necessary for the conspirators to recast their scheme of operations. Accordingly, the story runs, Rankovich met Rajk secretly in southern Hungary in October 1948 and unfolded a "brilliant new plan" through which Tito expected that he could "gradually turn the Jugoslav people against the Soviet Union and bring them into the camp of the Western imperialists." In the first phase, Tito would not criticize the Soviet Union but would continue to profess friendship for it and for its leaders. After a time, however, he would begin emphasizing that it was the Soviet Union which made it impossible for Jugoslavia to carry out the Five Year Plan and other Socialist reforms. When Jugoslav living conditions failed to rise as they ought to do under Communist rule, "the friendship of our people will turn to hatred" (Rankovich's purported words). Then Tito could secure popular approval for deserting Russia and aligning himself with the West. To complete the program, Rajk would arrange frontier incidents in which Hungary would seem to be the aggressor, and General Palffy and other "army Fascists" would carry out the "physical annihilation" of Hungary's pro-Soviet leadership, including Rakosi, Farkas and Gerö. Just in time the whole plot was discovered, said the charge, and "in the middle of May the arrests of the conspirators began."

Everybody confessed to everything. The confessions had been secured in advance, before the indictment was prepared or the trial began. Each defendant—or rather non-defendant, for none made any defense—seemed intent only on gaining credit by not merely admitting his alleged crimes but by magnifying them. Some interesting new details came out in this way. Brankov, for example, said that the plot for the West to wrest control of the Balkans from the Soviets was initiated in 1943 when the Western Allies began helping Tito, and that the instigator was Winston Churchill, assisted by various British and Americans, including Brigadier Maclean, head of the British military mission to Partisan headquarters, Allen W. Dulles, a director of OSS activities in several European resistance movements, and practically all the American and British officers known to have worked with the Partisans during the war. These were supposed to have succeeded in bringing around three members of the Jugoslav Politburo—Rankovich, Kardelj and Djilas—to the idea that postwar Jugoslavia should be a bourgeois capitalist state and that it should head a Balkan federation of similar states. Even Tito himself was supposed to have finally accepted the program. Indeed, he never had wanted Communism sincerely. One indication of this was that for a long time he rejected Soviet help in liberating Jugoslavia, though in the end he had been forced to ask for it.[2] His pro-Communist pose had been necessitated by the fact that of course the Jugoslav people did sincerely favor Communism. So Brankov testified. Palffy's chief contribution, beyond confirming everything that Rajk and Brankov had confessed, was the information that the date for the *putsch* in Budapest had been set definitely for May or June 1949 (incidentally the period of my visit, which would explain why Rajk was so busy).

The tale is worked out in ingenious detail, and parts of it may even be true. Rajk was known and feared in Budapest as a stern operator against class enemies, and in his dealings with foreign diplomats he was habitually cold, disagreeable and forbidding. These characteristics would not have prevented him, however, from opposing Moscow's domineering ways or sympathizing to some degree with Tito's efforts to prevent Jugoslavia from being exploited for Russia's benefit. But no operator is clever enough to participate in plots in which the principals suddenly shift sides without laying himself open to later accusations that he had played some sort of double game. To collaborate with class enemies as a matter of expediency (as Revai found quite natural) must be harrowing enough; for what is expedient today, you must be fully aware, will not be so considered forever, and when it is no longer there may be excellent reasons of expediency for making you "the goat." But what must be truly excruciating is to find that the ally with whose secret agents you have been working—as Rajk would have worked with the agents of Nazi Germany when she was Russia's ally—suddenly turns into an enemy. Almost surely you will have left some sort of incriminating evidence

[2] *Cf.* Chapter III for Pijade's description of Tito's futile appeals to "Grandfather" for help.

in the hands of your former colleagues. Worse, you know only too well that whether this is so or not those former colleagues of yours will in any case inform against you if this will ingratiate them with your master and persuade him to put them on his payroll and send you to the hangman. Rajk could not possibly have emerged from the morass of Nazi-Communist collaboration without leaving muddy footprints to the doors of a hundred suspicious characters and providing each of them with a motive to give evidence against him, equally damaging whether true or false.

The Jugoslavs reacted violently to the attack launched against them by the Cominform through Rajk. Their most telling argument was that the Hungarian Government was guilty of precisely the crimes which it attributed to Jugoslavia—pressure, threats, spying, border incidents—and that as it had no other means of defense it took the only possible course of accusing Jugoslavia first.

A series of government communiqués issued in Belgrade attempted to dispose of various questions of fact. For example, it was pointed out that the Jugoslav Communists whom Rajk had supposedly met in French concentration camps after the Spanish civil war were not in those camps; Bebler and Mrazovich, for example, had been seriously wounded, had been taken directly to Paris and transported from there to Jugoslavia. In reply to the charge that the Jugoslav Government plotted to overthrow the Hungarian Government, it was asked why in that case Jugoslavia had done so much to help Hungary consolidate her position economically and politically? Rakosi and the other Hungarian leaders had often come to Belgrade for help and advice, and they always had said publicly as well as privately how grateful they were for what they received. The Hungarian press had been lavish with expressions of gratitude to the Jugoslavs—that they had made such small demands on Hungary for reparations, that they had given Hungary credits without interest, that they had so loyally supported the Hungarian position at the Paris Peace Conference, oblivious of Hungary's many unjust acts toward Jugoslavia during the war. As to Rankovich's alleged meeting with Rajk in southern Hungary, it was stressed that the indictment "did not dare specify any exact date." Rankovich had been in

Belgrade throughout the period mentioned, and proof could have been brought forward that on any given date it was not physically possible for him to have been in Hungary.

Tito had the last word. He chose the moment when the Jugoslav autumn manœuvres were ending and he spoke in the defiant manner suited to an address to 600 army officers. "We have the right to say a falsehood is a falsehood," he said, "a lie is a lie." The Budapest trial had been a "deeply thought-out act of villainy against our country." He hinted at one possible reason when he said it had been planned "so as to make us out, at any time in the near future, to be aggressors, Fascists, men who threaten world peace, and so on." He suggested another reason when he said the trial had been used by the Soviets as a pretext for abrogating the Treaty of Friendship and Mutual Aid with Jugoslavia. As a third, he noted that the trial had been placed in Budapest—although it might just as easily have been staged in either the Soviet Union or any other East European country—because the Hungarian people "are deeply dissatisfied and discontented with the Soviet Union for several reasons, and it was necessary in some way to divert the dissatisfaction against Jugoslavia and to present this country as a great menace to the independence of Hungary."

Why had Rajk been picked? Tito said he was not sure. "Rajk was the very one we had least to do with. Most of our contacts were with Rakosi, Farkas and the others, while Rajk was always as silent as the grave." Tito said he had heard that at the time of the Cominform fight Rajk "at first wavered . . . because he did not like the methods being used against Jugoslavia." On account of that wavering Rajk had been taken to Moscow in 1948 "for overhaul." "I do not know all the parts of Rajk they 'overhauled,' " Tito remarked, "but he did go there and when he returned he became Minister of Foreign Affairs instead of Internal Affairs. In his place in the Ministry of Internal Affairs came another Minister—to organize this trial against Rajk." Tito concluded:

Thus all this was concocted in Moscow. Rajk was subsequently arrested and again sent to Moscow for "overhaul," together with Brankov. And there, according to some method they have there, they

were prepared for the trial. You saw that at the trial there was everything desired. How you achieve having people pile guilt on themselves,
I do not know, but that some monstrous method does exist is certain.

An acquaintance of mine who reported the trial for the London
*Times* said in one of his excellent long dispatches that Rajk agreed
"almost blandly" to everything of which he was accused, that his
tone throughout was quite impersonal and that he "spoke more as
one relating a narrative than as a man confessing." The account
reminds one of what observers wrote of the purge trials in Moscow
in the thirties. A few months before the Rajk trial, Cardinal Mindszenty, pleading guilty to a long list of charges, many of them highly
improbable, had made his answer to each in almost the identical
phraseology in which the police had stated it first. Rajk did the same.
The police accusations, he said, were all correct. He added that he
had done everything of his own volition, that he was his own
Mephistopheles. He asked to be hanged.

He received his request. He was hanged October 15. With him
were hanged Dr. Tibor Szonyi and an assistant. After Palffy's case
had been reviewed by a court-martial he was hanged too. The others
got off with prison sentences.

Mosha Pijade wrote in the Belgrade *Borba* [3] that it was "unimportant and accidental" that Rajk and Palffy happened to be the
accused, and hence unimportant and accidental that they happened
to be hanged. What was important, he said, was that the trial provided proof that "Great Russian chauvinism does not hesitate to use
any measures for its infiltration into the life of European nations and
for advancing Great Russia as the world nation—the leader." He
said: "It is the acme of malicious hypocrisy when someone in a
desire to hide his own crime ascribes that crime to the very one the
crime is directed against. Actually, that is the basic and character-
istic line of the entire struggle which has been waged for such a long
time against Socialist Jugoslavia by certain leaders of the Soviet
Union, supported obediently by their aides in the other People's
Democracies and in certain other Communist Parties." And he gave
in a single sentence his estimate of the cause and effect of this action:

[3] September 22, 26 and 29, and October 5 and 6, 1949.

"It is the fruit of the vain lack of reasoning which kills the most important fruit of the October Revolution, destroys the unity of the Revolutionary World Workers' Movement and the entire World Democratic Front and thus does the maximum service to world reaction."

# XXII

## "LET THE SPARROWS
## TWITTER"

> Governments are things that happen in
> cities.          Ignazio Silone, "Fontamara"

HAPPY, they say, is the people that has
no history. The history of the independent state of Rumania has
ended, but it would be brash to say that Rumanians are happy. They
are only mute.

The terminal date of Rumania's independence can be variously
fixed. She was an Axis satellite during the war, and was supposed
to have been liberated when Marshal Tolbukhin's armies drove out
the Nazis and their puppet government. Whether she ever truly regained her independence, and if so just when she lost it again, is a
question, but there will be little dispute that today she comes nearer
being a constituent member of the U.S.S.R. than any other of the
satellite states. Day by day the Rumanian bulge on the silhouette of
the Soviet boa-constrictor grows smaller and smaller as the Communist digestive juices do their work, and today it looms not much
larger than that caused by, say, the Ukraine. Moscow still permits
Rumania to receive American, British, French and other diplomats
in Bucharest; but their numbers are strictly limited, and they are
forbidden to enter about two-thirds of the Rumanian national territory, including the Banat, the Bukovina, Moldavia and the Dobrudja. Similarly, she is allowed to maintain diplomatic missions of
roughly equivalent size in the respective Western capitals. On the
other hand, though the Ukrainian People's Soviet Republic is not
qualified in Moscow's view to entertain foreign diplomats in Kiev
even *à la Roumaine,* it does approach independence closely enough

(as Stalin argued persuasively at Yalta) to deserve separate membership in the United Nations. The voice of the Ukraine is therefore
heard at Flushing Meadows—and is not to be despised, even though
it is the voice of Jacob rather than Esau, for usually it has been that
of Mr. Manuilsky, one of the most experienced revolutionary de-
baters extant. The voice of the Rumanian People's Republic is not
heard there and is not paid much if any attention anywhere.

Before long the question will come up whether Rumania deserves
even the title of satellite. This might be settled by Moscow's decision
to bring her into the Soviet Union as one of the constituent member
republics. Until now an argument against this has probably been
the hope that she might one day be elected to membership in the
United Nations, in exchange for Moscow's acceptance of some
Western-sponsored candidate like Ireland or Portugal. But meanwhile the orbit in which she moves has so much shrunk that she no
longer shines even by reflected light, and the chance that she might
be considered entitled to membership in any world assembly of independent nations has greatly diminished. Foreign newspaper men
no longer are allowed to report directly on what is occurring in the
country. If elements of national resistance still exist we hear little
or nothing of their activities.

Bucharest might have hoped to claim glory as the capital of the
Cominform, which she supposedly became when the organization
moved out of Belgrade. Even this is denied her, for the Cominform
no longer meets regularly, in Bucharest or anywhere else. Perhaps
the Soviet leaders see no further value in the organization. Perhaps
Stalin has made up his mind not to permit any alternate center of
power, even minor, to the Kremlin. Some persons think that the
Cominform was created originally in order to deal specifically with
the Jugoslav situation, and having fulfilled this function, though far
from successfully, is now retained simply as a paper organization for
possible use some time in the future. Today its principal activity is
as a printing press. To the extent that glory attaches to being a
printing press Bucharest has it. The Cominform journal, *For a Lasting Peace, for a People's Democracy!*, is printed there in some 15
languages.

The Cominform journal may even be written largely in Bucharest.

The typical articles by Communist leaders provide statistical material appropriate to the various circumstances, but whether they are signed by Signor Togliatti, M. Duclos, President Bierut, Herr Ulbricht or Mme. Ana Pauker they employ the standard vocabulary and are of standard cut. What might be called the ceremonial articles—marking anniversaries, hailing Stalin on his divine birthday, claiming this or that achievement of science or culture for Russia—are uniformly couched in a language of such vulgarity, turgidity, repetitiousness and monotony that they almost surely must emanate from a single brain. Possibly, of course, they merely reveal a uniform barrenness of thought and poverty of expression in Communist literary circles everywhere. If not, the central brain in Bucharest seems to be exhausted after executing so many changes of direction, doubling back so often on past tracks, discovering so many old enemies to be friends and firing the old epithets against so many old friends suddenly discovered to be enemies.

As I read through copies of *For a Lasting Peace, for a People's Democracy!* for chance statements of interest or indications of shifts of emphasis in the Party line I find myself wondering what would be thought of them by some master polemicist like Bukharin, Radek or another of the old professionals with a subtle mind, a knowledge of history and a feeling for human psychology. What would they have thought of this wearying succession of hammering adjectives as a method of conveying the power and sincerity of a great revolutionary purpose to the far parts of the earth? Certainly it is a convenience for us who fight that purpose that every great pen of the Russian revolution has been stilled by time or Stalin's hangmen.

The independence which Rumania was supposed to have regained when the Red Army occupied the country in August 1944 was formally guaranteed by the Declaration on Liberated Europe adopted by Roosevelt, Stalin and Churchill at Yalta. The same instrument guaranteed the Rumanian people their domestic liberties, including the right to choose their own government. But hardly were the "Big Three" back in their capitals from the Crimea before that independence and those freedoms were clearly jeopardized by the appearance of a Communist-dominated minority government in Bucharest. The manner in which this was accomplished was as significant as the result. The Soviet Vice-Commissar of Foreign Affairs, Andrei Vyshinsky, simply flew down to Bucharest from Moscow on February 27, 1945, and gave King Michael the necessary orders. By Vyshinsky's direction the King ignored the representatives of the two largest political organizations in the country, the National Peasant Party headed by Iuliu Maniu and the National Liberal Party headed by Dinu Bratianu, and entrusted power to the man of Vyshinsky's choice, Petru Groza. The United States and Great Britain protested. Informed of the painful impression which his interference in Rumanian domestic politics had created in Western capitals, Vyshinsky commented only: "Let the sparrows twitter."

Public opinion in the West was not well informed about this development, or indeed about current developments in any of the areas which came under the occupation of the Red Army. Few Western newspapermen were on the spot in Rumania or Bulgaria, and those who were had limited means of communication. So far as American public opinion was concerned, the State Department did not consider it wise, on the eve of the San Francisco Conference, to release the reports of highhanded Soviet actions which it was receiving from those countries. The hope was that when Soviet Russia had assumed her official place in world councils she would become responsive to world opinion and begin behaving like a responsible member of international society. It was considered inadvisable to exacerbate Stalin's feelings by too violent complaints of the farce being made of his Yalta promises at the very moment he was sending Molotov, Gromyko and Sobolev to a great international conference to assume world responsibilities in an organization based on the ideals of the Atlantic Charter and the Moscow Declaration of 1943. The State Department complained about violations of the Yalta Agreement in its notes to the Soviet Government; but officials refrained from stressing their anxiety and anger in comments to the press.

Western protests mounted in urgency as time passed and the Soviet halter, far from being released, was drawn closer around the necks of states occupied by the Red Army. In Rumania, Maniu and Bratianu had refused to submit to the minority control of the Communists and their stool-pigeons. At the time, Maniu in particular was criticized in liberal circles abroad for a lack of "realism" in failing to recognize that new "progressive" forces were at work and in refusing to coöperate with them. In Hungary, Ferenc Nagy's Smallholders Party coöperated with the Communists in a coalition government, and Petkov coöperated in the Fatherland Front in Bulgaria. These were applauded as signs of superior liberalism and far-sightedness. In neither case, as we have seen, was the end result satisfactory. It was not different in Rumania. The United States and British Governments made efforts to hold the governments concerned and their Soviet patrons to the terms of the Yalta Agreement. They succeeded only in revealing a distressing lack of power behind the written and verbal messages which their diplomats delivered at the respective foreign offices. To this extent it can be said that they actually damaged the native national forces which they aimed to help.

The Western Powers protested, as mentioned, against Vyshinsky's interference in Rumanian affairs and quite properly refused to recognize the Groza Government. Encouraged by this, King Michael in August 1945 appealed to the three signatories of the Yalta Agreement to help him create a "recognized democratic government." The Agreement provided that if differences arose about how democratic and representative régimes were to be created the three signatories should consult. The American and British Governments demanded that a consultation now take place about Rumania. Moscow replied that no differences existed except with regard to Rumanian domestic affairs and that therefore a consultation would be not only superfluous but highly improper. That was that. Soviet troops were in occupation of Rumania, and the Western Powers did not propose to go to war to replace Mr. Groza with Mr. Maniu. Other protests over other infringements of the Yalta undertaking were similarly rebuffed. It was right in one view to make them "for the record." The immediate result, however, was that the Western democracies lost face and non-Communist elements were weakened.

Simultaneously negotiations had been begun looking to the conclusion of peace treaties with Italy and the former Axis satellites. The peace conference opened in Paris on July 29, 1946. One staff member of the American delegation has said that the draft treaties there presented compared unfavorably with even the maligned treaties of 1919 and 1920.[1] The treaties as actually signed on February 10, 1947, were no better. The Western Powers tried to arrange that some respect be paid to the principle of self-determination, by plebiscite or otherwise, in settling the ownership of territories in dispute between former Axis states or between them and the victors. They met with no success.

In Rumania's case several important territories were at stake, including Bessarabia, a part of the Bukovina, the northern part of Transylvania and the Southern Dobrudja.

Bessarabia had come into Russian possession first in 1812; had been transferred to Rumania (largely on ethnic grounds) in 1918; and had been retaken by Russia in June 1940, pursuant to an agreement between Ribbentrop and Molotov a year earlier. Rumanians have since asserted that the Rumanian Government of 1940 did not formally consent to the Russian annexation but merely evacuated the territory under threat of force. At Paris the Soviet delegates referred to the 1940 transfer as "an agreement," said it had been confirmed by the armistice and made clear that possession was nine-tenths of the law. The peace treaty confirmed this reasoning. The case of Northern Bukovina was somewhat different, though the decision of the peace conference regarding it was the same. Northern Bukovina never in history had been Russian. The province had not been specifically mentioned in the Molotov-Ribbentrop deal of 1939; but Germany had not protested when the Soviets took it over in 1940. The Soviets argued that, as in the case of their territorial demands on the Czechs and the Finns, they required the area for strategic purposes of defense. The bear must protect itself against the carnivorous lamb.[2]

One decision was to Rumania's advantage. In 1940 Ciano and Ribbentrop had handed over the northern part of the Rumanian province of Transylvania to their protégés the Hungarians. When Vyshinsky installed Groza in power in Bucharest on March 6, 1945, he felt that he must give the new Prime Minister some success to

[1] John C. Campbell, "The United States in World Affairs, 1945–1947." New York: Harper's, for the Council on Foreign Relations, 1947, p. 134.

[2] Rumania ceded the Southern Dobrudja to Bulgaria September 7, 1940. The Peace Conference confirmed this also. The United States had favored this arrangement in 1919 and approved it in 1940.

advertise to the Rumanian masses, most of whom had never heard his name. On March 8, therefore, Groza was told to ask Stalin for northern Transylvania, and by return telegram he received it as a "present." The Nazis had not yet been expelled from Budapest, so there was nobody there for Moscow to take into account. The Western Allies were not consulted. As a matter of fact, they had no objection to the return of at least most of Transylvania to Rumania, but would have preferred that it be done after study as to whether or not there should be frontier rectifications in favor of Hungarian ethnic groups; and they certainly would have considered it more suitable that the transfer be made after agreement among the Allies rather than unilaterally by one of them.

The steps by which the Communist-dominated Rumanian Government became an absolute Communist dictatorship need not be detailed here.[3] In the beginning there certainly were some non-Communist elements which favored a clean sweep of the old order even though the representatives of the new order were Communists and protégés of the hated Russians. Seizure of the large properties still left in Rumania after the land reforms following the First World War was popular in principle. Rumanian régimes of the inter-war period had not been noted for efficiency or probity, and the Communists hastened to identify all Rumanian statesmen who held democratic beliefs and had a Western orientation with the "old gang" of profiteers and politicians who had mocked the Constitution in the dissolute days of King Carol and had ended by taking Rumania into the war as the ally of the Nazis. The fact that Maniu, the country's leading statesman, was famous for his incorruptibility and stubborn devotion to the Constitution did not deter Communist propaganda from picturing him also as a corrupt relic of the old dictatorial order. The Socialists were, of course, completely outbid by Communist promises of pie in the sky.

But although these tactics had some success at first the only one of them that was based on anything substantial, the gift of land to

[3] For a fuller outline of the postwar evolution in Rumania as well as other parts of Eastern Europe, and of relevant negotiations (if they can be called that) between the Soviets and the Western Powers, see Campbell, *op. cit.*, also volumes for 1947–48 and 1948–49 in the same series by the same author, and the volume for 1949 by Richard P. Stebbins.

the peasants, was a boomerang. The land reforms of 1919–21 had distributed about 14 million acres among about 1,400,000 peasants. The new Communist expropriations distributed an additional 2,750,000 acres among about 1,100,000 peasants. It has been calculated that as a result more than half of the land holdings in Rumania consisted of less than seven and a half acres per family. Most farms of this size were insufficient to support independent farmers. Now this may have been as the Communists planned, for it enabled them to point out the advantages of collectivization to peasants who lacked even the minimum of tools and draft animals to cultivate their small private holdings. But when they did so they lost the popularity they had gained, both with peasants who worked ancestral lands and with those who had just shared in the expropriated estates.

The Communists thus felt it necessary to make their political position more secure, in particular to head off their natural rivals in the countryside, the formidable National Peasant Party headed by Maniu. In December 1945 a correspondent of the London *Times* had written critically of Maniu's "rigidity" and unwillingness to accept a modern "radical policy," and had blamed his "unbending attitude" for the "inevitable" political crisis. Less than a year later (October 18, 1946) the same or another correspondent of the *Times* reported from Bucharest that Maniu was "more popular than ever in his long career." The dispatch continued: "His past mistakes and weaknesses are forgotten. He stands now not for any program or ideology but for the idea of national independence. He is the symbol of the Rumanian nation."

As the Rumanian nation was to be destroyed, Maniu had to be destroyed.

This was the period for dealing with peasant rivals to the Communists in all the agrarian satellite states. In Bulgaria, the leader of the Peasant Party, Petkov, was arrested in June 1947 and hanged in September. In Poland, the leader of the Peasant Party, Mikolajczyk, was harried from the political scene and in October 1947 was forced to flee to London. In Hungary, the Soviets had made the mistake of permitting free elections and had lost them to Nagy's Smallholders Party; but they had stipulated that regardless of the electoral results a coalition government should be set up, and in this they secured the Ministry of the Interior and thus made ready to stage a coup at the opportune moment. That moment came in May 1947. Maniu's turn came in July 1947. He was arrested, the National Peasant Party was dissolved, and three months later he was put on trial before a military court presided over by Colonel Alexandru Petrescu. This officer had worn many uniforms and (as W. H. Lawrence who covered the trial for *The New York Times* recalled) had once filled the same judicial office under the pro-Nazi Antonescu dictatorship when the prisoners in the dock usually were Jews or were charged with being Communists or anti-Fascists, equally reprehensible in those days. After a two-week trial which travestied anything that we would call a judicial proceeding, Maniu was convicted and given solitary imprisonment for life. With him were sentenced Ion Mihalache, Vice President of the National Peasant Party, and other associates.

By the end of 1947 the Communists had dealt with all political rivals in Eastern Europe who had particular influence with the peasant masses. Whether the peasant leaders temporized or were rigid, collaborated or fought back, their fate was different only in degree: for some death, for some prison, for some exile.

Six weeks after Maniu was sentenced, King Michael, who had struggled to diminish his royal prerogatives to the point where they might be combined with a Communist dictatorship, and who occasionally seemed to be succeeding, was ordered to abdicate and leave the country. The Rumanian People's Republic was proclaimed December 30, 1947. No political focus of opposition was left—reactionary, bourgeois, agrarian, democratic or Socialist.

Moscow even so did not feel that the situation in Rumania was all it should be. A core of nationalist sentiment seemed to remain inside the Communist organization itself, and it was ordered cut out. The man selected to serve as an example was an old Party stalwart and cabinet member, Lucretiu Patrascanu. He had been a Communist member of Parliament in the twenties, a leader of the Communist underground during the war and head of the commission sent to Moscow to negotiate the Rumanian armistice. In the cabinets preceding Groza's he had been Minister of Justice, and Vyshinsky thought him sufficiently reliable to allot him the same important position in the new setup. *The Daily Worker* [4] praised him in those days "for his staunch defense of leading anti-Fascists, such as Professor Constantinescu-Iasi, Ana Pauker and the railway strike leaders before the military and civil Rumanian tribunals," and added the information that he had joined the Rumanian Communist Party when it was first organized in 1920 and had been editor of the official Party organ, *Scanteia,* from 1921 to 1924. Patrascanu's administration of the Rumanian judicial system continued to be satisfactory at least to the end of 1947, for he was retained in the same post in the new republican cabinet formed after Michael's abdication.

Less than two months later, at a Congress when the rump groups still calling themselves "Social Democratic" joined the Communists to form the new Rumanian Workers' Party (Communist), Teohari Georgescu, Minister of the Interior, suddenly rose to assail Patrascanu as a deviationist. Like the accused, the accuser was a member of the Central Committee of the Party. Georgescu's complaint was that Patrascanu had fallen "under the influence of the bourgeoisie" and "had become an exponent of bourgeois ideology." As this happened at the end of February 1948, when only the innermost circle of Cominform authorities knew that Moscow was stigmatizing Tito as a bourgeois deviationist, we cannot tell whether the two developments were connected or whether Patrascanu merely happened to reveal some tendency toward independence at an unfortunate moment.

Tito had been in Bucharest at the end of December 1947 to sign the Jugoslav-Rumanian pact of friendship and mutual assistance, and half a million persons had assembled at an open-air rally to hear him speak. "It was a great triumph," Mosha Pijade has written—in fact, Pijade admits, too great a triumph, "for it started personal jealousy where none of us expected it." He adds: "When Comrade Tito achieved triumphs during his visits to Warsaw, Prague, Sofia, Bucharest and Budapest, it was too much for them. Sick vanity threw the interests of world Socialism into the dirt." [5] If Patrascanu

[4] New York, November 11, 1944.
[5] *Borba,* Belgrade, September 26 and 29, 1949.

had not heard that Tito was in danger, he might have made up to him too openly. Maybe he happened to be one of those to whom Tito mentioned the troubles he was having with the Soviets, and maybe some informer transmitted a sympathetic comment to Moscow. A few days after Tito left Bucharest, Dimitrov arrived to sign a similar treaty of friendship on behalf of Bulgaria. This was the occasion where the exuberant Rumanian welcome is supposed to have gone to Dimitrov's head, leading him to speak imprudently about forming a wide federation of East European states as an offset to Soviet hegemony. Was Patrascanu implicated in the indiscretions for which the Bulgarian Prime Minister apologized so abjectly after returning to Sofia? Perhaps the international events merely coincided with Patrascanu's fall. Perhaps he was purged simply because his background was Rumanian rather than Muscovite (he apparently never was in Moscow until 1944), and suspects were being gotten rid of everywhere in preparation for the showdown with Tito. He had spent the war in the Rumanian underground and Rumanian jails and knew the country as Ana Pauker, Vasile Luca and other Moscow-trained Communists did not. He may easily have had ideas about the importance of Rumanian national feelings and perhaps even a feeling of his own for Rumanian national interests which would have been alien to the Muscovites. Whether this or something more specific accounts for his disgrace must remain speculation. What is on record is that he was denounced as a bourgeois and nationalist and expelled from the Party to which he had belonged for 28 years.

The purge begun with Patrascanu went wide and deep. In the Cominform journal for February 10, 1950, the Secretary-General of the Central Committee, Alexandru Moghiorosh, reported that the "ever sharpening class struggle" had necessitated a thorough house-cleaning of "bestial, alien and opportunist elements." In all, he said, 18 percent of the Party members had been dropped. On the date when the remnants of the so-called Social Democratic parties merged with the Communists, the combined strength of the new Rumanian Workers' Party was said to be about a million. This would indicate a purge of something like 180,000 individuals found to be lacking in Communist zeal or trustworthiness. Moghiorosh warned that "the

Anglo-American imperialists and their Titoist agents" would try to disrupt the Party in the future as in the past, and he asked for redoubled revolutionary vigilance against "all deviations from the Party line."

Those who were not purged were vigorously educated in the same ideas which Dimitrov, Bierut and Revai had brought to the attention of their followers. They were informed that in Rumania as elsewhere one of the touchstones of conformity to the new Moscow line was to be the attitude of the Parties toward the peasants. In the early days of their power, the Rumanian Communists had aimed to make private ownership of land unpopular by proving it unprofitable. As in the other satellites, they had set high tax rates on land, imposed high indirect taxes on salt, matches and other commodities which the peasant could not avoid buying, fixed high prices for manufactured goods in comparison with agricultural produce, offered special favors to peasants who joined collectives and in other ways demonstrated the hazards and costs of independent farming with a view to bringing the peasants to favor collectivization, as it were of their own accord. Minister of the Interior Georgescu signalled the end of this era of persuasion, if it can be called that, in the spring of 1949.

Georgescu joined the ranks of Dimitrov, Bierut and Revai with a contribution to the Cominform journal for June 1, 1949. As an article there would be read abroad as well as at home he used more discreet language than, for instance, Revai had felt necessary in addressing the comrades in Budapest. In the main, however, his definitions and instructions followed the same pattern. There was to be "a sharpening of the class struggle in town and countryside," and he made plain, as Revai had done, that although "the main ally of the working class is the working peasantry" the working class always reserves to itself "the leading rôle." He also agreed that a civil war would not be necessary to bring in the full dictatorship of the proletariat. In Rumania as in Hungary the Soviet Army was always there "to support us." Vasile Luca, Secretary of the Central Committee of the Rumanian Workers' Party (Communist), followed soon afterwards with an article speaking of "the ever sharpening class struggle" and "acute class struggle in the countryside in particular," and referring to the workers "as the sole guiding force in the country." [6] Nevertheless he seemed slightly on the defensive over the fact that after having had a free hand longer than any other Party in Eastern Europe the Rumanian Communists had only succeeded in forming to date 6,732 coöperatives of all types (consumer as well as producer coöperatives). He stressed that "mass collectivization" must wait on increased industrialization to supply needed farm machinery. And as if to forestall the jibes of Jugoslav Communists he attacked their achievements in collectivization as not only wrong in substance but as having been produced at a wrong tempo.

The hope of basing Communist rule on the dominance of the industrial proletariat over the peasantry seems especially ambitious in Rumania, where only about five percent of the population are industrial workers and 80 percent are peasants. It is true that agrarian overpopulation exists in Rumania and therefore a gradual shift of some rural elements to city pursuits must occur. The Communist expropriations failed (as the Communists had expected) to solve the agrarian problem because the properties still remaining undivided were insufficient to supply all landless peasants with land or to give those receiving land sufficient acreage to make them self-supporting. Mechanization of agriculture, so much emphasized in the satellite countries, will not solve the problem but will merely aggravate it by increasing the peasant's dependence on a single crop marketed under strict state control. The solution is to raise the standard of living of the peasants. This could be done by improving seeds and livestock, diversifying crops, developing home industries, improving methods of marketing, building roads, providing facilities for local food processing to avoid wastage, and consolidating separated family strips of land into efficient farming units. As rural living standards rise productivity would increase, and this would permit concurrent rises in the living standards of the industrial workers. These objective facts of the Rumanian economic structure rule out any other procedure unless it is frankly based on injustice and is indifferent to human unhappiness on a tremendous scale.

The Communists cannot, however, favor a program like the one

[6] *For a Lasting Peace, for a People's Democracy!*, Bucharest, August 1, 1949.

outlined. In the first place it would be slow and costly to carry out. Secondly, it would call for skills which Communist régimes do not possess and foreign scientific information which they boast of despising. Thirdly, they in principle oppose measures for improving small-peasant agriculture, for if they succeeded the peasants would merely become more independent and recalcitrant. They therefore prefer to favor industry and neglect agriculture,[7] calculating that misery on the farms will make the peasants more amenable to collectivization or force them into great slave-labor projects like the Danube-Black Sea canal. In any case, they have not cast Rumania to play an agricultural rôle in the family of Sovietized states. Nature did so, but they are going to improve on nature.

In Stalin's original plans Jugoslavia and probably Bulgaria were destined to remain agricultural in the main and to supply the other members of the family with raw materials. Rumania, although so heavily agricultural, was to be largely industrialized. The reason for this arbitrary allotment of functions is not entirely clear. Rumania has oil and timber, as well as reserves of soft coal and natural gas in Transylvania, all of which can be developed without running counter to economic law. She also has a large reservoir of unskilled labor. But otherwise she is not adapted by natural resources and native skills to proceed with very speedy or very extensive industrialization projects, and she seems especially unsuited to becoming a center of heavy industry in view of the scarcity of her metallurgical reserves. In any case, the improvement and development of agricultural production would be the right preliminary to ambitious enlargements of the industrial plant such as are projected in the new Rumanian Five Year Plan, to end December 31, 1955.

Ana Pauker has called the new Plan "majestic." Its main purpose, she has written,[8] is "the industrialization of the country . . . on a new, advanced technical basis . . . which will insure the success of the Socialist offensive against the capitalist elements." Industrial output is to be increased twofold, with emphasis on what she called "the Stalin method" of developing heavy industry in particular.

[7] Of the Rumanian investment program for 1950, 47 percent was allocated for industry, 20 percent for transportation and 9 percent for agriculture.
[8] *For a Lasting Peace, for a People's Democracy!*, Bucharest, August 18, 1950.

Output of oil is to be doubled, of iron and steel nearly doubled. Though the socialization of agriculture is of course to be pushed, Mme. Pauker said nothing about class warfare in the villages nor did she emphasize the leading rôle of the industrial proletariat, as had been done by other satellite leaders as well as by her own colleagues in the Central Committee, Georgescu and Luca.

Perhaps geography supplies an answer to why Moscow slated Rumania but not Jugoslavia and Bulgaria for industrialization. The latter are more distant from Soviet Russia and would be much more exposed to enemy air attack in case of war. Rumania adjoins the Soviet Union; and although it is true that her oil fields were bombed from North Africa and Italy in the last war, they could be given air protection more easily than could the industrial installations in the other two countries. The same considerations apply, though in less degree, to Hungary; but in any case industrialization there was already considerably advanced. Rumania and Hungary, moreover, were destined in the Soviet planning to remain indefinitely under occupation by Soviet troops.

The favor shown by Soviet planners for developing heavy industry even in situations where it seems particularly unnatural, as in Rumania, is partly inspired, of course, by their desire to proletarianize the population as quickly as possible. But more important, perhaps, it also will increase the dependence of the satellites on the Soviet Union. Where else but in Russia can they hope to dispose of the product?

Despite all their adversities, present and planned, the peasants nevertheless remain the great—probably the only—obstacle to Rumania's full Sovietization. All over Southeast Europe farming is more a way of life than an occupation, and nowhere is this truer than in Rumania. Coercion will gradually break the Rumanian peasant of this way of life. As we have seen, however, the régime has so far made no claims to spectacular progress. Evidence that formidable difficulties are being encountered is found in the fact that while Georgescu, Luca and others stress complete proletarianization as the goal and hint at violent methods to attain it, they make excuses for not proceeding faster; and at the same time there continues to be conciliatory talk about getting the "freely given consent of the peasants."

Evidently this is only one of the *façons de parler* which Revai explained are permissible when it is inconvenient to call things "by their real names." Someday naked force will become convenient, and then the peasants will have to give in or starve. Their remarkable toughness is shown by the fact that they have been able to sustain their present position so long. With an egg selling at 2 lei and shoes costing 2,400 lei, a farmer must sell a hundred dozen eggs to get himself a new pair of shoes; and it takes a year's crop of wheat (in a good season at that) for the owner of an average-size farm to pay for a suit of store clothes. Tough as they are, the majority who still stand aside will have to knuckle under eventually and give up their land. Others will be channelled off to work on state construction jobs, and others again will be absorbed into factories. Some doubtless will hold out to the end—angry, bewildered and inarticulate, helpless to do anything but die. Millions died in Russia.

Nationalism will also continue to be something of a factor, but in Rumania it probably will not give the Communists particular trouble. Rumanians have always considered Russia an enemy of the Rumanian nation. But if nationalism can be held in check in countries with much greater native capacities of resistance, Poland for instance, how much less chance is there for it to remain alive and aggressive here in Rumania—the first of the satellites to come under Soviet occupation, the first to receive a Communist-controlled government imposed by Moscow, the one which today comes closest to being on the same political level as the Ukrainian or the Usbek Soviet Socialist Republic?

In March 1950 Patrascanu's name came back into public discussion as a result of reports in *Borba* and other Belgrade journals that he was to be made the chief performer in a spectacular trial on the Rajk and Kostov model. The reason these predictions did not materialize probably was that Moscow did not see pressing reasons to give Rumania any more lessons for the present. If Patrascanu should be tried later for nationalism, Titoism or spying for the West it would be because the people were starving and because when bread is lacking they must be given a circus. It will not indicate that there is (or probably ever has been) a very strong current of inde-

pendence inside the Rumanian Communist Party, as there was and
probably still is inside the Polish or Czechoslovak Parties or even as
there was inside the Bulgarian or Hungarian Parties. Moscow
secured political domination too early and brought it to completion
too fast for there to have been time for Rumanian opposition to
develop deep roots.

Pijade says that one of the statesmen from Budapest who visited
Belgrade while the two capitals still were on speaking terms reported
that the Rumanians were complaining that "the Russians skinned us
four times." After four skinnings, not much is left of the substance
for resistance.

# XXIII

## STALIN ON THE DEFENSIVE

The force of habit of millions and tens of
millions is a terrible force.

Lenin, "Left-Wing Communism," quoted in Stalin's "Problems of Leninism"


THE story has now been told of how from
the Cominform schism of June 1948 there grew and spread the very
thing which Stalin must have wanted most fervently to avoid—a
heresy with a general and lasting appeal.

Once Stalin had decided that Tito must be removed, and once
Tito had indicated his unwillingness to go quietly, there were two
ways of getting rid of him—by assassination, or by the "legal" if
fraudulent method of invoking the judgment of his captive peers in
the Cominform. The former would be final but it risked making Tito
a national martyr. In any case Stalin probably did not credit the
idea that Tito would or could hold out against the combined pressure
of the Cominform Parties, marshalled under his own leadership. Tito
could and did. Instead of eliminating himself, and taking his personal adherents with him into prison or the grave, he clapped into
jail the two of his cabinet ministers who showed a partiality for
Moscow, set aside the influential Partisan commander whom the
Russians had just carefully indoctrinated, and with the backing of
the vast majority of his Party and Army defied the Kremlin to do
its worst. In this situation it would no longer do for Stalin to accuse
Tito of mere ingratitude and lack of discipline, thereby revealing
that in essence the dispute was one for personal power—an affair in
which it was beneath Stalin's dignity to participate. He therefore
developed the attack against Tito on ideological grounds, pontificat-
ing as sole authorized interpreter of Marxist truth. This auto-

matically widened Tito's significance. Now he stood forth not simply as champion of the equality of all Communist Parties, the independence of all Communist states and the individual value and authority of all Communist leaders; the way was open for him to become the competing prophet of a schismatic Communist church.

We have seen what a deep impression the Tito heresy made on the Communist leaderships of Eastern Europe. To keep it from spreading, Stalin in 1949 added the obviously improbable charge that even while Tito was fighting the Nazis alone in the mountains, and earlier still, while he was a trusted Moscow agent, he had been a false Communist and actually in the service of the reactionary Western Powers. To make the charge stick, Stalin ordered that selected Communist leaders who were or might be suspected of sharing Tito's nationalist views be accused as members of a great Titoist "conspiracy." Kostov, Rajk and others were accordingly tried and hanged. As a method of intimidating East European Communists and facilitating the final Communization and Sovietization of the whole area these trials were probably effective; and wherever they are found not to have been, other trials can easily be supplied.

Inevitably there has been resentment among local Communist leaders that they are shorn of real authority, as well as envy of Tito for having been able to retain his. But while Soviet armies are nearby there can be only secret insubordination. The situation is different in countries where the Communist Party is not in power, or even in a country like China where it has gained control but without becoming physically the prisoner of the Soviet Army. In both cases the Jugoslav Communists have been on the lookout for possible allies. They have received intellectual support from nationalist dissidents in many other Parties; and they hope for something more than that from Mao Tse-tung, not immediately, perhaps, but under the teachings of the same experience which Tito has had with Moscow. Meanwhile they watch the situation in the whole Far East with particular attention.

Their experience with Ho Chi Minh, Communist head of the Viet Nam rebels in Indo-China, began encouragingly when he took the initiative in inviting Jugoslavia to recognize his régime in February 1950. The United States urged Tito not to comply, but he saw that it would embarrass Moscow and he naturally hastened to do so, emphasizing that he was acting in accordance with the principle of "respecting the rights of every people to independence and sovereignty." Perhaps the American intervention was unwise, not merely because it was certain to be ignored but because it was a departure from our established attitude of not interfering in Jugoslavia's political affairs, domestic or foreign, a point on which Tito is understandably touchy after his experience with Stalin. In any case, the Belgrade objective was to encourage Ho Chi Minh to maintain something like a middle position between independence and subservience to Moscow, a goal which (whether practicable of attainment or not) was not incompatible with American interests. Although relations were established in a formal sense, no diplomatic representatives had yet been exchanged nearly a year later.

Communists in Belgrade have no opportunity for direct relations with their Japanese brethren but they follow developments in the Japanese Communist Party closely. The real power there is supposed to be Sanzo Nosaka, who from the middle of the thirties until the end of the war spent most of his time with the Chinese Communists and became a close confidant of Mao Tse-tung. The Cominform journal, *For a Lasting Peace, for a People's Democracy!*, accused Nosaka on January 6, 1950, of being anti-democratic and anti-Socialist, and criticized him especially for asserting that he had "naturalized Marxism-Leninism on Japanese soil"—a claim which smelt of Titoism and ran counter to the Bolshevik position that Communism gains power only where the right conditions have been prepared by Soviet troops. The Jugoslavs noted not only that Nosaka was not dropped from the Japanese Communist Party but that several of his opponents were. Moscow apparently hesitated to purge him for fear of breaking the Party up, or even to press him too hard to conform for fear that he then might join the Titoist camp openly.

The sight of one of Mao Tse-tung's cronies being attacked in the Cominform press gave the Jugoslav Communists real pleasure as one more sign that Chinese nationalism may in the end rebel against domination by the Kremlin. Almost every conversation which I have had with Jugoslav officials, in Belgrade or abroad, has come around sooner or later to China, and always the hope is expressed that Stalin will violate Chinese national interests so flagrantly that the Chinese Communists will be unable to tolerate it, will take advantage of the fact that they are physically able to reject it and then will coöperate tacitly and perhaps openly with the Jugoslav Communist Party. Their arguments for hoping this are not entirely farfetched. But when a picture is drawn of an anti-Cominform axis with one pole in Belgrade and the other in Peking I recall a story that used to be told during the Balkan Wars about a boastful Montenegrin who when reminded that after all Montenegro was rather a small country said: "Ah, but we and the Russians—we are 180 millions!" Sometimes the Jugoslav Communists seem to find comfort in looking across Asia and saying: "Ah, but with the Chinese we are 450 millions!" Nobody can prove, of course, that the Chinese Communist movement will not remain strongly nationalist or that if so it may not draw close to other Communist nationalists, to Moscow's great disadvantage. Even a faint hope of restricting Soviet power, in China or anywhere else, is not to be lightly dismissed.

Many experts on China deny that there is any ideological or practical difference between Russian and Chinese Communism. Tito believes that this view takes no account of the fact that Stalinism is not what he calls Communism, and that it is not what he believes many Chinese Communists will call Communism when they experience it. He maintains that Chinese Communists are sure to show that they are different from Stalinist Communists simply because they are in a position to do so. His own case demonstrated, he points out, that acute divergencies in ideology and practice do exist inside the Communist world, and that what brings them to the surface is the Stalinist refusal to recognize the right of Communist Parties and states to autonomy. Since China's geographical situation would permit her Communist leaders to break away from Moscow if other political and economic conditions were favorable, he argues that the American and other anti-Stalinist governments should emphasize differences between Mao and Stalin instead of lumping them together and forcing Mao to turn to Stalin for the means of Chinese reconstruction and development. Some Jugoslav officials go so far as to believe that Stalin launched the Korean war in order to sow trouble between Peking and Washington and prevent the Chinese People's Republic from securing a place in the United Nations for presenting its nationalist aspirations.

It seems to be agreed that in the early thirties Mao Tse-tung was not on good terms with the Soviets. He successfully resisted Moscow's efforts to oust him and organized his Communist armies without much Soviet help. For a time there were two rival Central Committees of the Chinese Communist Party, one in Moscow, the other led by Mao in China. As the Jugoslavs stress, also, China actually has a larger population than Russia's; potentially at least she is a World Power; the present Communist leaders are mainly China-bred; they rose to power by their own efforts and strategy; and they have several million men under arms. Moreover, nationalism was a basic tenet of the Chinese revolution from the time Sun Yat-sen enlisted Communists in the service of the nationalist cause, and it was one of the main slogans used by the Communists to encourage resistance to the Japanese in the thirties when even Chiang Kai-shek temporized with them. Recently, it is true, the chief theoretician of the Chinese Communist Party, Liu Shao-chi, Secretary of the Central Committee, has expounded the idea that nationalism is a manifestation of bourgeois reaction, to be encouraged only in colonial areas where it can assist in overthrowing imperialism. Since the new China is anti-imperialistic, his argument runs, it has no need for nationalism and is free to practise internationalism.[1]

To which the answer might be that Stalin permits the practice of internationalism only where it does not damage Russian interests, and that eventually he will make this clear in Peking. The relations of a Communist state with Moscow are the litmus paper by which the sincerity and orthodoxy of its Communist leadership are determined. The Jugoslav Communists ask how long Mao as a sincere and idealistic Communist (which they claim he is) will pass the test. Conditions in China are becoming like those which provoked the Jugoslavs first to complaint and then to resistance. Soviet technicians are in the country by the hundreds. Soviet officers are advising on the organization of the Chinese Army, prescribing its tactics and

[1] Cf. "Communism and Nationalism in China," by C. M. Chang, *Foreign Affairs*, July 1950.

offering to supply Russian matériel to the extent that their advice is accepted. Soviet planners are taking the Chinese economy in hand, and by the analogy of what has happened elsewhere they will develop it to serve Russia's needs first and China's second. Some observers believe that they plan to develop industry only in Manchuria and border areas easily controlled by Russian forces, and will maintain the agricultural character of the rest of the country.

According to one Jugoslav official, Mao Tse-tung will experience his greatest difficulty in fulfilling Moscow's demands on the agrarian sector of the Communist front, where Stalin has often chosen to fight key ideological engagements with rivals from Bukharin to Tito. Mao wrote in his "New Democracy" in 1940 that his aim was "not to establish a Socialist agricultural order but rather to enable the peasants to own their own private properties." The next year he made a speech in Yenan in which he said that principles of Marxism-Leninism could bear fruit only when combined with a study of the "objective facts" of every country, and that these differ so markedly that even within the limits of one country they cannot be applied in an *a priori* manner. The similarity between such views and those for which Tito was later rebuked is so striking that a Jugoslav magazine, *Thirty Days*, which reprinted the article in July 1949, did not even feel the need to point it out. As lately as December 1947 in a report to his Central Committee Mao said that there "must absolutely be no repetition of the mistake of adopting the ultra-leftist policy of dealing with the economic elements represented by the small-property class and the medium-property class," as had been done in 1931-34.

Will Stalin's principles and interests permit the Chinese Communists to temporize with the peasant problem indefinitely, and if not shall we see this problem become once again a cause of serious friction? Even if he feels called on to curb Mao's nationalist tendencies, Stalin will surely act against him more cautiously than he did against Tito. Perhaps rumors that Mao is being elevated to the position of a figurehead are a sign that Stalin's hand is already at work. Even though there may be divisions of influence inside the Chinese Politburo, the fact remains that in the Korean affair the Chinese Communists are, as I write, acting to support a Soviet foreign adventure, at the risk of becoming involved in a new war when the country has hardly begun to recover from the last one. In the long run, Mao may resent that China was used against her own interests in further-ance of Russian aggressive policies, and either be purged or rebel. But in the first stage Stalin has had his way in China enough to dis-concert some of his enemies, the Jugoslavs especially. We saw an indication of this in Tito's statement after Chinese troops appeared in North Korea that he would support the United Nations in any action it might have to take to liquidate the Korean war.

In countries where Communism does not rule it has always been hard for Communist theoreticians to explain away the fact that Stalin identifies the interests of international Communism with the interests of Russia. The assertion that a Communist Party member's attitude toward Russia is the measure of his Communist faith indi-cates that when his own country's interests and those of Russia con-flict he must, if he is a true Communist, put his own country's inter-ests second. Sometimes he is asked to proclaim the treason that under no conditions would he fight for his country against the Soviets.

Tito not merely has proved that Soviet Russia's interests and those of other Communist countries are not necessarily identical; he has advertised that they may be diametrically opposite, and that when they are it is Russian interests which will be served exclusively—politically, economically, strategically. By rebelling against Russian hegemony and exploitation he has broken much of the force of Soviet propaganda against alleged Western imperialism and selfishness. The Cominform blockade and the threat that it might be followed by military measures have broken the force of the Moscow propaganda that it is the West which endangers the peace. Wherever the facts of the Tito-Stalin struggle are known, the Soviet dove—whether Picasso's or another—looks bogus. It is not a coincidence, I believe, that the strength of the Communist Parties in every West European country has fallen in the period since the story of Tito's effort to sur-vive began causing such embarrassment to Cominform propagand-ists. This is the same period in which the Marshall Plan began to produce results. By putting the Communist Parties on the defensive politically Tito has aided the Marshall Plan, I think, in putting them on the defensive economically and socially.

His duel with Stalin has not affected Party leaderships in Western

Europe so much as the rank and file. It nevertheless placed Thorez, Duclos and the other rather tame heads of the French Communist Party in an awkward position. While they held ministerial office under de Gaulle in 1945 and later they had to pretend to accept the régime. The insurrectionary strikes of 1947, ordered by Moscow with the object of crippling the Marshall Plan, were in sharp contrast to the Party's earlier attitude and were most unpopular with a large section of the Party membership, particularly after they had failed. But when the Tito affair convinced Moscow that appeasement of nationalist sentiments could no longer be permitted in Communist Parties anywhere the French leaders were compelled to adopt a categorical attitude. In December 1949 the Central Committee published a resolution denouncing Titoist and Trotskyist elements in the Party and starting a campaign against them, especially in two cities where Communism had always been particularly strong—Lyon and Bordeaux. The following spring *Les Cahiers du Communism,* the authoritative French organ on Communist theory, indicated that the campaign had not gone well because the danger had been imperfectly understood. Titoism was not a mere deviation but actually "the last stand of Trotskyism," which was serving "spies and assassins under the orders of imperialist war-mongers." But although the French leaders saved their positions by toeing the Moscow line they lost members, and the Party newspaper, *L'Humanité,* lost circulation. The most notable of the individual rebels was perhaps Jean Cassou, a French intellectual who had been prominently identified with the Communist cause; he attacked the Cominform in the French leftist monthly, *Esprit.*

Jugoslavia's immediate neighbor, Italy, is the country where her anti-Cominform propaganda has naturally been busiest. Italian Communism is almost exclusively a laboring class movement and includes few intellectuals who would understand or be worried by the issues raised by the Cominform fight. The Trieste question is also an adverse factor from the Jugoslav point of view; Italians care about it so passionately that they are reluctant to identify themselves in any way with either Jugoslavia or Tito. Nevertheless Tito's fight for independence seems to have had some effect both in Palmiro

Togliatti's Communist Party and in the ranks of the pro-Communist group of Socialists led by Pietro Nenni. At a great Communist rally held in Rome in October 1949, Alexander Fadeyev, President of the Union of Soviet Writers, was at pains to emphasize that Lenin and Stalin taught respect for the independence of all peoples and that friendship with Soviet Russia constituted the surest guarantee of Italian independence. As an offset to this, Mosha Pijade addressed an appeal to the Italians to defend themselves against Soviet attempts to subjugate them and establish an oppressive Russian hegemony throughout Europe. He implied that the French and Italian Communist Parties had been reduced to the level of "fifth columns" awaiting the arrival of Soviet troops. On December 14 Togliatti admitted that there was considerable "bewilderment" as well as "ideological disorientation" in the Party. A few days later the first member was formally expelled on charges that he was propagating Titoist ideas. A group of Nenni Socialists visited Jugoslavia in the summer of 1949 and came back with favorable reports. Ten of them were purged or otherwise disciplined. Titoist Communists and pro-Communist Socialists have been especially active in the south of Italy. Trieste is not such a burning question there and a few remaining Jugoslav Partisans who had headquarters in Bari and Palermo during the latter phases of the war conduct a strong anti-Cominform propaganda.

Other Communist Parties have suffered from the Tito heresy. The Norwegian Communist Party split in two in December 1949, and later the former Secretary-General, Peder Furubotn, was expelled along with 21 of his followers on the charge of "Titoist deviationism." The Austrian, Swedish and other Parties have had somewhat similar experiences. Edgar Lalmand, Secretary-General of the Belgian Communist Party, complained rather quaintly in January 1950 of an "excess" of Titoism in the membership. The difficulties experienced by various German Communist leaders in satisfying their German determination to resist Russia while following the Moscow line have been described in an earlier chapter. Everywhere the strengthening of the European economy by Marshall aid and of West European defenses by the Atlantic Pact have been facilitated by the confusion which Tito caused in the strongholds of opposition to these two American objectives.

The effect on fellow-travellers and social do-gooders has also been noticeable. Many of the restless individuals flitting about uncertainly in the half-lit wings of the Communist stage—whether bemused "progressives" like the Rogges and Zilliaci, or more conscious "fronters" for the C.P.—had been shocked to find that their association with avowed Communists had landed them in a political limbo. Suddenly they found a way of regaining something like respectability, at least to the extent of demonstrating that intellectual sympathizers with "progressive" aspects of Communism did not necessarily refuse under any conditions to fight for their country. By flocking to Belgrade and proclaiming how well Communism can work on an independent basis they have retrieved a degree of their reputation for patriotism while retaining their places in the avant garde. Tito has received their advances warmly. Probably he exaggerates their political and intellectual weight at home in his pleasure at obtaining respectable foreign support which can be advertised to offset the Cominform assertion that he continues to live only because he has sold out to the capitalist West.

This does not presage, however, the creation of a new anti-Stalinist international. One of Tito's most authoritative spokesmen, Milovan Djilas, a member of the Jugoslav Politburo, explicitly disclaimed any such intention in an interview printed in *The New York Times,* November 4, 1949. His reasons were that "workers' and democratic movements should develop independently, on the basis of the conditions prevailing in, and the situation of, their countries," and that "the formation of any centralized leadership, in which any given country or any given movement would have a leading rôle, would only hamper actual coöperation." He added: "Every people should achieve Socialism by its own forces without foreign intervention." This is the reverse, of course, of the position taken by the Bolsheviks in their letters to Tito in 1948, and goes even further than Mosha Pijade did in rebutting the Bolshevik claim that Communism can secure power in a country only after the Soviet Army has created the right conditions and can maintain itself only with the continued assistance of the Soviet Union. I was assured in Belgrade that Djilas was correct and that Tito has no idea of rallying other dissident Communists in a new international organization. He probably does not read Anatole France. If he did, he might have been warned by recalling how in "The Revolt of the Angels" Satan triumphant becomes God—and in turn is the object of a new rebellion by the Archangels.

# XXIV

## IF STALIN TAKES
## THE OFFENSIVE

The secret of liberty is courage.

Pericles

THE break between Belgrade and Moscow transformed the military strategy of Europe and necessitated changes in the plans of every Power which might become engaged in hostilities there.

The lands which make up the Jugoslav state have always been important strategically. Spread in a great east-west arc above the mountains of Bosnia and Serbia lie the Save and Danube plains. Southward the Morava and Vardar valleys lead to the Aegean. On the west is the almost impenetrable Adriatic coast land of Karst and Dinaric Alps, with the so-called Ljubljana gap at the northern end, the historic gateway for barbarian incursions into northern Italy. Any change in the status of this territory and in the allegiance of the strong fighting people who inhabit it alters the strategic pattern of Europe as a whole.

Tito's declaration of independence, and Stalin's reply that this made Jugoslavia an enemy, took Jugoslavia out of the Soviet camp and subtracted her army from the total of forces on which the Moscow strategists could count in case they invaded Western Europe. Jugoslavia was not thereby automatically committed, however, to the Western camp. In talking with me in the spring of 1950 Tito phrased his remarks on this point very carefully. He was not on our side, he said; we simply were on the same side for a certain realistic purpose. Since this common purpose is nothing less than to deter or if required defeat Soviet aggression the shift indicated by Tito's remark is sufficient. Indeed, it is extraordinarily important, and not only in over-all strategy but in actual manpower as well; for apart from the Soviet Army the Jugoslav Army is the strongest single land force today on the European continent.

Since nothing is certain in politics, there is no absolute certainty that if the Western Powers became involved with the Soviet Union in hostilities anywhere in Europe they would have the instant collaboration of the Jugoslav Army—unless, of course, Jugoslavia herself were directly attacked. But it became increasingly likely month by month after June 1948 that this would be the result, and the Korean affair has made it next to certain.

The Jugoslav representative on the Security Council, Dr. Bebler, perhaps without having had time to consult Belgrade, voted against the resolution of June 27, 1950, which called for the use of armed force to repel the North Korean attack. This first attitude was not maintained. On subsequent votes Dr. Bebler abstained, except that he backed the Indian effort at mediation. Then on September 5, just before leaving for New York to attend the General Assembly, Dr. Bebler's chief, Foreign Minister Kardelj, issued a carefully prepared policy statement which condemned the North Korean aggression as endangering world peace and not calculated to "lead toward a real liberation of the Korean people." The clamor of Soviet Russia and her satellites about peace, he said, "will not hide their responsibility for Korea and its threat to world peace." The evolution in Jugoslav thinking is clear. The first instinctive reluctance of a Communist régime to become involved against another Communist régime unless directly attacked by it gave way first to doubts as to whether the North Koreans were really fighting a "revolutionary" war and then to the realization that something more important than the ideological character of the contestants was involved—that the essential thing at stake was the principle of collective security on which Jugoslavia must rely for help in case she herself were attacked by the Soviets or by a Soviet satellite. If the Jugoslav Government took the attitude that aggression was to go unrebuked and undefeated in one area simply because the culprit was a Communist why should not the non-Communist members of the United Nations be expected to argue that the victim of aggression in another area might properly be left to perish alone simply because he was a Communist?

It is easy to be cynical about the intensely practical nature of this appraisal of the situation and the cold-blooded statement which Foreign Minister Kardelj issued as a result. But the effect produced can hardly be exaggerated. Soviet hostility toward Jugoslavia was if possible further deepened, and the likelihood was increased that if there were a general war in Europe, whatever the cause and wherever the first arena of conflict, the Soviet Union would spontaneously attack her. Indeed, it would appear that Tito and his Foreign Minister felt that this likelihood was already so great that the risk of increasing it could not be allowed to weigh against the risk that when the attack came Jugoslavia might have to face it alone. Then came, in November 1950, Kardelj's resolution in the General Assembly designed to pin responsibility on an aggressor more promptly and clearly. The result still was not, as I see it, to bring Tito onto "our" side, even supposing that this would really be to our interest; but it certainly made the basis for our common action on the same side more secure.

A vital point for us to remember (as more than one military expert has stressed to me, in Scandinavia among other places) is that if Soviet Russia ever should decide to move in Europe she will give no more notice than she did when her puppet armies attacked in Korea. She will avoid taking even such routine preparatory steps as concentrating troops at strategic points or constructing new strategic railways or marshalling yards, knowing that these would soon figure in foreign intelligence reports and give warning of her intentions. The Russian high command will always consider that the general strategic advantage of surprise far outweighs the tactical advantages to be derived from placing certain troops at certain points. The Soviet attack will be in the mass, and the Russian commanders have such quantities of men at their disposal that they will gladly spend a few hundred thousand of them if necessary to rectify the disadvantages of a take-off which is not well prepared locally but catches the enemy by surprise everywhere. With the development of atomic warfare the advantages of complete surprise of course increase. It is good for us never to lose sight of the fact that it takes only one to start a war, and that the one who chooses the place and time will not tell us in advance.

If Stalin attacked the Western Powers directly, in Germany for example, or by atomic bomb, he conceivably might try to avoid provoking Jugoslavia. This seems improbable, however, for he could hardly tolerate Tito as a neutral any more than he could accept him as a friend, and he must calculate that Tito would probably join the fray of his own accord, knowing that he was simply being left for the second bite. But on the supposition that Jugoslavia might not be in the conflict in the first phase, her divisions would nevertheless remain subtracted from the total of Soviet forces which had been arrayed on the Soviet side before 1948 and the strategic Jugoslav area would be neutralized for the time being and would be a barrier to any Soviet operations in southwest Europe. The Allied armies would still have to meet the main Soviet thrust across Western Germany towards the Low Countries, France and the Channel. But the front would be narrowed and their right wing would be secure. The secondary Soviet thrust through the Ljubljana gap and thence by the passageway between Venice and the Alps into the plains of Lombardy and onward into southern France would have to be postponed.

The more detailed consequences of Jugoslav neutrality can be merely indicated. Trieste, instead of being a spear at Italy's throat, which it was while Tito and Stalin were allies, would become a strong point in the opposite sense; the American and British forces there would not be doomed to fight a rearguard action but could be strengthened. The Communist fifth column in Italy would not receive direct support from without and could be disarmed. The Adriatic would not be closed to Allied shipping or Allied naval movements; Greece would not be directly menaced; Albania would become untenable as a Soviet advance base, either naval or air. The Allies could continue to base their bombing operations on Italy instead of drawing back to North African airfields.

We continue to enjoy these advantages, temporarily at any rate, in the event that Jugoslavia is attacked by Russia at the same time we are; and we gain in addition the support of the largest land force in Europe after the Soviet Army itself. This statement of the Jugoslav Army's unique position will be almost incredible to those who still think in terms of the last war, or indeed in terms of any previous situation on the Continent. But if the reader will check over in his mind the armies of the traditional Great Powers—France, Britain, Germany and Italy—he will find that the Jugoslav Army is the only presently effective European fighting force outside the Soviet bloc. Tito now has under arms between 30 and 35 highly trained divisions of approximately 10,000 men each. Including militia and various other units, he maintains a total of something close to half a million men in a state of war readiness. His trained reserves number upwards of three-quarters of a million—a large proportion of them trained in actual combat. In the event of war, and provided he had time for full mobilization, the total strength of his forces would be about a million and a quarter.

The Jugoslav Army is not, by standards of conventional warfare, a well balanced army. It is not strong in the air, it does not have many tanks and it does not possess heavy-caliber weapons in quantity. Much of its equipment is no longer in prime condition and it lacks spare parts. Some of it is of Soviet manufacture, and no replacements will be possible. The Jugoslav Army is not sustained by a strong heavy industry; specifically, domestic Jugoslav facilities for manufacturing armaments are meagre. But Tito does not intend to use his army in a conventional way. It is a guerrilla force par excellence, and Tito's strategy would not be to employ it against an invasion by the Soviet Army and its satellite allies as the Jugoslav Army was employed against the Germans in 1941. He would not attempt to defend the Jugoslav frontiers or give battle on the plains of Croatia and the Voivodina. His operations there would be to force the invading armies to deploy and to delay them long enough to permit full Jugoslav mobilization. He would fight the war mainly in the Bosnian and Serbian mountains, where he and many of his soldiers would be quite at home. Already the bulk of his forces and his supply depots are in the strategic areas found best suited to defensive operations in 1941–45. His forces have adequate equipment and ammunition for the first phase of a mountain war. In dealing with Soviet aggression he would expect to receive assistance from other United Nations members. I am told that with a steady supply of arms from the West he calculates that he could exist and resist indefinitely. During the last war there were as many as 20 German divisions in Jugoslavia. The Partisan forces which kept them busy were inferior in size, train-

ing, armament and organization to the present Jugoslav Army. Tito
seems to think that it would give as good an account of itself in
guerrilla fighting against the Russians as the Partisans did against the
Germans. He remarked to me that although arms are important they
are not everything. The Jugoslav Army which met the Nazi invaders
in April 1941 was well armed, but it lasted less then ten days in the
field; the Partisan forces which disputed the possession of large areas
of Jugoslavia with the Nazis and Italians were never well armed, but
in three years they were never effectively dispersed.

It is conceivable that instead of attacking directly Stalin might
dispatch only his satellite armies against Jugoslavia, on the assumption that the Western Powers would remain neutral in a local war.
Tito would expect to do much better against the satellites alone, and
he would hope in any case that the United Nations would stick by its
principles as it did in Korea and come to his aid.

The armies of the four neighboring satellites, Bulgaria, Rumania,
Hungary and Albania, are inferior to the Jugoslav Army individually
and probably collectively. Before the Korean war one would have
omitted the "probably." We do not know, however, how much the
Soviets have stiffened them (as they did the North Korean Army)
with tanks and other equipment; but we can be sure that Moscow
will have profited by its Korean experience and that future adven-
tures of the sort will be better prepared. Moreover, although American control of the air proved less important in Korea than American
military experts would have expected, we must assume that air
power is not being neglected. We know that the Hungarian air force
in particular is being strengthened. Of the three, Bulgaria is the most
respected militarily by the Jugoslavs and she is reported to be the
chief beneficiary in Russian matériel, especially tanks. This would be
natural, for she is the most trusted of the Soviet satellites and she
holds a key turntable position for possible operations against not
only Jugoslavia but Greece and Turkey as well. Furthermore, if the
satellite hostilities against Jugoslavia took the form of infiltration and
guerrilla warfare the place to start would be Macedonia. Rebel
bands could be organized and supplied from Bulgaria, as was done
in the Greek civil war; and if the operation were disguised as a "Free
Macedonia" movement, in accordance with Article X of the Jugo-

slav Constitution providing for the right of secession, the Soviets could call it a civil war and might hope to avoid intervention by the United Nations. In this they would be counting without Tito. He doubtless would throw in so many troops to suppress any rebellion in Macedonia and defeat any guerrilla forays that the operations would soon assume the character of an international war.

As the numbers of all the satellite forces are steadily increasing any current estimate is soon out of date. Their total strength (including the Polish, Czechoslovak and East German armies, which would not be available for use against Jugoslavia) was estimated late in the autumn of 1950 at from over three-quarters of a million to over one million men, divided as follows: Bulgaria, 125,000 to 150,000; Rumania, 210,000 to 230,000; Hungary, 45,000 to 100,000; Albania, 50,000 to 55,000; Czechoslovakia, 130,000 to 160,000; Poland, 300,000 to 350,000; East Germany, 80,000 to 100,000. These figures include regular troops, militia, security troops and frontier guards. The lower estimates are conservative. In addition, there were thought to be between 30,000 and 35,000 men in the satellite air forces, manning 700 to 800 planes, mostly "Stormoviks," as well as some small naval contingents. The air forces were reported to be increasing. About ten Soviet divisions totalling about 100,000 men were stationed in eastern Austria, Hungary and Rumania. The Soviet divisions in Hungary—including at least one mechanized division and one air division—were close to the Jugoslav border. All the satellite armies are now commanded or controlled by former officers of the Soviet Army, and would of course operate in time of war in accordance with a common strategic plan.[1]

Taking into account numbers, morale, equipment and terrain, Tito's belief that under the conditions of late 1950 the Jugoslav Army could stand off a purely satellite invasion successfully does not seem unreasonable. Our conclusion from this is that if Stalin wishes

[1] Soviet Russia's standing army was estimated late in 1950 at 2,500,000 men in 175 divisions, plus 20 artillery divisions and 20 antiaircraft divisions. To these would be added border and interior troops, signal troops and the forces of the MVD. Thirty days after full mobilization was ordered she could have over 8,000,000 men under arms. Her air forces as of the same date were estimated at about 600,000 men with 17,000 aircraft, and her navy at 600,000 men with about 300 submarines and some small surface craft.

to overthrow Tito by force he must sooner or later attack him with his own troops, which is another way of saying that he would have decided to run the most serious risk of starting another world war. In the moment when the Soviet Armies were launching out into a general war of unknown scope and duration, when they presumably would want to concentrate their strength for a knockout blow against France and Britain before American power became fully effective, they would have to divert a certain proportion of that strength to the Balkan theater. By the analogy of German experience in the last war they would need to send at least 20 divisions into Jugoslavia and arrange to munition them there indefinitely. The Russian strategists might not consider such a diversion of their assets of major importance in itself. But even if 20 Soviet divisions proved sufficient in combination with the satellite forces to capture and occupy large sections of Jugoslavia, the invaders would never be safe from guerrilla attacks and Soviet military operations westward across Jugoslav territory would never be free from sabotage. Soviet lines of communication to Italy and beyond would never be secure. The advantages to us would be of the same sort, but doubtless magnified many times, as those which we derived from the Jugoslav resistance to the Nazis in the last war.

But while it may be true that even after the Soviet invaders had driven Tito's army back into the mountains they still, like the Nazis, could not call the country their own, is not Tito's resistance likely to be undermined and threatened in the rear by hostile Jugoslav elements? The official Jugoslav view is that pro-Cominform or "reactionary" elements in the country are insignificant and could not create difficulties even in wartime; instead, all Jugoslavs regardless of class origin or previous sentiment would rally to fight the invader. Even violent anti-Communists would probably do so, in this view, for two main reasons. In the first place, at least two of the invaders— Hungary and Bulgaria—would be old enemies who in the past war seized Jugoslav territories and since then have given the Jugoslav nation as a whole, and not just its Communist government, additional cause to fear and hate them. In the second place, bourgeois "reactionaries" detest Stalin even more than they do Tito and would fear the Soviet Army and the ruthless rule of Soviet commissars more than they do the present Communist régime. Belgrade officials deny, of course, that any considerable sentiment for Stalin or even for Russia survives in the Jugoslav Communist Party. The severity of the measures against those even suspected of disloyalty to Tito belie the assertion; but the very severity does mean that any Cominform elements remaining after the arrest of Hebrang and Zhujovich in 1948 and the purge in the Croat government in the autumn of 1950 will have had great difficulty in maintaining even a skeleton organization. Bourgeois opponents of the régime have been receiving less attention than formerly, but this does not signify that they have regained any influence. On the contrary, they had been rather thoroughly liquidated or cowed before 1948, and since then one hears less about their sins not only on that account but simply because the police are not numerous enough and the jails are not large enough to permit the government to deal with them and its pro-Cominform enemies at the same time, and the latter are considered more insidious. Many representatives of the old order are abroad or dead; some innocuous individuals have been given minor posts or small pensions; and such hardened democratic or monarchist leaders as remain and are considered sufficiently important are kept under surveillance or find that room can still be made for them in prison.

What would begin to happen in the Russian rear after the Soviet armies had marched on Western Europe? We have seen evidence in one conquered country after another that though the Soviet rule is supreme it has not yet been consolidated and that though opposition elements are impotent under present conditions they have not yet been subdued. Would the opposition be able to assert itself in time of war to the extent of causing serious trouble to the local administration or interfering with the operations of the Soviet armies? The answer is yes, though within limits. The changes and chances of a great cataclysm would bring every latent hatred of the Russian dictatorship to the boil.

It is said that "people get the government they deserve." Usually it is said by people who have a fairly good government or at any rate are tolerably well satisfied with it. It does not lie well with us, I think, who are free to speak, choose, vote and repudiate, to criticize those who by the chances of historical evolution or geography or by ill

fortune in war are not free to do any of those things and have no
possibility of becoming free by any present acts of courage or sacrifice. In Soviet Europe the masses labor to create or recreate self-
respecting lives and to rebuild the material foundations of their
nations on the ruins of war. But neither individual lives nor national
lives are part of the Stalin plan. Individuals and nations are being
reduced to a gray amorphous mass, without character, integrity or
personality and almost without hope. How strong and brave can the
strongest and bravest of the surviving individualists and patriots be,
and with what results?

In his school days in Gori, Stalin felt a nostalgic sense of his
Georgian past well up in his breast; but it soon subsided, and we
may doubt whether it was in any event more than distant kin to the
sort of nationalism which he undertook to deal with in the countries
of Eastern Europe when he ordered them Communized and Sovietized. He had seen nationalism in the Ukraine become little more
than a sense of cultural identity. Nationalist slogans in the Great
Patriotic War had been useful in rousing a fighting spirit among the
Russian peoples, and this had been sustained afterwards by the constant stress on Russia's primacy in all fields of culture and science.
But in Poland or Jugoslavia nationalism was not something vague
and nostalgic, not a mere sense of cultural identity and not a chau-
vinistic slogan. Nationalism was the same thing as liberty—a concrete prize which had been fought for and won only yesterday and
was still the subject of universal and daily pride from cradle song to
old man's reminiscence. Now new Tsars and Hapsburgs, new
Fuehrers and Duces, lived in the palaces of the former "bloodsuckers
of the people" and rode about in Cadillacs with shades drawn behind
bullet-proof glass. No end of statistical charts to evidence every conceivable kind of progress are shown to visitors and published in the
Cominform press. Anyone who knew these countries of old had many
criticisms to make of their political régimes; but if he troubles to
make comparisons of a more than superficial sort today he must conclude that the over-all result of Moscow's rule is not a general lifting
up but a constant pressing down. For the favored industrial workers
there are inducement bonuses. Production is never satisfactory to the
government bosses, however; threats of punishment go hand in hand

with rationing privileges and paid vacations, and an atmosphere of pressure and tension pervades the factories and mines. The church, the farm, the school, the university, the independent trade union, the press—every agency, forum and prop of the traditional way of doing things, the national way, and give-and-take way, the way of people with individual consciences and interests and ideas, the non-Communist way, are perverted, destroyed or under constant attack. What can be done? Can anything be done?

The masses of the people resist in the only practical way, passively. They go to church, they hold on to their farms, they cling to their little shops, they work and struggle and save. Their priests are arrested as they stand in their robes before the altar or prepare to hear confessions; their produce is requisitioned and if they cannot get seed for a crop or credit to pay for it or the use of machines to cultivate it they are told to join a collective; their shops are nationalized, their stocks confiscated against insignificant indemnity and they take to manual labor if they are able and starve if they are not; they are worn out with appeals to be Stakhanovites in their working hours and to march in parades or attend Party lectures in their time off; their savings become valueless or a way of laying hands on them is soon found. They have no means of communication with each other, and would not know what to plan if they had. They are unarmed. They are without direction or leadership. Their aim, except in the most unusual cases, gradually becomes simply to live through. Summoned to vote in a plebiscite, they may turn in blank ballots if they are sure there is no risk of detection; but usually there is, and they help to register the ninety-nine percent which the Communists would announce in any case. They hate the strangers whose names are on the ballots, just as they hate the powers, near and distant, that force them to vote for them. But they know there is no possibility of improvement through political action any more than through violence. Nothing that the régime tells them is believed and they take no stock in its promises. Indeed, they have lived through too many struggles and hardships, run too many dangers, suffered too many injustices, to be greatly swayed by either promises or threats.

This is the mass of the middle-aged and the elderly. Their Com-

munist rulers cajole, discipline, work and punish them, but hardly try
to indoctrinate them. It is the next generation on which they concentrate their efforts and threats. They form Communist youth clubs
and youth brigades; they reward enthusiasm and put those who are
too bright to be enthusiastic in the same group with those who are
too dull to care and allot both the same destiny, a life of work in
mines, factories or fields. The wastage of ability and talent is
enormous, but the objective is uniformity and obedience, not individ-
uality and excellence. In one Communist country a cousin of an
acquaintance of mine, a girl about to finish her last year in medical
school, was dropped three months before her final examinations. She
stood near the top of her class, but the political authorities decided
in a final screening that she was not fitted ideologically to be a leader.
She had never taken any part in subversive activities; she simply had
taken no part in political activities. She was barred from a life of
service because she had spent her evenings in the lab or in hospital
wards instead of attending Party rallies with her classmates. An occasional example like this teaches all but the most stiff-necked individualists to conform to the Party line.

Beyond punishments and rewards the Communists rely on ignorance as their main weapon to make the coming generations conform.
There will never be an end of young idealists, boys and girls like the
Prague students who marched up Hradčany to protest the end of the
Masaryk republic. When they show themselves openly in that way
they can be knocked on the head or picked up quietly the following
night in their homes and dispatched to a labor camp. More difficult
to ferret out are those who are brought up with some secret feeling
for national traditions and personal liberty and who have been
warned in time that sportsmanship or intellectual argument are ineffective weapons against a secret police. The men who might inspire
or instruct them, however, become fewer and fewer—the professors
who know history, the clergy who combine civic with spiritual
admonition, the writers, journalists or artists who have travelled. All
such having positive records of leadership were removed long ago
from public life. Now periodic sweeps are made of those who simply
seem potential carriers of the virus of individualism. They are arrested without warning, held without habeas corpus, tried in secret

and never heard of again. History shows, however, that men's most dangerous thoughts are those they must think in secret. Through all the past century and a half large areas of Eastern Europe were under oppressive rule, but there always was a Karageorge or Kossuth or Mavrocordato, and when he was exiled or died another took his place. Their successors in the present undergrounds will have to be excessively cautious, patient and wily, for behind the façade of social generosity and reform their new masters are less regardful of human impediments in their way than any conquerors since the days when Jenghiz Khan brought Asia beyond the Dnieper.

We should be under no delusions about the ability of the Soviet command to use the satellite armies as they wish in time of war. But the population of occupied countries will not work well and produce on schedule for their national enemies, and firing squads and hangmen will not keep resistance groups from forming or individuals from performing deeds of daring. There will be sabotage in factories and mines in Poland and Czechoslovakia and Hungary and Rumania and Bulgaria. One in ten men or women will be an eager spy. Rail communications will be cut and bridges blown up. Military commanders and administrators will be assassinated. The watchword will be "One more Heydrich!" The further the Soviet armies sweep westward, the broader the band of hostile peoples separating them from their home bases of supply. The prospect may be a minor deterrent in the minds of Russian leaders estimating the hazards and chances of a war with the West, but any deterrent however minor is welcome.

The contribution made by Tito in this connection is not negligible. Beyond the strategic effects of his defection from the Soviet camp are psychological consequences which in the long run may prove equally important. In every Communist-ruled country a stir is audible, a whisper of doubt runs through even the Communist leadership. Tito may not be responsible for starting this. Perhaps it is only an automatic reaction to the same universal stimuli to which he responded. But certainly the malaise now pervading every Communist Party and cell all over the world, from Warsaw to Paris to Peking, has been aggravated by Tito's propaganda and above all by the simple fact of his continuing to remain alive after Stalin had marked him for destruction. The people themselves would have sensed this even if the terror trials had not advertised it, and they are in some little measure grateful to the man who is abused in the Cominform press as the traitor to Communism who started all the trouble. They were glad to see Tito prove that Stalin was not infallible and all-powerful, and the more their Communist rulers attack him the more they tend to forget that he is a Communist and think of him mainly as a nationalist and the enemy of their archenemy. If he survived a Soviet military attack his example would give them fresh enthusiasm and hope. The picture which they paint of Tito in national colors may idealize him beyond his true deserts. But pictures and slogans are necessary to vitalize popular movements, and Tito has provided them for nationalist resisters to Soviet imperialism and exploitation everywhere. The occupied nations are cut off from spiritual nourishment from outside and their own wellsprings of cultural and patriotic expression have been polluted. They will slowly begin again, history has shown, the ceaseless "climbing up the ever-climbing wave" toward freedom—not the precise freedom they used to know, necessarily, that will become dim in their memories—but freedom as such, needing no precedent, immanent in human hearts, something to be discovered and won. If the Soviets and their rulers in Eastern Europe ever put themselves to the ordeal of battle they will find this will to freedom woundingly alive as guerrillas gather in forests and swamps and terrorists plot in back rooms and on isolated farms.

On many counts, then, it is to our direct interest that Jugoslavia shall remain independent. At present she can remain independent only under Tito. If he falls, Stalin takes over; that would be a worse fate even for the Jugoslav people. We cannot risk helping Tito build up a war potential which some successor put in his place by Stalin might use against us, but short of that, as practitioners ourselves of the theory of equality and independence among nations, we can properly help him keep the Jugoslav people alive and help him maintain his army in a state of readiness against the same potential aggressor who menaces our own peace and security. We cannot force him to change the nature of his régime; and we should not try—except by whatever virtue there may be in our own example—to per-

suade him to change it. Pressure will not succeed with a man who
has staked his life on his ability to resist pressure. Nor do we need to
beg him to "join the West." It is enough that intercourse in ideas
between Jugoslavia and outside nations is possible. Here is a Communist country with doors open to visitors. The clue to the importance of this is the ferocity with which the Communist dictatorship forbids it in Russia.

In Tito's own case we can hope that direct experience with the
West may in time be as educational as it occasionally has been for
others brought up in totalitarian doctrine. We may properly call to
his attention that we have ourselves been passing through a social
revolution since Wilson proclaimed the "New Freedom" and that it
has been neither insincere nor ineffective simply because it has been
bloodless. A Jugoslav delegate to the United Nations who was visiting the United States for the first time told me of his surprise in
finding how broad and deep the roots of capitalism are here. "It is
not the country I read about," he said. Reports to Tito by colleagues
who no longer must judge American life at second hand may carry
forward the educational process inaugurated by Stalin. The thought
makes the indiscriminate provisions of the Internal Security Act of
1950 barring all adherents of totalitarian régimes from visiting the
United States seem not merely senseless but positively harmful. We
shall never keep out professional spies or foreign agents by such crude
methods; and we lose the chance to show foreigners who have never
known the meaning of free competition and a free press how liberty
really functions.

Americans do not claim that the American theory of government
is perfect or that their practice of it has attained perfection. We
know and admit that neither is true. If certain Communist leaders
and groups make that same admission regarding Communist theory
and practice, and will work to improve both the theory and the practice as we know that we must work to improve ours; and if in this
somewhat more humble frame of mind they abandon the pretension
of other Communist leaders that they have the right and duty to
compel all the peoples of the earth, regardless of their stages of political and social development, to submit to a particular discipline as
revealed in the writings of one man and interpreted by another—

then distinct progress will have been made toward the day when different social systems can live side by side in mutual accommodation and peace. Americans have built their society on the premise that there is no absolute truth in human affairs, and that the way to make progress is to debate differences. We can meet the representatives of different social systems on a plane of complete equality and even understanding provided they will accept the same principle: live and let live. Tito has said that this is his aim and desire, and since it is the declared basis of his struggle against Stalin he may really mean it. Inside his own country he has given signs that he would like to strengthen his position with the people by modifying his bureaucratic and centralistic administration. One notices, however, that he explains any relaxation in his methods as a reversion to pure Marxist precepts which had been perverted by Stalin. In abolishing the special privileges enjoyed by the Party and state hierarchy he referred to them as excrescences on true Marxist practice, transplanted from Soviet Russia. The paradoxical question that arises in connection with any domestic reform in Jugoslavia is whether Tito could gain in popularity without losing political control. So long as he has to choose between them he will hold to political control, but the conditions in which a choice is necessary may not be permanent. In a long crisis pointing to war, for example, he might find it desirable to make the switch and possible to make it successfully.

Meanwhile we continue to profit from the discord spread by the Tito heresy through all the Communist world. Since the middle of 1949 the Moscow propaganda machine has devoted all its resources to diverting attention from the fact that Titoism is not a Jugoslav phenomenon but a Communist phenomenon. This frantic effort informs us how valuable Tito's movement is in its broadest sense. The United States does not seek out Communist states as partners. So long as Communist states exist in the world, however, we are glad to know that there can be differences between them. We are glad to see that whether because of genuine dispute as to true Marxist teaching, or because of the diversity of national interest which Bukharin was wrong in calling an impossibility, we find it easier to live alongside certain Communist states than we have been able to do in the case of the absolutist, monolithic, imperialist and reactionary government of Soviet Russia. We shall not need to judge between them in their doctrinal disputes. It is enough for us to have had a demonstration of what we ourselves believe to be unalterably true—that there is a great diversity in the wishes and capacities of peoples with different histories and environments, that they can make contributions to human progress and their own contentment by many different methods, and that this is in fact best. Even if there were some infallible man to draw an infallible plan for making all men over and all alike, diversity would still bring civilization to a richer flowering than uniformity.

When I asked Tito whether, looking back, he would act differently if he had it all to do again, he paused as if recapitulating in his mind the steps by which he had earned Stalin's implacable hostility and had been driven in the end to disrupt the Cominform. "No," he said deliberately. "It was fated. It could not have been otherwise. There was one conception there, another here. No compromise was possible, and none is now." The clash may not have been so inevitable as Tito now likes to think; the motivations which produced it may have been less concerned with principle than with personal interest. The fact remains that the forces vowed to world revolution have been split and that one segment of them vows it no longer. Pijade said that the authors of the Cominform anathema against Tito had no idea, when they set that wind of faith blowing, of the kind of tempest it would prove to be, and he quoted the following warning by Engels, written to Kautsky in 1882: "The victorious proletariat cannot impose on any people happiness and at the same time not undermine their own victory." How much more, we can add, when they impose unhappiness.

# INDEX

Acheson, Dean, 107
Albania, 5, 39, 93, 103, 191, 193, 208,
  209, 223 ff., 230, 287; annexed by
  Italy, 9 n.; anti-Tito policy, 91, 227;
  army, 226, 227, 289, 290; Communist Party, 145 n., 224, 226, 229, 233;
  elections, 230; and Greek civil war,
  227-228; minorities, 230, 231; nationalism, 229, 230; People's Assembly, 100; purge, 231-232; relations
  with Czechoslovakia, 176; with Jugoslavia, 224-235 passim; strategic importance to Soviet Russia, 228-229;
  territorial claims, 230; Western diplomatic representation, 223
Alexander, Prince Regent, 9
Allied High Commission, Germany,
  128
Anti-Fascist Council of National Liberation (AVNOJ), 24, 25, 30, 41,
  43, 187
Antonescu dictatorship, 264
Arutiunian, A. A., 69
Assmann, Vice Admiral Kurt, 10 n.
Atlantic Charter, 44, 259
Atlantic Pact, 104, 161, 281
Auchinleck, General Sir Claude, 26 n.
Austria, 6, 39, 290, see also Carinthia;
  Communist Party, 281

Baltic states, 40
Barbarossa, 10 n.
Barker, Elizabeth, 186 n.
Bebler, Aleš, 247, 252, 285
Bela Kun, 202
Belgian Communist Party, 281
Belgrade, 16, 20, 86, 88, 89, 257;
  bombardment of, 10, 11; capture of
  (1944), 33; Cominform headquar-
  ters, 67; May Day parade, 97-98;
  youth brigades, 117
Benda, Bohdan, 180
Beneš, Eduard, 5, 56, 173, 174, 182;
  government-in-exile, 180; provi-
  sional government, 180-181
Beran, Archbishop, 175
"Bereitschaften" (East Germany), 167

Berlin, blockade, 68; wartime destruc-
  tion, 131
Berman, Jakub, 145, 168; attitude to-
  ward Germany, 158-159; Tito, 157
Bernstein, Eduard, 73
Bessarabia, 40, 261
Bierut, Boleslaw, 4, 140, 145, 148, 149,
  153 n., 168, 237, 258, 267
Bofors, 126
Boldizsar, 241
Bonnet, Georges, 39
Bor, General, 155, 188
Borba (Belgrade), 15 n., 27, 77, 89,
  96, 105 ff., 120 n., 271, see also
  Pijade; on Jugoslav aid to Greek
  rebels, 193 n.; on Russian trade
  practices, 71
Borowy, Ryszard, 154
Bosnia, 18, 19, 31, 33, 284, 288
Bowman, Dr. Isaiah, 170
Brandt, Albert A., 211 n.
Brankov, Lazar, 246, 249, 250, 251,
  253
Bratianu, Dinu, 259
Broz, Josip, see Tito
Bucharest, 68 n., 238, 256 ff.; Comin-
  form Conference (June 1948), 79,
  147
Budapest, 132, 237 ff.; People's Court,
  247
Bukharin, Nikolai, 72, 73, 77, 78,
  83, 86, 150, 202, 235, 258, 278;
  execution of, 84; on relations of
  Communist states, vii, viii, ix, 4, 52,
  81, 299
Bukovina, see Northern Bukovina
Bulgaria, 5, 19, 36, 54, 65, 93, 103,
  104, 164, 174, 188 ff., 209, 212, 259,
  261 n., 289, 291, 296; Agrarian
  Party, 212; agricultural production,
  201, 217; and Albania, 225; anti-
  Jugoslav attitude, 91; army, 188,
  197, 289, 290; class war, 140, 215,
  216, 219; collectivization, 216 ff.;
  Communist Party, 59, 74, 187, 188,
  202, 204, 272; constitution, 200;
  elections, 210; Fatherland Front,

188, 212, 215, 260; Five Year Plan, 200; Grand National Assembly, 218–219; Macedonian question, 93, 185 ff., 190, 221; National Bank, 201; national Communism, 199, 219; nationalism, 221; Peasant Party, 263; peasantry, 216 ff.; purge, 211–212, 219; relations with Jugoslavia, 108, 208; with Rumania, 266; federation, negotiations with Jugoslavia, 67, 188–189, 203–204–207, 209; revolutionary movement, 214 ff.; socialism, 215, 216; Soviet demand for "security zone," 14 n.; Soviet policy in, 220, 269, 270; Soviet trade practices, 201; Sovietization, opposition to, 221–222; strategic importance to Soviet Russia, 221; in World War II, 9 n., 33, 188
Bulgarian Macedonia, 217
"Bulgarian system" (peasant coöperatives), 138
Byelorussian Soviet Socialist Republic, 145 n.
Byrnes, James F., 163

Les Cahiers du Communisme, 280
Campbell, John C., 44 n., 261 n., 262 n.
Carinthia, 65, 66, 103, 106, 107 n.
Carol, King, 262
Cassou, Jean, 280
Central European Observer, 181. See also New Central European Observer
Čepička, Alexi, 175
Chamberlain, Neville, 39
Chang, C. M., 277 n.
Chernokolev, T., 216, 218
Chervenkov, Vulko, 210, 217, 218, 220
Chetniks, 18, 22 ff., 42, 230
Chiang Kai-shek, 277
Chinese People's Republic, 274–278; army, 277; Communist Party, 145 n., 274, 277; nationalism, 275–276
Christo, Pandi, 232
Churchill, Winston S., 11, 22, 26, 32, 33, 35–36, 37, 41 ff., 64, 98, 155, 250, 258; in Moscow, 35, 43; policy toward Tito, 29, 30; World War II strategy, 29, 229
Ciano, Galeazzo, 14 n., 224, 261
Clausewitz, Karl von, 160

Clementis, Vladimir, 179–184, 191
Clissold, Stephen, 15 n., 32, 42
Coblentz, Gaston, 123 n., 195, 217
Collectivization, see individual countries
Cominform, 58, 59, 66, 69, 86, 88, 98, 99, 103, 125, 226, 257, 279, 282, 293, 297; and Macedonia, 193, 195; membership, 145 n.; organization of, 57, 67, 145, 146; resolutions (June 28, 1948), 80, 144, 147; (November 1949), 109–110; strategy against Rajk, 245
Cominform-Jugoslav correspondence, 61–81 passim, 91, 95
Cominform journal, see For a Lasting Peace, for a People's Democracy!
Cominform schism, 60 ff., 90–109 passim, 126, 190, 225, 273, 300; Tito-Stalin relations deteriorate, 4, 26, 28, 31, 37, 38, 56; evidences of impending break, 88–90; charges, countercharges, 63–71; Tito expelled, 60, 61, 78 ff., 86, 87, 212; ideological aspects, 72–83, 94; consequences, 129, 157, 172–173, 190 ff., 197, 214, 227–229, 249–250, 273–274, 279–282, 284–287, 296, 299, see also Titoism
Comintern, 39, 59, 67, 186, 188
Communism, 33, 42; collaboration with non-Communists, 44, 54–55, 77, 145, 154, 186, 212, 229, 242; early ideological controversies, 82–83; function of Soviet Army, 76, 94, 214, 267, 275, 282; and internal resistance to, 294–296; new Moscow line, 214, 237, 267; and internationalism, 57–58, 187, see also Bukharin; rôles of peasantry, proletariat, 49, 52, 77–79, 83, 85, 218 ff., 242 ff.; significance to, of Tito's fight, 2, 3, 82, 274; see also Marxist-Leninism, nationalism, Socialism, Soviet Russia, Stalin, Tito, and individual countries
Constantinescu-Iasi, 265
Council for Mutual Economic Assistance (CMEA), 133 n., 164
Council of Foreign Ministers, Moscow (1947), 163; (1949), 103
Crimea Conference (Yalta), 36, 43–44, 64, 169, 170, 258 ff.; Declara-

tion on Liberated Europe, 44, 45, 258

Croatia, 1, 20 ff., 85, 207, 288; feud with Serbs, 19, 21; government, purge in, 292; Peasant Party, 14, 21; *see also* Jugoslavia, Ustashi

Cvetkovich, Prime Minister, 8; government, 15, 16

Cyrankiewicz, Jozef, 147

Czechoslovakia, 5, 6 n., 39, 48, 52, 55, 71, 134, 164, 208, 209, 246, 247, 261, 296; army, 174, 183, 290; Communism, opposition to, 173, 174; Communist coup d'état, 56, 173 ff.; Communist Party, 179; and nationalism in, 177, 178, 182, 272; labor in, 175; political democracy in, 172–173; purge, 179–180; relations with Hungary, 178, 183; with Jugoslavia, 103, 108–109, 176; with Poland, 177–178; Roman Catholic Church, 174; Soviet control of economy, 175–176; standard of living, 176, 177; *see also* Sudeten Germans

*Daily Worker*, 265, *see also Worker*

Daladier, Edouard, 39

Danube, control of, 14 n.

Danube Conference, 89, 92

Dardanelles, 29

Daskalov, Dushan, 190

Declaration on Liberated Europe, *see* Crimea Conference

Dedijer, Vladimir, 30 n., 32 n.

De Gaulle, Charles, 280

Dekanozov, Soviet Ambassador to Berlin (1941), 11 n.

Dertinger, Georg, 164

Deutscher, Isaac, 84 n.

Dictatorship of the proletariat, 220, 242–244

Dimitrov, Georgi, 59, 89, 140, 191, 191 n., 199 ff., 211 n., 212, 213, 217 n., 219, 220, 237, 267; address (September 1946), 215; (December 1948), 214 ff.; and federation plans, 206 ff., 213, 266; orthodoxy, 213; visits Tito at Bled, 67, 189

Djilas, Milovan, 15, 31, 90, 96, 99, 209, 213, 236, 251; statement on possible anti-Stalinist international, 282–283; statement on Soviet Army, 62, 65

Dobrudja, Southern, 261, 261 n.

Donovan, Col. William J., 8

Dorian, Paul, 181 n.

Dragnich, Alex N., 88 n.

Drashkovich, 9

Duclos, Jacques, 258, 280

Dulles, Allen W., 250

East German Republic, 134, 161; accepts Oder-Neisse frontier, 164; admitted to CMEA, 164; National Democratic Front, 167–168; relations with Czechoslovakia, 183; with Polish Communists, 166; remilitarization, 166–167; S.E.D. (Communist) Party, 165, 167; Soviet policy in, 160, 165

Eastern Europe, Communist parties, 49–50, 54–55, 186, 263, 264

Eastern Galicia, 169, 170, 178

*Economist* (London), 119, 120 n., 201 n., 205 n., 217, 218 n., 220n.

Eden, Anthony, 26, 29, 30, 36, 37, 41

Egypt, 23, 26 n., 201

Eisenhower, General Dwight D., 26 n., 29, 30 n.

Engels, Friedrich, 78, 300

Espionage, *see* Rajk, Hungary, Jugoslavia

*Esprit*, 280

European Advisory Commission, 189 n.

Export-Import Bank, 125, 126

Fadeyev, Alexander, 281

Farkas, Mihaly, 250, 253

Federation plans, Balkans, 67, 188, 191, 207, 208, 212, 266, *see also* Bulgaria, Dimitrov, Jugoslavia

Federative People's Republic of Jugoslavia, *see* Jugoslavia

Field, Hermann, 180 n.

Field, Herta, 180 n.

Field, Noel, 180

*Figaro* (Paris), 8 n.

Finland, 40, 261

Foggia, 229

*For a Lasting Peace, for a People's Democracy!* 81, 89, 104, 141 n., 153 n., 196 n., 197, 201 n., 217 n., 218, 257–258, 266, 267, 268 n., 269 n., 275

*For a Socialist Jugoslavia* (Moscow), 102

*For Victory* (Warsaw), 102 n.
*Foreign Affairs,* 10 n., 147 n., 242 n., 243 n., 277 n.
*Forward* (Sofia), 102 n.
Fotich, Constantin, 24 n., 26 n.
France, 18, 39, 44, 161, 166, 223, 247, 287, 288, 291; Communist Party, 66, 76, 89, 94, 280, 281; resistance, 18; strikes, 280; trade mission to Belgrade, 124
Furubotn, Peder, 281

Georgescu, Teohari, 265, 267, 270
Georgevich, 13 n.
Georgiev, K., 206, 207
Germany, 6, 134, 158, 161, 186, 288, *see also* East German Republic, West Germany; collaboration with Soviet Russia, 11, 18, 163, *see also* Ribbentrop-Molotov pact; Communism, 165, 281; expellees, 119, 178; Tripartite Pact, 9; in World War II, 5, 6, 9, 10, 26 n.; invasion forces in Jugoslavia, 5, 17, 18, 19, 21, 288; Russian campaign, 10, 11, 13, 16, 18; Social Democratic Party, 73 n.
Gerö, Ernö, 250
Gestapo agents, 247, 248
Gheorghiu-Dej, Gheorghe, 59, 110
*Glos Ludu* (Warsaw), 148
Golubnitchy, I., 225 n.
Gomulka, Wladyslaw, 59, 149–150, 151, 152, 183, 191, 201, 249; address to Unification Congress, 149; attitude toward Peasant Party, 146; toward Tito, 144; career, 145–146; dismissal of, 148–149, 152; independence of, 144, 146, 147, 154–155, 156; and merger of Socialist and Polish Workers' Parties, 146; and socialism, 146; summoned to Moscow, 147
*Gorica* (Jugoslav freighter), 124 n.
Gorkich, 38
Gottwald, Klement, 4, 175, 179, 182
Great Britain, 8, 11, 39, 125, 159, 164, 166, 212, 249, 288, 291; agreement with Russia on Balkan spheres of influence, 35 ff.; on Jugoslavia, 43; and Albanian Communists, 229; army, Djilas' view, 62; attitude toward Greece, 230; toward Bulgaria, 204; toward federation plan, 207–

208; toward Mihailovich, 23, 26; toward Tito, 24, 26, 40; Labor Party, 216; military strategy, 229; trade agreement with Jugoslavia, 126; trade mission to Belgrade, 124; trade with Poland, 139; and Yalta agreement, 44, 45, 169–170, 259, 260
Great Patriotic War, 6, 18, 56, 187, 293
Great Russian chauvinism, 95, 254
Greece, 9, 10, 18, 36, 187, 188, 208, 226, 230 ff., 287, 289; army, 196; civil war, 103, 191 ff., 227, 228, 289; Communism in, 197; Communist Party, 186, 190, 191, 196, 228; and nationalism in, 192; ELAS revolt, 189; elections, 194; Free Greek Government, 191; frontier, 103, 193, 195, 196, 221, 228; minorities, 230, 233; nationalism, 197; People's Liberation Front, 192; and Macedonia, 190 ff.; railways, 195 ff., 221; relations with Albania, 233–234; with Jugoslavia, 194–195; territorial claim to Northern Epirus, 230
Greek children problem, 191, 195
Greek Macedonia, 191, 195
Grol, Milan, 43 ff.
Gromyko, Andrei, 259
Grosz, General Wiktor, 149
Grotewohl, Otto, 164, 165 n., 167, 168
Groza, Petru, 259 ff.
Gusev, Ambassador, 189 n.

Halifax, Lord, 35
Handler, M. S., 107 n., 109, 112 n., 194
Harwood, Admiral Sir Henry, 26 n.
Hebrang, Andrija, 61–62, 89, 90 n., 292
Heydrich, Reinhard, 296
Hitler, Adolf, 1, 5 ff., 16, 18 ff., 22, 26 n., 39, 40, 131, 155, 168, 187, 188
Ho Chi Minh, 274, 275
Horthy régime, Rajk's alleged activities in, 246
Hoxha, Enver, 91, 103, 208, 224–235; anti-Tito policy, 226–227; denounces Xoxe, 231–232
Hull, Cordell, 8, 11 n., 26, 35–37
*Humanité* (Paris), 280

Hungarian Workers' Party (Communist), *see* Hungary, Communist Party

Hungary, 5, 14 n., 19, 36, 48, 54, 93, 103, 107, 134, 164, 290, 291, 296; alleged espionage in, 108, 247, 249–251, *see also* Rajk; army, 246, 248, 249, 289, 290; bishops, 239 n.; Communist Party, 237, 242 n., 243 ff., *see also* Revai; and independence of, 272; elections, 241, 243 n., 263–264; Jews in, 240–241; Ministry of the Interior, police section (A.V.O.), 240; minorities, 178, 183; occupation by Soviet troops, 267, 270; peasantry, 243; relations with Jugoslavia, 103, 108, 249, 252; revolution in, 237–238; signs Tripartite Pact, 9; Smallholders Party, 243 n., 260, 263; Soviet plans for, 270; and Transylvania, 261, 262; working class, 243, 244

Husak, Gustav, 182

India, 285

Indo-China, 274

Internal Macedonian Revolutionary Organization (I.M.R.O.), 186

International Bank, 125, 128

International Monetary Fund, 125, 126

Ioannides, Yannis, 190, 192

Italy, 64, 65, 99, 161, 187, 188, 201, 223, 230, 270, 287, 288, 291; annexes Albania, 224; policy toward Albania, 233; and Communism in, 280, 281, 287; Communist Party, 66, 76, 89, 94, 281; and Jugoslavia, 280–281; Nenni Socialists, 281; strategic position, 228–229; trade mission to Belgrade, 124; and Tripartite Pact, 9; in World War II, 5, 6, 9 n.; Jugoslav resistance against, 17, 19, 21

*Izvestia*, 67

Jajce declaration, 187, *see also* Anti-Fascist Council

Japan, Chinese resistance to, 277; Communist Party, 275; and Tripartite Pact, 9

*Jezh* (Belgrade), 98

Jovanovich, General Arso, 68 n.

Jozwiak, Franciszek, 149

Jugoslav Communist Party, 10 ff., 35, 45, 46, 61, 62, 93, 168, 186, 188, 292; Croat members of, 90 n.; and development by Tito, 7, 38, 40; expulsion from Cominform, 60, 79, 80, 86, *see also* Cominform schism; Fifth Party Congress, 74, 91, 92, *see also* Tito; and formation of Cominform, 67; May Day proclamation, 1949, 97–98; membership, 38, 40; outlawed, 9; patriotism of, 6, 9 ff., 16–17; organization, 72, 74; and People's Front, 73, 74, 77, 89; Soviet criticism of, 72 ff., 78

Jugoslav Macedonia, 104, 185, 188, 193; Bulgarian claims, 93; *see also* Macedonia

Jugoslavia, 66, 75, 85–86, 99, 109, 128, 179, 289; alleged conspiracy against Hungary, 248, 249, 252, *see also* Hungary, Rajk; Anglo-Soviet arrangement, 35 ff., 43; army, 5, 15, 16, 20, 21, 46, 53, 62, 68, 70, 90, 105, 197, 285, 287 ff.; attitude on aggression, 285; toward Bulgarian Communism, 215; capitalism, 129; China, 275 ff.; to Dimitrov, 213, 214; Kostov, 213; labor, 116–118; to Stalin's Communism, 101, 105; and changing aspects of régime, 111–116, 299; class struggle, 48, 72–74, 77; collectivization, 48, 52, 120; Communism, 44, 45, 93–95, 98, 111, 129, 274; Constitution, Article X, 289–290; drought, 115, 123; economic problems, 48, 50 ff., 115, 118–120; elections, 45, 112; émigrés, 102; exports to United States, 126; and Far East developments, 274–276; federation negotiations with Bulgaria, 67, 188–189, 203–207, 209; Five Year Plan, 48, 52, 60, 68, 124, 128; foreign relations, *see* other countries; government-in-exile, 7, 22 ff., 41; and Greek civil war, 103, 191 ff.; *see also* Greek children, Greek frontier; health problem, 117–118; industrialization program, 47–48, 50–51; joint Soviet economic ventures, 69–70, 125; loans to, 125, 126, 128; and Macedonia, 187, 193, 195; monarchy, 41, 43, 45; National Committee of Liberation, 25, 41,

45; National Liberation Army, 41;
National Liberation Movement, 42;
nationalism, 6, 15, 16, 65, 79, 101,
293, 297; opposition to Tito, 291–
292; parliament, 112, 113; peasantry, 38, 49, 52, 79, 85, 119–123;
People's Front, 77, 89, 97, 112, 168;
policy on Korean war, 279, 285,
286; on religion, 114–115; Presidium, 113, 208; proposed judiciary
reform, 116; recognizes Viet Nam,
274–275; Republic proclaimed, 45;
and socialism in, 55, 75, 92, 104, 112,
140; Soviet economic policy for, 47–
48, 50, 68–71, 269, 270; Soviet military missions in, 31, 49, 53–54, 65;
and strategic position of, 3, 6, 39,
70, 284, 287– 288; territorial questions, 65, 66, 103, 106, 107 n., 187;
trade with Russia, 60, 71, 123, 124;
war potential, 287–289, 291; in
World War II, 5 ff., 19, 20; anti-
Axis coup, 9, 10; German invasion,
10; resistance, see Chetniks, Partisans; surrender, 10; and Tripartite
Pact, 9; youth brigades, 117, 118;
Zhivkovich government, 38; see also
Cominform schism, Croatia, Serbia,
Slovenia, Soviet Russia, Stalin, Tito
"Juspad," 69
"Justa," 69
Jusztusz, Pal, 246

Kachanowicz, Tadeuez, 154
Kalinin, Mikhail, 57
Kalinov, Cyrille, 11 n.
Kamenev, Lev Borosovich, 83
Karageorgevich dynasty, 7, 22, 37
Karageorgis, Constantin, 192
Kardelj, Edvard, 60, 69, 75 n., 76, 77,
80, 90, 127 ff., 193, 251; industrial
plan, 113, 114; in Sofia, 188, 189,
203–207 passim; on North Korean
aggression, 285, 286
Kautsky, Karl, 300
Kerentyi, Nosti, 232
Kidrich, Boris, 113, 123
Klinger, Evzen, 180
Kliszko, Zenon, 154
Kolarov, Vassil, 200, 201, 202, 209,
217 n., 218, 220
Kolishevski, Lazar, 193
Kolkhoz, 94, 138, 140

Kopecky, Vaclav, 175
Kopriva, Ladislav, 179, 180
Korean war, 111, 197, 276, 278–279,
285, 286, 289
Kossovo, 230, 231
Kostov, Traicho, 103, 150, 189, 209,
211, 212, 213, 218–219, 236, 241,
242, 274; attitude toward Tito, 204;
in Belgrade, 204; execution of, 210;
expulsion of, 199, 200–201; functions of, 200; indictment of, 202–
204; nationalism of, 200–201, 214,
221; and proposed federation,
203 ff.; trial of, 205, 206, 209; and
political implications, 214, 219
Kowalewski, Stanislaw, 154
Kreachich, Lt. Gen. Otmar, 70 n.
Kulaks, 79, 80, 205, 218

Lalmand, Edgar, 281
Lane, Arthur Bliss, 153
Law, Richard, 26
Lawrence, W. H., 264
Lechowicz, Wlodzimierz, 154
Lenin, vii, ix, 55, 73, 77 ff., 85, 115,
243, 281
Leningrad, 57
Lenski, Arno von, 167
Libya, 26 n.
Litvinov, Maxim M., 39
Liu Shao-chi, 277
Ljubljana, 14, 29, 284, 287; Tito's
speeches in, 64, 100 n.
Loebl, Evzen, 180
London, 131
Luca, Vasile, 266, 267, 270
Lysenko theories, 175

McCormick, Anne O'Hare, 162
Macedonia, 19, 65, 185–195 passim,
289–290; see also Bulgaria, Bulga-
rian Macedonia, Greek Macedonia,
Jugoslav Macedonia
Macedonian People's Republic in Ju-
goslavia, see Jugoslav Macedonia
Machek, Vlatko, 14, 21
Maclean, Brigadier Fitzroy, 11, 26, 29,
30, 31, 32, 250
McNeil, Hector, 107
Malta, 23
Manchuria, 278
Maniu, Iuliu, 259 ff.; arrest of, 264
Manuilsky, Dmitry Z., 257

Mao Tse-tung, 168, 274–278
Markos Vafiades, General, 191–194
Marshall, George C., 163
Marshall Plan, 161, 173, 183, 279, 280, 281
Marty, André, 18
Marx, Karl, 78
Marxist-Leninism, 49, 72, 73, 77 ff., 92, 99, 104, 275, 278, 299
Masaryk, Jan, 56–57, 171, 173, 174, 180, 181
Masaryk, Thomas G., 171, 173, 184
Mediterranean area, strategic importance of, 228–229
Mensheviks, 72, 73, 77, 80
Michael, King, 259, 260, 264
Middleton, Drew, 165
Mihailovich, Drazha, 24, 30, 32, 33, 41 n., 43; Allied policy toward, 23 ff., 30; charges against, 22, 26, 29; death sentence for, 34; as Minister of War, 22, 42; part in coup, 9; resistance activities, 18; rivalry with Tito, 22–33 passim; see also Chetniks
Mihalache, Ion, 264
Mikolajczyk, Stanislaw, 155, 263
Minc, Hilary, 133, 139 ff., 147, 153, 164
Mindszenty, Cardinal, 137, 254
Minorities, see Albania, Greece, Hungary, Slovakia
Moghiorosh, Alexandru, 266
Molotov, Vyacheslav M., 19, 26, 30, 33, 35, 36, 60, 63, 75, 164, 168, 169, 259, see also Ribbentrop
Monde (Paris), 104
Montenegro, 19, 22, 27, 207, 276
Morrow, Edward A., 141 n., 153 n.
Moscow, in German campaign, 10
Moscow Conference, 36
Moscow Declaration, 259
Moscow purge trials, 254
Mosely, Philip E., 172 n., 189 n.
Mostar, Bishop of, 114
Mrazovich, Karlo, 247, 252
Mueller, Kurt, 165
Mueller, Vincenz, 167
Munich crisis, 18, 39
Mussolini, Benito, 8, 20, 22, 39, 224, 230

Nagy, Ferenc, 243 n., 260, 263

National Zeitung, 167 n.
Nationalism in Communist countries, viii, ix, 7, 19; see also Communism and internationalism, countries, persons, Great Patriotic War
Nedich, General Milan, 20, 22, 26
Nenni, Pietro, 281
Neue Zeitung (Berlin), 165
New Central European Observer, 196 n.; see also Central European Observer
New Fight (Prague), 102 n.
New Times (Moscow), 202 n., 246 n.
New York Herald Tribune, 70 n., 218 n., see also Coblentz, Newman
New York Times, 70 n., 120 n., 124 n., 182, 205 n., 282, see also Handler, Lawrence, Middleton, Morrow, Schmidt, Schwartz, Sulzberger
Newman, Joseph, 167 n., 168
Ninchich, Olga, 32
Northern Bukovina, 40, 261
Northern Epirus, 230, 233
Norwegian Communist Party, 281
Nosaka, Sanzo, 275
Novikov, General, 197
Novo Vremye (Belgrade), 13 n.
Novomesky, Ladislav, 182
Novy, Vilem, 179
Nowe Drogi (Warsaw), 149, 153 n.

Ochab, Edward, 154
Oder-Neisse line, 161, 163, 164, 170
Otechestven Front, 217
Oumansky, Constantine A., 11 n.

Padev, Michael, 217 n.
Palffy, Lt.-Gen. Gyorgy, 246–254 passim
Panchevsky, Lt.-Gen. Peter, 197
Pan-Slavism, 22
Papagos, General, 196
Paris, 296; Peace Conference (1919–1920), 169; (1946), 252, 260–261
Partisans, 7, 16, 17, 21 ff., 31 ff., 40, 49, 52, 53, 65, 66, 94, 188, 224, 229, 247, 281, 288–289, see also Anti-Fascist Council of National Liberation, Tito
Pasich, Premier, 9
Patrascanu, Lucretiu, 264, 271; expulsion, 265–266
Pauker, Ana, 4, 258, 265, 266, 269

Paul, Prince Regent, 8, 13, 16
Pavelich, Ante, 20 ff., 33
Pavlov, Nikola, 203
Peace treaty negotiations (1946), 66, 260–261
Peking, 168, 296
People's Democracy, 237, 242, 244
Perventsev, Arkadi, 233 n.
Peter, King, 9, 21, 25, 40 ff.; visit of, to United States, 23
Petkov, Nikola, 260; execution of, 212, 263; nationalism of, 221
Petrescu, Col. Alexandru, 264
Pieck, Wilhelm, 161 ff., 165, 165 n.
Pijade, Mosha, 24 n., 28, 67, 73 n., 76, 90, 95, 98, 99, 105, 107, 208, 213, 234, 265, 272, 281, 282, 300, see also Borba; and Anglo-Soviet agreement on Jugoslavia, 35–37; and Bulgarian-Jugoslav negotiations, 206, 207; on Clementis, 183 n.; correspondence with Tito, 27–28; on Jugoslav theory, practice of Marxism, 93–95; on Kostov's execution, 210; meeting with Tito, 38; on Rajk trial, 254–255; on relationship of Communist Party and People's Front, 89; on Soviet Army's function, 94
Plastiras, General, 194, 195
Poland, 19, 39, 40, 48, 52, 55, 130, 164, 169, 208, 221, 296; army, 151 ff., 161, 290; Home Army, 155; and attitude toward Germany, 158; Beck régime, 5; class war, 141, 143; collectivization, 132, 134, 138–143; Communist Party, 59, 74, 140, 144, 146 ff.; deviationism in, 130, 152 ff., 272; dismissal of Gomulka, 152, see also Gomulka; first congress, United Workers' Party, 139, 149; and Czechoslovakian industries, 177–178; and economic relations with West, 133–134, 139, 142; economy of, 133; expulsion of Germans, 163–164, see also Oder-Neisse line; factors for national continuity, 134–135; frontier problem, 163, 169; geographical position, 134; government-in-exile, 155; industrialization program, 139; labor, 139; loan to, 125; Lublin government, 145, 155, 169; nationalism in, 168, 271, 293;

nationalization of business, industry, 132–133; Peasant Party, 263; peasantry, 134–135, 138, 143, 154; reconstruction, 131–132; relations with East Germany, 164, 166; with Jugoslavia, 103, 108; resistance to Nazis, 5, 145; to Sovietization, 130, 156, 168, 170; Roman Catholic Church, 134–137, 138 n.; Six Year Plan, 139, 141, 142; Socialist Party, 146, 147, 149; strategic significance to Russia, 134, 161, 163; Three Year Plan, 140; war potential, 134; wartime destruction, 131; youth brigades, 132
Polish Workers' Party (Communist), see Poland
Polska Zbrojna, 141
Popovich, Miladin, 224
Potsdam Agreement, 163 ff.
Prague, 171, 172, 238
Pravda, 67, 102, 149, 191 n., 212; on Balkan federation plan, 208; on Dimitrov, 206; on Kostov, 205

Rabotnichesko Delo (Sofia), 217
Radek, Karl B., 258
Rajk, Laszlo, 103, 108, 150, 154, 234, 236, 241, 244 ff., 252, 253, 274; career, government offices, 241, 245–247, 249, 253; character, 251; confession, 250–251, 254; execution, 254; indictment, 245–248, 250; trial, 245–255 passim
Rakosi, Matyas, 237, 250, 252, 253
Rakosi Battalion, 246
Rankovich, Alexander, 105, 204, 208, 249 ff.
Reams, R. Borden, 88 n.
Reiman, Milan, 180
Reimann, Max, 165
Revai, Josef, 251, 267; on Hungarian Communist Party program, 237–244 passim, 271
Ribbentrop, Joachim von, 13–14, 19, 163, 169; -Molotov Pact, 19, 155, 181, 261
Rokossovsky, Marshal Konstantine K., 152, 155, 161, 163, 188
Roman Catholic Church, see Czechoslovakia, Jugoslavia, religion, Poland
Roosevelt, Franklin D., 8, 23, 29, 30, 36, 40, 44, 155, 170, 258

Rosa, Ruth Amende, 56 n.
*Rude Pravo,* 109, 179
Rumania, 5, 36, 103, 107, 164, 174, 209, 256 ff., 259, 290, 296; agrarian problem, 263, 267 ff.; armed forces, 289, 290; class struggle, 267; collectivization, 267, 268; Communist Party, 59, 265, 272; consolidates position, 188, 258, 259, 262 ff.; nationalism in, 264; purge of, 266; and diplomatic relations with West, 256; Five Year Plan, 269; industrialization program, 269–270; investment program, 269 n.; land reform, 262, 263; National Liberal Party, 259; National Peasant Party, 259, 263, 264; nationalism, 271; occupation by Soviet troops, 258 ff., 267, 270; opposition to Sovietization, 270 ff.; peace treaty, 261; peasantry, 263, 267, 270–271; proletarianization as goal, 270; relations with Jugoslavia, 108, 265; signs Tripartite Pact, 9; Soviet interference in, 259, 260; Soviet policy for, 269, 270; surrenders, 33; territorial questions, 261; Western public opinion on, 259; working class, 267, 268
Rumanian Workers' Party (Communist), *see* Rumania
Rykov, A., 108

Salonika, 9, 10, 26 n., 190, 192, 195; railway line, 197
San Francisco Conference, 259
Sapieha, Cardinal, 138 n.
Saseno naval station, 228, 229
*Scanteia,* 265
Schmidt, Dana Adams, 179
Schoenfeld, H. F. Arthur, 243 n.
Schwartz, Harry, 142 n., 217 n.
Serb Orthodox Church, 114
Serbia, 7, 18, 20, 22, 26 n., 207, 284, 288; feud with Croats, 19, 21; landowners, 1, 85; *see also* Chetniks, Jugoslavia
Seton-Watson, R. W., 134 n.
Sforza, Count Carlo, 233
Shehu, Mehmet, 232, 233
Shubashich, Ivan, 40–41, 44, 45; becomes Prime Minister, 41 ff.; *see also* Tito, agreements with

Silesia, 132, 133, 166
Simich, Stanoje, 89
Simon, Helen, 225 n.
Simovich, General Dushan, 9, 10; government of, 15, 16, 21
Siroky, Viliam, 181–183
Slansky, Rudolph, 177, 182
*Slavyanye,* 102
Slovak Communist Party Congress, 181–183
Slovakia, 178 ff.; minorities, 183; nationalism, 182–183
Slovenia, 1, 19, 29, 64, 65; *see also* Jugoslavia
Sobolev, A. A., 259
Socialism, 82, 83, 95, 100, 140, 144, 282
Sofia, 238
*Soviet Press Translations,* 103 n.
Soviet Russia, 6, 39, 40, 44, 52, 68, 161, 188, 253, 261, 281; agrarian program, 84, 219; agreement with Great Britain on Balkan spheres of influence, 35 ff.; All-Union Party Congress, 73 n.; ambassador's functions in satellite states, 74, 76, 91; annexation of Bessarabia, 261; attitude toward federation plans, Bulgarian-Jugoslav, 204, 206–209; east European, 67, 191; Bolshevik Party, 93, 145 n.; Politburo, 56, 57, 62, 67, 150; and break with Tito, *see* Cominform schism; famine, 84; military strategy, 228–229, 284–291 *passim*; *muzhiks,* 85; M.V.D., 144, 154, 290 n.; nationalism, 6, 57–58, 187, 279, 293; N.E.P., 85; N.K.V.D., 86; opposition in, 292; peasantry, 38–39, 84; policy in China, 275–278; in East Germany, 160, 163, 166; toward satellites, 47–55 *passim,* 58, 133, 152, 178, 197, 214, 221, 237, 242, 269, 270, 289, 290; Albania, 224–229 *passim;* Bulgaria, 189 n., 214, 220–221; and Soviet trade practices with, 201–202; and Czechoslovakia, 175–176; toward Greece, 191; and Greek civil war, 194, 196; toward Macedonia, 185–186, 188, 190; toward Poland, 134, 151, 152, 163, 166, 168; toward Rumania, 220, 256 ff., 264–265, 269, 270; Red Army, 5, 6, 33, 65, 152, 155,

180, 199, 258, 259, *see also* Soviet Army; relations with Germany, 13–14; with Jugoslavia, in World War II, 8, 10–11, 13; economic policy toward, 50, 68–71, 123, 269, 270; and Jugoslav territorial claims, 103, 106, 107 n.; and military missions to Tito, 31, 49, 53–54, 65; and plans for Jugoslav Army, 68; and treaty of friendship with, 47, 63; and abrogation of, 108, 253; *see also* Cominform correspondence, Cominform schism, Stalin; revolution, 38, 84–85, 255; Soviet Army, 62, 68, 70, 103, 107, 134, 151, 152, 156, 160, 161, 183, 227, 244, 267, 274, 282, 285, 287, 288, 290 n., 291; and function of, in Communist achievement of power, 76, 94, 214, 267, 275, 282; *see also* Red Army; United States, British warning of impending Nazi aggression, 11; *see also* Communism

Spanish civil war, 38, 246–247

Spychalski, General Marian, 153, 154

Stakhanovites, 294

Stalin, Joseph, ix, 1 ff., 9, 11, 19, 22, 24, 29, 32, 40, 43, 53, 58, 63, 64, 75, 97, 98, 115, 144, 145 n., 150, 155, 168, 180, 209, 243, 257, 258, 262, 281, 291, 292; agrarian policy, 84; approves Jajce declaration, 187; assessment of Tito, 4, 86, 87; attitude toward Bukharin, vii; denounces Bukharin, 83–84; attitude toward Partisans, 10 ff., 26 ff., 37; toward Mihailovich, 29; toward peasants, 38, 143; his claim to authority, infallibility questioned, 59, 82, 96, 130, 155, 184, 235–236, 279, 297; controversy with Tito, *see* Cominform schism; ideology, tactics, 49, 54–56, 80–81, 83, 140, 276, 277, 279; and Karageorgevich dynasty, 37; message to Pieck, 162; nationalism, emergence of, 6, 187, 293; and Communist international objectives, 57–58, 187; Tito's attitude toward, 100; policy toward Mao Tsetung, 278; at Yalta, 44, 64, 169, 259

Stambuliski, Alexander, 212

Stavincha, Josef, 180

Stebbins, Richard P., 44 n., 262 n.

Stefan, Charles G., 88 n.

Stefanov, 202

Stepinatz, Archbishop, 115, 137

Stettinius, Edward R., Jr., 43, 44 n., 64, 170

Stines, Norman C., 88 n.

"Stormoviks," 290

Styria, 66

Sub-Carpatho Ruthenia, 180

Sudeten Germans, 178, 183

Sulzberger, C. L., 115, 226

Sun Yat-sen, 277

Sweden, 126; Communist Party, 281

Switzerland, 248

Szonyi, Dr. Tibor, 246, 254

*Tarsadalmi Szemle*, 242 n.

*Tass*, 124

Tedder, Air Marshal, 26 n.

Teheran Conference, 29; decision to aid Tito, 30, 31, 33

Temperley, H. W. V., 170 n.

Teschen, 178

*Thirty Days*, 278

Thorez, Maurice, 18, 59, 280

*Times* (London), 263

Tirana, western diplomatic missions in, 223

Tito, Marshal (Josip Broz), ix, 1 ff., 15, 21, 26 n., 31, 32, 52, 59, 66, 76, 142, 145, 148, 187, 188, 191, 202, 249, 278, 282–283, 291, 292; addresses, at Ljubljana (May 1945), 64–65; at Belgrade (Sept. 1947), 58, 66; at Fifth Party Congress (July 1948), 11–12, 15–16, 22 n., 32, 39, 41 n., 42, 44 n., 92–93; at Ljubljana (Nov. 1948), 100 n.; at Third People's Front Congress (April 1949), 104; on Rajk trial, 253; to Macedonians, 194; at Skoplje (August 1949), 105; at National Assembly (April 1950), 208–209; and agrarian policy, 84, 112; agreements with Shubashich, 41–45, 63, 64; aliases, 9; attitude, May Day parade, 98–99; to capitalism, 126–127; toward Chinese Communism, 276; to Dimitrov, 213; to Jugoslav Army, 53, 68; to Kostov, 204; to religion, 114, 115; to peasants, 38, 77–78, 123; birth of, 37; character, 7, 37; childhood, early career, 37; Communist beliefs, 9, 21, 37, 38, 50–51, 63, 77, 78, 93, 111, 127; controversy with Stalin, see Cominform schism; correspondence with Pijade, 27–28; with Stalin, 27–28, see also Cominform correspondence; development of Communist Party, 7, 38, 40; early Communist activities, 38; economic, financial problems, 68–69, 124; election campaign, 112; federation plan, 202 ff., 207, 209; feud with Mihailovich, 22–33 passim; heads provisional government, 25, 43; heresy, see nationalism; Marshal of Jugoslavia, 25, 30, 41; military strategy, 288 ff.; modified character of régime, 111–116; nationalism, 2, 39, 42, 55, 72, 80, 81, 84, 100–102, 154, 265, 274, 297; position in Party, 19, 45–46, 156; and Rajk case, 108, 242, 245, 248–251; relations with West, 104, 124 ff., 129; resistance to Germans, Italians, 13, 18, 19, see also Partisans; rôle between East and West, 104, 127, 284, 286, 287; significance to Communism, 2, 3, 82, 129, 274; his Socialism, 100, 140, 144; visit to Bucharest, 265, 266; to Moscow, 33, 47, 53, 189; Sofia, 189, 204, 208; at Vis, 31 ff., 41

Titoism, 201; in Albania, 231, 236; Austria, 281; Belgium, 281; Bulgaria, 217; Czechoslovakia, 178, 179; France, 280; Germany, 165, 281; Greece, 192; Hungary, 241; Italy, 280–281; Norway, 281; Poland, 147, 148, 152; Sweden, 281; see also Cominform schism, consequences

Togliatti, Palmiro, 59, 64, 99, 258, 280–281

Tolbukhin, Marshal, armies of, in Balkans, 188, 189; in Jugoslavia, 33, 65; Rumania, 256

Transylvania, 14 n., 261, 262, 269

Trieste, 53, 64, 65, 280, 281, 287

Tripartite Pact, 9, 10, 15

Trotsky, 62, 72, 78, 79, 83, 87

Trotskyism, 92, 202, 232, 248, 280

Trud, 224, 225

Truman, Harry S., 98

Truman Doctrine, 197, 230

Tsaldaris, Constantin, 194, 195

Tukhachevsky, Marshal, 154, 248

Turkey, 188, 208, 221, 289

Ukraine, nationalism in, 293

Ukrainian Soviet Socialist Republic, 145 n., 256–257, 271

Ulbricht, Walter, 164 ff., 258

Under the Banner of Internationalism (Bucharest), 102 n.

Union of Soviet Writers, 281

United Nations, 125, 128, 257, 277, 279, 288 ff.; General Assembly, 127, 179, 286; and Greek civil war, 193, 194, 196; Economic and Financial Committee, 69; Security Council, on Greece, 195; on Korean aggression, 285

UNRRA, 68

United States, 161, 164, 166, 212; alleged complicity in Rajk case, 248 ff.; and Declaration on Liberated Europe, 44, 45, 259, 260; Internal Security Act (1950), 298; Jugoslav exports to, 126; military strategy, 229, 296 ff.; National Security Council, 124; Office of Strategic Services, 20, 40, 250; policy in Balkans, 36; toward Albania, 229; and cession of Dobrudja to Bulgaria, 261 n.; policy toward Greece, 196, 230; toward Jugoslavia, 128, 275, 297–298; economic, 124 ff.; wartime, 8, 20, 23, 40; policy toward Poland, 169, 170; protests Petkov trial, 212; on Rumanian developments, 259; warns Russia of impending Nazi attack, 11; Embassy, Belgrade, 88, 90; Moscow, 90; State Department, 31, 88, 90, 166, 259

United Workers' Party, see Poland

Ustashi, 19, 21, 25

Vatican, see Poland, Roman Catholic Church

Velebit, General, 30 n.

Venizelos, Sophocles, 195

Vienna, 171, 172

Vienna award, see Ciano, Ribbentrop

Viet Nam, Jugoslav recognition of, 274–275

Vikentije, Patriarch, 114

Vilfan, Dr. Josef, 69

*Völkischer Beobachter,* 13 n.
Voice of America, 169, 170
Voivodina, 119, 288
Vollmar, Georg, 73
Vorobyev, N., 216 n.
Vyshinsky, Andrei, 103, 108, 116, 206, 207, 261, 264–265; interference in Rumanian affairs, 259, 260

Warsaw, 168, 238, 296; destruction of, 131; youth brigades, 117
Welles, Sumner, 11 n.
Western Germany, 128, 164, 287; national Communism in, 165
Western powers, diplomatic representation in satellite states, 90, 223, 256; and German problem, 159; policy toward Tito, 104, 124 ff., 129; potential military aid to Tito, 288; protest Vyshinsky's Rumanian interference, 259, 260
Wilson, Sir Horace, 39
Wilson, Sir Henry Maitland, 32
Wilson, Woodrow, 173, 298
*Worker,* 225, 234; *see also Daily Worker*
World War I, 29

World War II, 5, 8, 18 ff., 23, 26 n., 29, 30, 33, 65, 188, 189, 256
Wyszynski, Archbishop, 137, 138 n.

Xoxe, Lt. Gen. Koci, 231–236 *passim,* 241, 242

Yagoda, OGPU chief, 248
Yalta, *see* Crimea Conference
*Yugoslav Fortnightly* (Belgrade), 206 n., 208 n., 209 n.
Yugov, 206

Zachariades, Nicolas, 192, 197
*Zadruga* system, 85, 120
Zagreb, 9, 20, 33, 38
Zambrowski, Roman, 140, 141
Zapotocky, Antonin, 177, 180
Zhdanov, Andrei, 57 ff., 83, 86
Zhujovich, Sretan, 61–62, 89, 90 n., 292
Zhukov, Marshal George, 152 n.
Zilliacus, 215
Zinoviev, Gregory E., 83
Zog, King, 224
Zorin, 206, 207 n.
Zymierski, Marshal, 153

Gazier, Georges. *Les Maisons Natales de Fourier et de Proudhon*. Besançon, 1905.

Guy-Grand, Georges. *Pour Connaîte la Pensée de Proudhon*. Paris, 1947.

Halévy, Daniel. *La Jeunesse de Proudhon*. Paris, 1913.
(A revised edition of the above, together with Sainte-Beuve's P.-J. Proudhon, appeared in 1948, in Paris, under the title of *La Vie de Proudhon*.)

Halévy, Daniel. "Proudhon d'après ses Carnet inédits, 1843–1847." *Hier et Demain*, No. IX, 1944.

Haubtmann, Pierre. *Marx et Proudhon*. Paris, 1947.

Labry, Raoul. *Herzen et Proudhon*. Paris, 1928.

Lossier, Jean. *Le Rôle social de l'Art selon Proudhon*. Paris, 1937.

Lubac, Henri de. *Proudhon et le Christianisme*. Paris, 1945.
(This book appeared in an English translation by R. E. Scantlebury, under the misleading title of *The Unmarxian Socialist: A Study of Proudhon*, London, 1948.)

Marx, Karl. *La Misère de la Philosophie*. Paris, 1847.

Mirecourt, Eugène de. *Proudhon*. Brussels, 1855.

Mülberger, Arthur. *P.-J. Proudhon, Leben und Werke*. Stuttgart, 1899.

Pirou, Gaëtan. *Proudhon et Syndicalisme Révolutionnaire*. Paris, 1910.

*Proudhon et Notre Temps*. A symposium with an introduction by C. Bouglé. Paris, 1920.

Puech, J.-L. *Le Proudhonisme dans l'Association Internationale des Travailleurs*. Paris, 1907.

Raphaël, Max. *Proudhon, Marx, Picasso*. Paris, 1933.

Sainte-Beuve, Charles Augustin. *P.-J. Proudhon, Sa Vie et Sa Correspondence, 1838–1848*. Paris, 1872.

Sudan, Elisan. *L'Activité d'un Socialiste de 1848*. Fribourg, 1921.

Thuriet, Ch. *Le Dernier Voyage de Proudhon à Besançon*. Besançon, 1896.

# BIBLIOGRAPHICAL SUPPLEMENT TO THE 1972 EDITION

The years immediately preceding the publication of my *Pierre-Joseph Proudhon* in 1956 were a time of special activity in the study of Proudhon, particularly in France; the many books on him and the collections of his fugitive writings that appeared during the 1940s and the early 1950s are noted in the bibliography of the original edition of that work. The rediscovery of Proudhon played an important part in France's rediscovery of itself during the years of resistance and the first decade of liberation.

Since 1956 the works on Proudhon himself have perhaps been less important than the general histories of anarchist thought and action that have sought to establish his position in the libertarian tradition. Among these are my own *Anarchism* (Cleveland, 1962) and James Joll's *The Anarchists* (Boston, 1964), both of which devote chapters to Proudhon and his influence, and Daniel Guerin's *Anarchisme*, which English version (*Anarchism*, translated by Mary Klopper) appeared in New York in 1970.

The English studies of Proudhon which have some importance during the last decade and a half are *Marx, Proudhon and European Socialism* by J. Hampden Jackson (London, 1958) and *The Political Thought of Pierre-Joseph Proudhon* by Alan Ritter (Princeton, 1969). *The Teaching of Charles Fourier* by Nicholas J. Riasonovsky (Berkeley, 1969) provides important information on the background out of which Proudhon's own teachings developed, and a neglected aspect of his thought—the aesthetic philosophy that linked him with Gustave Courbet and the Impressionists—is discussed in some depth by Donald G. Egbert in *Social Radicalism and the Arts: Western Europe* (New York, 1970).

Most of Proudhon's own works had been rediscovered and republished by the time my *Pierre-Joseph Proudhon* appeared, and undoubtedly the most important new item since that time has been the three-volume edition of his unpublished *Carnets,* issued from 1960 at intervals in Paris, under the editorship of Abbé Pierre Haubtmann; a translation has not appeared, but recently I devoted a long essay in *Encounter,* entitled "The Solitary Revolutionary," to these notebooks. I also wrote the introductory essay to the sole recent reissue of a complete Proudhon text in English, *What is Property?* (New York, 1970). The only recent new translation of any significance—and the first broad selection of Proudhon's works to appear in English—is *Selected Writings of Pierre-Joseph Proudhon,* edited by Stewart Edwards and translated by Elizabeth Fraser (Garden City, N.Y., 1969).

Proudhon also finds his way into one of the two important recent anthologies of anarchist writings—*The Anarchists,* edited by Irving L. Horowitz (New York, 1964). He is represented only indirectly, through the lens of Charles Dana's interpretation of his People's Bank, in the rival collection, *Patterns of Anarchy,* edited by Leonard I. Krimerman and Lewis Perry (Garden City, 1966). The lack of good English translations, now as in the past, is not difficult to understand, for Proudhon is rather like one of those extraordinary French provincial wines that taste magnificent in their own *pays,* but travel badly; no work can be more exciting to read in the original than his masterpiece, *De la Justice,* but to turn it into English acceptable to even a readership of devotees is a task that for more than a century has intimidated all translators. I intend to make it the challenge of my retirement.

G. W.

# INDEX

Ackermann, Louise Victorine, 158
Ackermann, Paul, 28, 31, 42, 52, 55–7, 59, 61, 65, 68, 80–4, 86, 95–6
Agoult, Comtesse d', 101, 109–10, 124, 173, 255
Alembert, Jean d', 26, 204
Alexander II, Tsar, 195
Alton-Shée, Comte d', 160
Anarchism, 21, 25, 27, 35, 50–1, 55, 128, 171–2, 182, 203, 231–2, 249, 252, 269, 275–9
*Annales Franco-Allemandes*, 87, 90
Arago, Etienne, 229
Art, 256–9
*Avertissement aux Propriétaires*, 61–6, 239

Bakunin, Michael, 41, 49, 87–90, 109, 153, 203, 239, 266, 275–8
Bank of Exchange, 122–3, 128, 142–3
Barbès, Armand, 121, 127, 164, 166
Baroche, Pierre, 164
Bastiat, F., 142
Bastide, Jules, 251–2
Baudelaire, Charles, 98, 128, 142
Benoît, Joseph, 73
Bergier, 25–8, 41,
Bergmann, F.–G., 43–4, 49, 53–7, 62–5, 67–8, 80, 83, 86, 95–6, 108, 110–2, 192, 229, 257, 267
Beslay, Charles, 181, 184, 201, 245, 250, 262, 265, 274, 276
Blanc, Louis, 45, 54, 61, 84, 123, 135, 143

Blanqui, Jerome, 54–5, 59, 60–1, 109
Blanqui, Louis, 41, 51, 121, 127, 164, 224, 229, 230, 241, 260, 271, 276
Boileau, 68
Bonaparte, Jerome, 110, 185, 188, 198–9, 241
Bonaparte, Louis. See Napoleon III
Bradlaugh, Charles, 205
Brisbane, Arthur, 179
Brissot, 45
Buchon, Max, 258
Buzon, 236, 243, 248, 251–2, 254–5, 263, 265, 267

Cabet, Etienne, 73, 83–5, 109–10, 155
Camélinat, R.Z., 261–2, 275
*Capacité Politique des Classes ouvrières, De la*, 267, 273–5
Carlier, 149, 152
Cavaignac, General, 131, 133, 137–8, 140–1,
*Célébration du Dimanche, De la*, 39–40, 42
Chambord, Comte de, 107–8
Changarnier, General, 128
Charles X, 12, 119, 163
Châteaubriand, 28
Chaudey, Gustave, 217, 226, 235, 245, 250, 257–8, 267, 269, 274
Chevalier, Jules le, 120, 143–4, 147
Cobbett, William, 271
*Commune de Paris, La*, 142
Commune of Paris (1871), 261, 276–7

289

Communism, 45, 48–51, 76, 85, 100, 124
*Communist Manifesto*, 79
Comte, Auguste, 67, 77
*Confessions d'un Révolutionnaire, Les*, 129, 155–7
Considérant, Victor, 60–2, 142, 155, 220
Conspiracy of the Seasons, 43, 121
*Contradictions Economiques, Système des*, 11, 40, 83, 86, 95–103, 112–3, 169
Cornut, Romain, 189
Courbet, Gustave, 2, 110, 173, 187, 256–9, 276
*Création de l'Ordre dans l'Humanité, De la*, 49, 76–80, 83, 85, 90
Crémieux, 165, 218
Cretin, Dr., 200–1, 217, 245, 250, 263–5, 267
Crimean War, 194–6

Dameth, Claude-Marie-Henri, 62
Darimon, A., 76–7, 104-5, 120, 128, 142, 146, 148, 154, 161–2, 168, 229, 241, 245, 248
*Débats, Les*, 241
Debock, 120, 276
Defontaine, 253
Delarageaz, 76, 231
Delescluze, Charles, 141
Delhasse, Felix, 221–2, 238, 242, 263, 265–7
*Démocrates Assermentés, Les*, 251–2
Democratic Socialists, 138–9, 156, 184
*Démonstration de l'Existence de Dieu* (Fénélon), 7–8
Dentu, 233, 247
Desjardins, Arthur, 44
Diderot, Denis, 15, 204
Donoso-Cortes, 136
Dostoevesky, Fyodor, 205
Droz, Joseph, 36–7
Duchêne, Georges, 120, 146, 191, 262, 269, 274, 276
Dufraisse, Marc, 167–8, 173, 175, 180

*Economic Contradictions, See Contradictions Economiques, Système des*
Edmond, Charles, 89, 153–4, 165, 169, 177–9, 194–5, 218, 238, 239
Elmerich, 52
Enfantin, Père, 59
Engels, F., 41, 78, 90, 124
*Essai de Grammaire Générale*, 27–8
Etex, Antoine, 136
Ewerbeck, 87

Fallot, Gustave, 13–9, 26–7, 29, 56
Falloux, de, 130
Fauvety, Charles, 111, 120
Federalism, 21, 246–51, 260, 273, 275, 276
*Fédération et l'Unité en Italie, La*, 246–7, 276
Ferrari, Joseph, 186
Flocon, 119
Fourier, Charles, 13, 21, 34, 41, 48, 61, 77
*France Libre, La*, 142
Fribourg, 274

Garibaldi, 230, 242–3
Garnier, Joseph, 85–6
Garniers (publishers), 182, 191, 202, 217, 218, 227, 233, 236, 266
Gauthier (printing house), 9, 13, 14, 25–6
Gauthier, Antoine, 9, 59, 68, 113, 141, 148, 180, 245, 247
Gauthier Frères, 71, 81, 103–4, 112–3, 187
*General Idea of the Revolution.* See *Idée Générale de la Révolution*
Gide, André, 14
Girardin, Emile de, 137, 142–3, 166, 189, 252
Godwin, William, 40, 50, 106, 274
Goethe, 68
Goudchaux, 129, 184
Gouvernet, 224, 235, 236
Granovsky, 153
Greppo, 73, 135, 139, 241

Gruen, Karl, 41, 49, 87–8, 90, 220, 222
Guerre et la Paix, La, 233–8, 240
Guild Socialism, 279
Guillaumin, 86, 95–6, 100, 102, 103, 113
Guillemin, 143, 146–7, 153, 158, 180, 185, 201, 264
Guizot, 118, 121

Halévy, Daniel, 16
Haubtmann, Pierre, 74–5, 90, 102
Hegel, 41, 48–9, 67, 88–90, 97, 99, 101
Heine, 87
Heraclitus, 41, 46, 96, 190
Herzen, Alexander, 24, 41, 80, 88–9, 109, 146, 153–4, 166, 194–5, 213, 228–9, 238–9, 278
Homer, 68, 233
Huber, 127, 164, 188
Hugo, Victor, 128, 130, 134, 162, 176, 229
Humboldt, Alexander, 86

Idée Générale de la Revolution, 52, 169–172, 205
Impartial, L', 21
International Workingmen's Association, 35, 76, 228, 260–1, 274–8
Italy, 239, 242–3, 246–7, 249

Janzé, Baron Charles de, 137
Javel, Auguste, 22–4, 139
Journal des Débats, 132
Justice, 40, 44, 46, 206–16
Justice dans la Révolution et dans l'Eglise, De la, 11, 20, 32–3, 89, 90, 155, 167, 173, 190, 197, 202–17, 220, 228–9, 231–3, 246, 256
Justice Poursuivie par l'Eglise, La, 221–2

Kant, 40–2, 67, 80, 97
Kierkegaard, 205
Kropotkin, Peter, 277–8

Lacordaire, 132
Lamartine, 118
Lambert, 26–30
Lamennais, 12, 55, 57, 61, 67, 132, 139
Langlois, J.–A., 41, 120, 150, 164, 227, 250, 262, 267, 269, 274
Lebègue, 221, 242, 245
Ledru-Rollin, 139–41, 150
Lefrançais, Gustave, 124, 268
Leroux, Pierre, 59–60, 77, 80, 84, 128, 139, 189, 255, 271
Lettre à M. Blanqui, 55–9, 61
Limousin, Charles, 261, 274
Longuet, 276
Louis-Philippe, 55, 58, 63–4, 104, 115, 118–9, 163
Lubac, Pierre de, 196–7, 205

Madier-Montjau, 185, 198–9, 220, 222
Maguet, Dr., 136, 145–7, 155, 167, 189, 195, 201, 264, 267
Mairet, Joseph, 120
Mairet, Nicholas, 120
Majorats Littéraires, Les, 253, 256, 259
Malon, Benoît, 103
Malthus, 23, 40
Manifesto of the Sixty, 259–62, 273
Marx, Karl, 41, 44–5, 47, 49, 51, 67, 75–6, 78–9, 87–93, 96, 101–3, 124, 135, 203, 260, 270, 274
Mathey, 143, 146–7, 164, 201, 218, 226–7, 232
Mathieu, Cardinal, 197, 216
Maurice, 27, 29, 39, 69, 72–3, 84, 100–1, 112–3, 119, 143, 145, 150, 168–9, 177, 199–201, 217, 223, 254, 266
Maximilian, Emperor of Mexico, 198
Mazzini, 173, 230, 242–3, 246
Metternich, 204
Micaud, Olympe, 14, 16, 87, 157, 160, 201
Michelet, Jules, 41, 111, 169, 171, 173–4, 213, 227, 230
Milliet, 10, 249

Mirecourt, Eugène de, 196–7, 203
Molière, 44
*Moniteur, Le,* 138
Montaigne, 15
Montalembert, 178
Morny, Duc de, 178
Morris, William, 203, 259
Muiron, Just, 21–2, 27–8, 62
Mutualism, 21, 74, 99–100, 122, 191, 260, 273–80
Mutualists of Lyons, 73–4, 76, 95

Nadaud, Martin, 83–4
Napoleon I, 41, 182, 218
Napoleon III, 122, 124, 128, 137–8, 140–5, 150, 153, 166–7, 175–8, 180–6, 194–5, 203–4, 223–5, 235, 243
*National, Le,* 117, 124, 142
Nationalism, 237–9, 242–3, 246–7
Negrier, General, 130
Normanby, Lord, 134
*Nouveau Monde Industriel et Sociétaire, Le* (Fourier), 13

*Office de la Publicité, L',* 242, 245
Ogarev, 154
Orsini, 204
Owen, Robert, 40

Pascal, 178
Pauthier, Jean-Pierre, 14, 29, 40, 80, 82, 85
Penet, 255–6
People's Bank, 76, 122, 142–4, 146–8, 173, 187, 272
Pereire, 188–9, 199
Pérennès, 13, 29–30, 36, 43, 56
*Peuple, Le,* 110–2, 116–8, 137, 141, 145–8, 150–3, 165–7, 169
Phalansterianism, 13, 57, 59, 61–2, 64, 73, 75, 77, 84, 120, 162
*Philosophie du Progrès,* 51, 189–91, 211–2

Piégard, Euphrasie. See Proudhon, Euphrasie
Pilhes, Victor, 152, 220, 237
Plato, 41, 96, 258
Poland, 238–9, 253, 266
*Political Justice* (Godwin), 40, 50
*Populaire, Le,* 83–4
Positivism, 77
*Poverty of Philosophy, The* (Marx), 89, 101–3
Prével, 143
*Presse, La,* 137, 142, 189, 239, 252
*Principe de l'Art, Du,* 256–9
*Principe Fédératif, Du,* 248–50
Property, 39–40, 43–52, 54, 57–8, 64, 93, 97, 239–40
Proudhon, Catherine (mother of P.-J.), 1–7, 17–8, 20, 94–5, 103, 113–4, 168
  Catherine (daughter of P.-J.), 168–9, 179, 183, 187, 201, 237, 247, 266–7
  Charles, 3–4, 94, 152, 163, 199, 230–1
  Charlotte, 201–2
  Claude-François, 1–9, 17–8, 94–5
  Euphrasie, 105–9, 113–4, 147–8, 157–9, 161–4, 168, 173, 178–9, 192, 200–1, 220, 222–6, 236–8, 241, 244–5, 247, 257, 263–7
  François-Victor, 2
  Jean-Baptiste, 2
  Jean-Etienne, 3–4, 20, 24–5
  Marcelle, 179, 183, 187, 192–3
  Melchior, 2, 201, 230–1
  Pierre-Joseph: birth and family, 1; childhood, 4; education, 5; apprenticed to printing, 9; meets Fourier, 12; meets Fallot, 13; first journey to Paris, 17; becomes master printer, 26; publishes first writing, the *Essai de Grammaire Générale,* 27; gains Suard Pension, 30; on women, 31; goes to study in Paris, 36; writes *De la Célébration du Dimanche,* 39; formative influ-

Proudhon, Pierre-Joseph—*continued* ences, 40; publishes *Qu'est-ce que la Propriété?*, 44; proclaims himself an anarchist, 50; dispute with Besançon Academy, 53; publishes *Lettre à M. Blanqui*, 57; meets Pierre Leroux, 59; publishes *Avertissement aux Propriétaires*, 63; acquitted on charges arising out of *A. aux P.*, 66; sells printing house, 69; becomes transport clerk in Lyons, 71; encounters socialist groups in Lyons, 73; his debt to the Mutualists, 74; ideas on association, 75; publishes *De la Création de l'Ordre dans l'Humanité*, 76; begins diary, 81; on the theatre, 81; relations with Cabet, 83; meets Marx and Bakunin, 87; attitude to Hegel, 88; correspondence with Marx, 91; death of father, 94; writes *Système des Contradictions Economiques*, 95; attacks idea of God, 98; is attacked by Marx, 101; courts Euphrasie Piégard, 104; corresponds with Madame d'Agoult, 109; plans a periodical, 110; leaves employment in Lyons, 112; death of mother, 113; attitude towards February Revolution of 1848, 116; activities during Revolution, 118; accepts editorship of *Le Représentant du Peuple*, 120; elected to National Assembly, 128; attitude to June insurrection, 130; defends proposition for moratorium, 133; is censured by National Assembly, 135; founds *Le Peuple*, 137; meets Louis Bonaparte, 137; upholds Raspail's candidature for Presidency, 140; fights duel with Pyat, 141; attitude towards election of Louis Bonaparte, 141; founds People's Bank, 143; sentenced to imprisonment for article against L. Bonaparte, 145;

Proudhon, Pierre-Joseph—*continued* goes into hiding, 146; liquidates People's Bank, 146; arrested and imprisoned, 149; collaborates with Herzen in founding *La Voix du Peuple*, 153; publishes *Confessions d'un Révolutionnaire*, 155; marries Euphrasie Piégard, 158; transferred to fortress of Doullens, 163; acquitted on further charges, 165; publishes *Idée Générale de la Révolution*, 169; meets George Sand, 173; relationship with Michelet, 174; attitude to Louis Bonaparte's *coup d'état*, 175; liberated from prison, 180; publishes *La Révolution sociale*, 181; experiences financial distress, 186; publishes *Philosophie du Progrès*, which is banned, 190; publishes *Stock Exchange Speculators' Manual* anonymously, 191; afflicted by cholera, 192; death of daughter Marcelle, 193; on Crimean War, 194; attacked by de Mirecourt, 196; relationship with Jerome Bonaparte, 198; death of daughter Charlotte, 202; advocates abstention in elections of 1857, 202; publishes *De la Justice*, 204; sentenced to imprisonment for *De la Justice*, 217; flees to Belgium, 218; publishes *La Justice poursuivie par l'Eglise*, 221; second edition of *Justice*, 228; growing international reputation, 228; visited by Tolstoy, 229; wins Lausanne prize for *Théorie de l'Impôt*, 231; pardoned by Napoleon III, 235; tours Rhineland, 238; arouses Belgian hostility by articles on Italian unity, 243; returns to Paris, 244; publishes *La Féderation et l'Unité en Italie*, 246; writes *Du Principe Fédératif*, 248; campaigns for abstention from voting, 250; writes *Du*

Proudhon, Pierre-Joseph—*continued*
  *Principe de l'Art*, 256; welcomes
  *Manifesto of Sixty*, 260; makes
  last journey to Franche-Comté,
  263; last meeting with Bakunin,
  266; works on *De la Capacité
  Politique des Classes ouvrières*, 267;
  last illness and death, 267; his
  character, 270; his influence,
  274; his significance, 279
  Stephanie, 189, 201, 226, 247
Pyat, Felix, 141

*Qu'est-ce que la Propriété?*, 43–55, 57,
  59, 139, 272

Rabelais, 15
Raspail, 86, 108, 127, 139–41, 164
*Réforme, La*, 83, 110, 117, 119, 154
Regnault, Elias, 239
Renan, Ernest, 41
*Représentant du Peuple, Le*, 111–3,
  120, 123–7, 132–3, 136–7, 143
Revolution of 1789, 2, 17, 40–1, 46,
  156, 170
  of 1830, 12, 17, 156
  of 1848, 103, 109, 115–49, 156,
  176
*Révolution Sociale démontrée dans le coup
  d'état du 2 Décembre, La*, 181–3
*Revue des Economistes*, 85, 113
*Revue du Progrès*, 54
*Revue Rétrospective*, 121
Ribeyrolles, 110
Robespierre, 2, 41, 119, 172, 250
Roland, Mme, 150
Rolland, 226, 230, 235, 241, 245
Rossini, 81
Royssen, Théodore, 51
*Rouge et Noir, Le* (Stendhal), 11
Rousseau, 15, 34, 40, 172, 266
Ruge, Arnold, 87, 90
Ruskin, John, 258

Sagra, Ramon de la, 144
Sainte-Beuve, 28, 39, 63, 69, 155

Saint-Simon, 34, 41, 48, 59, 73, 84,
  188, 198, 273
Sand, George, 33–4, 84, 173
Sazonov, 153–4
Serialism, 13, 77–8, 80
Senart, 132, 139
*Siècle, Le*, 241
Simonin, Jean-Claude, 2–3
Smith, Adam, 41
Sobrier, 127
Social Contract, 40, 111
Social Credit, 279
*Solution of the Social Problem, The*, 121
Spinoza, 179, 220
Staël, Mme de, 34
Stendhal, 11
Stirner, Max, 78
*Stock Exchange Speculator's Manual*,
  191–2
Stoicism, 41
Syndicalism, 252, 277–9
*Système des Contradictions Economiques.*
  See *Contradictions Economiques.*

Taschereau Affair, 121, 164
*Théorie de la Propriéte*, 230–40
*Théorie de l'Impôt*, 231–2, 240
Thiers, 116, 128, 134
Tissot, 40–2, 49, 53, 59, 67, 80, 85,
  159, 201
Tocqueville, Alexis de, 116
Tolain, Henri, 76, 261, 274
Tolstoy, 51, 110, 166, 229, 278
Tourneux, 74, 86, 104
*Tribune Nationale, La*, 128, 142
Tristan, Flora, 73, 75

Utopianism, 97, 170–2

Varlin, 76
Vasbenter, 120
Viard, Jules, 111, 120
Vivien, 54–5, 139
Vogt, Karl, 89